Visualizing with Text

AK Peters Visualization Series

Series Editor: Tamara Munzner

University of British Columbia, Vancouver, Canada

This series aims to capture new developments and summarize what is known over the whole spectrum of visualization by publishing a broad range of textbooks, reference works, and handbooks. It will contain books from all subfields of visualization, including visual analytics, information visualization, and scientific visualization. The scope will largely follow the calls of the major conferences such as VIS: techniques, algorithms, theoretical foundations and models, quantitative and qualitative evaluation, design studies, and applications.

Visualization Analysis and Design
Tamara Munzner

Information Theory Tools for Visualization
Min Chen, Miquel Feixas, Ivan Viola, Anton Bardera, Han-Wei Shen, Mateu Sbert

Data-Driven Storytelling
Nathalie Henry Riche, Christophe Hurter, Nicholas Diakopoulos, Sheelagh Carpendale

Interactive Visual Data Analysis
Christian Tominski, Heidrun Schumann

Data Sketches
Nadieh Bremer, Shirley Wu

Visualizing with Text
Richard Brath

For more information about this series please visit: https://www.crcpress.com/AK-Peters-Visualization-Series/book-series/CRCVIS

Visualizing with Text

Richard Brath

CRC Press
Taylor & Francis Group
Boca Raton London New York

CRC Press is an imprint of the
Taylor & Francis Group, an **informa** business
AN A K PETERS BOOK

First edition published 2021
by CRC Press
6000 Broken Sound Parkway NW, Suite 300, Boca Raton, FL 33487-2742

and by CRC Press
2 Park Square, Milton Park, Abingdon, Oxon, OX14 4RN

ISBN: 9780367259303 (hbk)
ISBN: 9780367259266 (pbk)
ISBN: 9780429290565 (ebk)

Typeset in Minion
by Deanta Global Publishing Services, Chennai, India

In honor of my deceased father, for whom a task was not worth doing if it was not worth doing well. And then, to my highly supportive Bayla, Abe, and Hana, who gave me the time and opportunity to pursue this endeavor thoroughly and deeply, in the hopes of doing it well.

Visual Table of Contents

The first step is to **define visualization with text, Part I** (Chapters 1–4). First, *Why Visualize with Text* (Chapter 1)? Some problems, such as translation, bot detection, and phishing, are text-centric. However, since the printing press, text and visuals have been separated (Section 1.2), yet many specialized uses deeply weave graphically enhanced text and visuals together, as shown in many examples (1.3):

The current *Design Space of Visualization with Text*, Chapter 2, emphasizes perceptions of patterns over other roles (2.1). The current visualization pipeline either does not consider text (2.2), or preprocesses text for use with existing visualizations (2.3). With the cross-domain view, the visualization pipeline can be extended (2.4), as indicated in this diagram in **red** (from Figure 2.13):

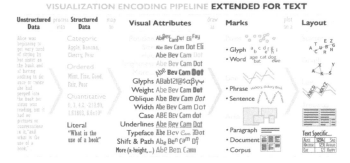

Chapter 3, *Characterizing Text*, describes literal data (3.1); qualities of typographic (3.2) and visual attributes (3.3); scope from characters to paragraphs (3.4); alternative layouts (3.5); and interactions (3.6):

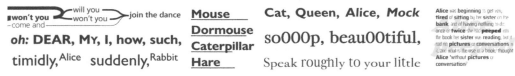

New visualization opportunities are outlined in Chapter 4, *Using the Design Space*, for: structured data (4.1); unstructured data and natural language processing (4.2); encoding with multiple attributes (4.3); enhanced supporting roles, such as tick labels, notes, and narratives (4.4); and new application areas, such as monitoring, search, and so on (4.5):

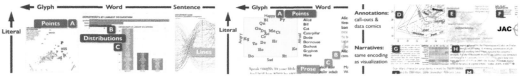

Next, in **Part II, Labels**, visualizations use literal text. In Chapter 5, *Point Labels* replace point marks for faster identification, and range from codes to various strategies for handling long labels or many labels.

In Chapter 6, *Distributions* are made with alphanumeric stacks, such as stem and leaf plots, with attributes to add data. Literal leaves and literal stems create variants of bar charts and hierarchies.

In Chapter 7, *Microtext Lines* use text on paths to show detailed content and aid disambiguation. Text can be a long string of microtext replacing the line or sparse, like river labels on a map. Interactions aid search and legibility.

Then, in **Part III, Formats** convey data. In Chapter 8, *Sets and Categories* use typographic formats to convey categoric data in Venn diagrams, graphs, scatterplots, mosaic plots, and bar charts.

Maps and Ordered Data, Chapter 9, address problems with thematic maps by showing one or more ordered variables in typographic labels, including long labels, various layouts, and other visualizations.

In Chapter 10, *Ratios and Quantitative Data* are embedded into text by marking a proportion of a word, phrase, line, or area with one or more formats. Alternatively, the position of the format can mark these values.

In **Part IV, Text Layouts**, data is embedded directly into words in text. In Chapter 11, *Prose and Prosody*, reading is enhanced and words formatted for skimming. Individual letters are formatted to aid pronunciation, spelling, and prosody.

SparkWords, Chapter 12, embed data into words using formats, in narrative text, such as explanations, hierarchical codes, or data comics; in lists; or in tables to show orders of magnitude or a dialog matrix.

Opportunity and Checklist, Chapter 13. With a vast new design space there are many opportunities for new ways to transform visualization. There are also challenges that can be mitigated as outlined in checklists.

References, Chapter 14, has acknowledgments, research, the bibliography, and the index.

Contents

List of Figures and Credits

IMAGES WITHOUT CREDIT WERE created by the author. Digital versions of the author's images can be viewed on-line at www.crcpress.com/Visualizing-With-Text/Brath/p/book/9780367259266

Foreword

Outside the mind,
it undresses to nothing.
To visualize, narrate its story.

VISUALIZING IS FORMING A MENTAL IMAGE; it is to register inside the mind. It is a process as old as creation itself, which stimulates senses of sight, hearing, touch, or taste to communicate. Today, visualization is a discipline in tandem with others that uses the processing power of computers to transform complex data into visual imagery for comprehension, communication, and decision making.

The field of visualization has progressed dramatically since the late 1980s, when the National Science Foundation commissioned a report entitled "Visualization in Scientific Computing"* that proposed a framework defining it as a discipline within the field of science. From then on, it has touched subfields such as information and knowledge: fields that may be further differentiated into theme-specific areas, for example, geo-, biomedical-, software-, and humanities visualization, to name but a few. From molecules to galaxies, visualization tools and techniques have enabled researchers to "see" their complex data in a different light. Nowadays, it has become not just an essential component of scientific discovery, but it has also become a necessary component to "comprehend" the story behind the data. Such a paradigm shift makes this book timely, which expands the design space for visualization with text.

The future impact of visualization will be from the continued development of methods that lead from visual form to information and knowledge. It is often revealed as part of storytelling through visuals that are placed within the wider context of knowledge transfer, characterized by a sense of story that is often remembered long after it has been told. This degree of engagement remains a challenge to contemporary visualization. Some notable examples are in the early visualizations discussed and analyzed in the early chapters of this book. These hint at the rich aspects of visualization that complement the story. It also draws a lesson from such records for adaptation to the computer-aided medium that enriches with wider choices. As such, these examples are from varied disciplines from the pre-computing era. It highlights one of the key messages of this book that an interdisciplinary approach is rich, not just for better understanding, but also for knowledge

---

* B. H. McCormick, T.A. DeFanti, and M.D. Brown., Computer Graphics, vol 21, no 6, ACM SIGGRAPH, 1987.

diffusion to lead to new designs and products. It provides ample examples from typography, cartography, and elegant examples from the field of chemistry and biology, as well as pushes the boundary to less exposed areas of humanities.

Text, like visualization, has a rich history. It is one of the landmark innovations closely linked to language, cultural development, and recording. Unlike visualization that is boundless and language-independent, it does require a lot of effort and attention to comprehend and read; it is also language-dependent. Yet most communication, written or spoken, are text-based.

The theme of this book is based on the research work undertaken by Dr. Richard Brath for the last 20 years, creating and designing visualization tools for numerous companies in a different field, as well as academic research and publications. The premise and approach are novel in the way the subject is approached and demonstrate a much deeper and wider understanding of how visualization is applied. It demonstrates the wider potential that visualization with text has to offer in many other text-rich disciplines. In short, visualizing with text provides not only an additional layer of functionality to the visualization design pipeline, but, by default, it also offers text enhancement, text annotation, and data narrative.

From a design perspective, it illustrates how the design space of visualization is enriched by introducing literal text as a data type to the design pipeline. Then, rich visual text attributes together with additional marks (glyph, word, phrase, sentence, paragraph, document, and corpus) provide the potential for text-specific layouts. It provides an enhanced visualization encoding pipeline, with a vast range of illustrations.

The other underlying theme is the functional benefit of text to reduce cognitive load and increase information density. For example, the perceptual advantages of interaction are examined against micro-readings supported by fast and automatic word recognition. Ultimately, the degree of adaption will be dependent on reducing cognitive overload against the effectiveness of aid to reasoning. Though it argues language-dependency, nevertheless ideas are adaptable across languages with minor modification.

By exploring each phase of the visualization pipeline, it shows systematically how textual data can be used. For this, typographical characteristics of text are analyzed through a visualization lens for both text-based as well as non-type visual attributes. In the layout phase, it is demonstrated with prose, tables, and lists. All these are explored with application cases, for example, treemaps, parallel coordinates, ternary- and radar-plots, self-organizing maps, and networked graphs.

An inventive source for a number of features for applications is discussed, such as sentiment, topic, and similarity analysis, which are based on Natural Language Processing (NLP) and underpinned with Machine Learning (ML). It projects how to apply all the above to unstructured text data, by ample illustrations of markup using NLP applications, to assist skimming, reveal structure, indicate errors, support close readings, knowledge mapping, and many more. Most of the above are illustrated with practical examples of how Bertin's Permutations can be adopted and presented using visualization in text. This is elegantly presented with quantitative, ordered, categoric, and literal data and using textual markers including words, sentences, and paragraphs.

In Part II of this book, the focus is on labels and how to visualize with literal text. Again, the emphasis is to reduce cognitive load and increase information density. To illustrate the point, it gives examples of point labels with multiple and massive data labeling. Distributions of data in layouts of bar charts and treemaps are enriched with highlights of different statistical details, and in stem and leaf plots with a variety of text attributes. Another key contribution is Microtext Lines: text-enhanced line charts with the potential use for time series analysis, and enhanced decipherability, especially when lines of the chart are too many to read. Removing the need for legends helps reduce cognitive loads; it also offers the potential for annotating other statistical details to enhance information density.

Part III, Conveying Data with Typographic Attributes, examines data added within the context of text. Set analysis refers to some of the challenges, such as identifying elements and membership, within set visualization. Using text attributes for membership provides multi-layered Venn-type diagrams with enhanced information density.

The author provides a number of elegant examples to address solutions to the problems of thematic maps, such as map scale, disproportionality, and information loss due to area restrictions. Thematic maps are shown with multi-variate topics using typographically enabled theme-based mapping to address the above problems in a number of application domains. This is particularly useful in geographic and thematic map design industries.

Ratios and quantitative typographic attributes can be used with text to represent proportional data. This can be applied to words and phrases and has application for giving context to ratios, ranges, and other distributional measures relating to the text contents. The examples of opinion analysis and review scores are particularly useful for increased rate of information capture. It can lend itself to multiple proportional comparisons.

Part IV of this book provides unique ways to merge visualization and text data. This is demonstrated with formatting to aid skim reading – with potential application for automating skim reading, or tools for dyslexics and other reading disabilities. It has the potential for synopsis of large documents. It provides potential applications for pronunciation and spelling tool developments, which are useful for language education. With SparkWords, running text can be enhanced with visual encoding of extrinsic data to increase information density and rate of capture.

This book provides a unique insight into visualization with text. Its collection of ideas and the interdisciplinary angle are a unique source for applications and further research for the advocates of visualization, typographers, cartographers, linguists, and data scientists. The last chapter highlights the future research, development, and adoption criteria. With many elegant examples, it is a clear invitation for collaborative work from a number of multi-disciplinary domain experts.

Dr. Ebad Banissi,
Professor Emeritus,
Computer Science and Informatics,
London South Bank University

Preface

THIS BOOK ORIGINATES FROM a desire to re-assess the foundations of visualization science with respect to text. Visualization has become popular in the last decade with point and click visualization software, amazing data journalism, highly flexible programming tools, and so on. But the foundations of data visualization were boot-strapped 50 years ago by bringing together research from fields such as cartography, statistics, and perceptual psychology. Text was bypassed because the origins of visualization were *data* visualization – not text visualization.

The time is now appropriate to dig down and reconsider how text fits with visualization: to enable richer, more expressive visualizations of *data* or *text*. This book not only argues for visualizing with text, it also shows real examples; the book has more than 100 historic examples and more than 80 new variants, for a total of more than 250 example images.

This book is about a design space. The visualization design space is an organization of the many parameters and alternatives that a designer can manipulate when creating a visualization. Attempting to divine and organize the constituent elements of a design space is somewhat arbitrary based on the author's reasoning. In this attempt to organize how text fits within visualization, this design space is built on the foundations established by prior visualization researchers, starting with Jacques Bertin and extended by researchers such as Cleveland, Mackinlay, Shneiderman, Wilkinson, Ware, Heer, and Munzner. To see further, one must stand on the shoulders of giants.

But defining a broad extension to a design space is to venture into uncharted territory. What method should be used? Fortunately, with text, one can look back across a thousand years of documents and the related contemporary research. This cross-disciplinary approach is informed by domains such as cartography, (from Mercator to MacEachren), typography (from Warde to Unger), and others. Many wonderful historical examples are highly inspirational, and there is space in this book for only a small number of them. This analysis forms the first part of the book and defines the design space.

And what is the use of a design space without any pictures? The rest of the book is filled with many examples, deliberately focused on different types of visualizations, to show that the design space has broad applicability. Just as many of the ideas in this book emerge from collaborative cross-disciplinary investigations, most of the examples are transferrable to other applications and domains. There are examples that should be of interest and inspiration to people focused on business intelligence, statistics, visualization, computational linguistics, natural language processing, humanities, cartography, and graphic design. And, even if none of the examples quite fit the reader's specific need, the design space defined in **Chapter 2** is a useful conceptual framework for thinking about textual and typographic variables, with the many examples throughout the book simply inspirational points of departure.

Richard Brath

About the Author

Richard Brath has been actively involved in the research, design, and development of data visualization and visual analytics since 1990. His research interests include exploration of the boundaries of visualization – such as this book regarding text and visualization – as well as graph visualization, automated insights, 3D, spreadsheets, aesthetics, and machine learning. From a commercial perspective, Richard focuses on the creation of unique, innovative visualizations that are in use by hundreds of thousands of users.

Richard originally acquired a degree in architecture and worked in industrial design, special effects, and 3D animation. With the opportunity to solve business challenges with interactive computer graphics, Richard switched to visualization, creating one of the first interactive 3D financial visualizations on the web (1996). Richard is a partner at Uncharted Software, where his team creates a wide variety of visualizations, ranging from small mobile screens to multi-screen video walls. These visualizations are used in domains such as financial markets, professional sports, health care, journalism, and customer analytics. Richard has a personal blog at richardbrath.wordpress.com.

I

Defining Text Elements

CHAPTER 1

Why Visualize with Text?

Fake news. Voice-based interfaces. Chatbots that answer the wrong questions. Automated transcription. Phishing emails. Underutilized customer feedback. Trolls posting hate speech. Incorrect translations. Algorithms that inadvertently promote extremism. Product reviews posted by bots. These are some very real text-oriented problems confronting 21st-century society. In the past 20 years, the visual display of quantitative information has significantly enhanced the analysis of measurements. There is now a pressing need to expand our visualization vocabulary and repertoire for the analysis of text using visualization techniques.

1.1 WHY TEXT?

Data visualization transforms data into visual representations such as size and color so that we can easily see trends, patterns, and anomalies across the display. Text, however, requires focused attention, sequentially perceived a few words at a time. Visualization leverages humans' automatic preattentive perceptual capabilities – where *preattentive* means that we perceive the patterns *before* we consciously focus on specific items in the view. Reading, by comparison, is slow. Therefore, the use of text inside a visualization seems counterintuitive.

So, why should text be used with visualization other than simple supporting roles, such as axes labels, legends, or explanations?

Consider some medieval visualizations. In Figure 1.1, part of a circular diagram is shown (Virgil 1405). Pie-chart-like, it is formed of wedges, with sequences of individual characters around the perimeter, sentences in each wedge, and a few character codes per wedge as well. Text color differentiates wedges and some individual characters are highlighted in yellow.

In the top image of Figure 1.2, a portion of a map of England is shown (Paris 1255). Text ranges from simple labels, to phrases to sentences. Text color varies: cities are brown, counties are red, some regions are entirely red (e.g. **DORSET**) or combinations of alternating red and blue letters (**NORTHFOLK**). Case varies: cities are lowercase, regions in uppercase. Colored boxes (brown or red) surround the text for many cities.

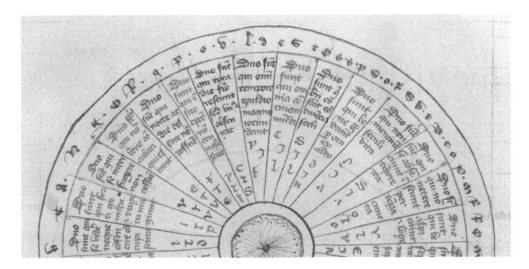

FIGURE 1.1   Portion of a text-heavy medieval circular chart from 1405 with sentences filling wedges, plus character codes and text around the perimeter.

At the bottom of Figure 1.2 is a genealogical diagram (Peter of Poitier 1205). Nodes are thumbnail portraits with colored names with connections sometimes labeled. The accompanying text is fluidly set out in relation to and adjacent to the nodes. This text will cross lines or squish into narrow spaces in order to be close, while not overlapping the nodes.

Clearly, medieval scribes were very flexible with regards to the textual content, graphical elements, and their composition. Text and visualization were not separate.

1.2   500 YEARS OF PUSHING TEXT OUT OF VISUALIZATIONS

How did text become separated from visualization?

Guttenberg's printing press of 1455 fundamentally changed the technical process of publishing. After the printing press, the text for a document is assembled from small pieces of movable type, arranged and locked together in a form. Images, on the other hand, were produced separately, such as carved wood blocks or engraved metal plates. The two technologies were not easy to mix. Blocks of text became separate from the blocks with images (with a few words carved into the image, if required). Figure 1.3 shows some early books with wood block images. In the second image, some minimal text has been carved into the blocks.

It is easier to print the text and image separately. Figure 1.4 shows an illustration of a watermill from the *Encyclopédie*, 1777, and the associated descriptive text (Diderot et al., Meunier, Planche II). Items in the illustration are marked with characters and numbers (A,B,C…1,2,3…), which are then cross-referenced in the descriptive text on separate pages at the beginning of the volume. Both the text and the image can be reproduced at high quality but use different technologies (cast metal type vs. copper plate engravings) and therefore printed on separate pages. However, the viewer is required to flip back and forth between the pages. The viewer needs to rely on short-term memory to keep track of

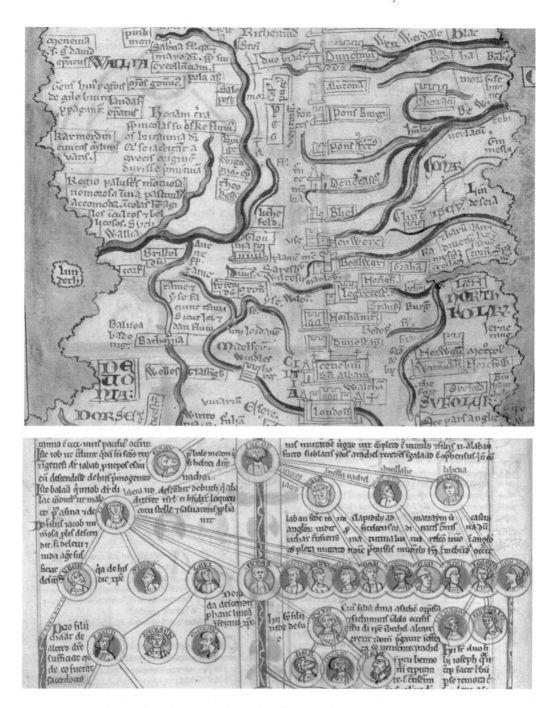

FIGURE 1.2 Early medieval map and graph. Text is fully integrated within the other visual elements.

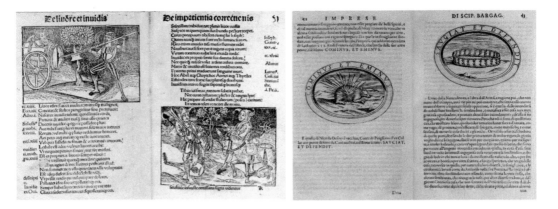

FIGURE 1.3   Early printed texts with woodblock images (Brant 1497, Bargagli 1589). Text is separate from image or otherwise minimal.

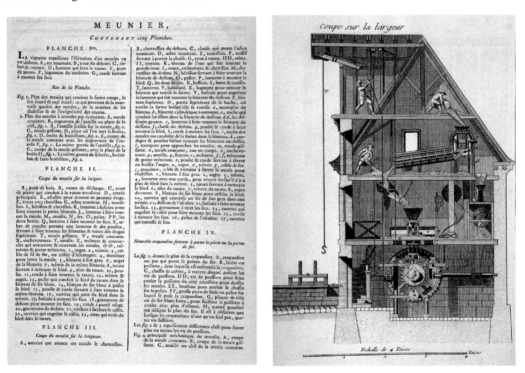

FIGURE 1.4   Explanation and illustration of a watermill are completely separated and cross-referenced with tiny characters. From *Encyclopédie* (Diderot et al. 1777).

references – for example, this one figure has 49 items labeled A–Z,1–23, discretely placed throughout the image.

In the early 1900s, this separation between text and illustration was also applied to charts and graphs. Figure 1.5 shows some example pages from a book by Briton (1919) on charts and their uses. All text is pushed away from the chart; even the axes titles and tick labels are pushed to the perimeter of these charts. Similar to the *Encyclopédie*, text in the

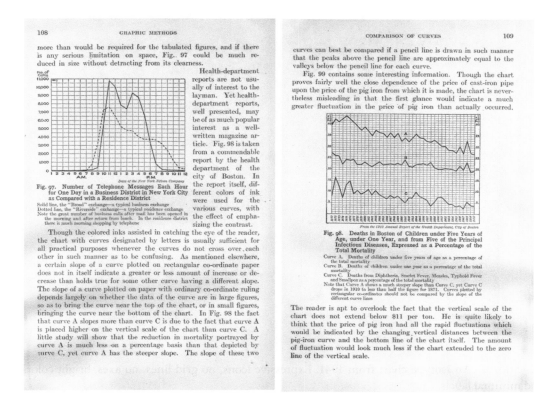

FIGURE 1.5   Charts in a book from 1919: text is pushed outside and away from the chart.

plot area is minimized; on the right chart, tiny labels in the plot (A,B,C) need to be cross-referenced with the text below.

By the 1950s, the *International Style* was sweeping across the world, promoting design that supported international trade and communication. At the core of the International Style was *modernism*, which emphasized simplicity, cleanness, and readability, as well as minimizing language-specific text in favor of non-language icons and symbols. Isotype was a visualization approach typified by expressive icons (see Burke et al. 2014). Isotype was created during the early formation of modernism. The Isotype example shown in Figure 1.6 is highly different from the earlier charts: with no grid lines or axes; a strong reliance on icons (which can be easily counted thereby not needing the axis); and strong use of color. The paired charts strongly suggest a correlation between overcrowding and infant mortality.

Isotype became broadly diffused with the International Style, for example, with standardized symbols for international signage, such as airports, Olympics, and road signs. Modernists responsible for communicating data graphically would prefer simpler thematic maps and icons, short concise labels, and reduced use of grid lines.

By the 1960s, the technological shift to photo-compositing lowered costs and reduced time, but also reduced the ability to show fine details; small text was difficult to reproduce. This continued the bias for the design of visualizations to reduce the amount of text.

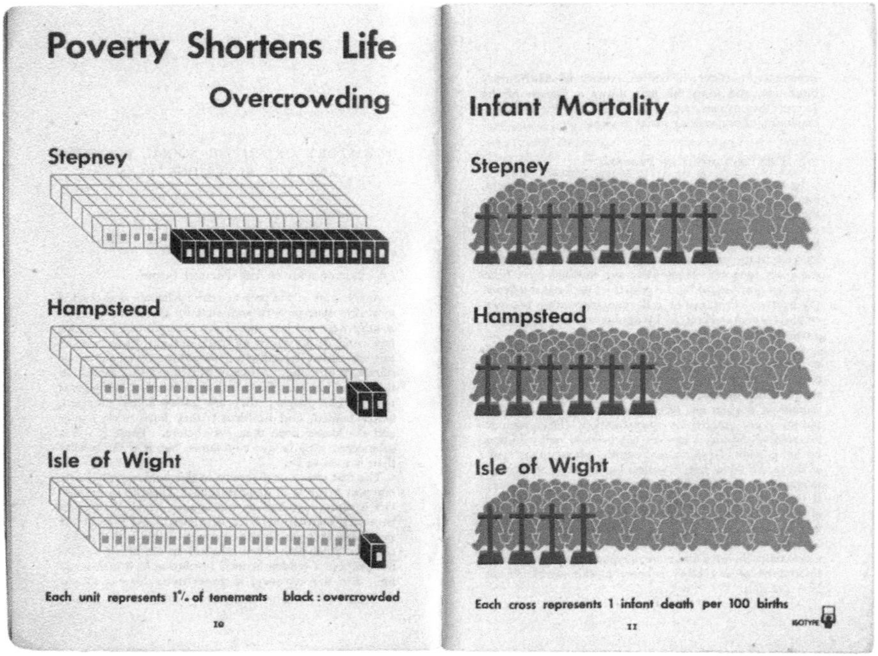

FIGURE 1.6 An Isotype chart from 1941. Expressive icons, no grid lines, no axes, bright colors, and minimal labels.

While the quality of phototypesetting improved, the 1980s introduced personal computers. With computers attached to monitors, visualizations could become interactive, but screens were small, and resolution was low (72–96 pixels per inch). Early graphical user interfaces used big icons and minimal labels. Text did not look good on early desktop computers. Adrian Frutiger (designer of the font *Univers*) said: "Coarse resolution would result in a stair-step effect on curves and diagonals that was referred to as the jaggies" (Osterer and Stamm 2014). Poor resolution required text to be large and limited the features of text that could be used. User interface guidelines from 1998 (e.g. Kahn and Lenk) recommended against the use of italics, weights, and small caps.

Only since Apple introduced Retina displays starting in 2012 did screen resolutions significantly increase so that individual pixels are no longer identifiable, making fine detail possible in interface design. Now that much higher pixel resolutions have become pervasive across devices, there are no longer technical constraints limiting the use of small text, typographic features, or mixing text directly into visualizations. However, 500 years of cultural conventions limit design thinking about text in visualization.

For example, many contemporary articles on news websites with charts tend to be long scrolling web pages with blocks of text interspersed with separate charts – conceptually similar to the layout in Figure 1.5. These visualizations may have typographically differentiated titles, legends, and axis labels, but the text within the visualization plot area is minimal or revealed via interactions such as tooltips or pop-ups.

Figure 1.7 shows three highly interactive analytical visualizations. All of these visualizations are about textual data (clockwise from top left: relationships across social media, classified advertisement search interface, and building permit topics on a city map), and all do show some text in the plot area, but beyond the literal label, most of the data attributes are conveyed by the geometry behind the labels, for example, using size, color, shape, outlines, imagery, and so on.

Perhaps the most pervasive contemporary text visualization is the word cloud (also known as a tag cloud). Figure 1.8 shows a word cloud with the most frequent words from *Alice's Adventures in Wonderland*. While highly popular, most word clouds miss the opportunity to convey much information. Word color and word position are arbitrary in most word clouds – not based on data. Word size is indicative of word frequency, but since most word clouds do not provide a legend, the relative frequencies cannot be determined. Word clouds have many criticisms in the visualization and user experience communities, such as Jakob Nielsen's statement (2009): "A one paragraph summary [of each report] would

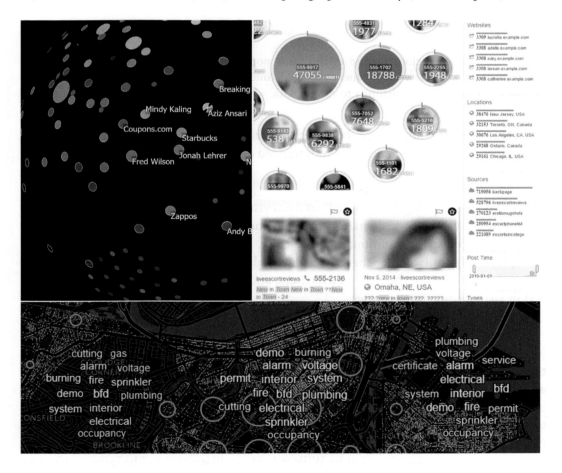

FIGURE 1.7 Contemporary analytical visualizations for interacting with millions of text documents: within the plot area text is simple, while marks behind convey data via color, size, icons, imagery, etc.

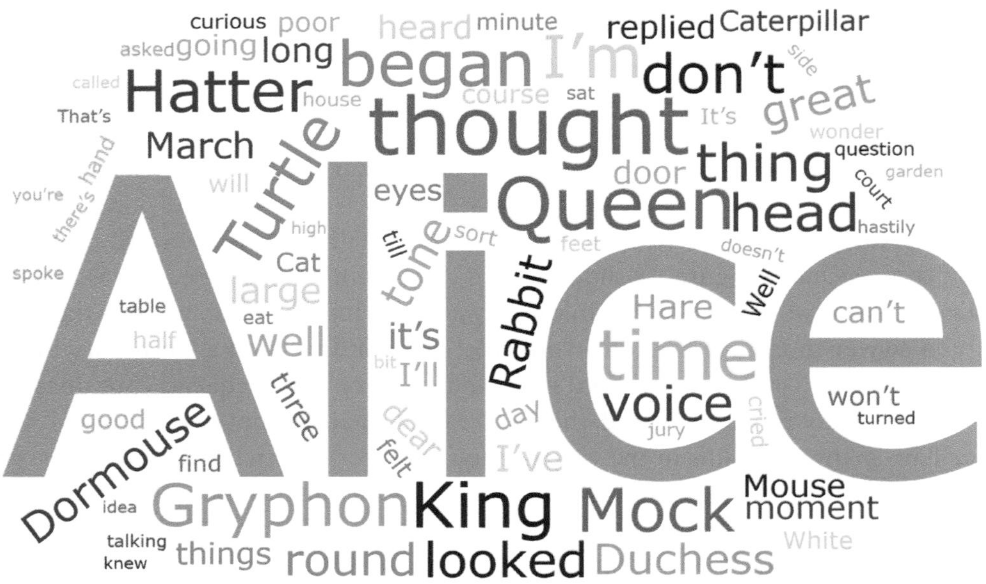

FIGURE 1.8   A word cloud is one of the most popular text visualization techniques. Word size represents data: the word frequency in a document. But, word location and color are often arbitrary – missing the opportunity to convey data.

probably be more enlightening, be faster to scan, and would take up much less screen space, allowing for more items to be summarized on any given page [than tag clouds]."

1.3   (RE)LEARNING FROM HISTORY

While text has been largely separated out from visuals over the last half millennium, there are examples in specialized domains where text encodes data beyond the simple literal text, for example, conveying additional data by color, case, and weight as shown in medieval examples in Figure 1.2. Since the medieval period, domains such as cartography, typesetting, art, mathematics, chemistry, advertisers, and more have continued to use enhanced text in visualization for centuries.

1.3.1   Cartography

Maps require text labels to identify features throughout. Cartographers have enhanced these labels to differentiate between various classes of entities on maps. The use of what are now called typographic attributes pre-dates the printing press, such as the Paris map using color, case, and weight in Figure 1.2. With printing, even the earliest maps continued to use typographic variation. Mercator, for example, wrote about type on maps in 1540 (Osley 1969).

Figure 1.9 shows part of a map by Willem Janzoon Blaeu (1629). The large text MARE MEDITERRANEUM at the top fills the sea, stretched with spacing between the letters (wide tracking). On land, most of the text is of uniform height, but differentiated such that regions are in small caps (e.g. SIMEON, DAN, JUDA), cities in plain (roman) text with a

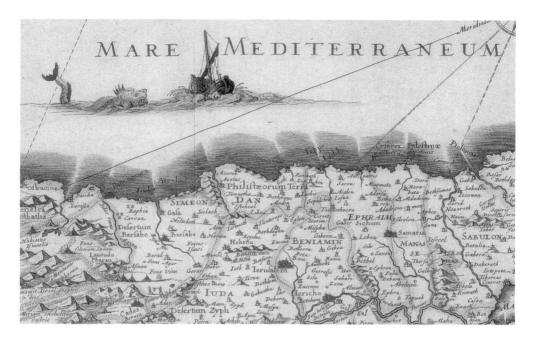

FIGURE 1.9   Early printed map (1629) using typographic variation to differentiate between entities.

leading capital (e.g. Hebron, Jerusalem, Jericho), smaller towns in italic (e.g. *Dora, Aialon*), and rivers set in an italic font following the path of the river (e.g. *Sihar rivus, Jordanes*).

The map in Figure 1.10 is from *Stielers' Atlas* (1905). This map is packed with labels at many sizes for different types of features. Regional features such as **O d e n w a l d** and *H o h e n l o h e r* are larger, spaced, and curved to indicate extents of the area. Rivers are labeled along their paths in a *reverse italic* such as Kocher, Elz, and Seckach.

Typographic attributes on city labels are ordered. For example, there is an ordering of underlines from dashed to solid to double underline indicating successive levels of administration (e.g. Buchen, Mosbach, Speyer). City populations are indicated by an ordering of formats: starting with small italics, to plain, to bold, to all caps bold with slight size increases (e.g. *Mudau*, Weinheim, **Heidelberg**, **MANNHEIM**).

There are other design features of interest. Long names are contracted to better fit the space available, e.g. Heidelbg for Heidelberg, Adelshm. for Adelsheim, and Eberb. for Eberbach.

At a macro level, the density of city labels is an indication of the density of settlements; note how the left side of the image has a greater number of labels than the right side of the image. This is further differentiated as the left labels tend to be mostly horizontal (i.e. point features, such as cities) whereas the fewer labels on the right side also have more labels at angles (indicating natural features such as rivers and extents).

1.3.2 Typography

Typographers also have requirements to order and organization information – using the tools available to them – i.e. text. The diagram in Figure 1.11 is from the preface of

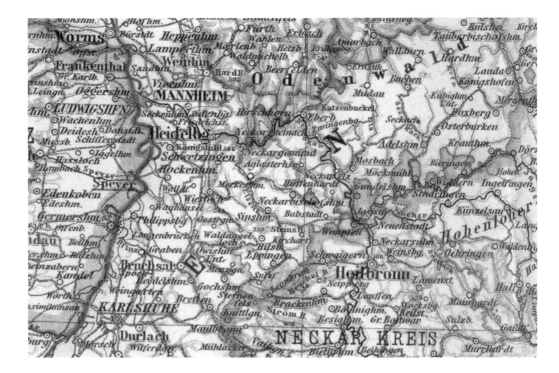

FIGURE 1.10 Map from 1905 packed with labels. City labels indicate data via size, weight, italics, and underline.

Chambers *Cyclopaedia*, first published in 1728. It is entirely text plus a few large parentheses. One may recognize it as a hierarchical representation with various branches. The most dominant word is on the far left, in uppercase with expanded spacing: K N O W L E D G E . This word is connected both visually (with a connecting line) and grammatically (with connecting words "is either") to the node "*Natural,* and *Scientifical,* which is either –." This, in turn, is connected to the next phrases, which in turn are eventually connected to target subjects such as METEOROLOGY[1], HYDROLOGY[2], ZOOLOGY[5], etc.

This textual hierarchy can be skimmed visually or read literally. Typographic formats differentiate key words: for example, italics are used to indicate broad topic areas, while small caps indicate specific subjects. Numeric superscripts are references to numbered sections on following pages. Clearly, this is a visualization, and this visualization is doing something quite different than representing data with shapes, sizes, and colors.

Figure 1.12 is a genealogical tree from 1820 (Carey and Lavoisne) composed entirely from moveable type. Glyphs within the tree, such as crowns, diamonds, and filled circles, indicate people. Background shading differentiates large branches of the tree.

The bulk of the visualization is composed of literal text, such as the names of branches, states, and individual people. A cross (+) indicates date of death. A section sign (§) followed by a phrase indicates continuation in a different tree. Additional details are revealed in phrases, such as "His posterity became extinct" or "made Elector 1623." These names and details can only be encoded with literal text – not shape, color, bold, or other visual attributes.

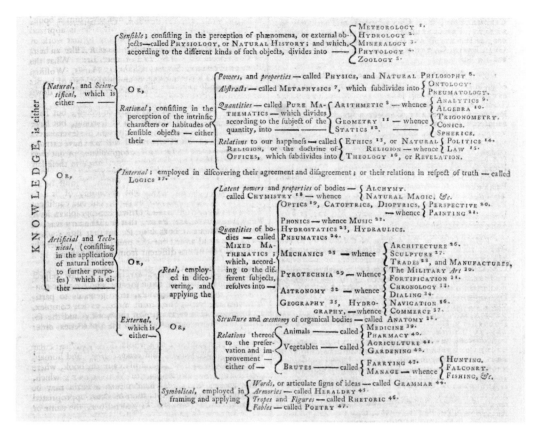

FIGURE 1.11   A hierarchical depiction of the contents of an encyclopedia (1728) as a readable paragraph, with broad topics in italics, specific subjects in small caps, and cross-references in superscript.

The text is further enhanced with typographic attributes. Large branches are indicated in big bold all caps, and states in plain all caps. Individuals are differentiated with rulers in small caps, siblings in roman (plain text), and spouses in italics.

1.3.3 Tables

Timetables are exemplars of information organization and visualization. Pervasive, data dense, and boring, they are easy to ignore. Figure 1.13 is part of a railway timetable from *Bradshaw's Railway Guide* (1906). Stations are listed vertically along the left edge. Each column lists one or more trains, with the earliest trains in the leftmost columns, latest rightmost. A sequence of times in a column defines a train (A). It creates a texture with a set amount of ink that establishes where trains occur. In a portion of a column where there is no train, only dots appear, creating a much lighter texture (B). The viewer can visually skim the table to see blocks of trains. And, unlike many other visualizations of schedules, critical micro-information is immediately accessible – passengers can immediately identify whether they are early or late for their specific train.

ELECTORAL HOUSE of BAVARIA.

1. OTHO I. the GREAT, of Wittelsbach, descended from Leopold first D. of Bavaria, was invested by the Emp. Frederick I. in 1180, + 1183 ; m. Agnes of Wasserburgh.

2. LOUIS I. assassinated 1231 ; m. Ludomilla of Bohemia. ◊Sophia ; m. Herman I. Landgrave of Thuringia. ◊Matilda ; m. Rapoten, Lord of Craiburgh.

3. OTHO II. the ILLUSTRIOUS, + 1253 ; m. Agnes of Saxony, Heiress of Henry the Long, Count Palatine.

4. LOUIS II. the SEVERE, + 1294; m. 1. Mary of Brabant, beh. 1256. ●Henry, Duke of Lower Bavaria. ●Gebehard, Count of ●Elizabeth, + 1270.
2. Anne of Glogau, + 1260. 3. Matilda of Hapsburgh, + 1323. ٭ His posterity became extinct,1340. Hirschburgh. § 1. Conrad IV. Emperor, assas. 1254.
2. Mainard, Count of Tyrol.

ELDEST BRANCH, surnamed Palatine.—24 Electors. | **YOUNGEST BRANCH**, surnamed of Bavaria.—5 Elec.

5. RODOLPH I. the STAMMERER, + 1319 ; m. 1. Matilda, daughter of Emperor | LOUIS III. elected Emperor 1314, + 1347.
Adolphus of Nassau, + 1315. 2. Matilda, daughter of Edward I. of England. | 1. Beatrix of Glogau, + 1322. 2. Margaret of Holland, + 1356.

6. ADOLPHUS, + 1327. 7. RODOLPH II. + 1353. 8. ROBERT L. + 1390. | Louis, elector of Bradenburgh, + 1361. ●Stephen, + 1375.
Ermengarde of Œtingen, Anne of Carinthia. 1. Isabella of Namur, | Margaret of Elizabeth of Sicily.
+ 1389. + 1382. | Carinthia. LANDSHUT.
9. ROBERT II. + 1398. ●Anne, + 1352. 2. Beatrix of Berg, | ●Mainhard,Count of ●Frederick, + 1393.●John the Pacific, + 1397.
Beatrix of Arragon, +1366. Charles IV. Emp.+1378. + 1395. | Tyrol, pois. 1363. Magdalene of Milan. Catharine of Tyrol.

10. ROBERT III. Emperor ◊Anne. ◊Elizabeth. | ●Henry the Rich, ●Ernest, +1438. ●William, go-
in 1400, + 1410. §William II. Count Procopius, Marquis of Moravia. | + 1450. Eliz. Visconti, verned joint-
Elizabeth of Nuremburgh, + 1411. of Berg. SIMMEREN. | Margaret of Austria. + 1432. ly with his
brother.

11. LOUIS III. + 1436. ●John, + 1443. ◊◊Three Stephen, + 1459. | ●George the Rich, ●Albert I. the Pious, + 1460.
1. Blanche of Eng. + 1406. § Catharine of Denmark. daughters. Anne of Weldentz, + 1439. | § + 1503. Anne of Brunswick Grubenhagen.
2. Matilda of Savoy, + 1438. See Map, No. 50. | ٭٭ He left only a
DEUX PONTS. | daughter and the suc-

12. LOUIS IV. ●13. FREDERICK I. ●Robert, Elect. ●Frederick I.+1480. ●Louis the Black, + 1489. | cession was seized by●Albert II. the Wise, gov. after his 2
+ 1449. § + 1476. of Cologne, Margaret of Gueldres, Jane of Croi. | Albert the Wise. elder brothers Johnand Sigismund,
Marg.of Savoy.§ Clara of Tetlingen, + 1480. + 1485. | + 1508 ; m. Cunegunda of Austria.
14. PHILIP, + 1508 ; m. Marg. of Bavaria. John I. + 1509. ●Gaspard, governed joint- | ●Alexander, + 1514. ●William I. the Constant, + 1550.
John II. + 1557. ly with his brother, and | Margaret of Hohenloe. Mary Jacqueline of Baden, + 1580.

15. LOUIS V. ●Robert, + 1504. ●16. FREDE- John II. + 1557. died soon afterhisfather. | Louis, + 1532. ●Albert III. the Magnanimous,
+ 1544. Elizabeth of RICK II. the 1. Beat. of Baden, +1535. Emilia of Brandenburgh. | Elizabeth of Hesse, + 1579.
Sibylla of Ba- Bavaria. WISE,+1556. 2. Mary of Œtingen. | + 1563. Mary, dau. of Emp. Ferdinand I.
varia, +1519. 17. OTHO-HENRY, Dorothy of 18. FREDERICK III. 1576. | ●Wolfgang ; + 1569. ●William II. the Religious, abdi-
+ 1559. Denmark. 1. Mary of Brandenburgh, + 1567. | Anne of Hesse,+1591. cated 1596, + 1626.
Susan of Bav. + 1543. 2. Amelia of Nevenauer, + 1602. | Renata of Lorraine.

NEUBURGH.
19. LOUIS VI. ●John Casimir. ◊Elizabeth. ◊Susanna Dorothy, + 1592. Philip Louis, | Charles, Duke of ●1. MAXIMILIAN the Great,
+ 1583. § John Frederick § Joha William of Saxony, + 1614. | Birkenfeld, + 1600. made Elector 1623, + 1651.
Elizabeth of Hesse, + 1582. of Saxony. + 1573. Anne of Juliers, | Dorothy of Brunswick. Mary Anne of Austria.
SULZBACH.

20. FREDERICK IV.+1610.◊Anne Mary, + 1583. ●Wolfgang William, + 1653. Augustus, | Christian I. Duke of ●2. FERDINAND MARY, + 1679.
Louisa of Nassau, +1644. § Charles IX. King of 1. Magdalene of Bavaria. + 1631. | Beschweiler, + 1654. Henrietta of Savoy, + 1676.
Sweden. 2. Catharine of Deux-Ponts. Hedwige of Hol- | Magdalene of Deuz-
3. Mary of Furstemburgh. stein, + 1657. | Ponts.

21. FREDERICK V.+1632.◊Elizabeth, + 1660. ●John, + 1690. 24. PHILIP WILLIAM, Christian Au- | Christian II. + 1717. ●3. MAXIMILIAN EMMANUEL,
Elizabeth of England, § George William, Elec- + 1690. gustus, + 1708. | Catharine of Rappel- + 1726.
+ 1662. tor of Brandenburgh, 1. Anne of Poland, +1651. Amelia of Nas- | stein, + 1683. 1. Mary Antonia of Austria, +1692.
+ 1640. 2. Elizabeth of Hesse, + 1709. sau, + 1669. | 2. Theresa Sobieski, + 1730.

22. CHARLES LOUIS, +1680. ◊◊See Map, 25. JOHN 26. CHARLES Theodore +1732. | Christian III. + 1735. ●4. CHARLES ALBERT, Emperor in
Charlotte of Hesse-Cassel, + 1686. § § No. 31. WILLIAM, PHILIP, Mary of Hesse- | Charlotte of Nassau- 1742, + 1745.
+ 1716. + 1742. Rhinsfeld, +1720. | Saarbruck, + 1774. Mary Amelia of Austria, + 1756.
23. CHARLES, Elizabeth, 1. Mary of 1. Louisa of John Christian, | Frederick, + 1767. ●5. MAXIMILIAN JOSEPH, + 1777.
+1685. § + 1722. Austria, Brandenburgh, +1733. | Mary of Sultzbach. Mary Anne of Saxony, + 1797.
Wilhemina of Philip, Duke of + 1689. + 1695. Henrietta, of La | ٭٭ His dominions went to Charles
Denmark. Orleans. 2. Mary of 2. Theresa Tour, + 1728. | Theodore.
+ 1701. Medicis. Lubomirski, 27. CHARLES THEODORE, + 1799. | ●28. MAXIMILIAN JOSEPH, born 1756.
+ 1712. Mary Leopold, of Austria, born 1776. | 1. Mary of Hesse-Darmstadt.
2. Caroline of Baden, born 1776.

●Charles Louis, b. 1786. ◊Augusta Amelia, b. 1788; m. Eugene Beauharnois, b. 1782. ◊Charlotte, b. 1792 ; m. Fred. Will. of Wirtemburgh.●Charles, b.1795.◊◊5 dau.

FIGURE 1.12 Text-dense 1820 genealogical tree with additional information in formats and symbols.

This established pattern can then be disrupted by inserting much darker blocks such as the dark line and the bold text **Stop** (C); text rotated 90 degrees and extra bold, such as **Wednesdays Only** (D); or a variety of big, individual extra bold characters (E) explained in the legend. The same approach of setting a convention and then breaking it happens in other places, such as the station list, using indentation to indicate a deviation – a branch line (F).

1.3.4 Science Classification and Notation

Text-heavy charts can also be found in the sciences. Figure 1.14 is a zoologic taxonomy from 1890. This visualization requires extensive text to be usable; all the nodes are explicitly labeled. The text is somewhat differentiated at each level; the root *ANIMAL KINGDOM* is set in all caps spaced widely. The first level, *BRANCHES*, is set in a smaller all caps. Thereafter each level is set in proper case (e.g. *Mammalia > Carnivora > Canidae*). Text at higher levels is usually larger than text at lower levels, depending on space available. Text

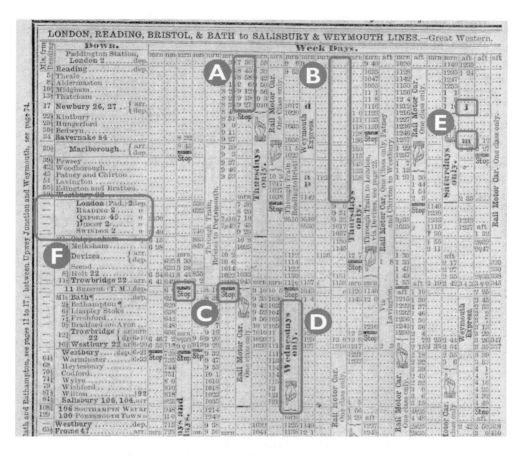

FIGURE 1.13   Portion of a 1906 railway timetable with macro-patterns (trains) and details (times, notes).

is set along arcs when space permits, and this text may be spaced widely, like area labels on a map (e.g. *I n s e c t a*). Color differentiates wedges corresponding to classes. Illustrations around the perimeter are purely decorative; they are ordered but otherwise do not line up with corresponding families.

The *periodic table of the elements* is a 19th century invention. Each cell corresponds to an element, identifying the element with a symbol (a one or two letter code) and the element name. The rows and columns of the table organize elements such that characteristics of the elements are related to adjacent cells. Therefore, it may be desirable to show these character-istics directly in the table cells, such as Figure 1.15. These characteristics may be represented as numeric text with a high degree of accuracy (useful as a reference) or encoded with a visual attribute, such as color (useful to reveal a pattern across rows and columns). Each cell in this table displays six characteristics as text, in addition to the identification and color. In this table, the only typographic differentiation is text size and font weight – although there are many, many different variants of encodings used across periodic tables.

The periodic table introduces the element codes which are used in chemical formulas. Each element is uniquely identified by a one or two letter code. The first letter is always

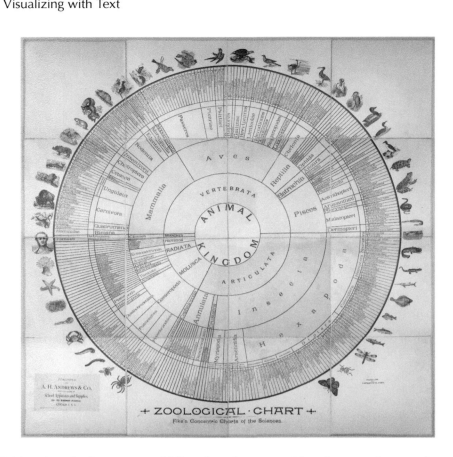

FIGURE 1.14   A zoologic taxonomy folding chart from 1890. Note the extensive use of text.

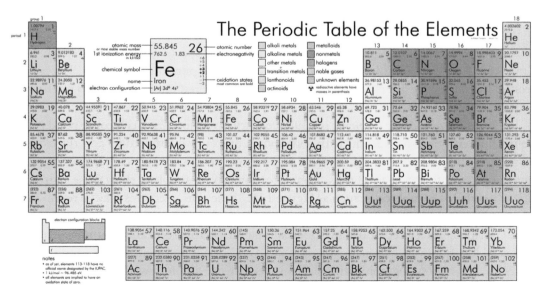

FIGURE 1.15   Sample contemporary periodic table of the elements, mostly made of text and numbers.

uppercase, the second letter always lowercase. Chemical formulas sequence these codes, plus numeric values and symbols, to encode information regarding a molecule. This includes:

- *Preceding superscripts* denote isotopes, e.g. ^2H, ^{235}U.

- *Trailing subscripts* denote the number of atoms in the molecule, e.g. H_2O, $C_6H_{12}O_6$.

- *Trailing superscripts* denote the charge on an ion, e.g. Na^+, or Cu^{2+}.

- *Paired brackets* indicate ionic compounds which are not discrete molecules, e.g. $[SO_4]^{2-}$. Paired parentheses indicate repeating units.

- *Symbols* may be used to indicate structures, such as double bonds with =, e.g. $H_2C=CH_2$, or @ to indicate a trapped atom, e.g. $M@C_{60}$.

These codes can be sequenced to create chemical equations, e.g. $CH_4 + 2O_2 \rightarrow CO_2 + 2H_2O$. One percent of a massive biochemical pathways flowchart (Michal 2017) is shown in Figure 1.16, filled with chemical notations, connections, and annotations.

Mathematical notation similarly uses alphanumerics and symbols to express algebraic equations. Conventions include:

- *Alphanumerics* represent quantities (e.g. 3, 1.618) and unknowns (e.g. x, y) or constants (e.g. π, c).

- *Parentheses, brackets, etc.* are used for grouping symbols, e.g. $f(x)$, [], {}.

- *Symbols* are used extensively as arithmetic operators (e.g. +, −, /, =, <) and set operators (e.g. $\in$, $\cap$, $\cup$).

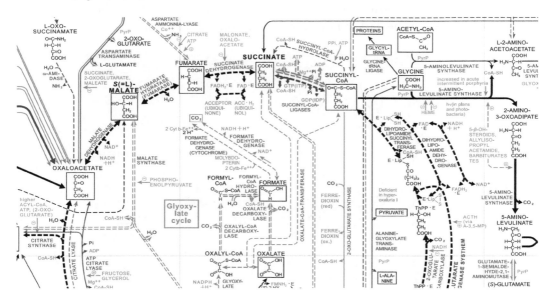

FIGURE 1.16 Tiny portion of a modern biochemical chart. Dense with text and chemical formulas.

- *Line* (viniculum). Used as a divider for stacked numerics and an operation, e.g. a list of numbers to be added, or as division. The line, used as division, can be used to group symbols. The line is similar to a text underline but treated independently.

- *Superscripts and subscripts*, for example, as exponents x^2, 2^x.

- *Typefaces and alphabets*. Latin and Greek letters (e.g. α, β, Σ) are used as well as different typefaces, such as script (i.e. calligraphy, e.g. $\mathscr{H}$, $\mathscr{R}$), blackletter (i.e. Fraktur, e.g. $\mathfrak{H}$, $\mathfrak{R}$) and a blackboard bold (e.g. $\mathbb{H}$, $\mathbb{R}$). Glyphs may be reoriented or have added marks to create a unique meaning (e.g. $\forall$, $\exists$, $\nexists$, $\varnothing$).

As with chemical equations, some mathematical equations can be expressed in a line of text, such as $a^2 + b^2 = c^2$ or $A = \pi r^2$. More generally, many formulas may require more space than a single line of symbols and follow different layout rules than running text.

1.3.5 Code Editors

Software code, like notation systems, is highly structured. Code conventions and automatic formatting of code increases the visibility of the structure, differentiates types of tokens, and highlights syntax errors. Baecker and Marcus (1989) systematized typographic formatting of computer code (based on earlier *pretty print* programs). In turn, these many conventions are now commonplace in modern code editors, such as Figure 1.17. In this snapshot, some examples of formats include:

- *Foreground color* differentiates token type, e.g. comments are in green text, function names in yellow, global variables in purple.

- *Background color* is used to highlight a range of text, such as a full line for breakpoint (line 50), the small boxes indicating parameters (e.g. light gray box behind *key* and *def* on line 39), or the dark yellow warning box on the same line.

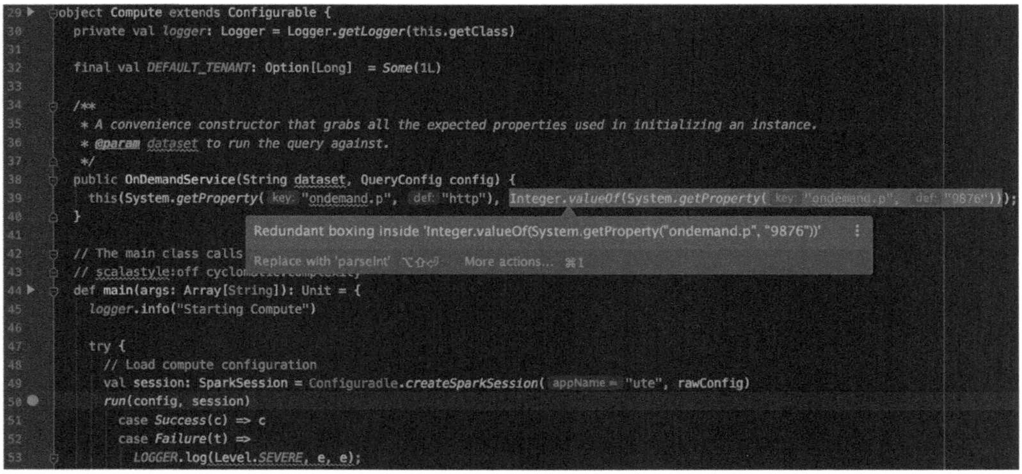

FIGURE 1.17 Modern code editor with formats and conventions indicating syntax, errors, and scope.

- *Bold* is used to pop-out some tagged text, e.g. @param (on line 36).

- *Italics* indicate commented-out code blocks (lines 34—37) and globally accessible variables and functions (e.g. *getLogger* line 30)

- *Underlines* can be straight or wavy, for example to indicate function errors (line 53) or potential spelling errors, e.g. dataset (line 36).

- *Symbols* and *delimiters* are intrinsic to the programming language. In this example, colon, equal, period, slash, and star denote syntax such as comments or assignment; while parentheses, braces, and brackets define several types of scope.

- *Capitalization* is used by the programmer to differentiate between variables (e.g. constant or global) or camelCase to improve readability.

1.3.6 Alphanumeric Charts

Alphanumeric charts use characters to plot data points. Stem and leaf plots are one type of alphanumeric chart. Alphanumeric charts have a long history in financial services, starting in the late 19th century as *figure* charts, and have evolved in a variety of ways.

Figure 1.18 is a *market profile* chart used in financial services. Letters indicate the time of day that a commodity trades at a specific price level. A common encoding uses A–X, a–x to indicate half hour intervals starting at midnight, with uppercase for trades in the morning, lowercase for the afternoon. Characters are aligned vertically (by day) and stacked horizontally forming a histogram, enabling a macro-reading (the distribution) and a micro-reading (the individual characters). The use of letters allows for up to 48 unique half hour intervals to be shown.

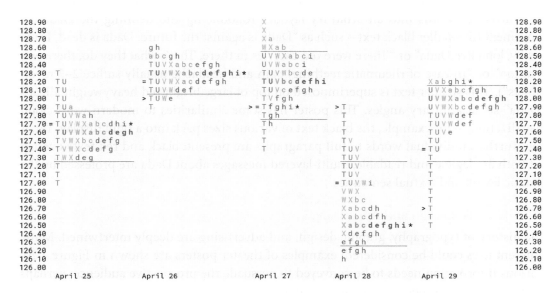

FIGURE 1.18 Sample contemporary *market profile* chart. Distributions are formed with stacked letters.

Much more data can be added. Symbols indicate price levels such as price at market open (>) and market close (*). Underlines indicate ranges, such as inner quartiles. Bold indicates *point of control*, which is the longest bar in the distribution. Color is used to indicate blocks of time (e.g. some markets trade in multiple sessions per day or in different time zones).

Modern interactive versions of market profile charts are produced by many commercial software vendors (e.g. Bluewater Trading, CBOT, CQG, E-Signal, Market Delta, Pro Realtime, Sierra Chart, and Windotrader), implying an economic validation of the approach. Each vendor may have unique extensions, such as the use of color (foreground letter color or background square); superscripts; micro-scale fonts (down to three points, i.e. approximately 1mm high); added shapes; added outlines; vertical lines (indicating a range); aligned distributions (either underneath or adjacent); interactive splitting or merging of columns; interactive highlights across rows; and so on.

1.3.7 Art and Poetry

Artists and poets have long used typography and text layout as elements to enhance or add semantic meaning beyond the literal words. While not directly encoding categorical or quantitative data, they add semantics through type manipulation.

Concrete poetry, such as the *Calligrammes* by Apollinaire (1918) adjusts lines of text, such as curving text along paths, wrapping text, adjusting sizes, capitalization, and so on. These form figurative images, such as a bird or fountain, in the example poem *The stabbed dove and the water fountain* shown in Figure 1.19. More generally, fitting text into arbitrary shapes can be done computationally such as micrography (adjusting text layout to fit, e.g. Maharik 2011) or calligraphic packing (adjusting letterforms to fit, e.g. Xu and Kaplan 2007).

The Dada poster by Theo van Doesburg (1923) in Figure 1.19 (right) assembles somewhat arbitrary words into an arbitrary layout pronouncing and defining the Dada art movement (in smaller black text – such as "Dada is against the future, Dada is dead, Dada is silly, long live Dada" or "There were red cherries in there, That's what they do, there was that too" or "In case of rheumatic teething, pain and headache usually suffice 2–3 revon tablets"). This smaller text is superimposed on top of large bright red heavyweight allcaps "Dada" set at arbitrary angles. This poster has some similarities to modern word cloud visualizations – for example, the black text of various sizes pack into a tight display. Yet, it goes further: individual words to full paragraphs are present; black and red texts overlap yet both are legible and readable; multi-layered messages about Dada are professed by the chaotic layout and textual semantics.

1.3.8 Graphic Design and Advertising

The history of typography, graphic design, and advertising are deeply intertwined. Many different uses could be considered: examples of theater posters are shown in Figure 1.20. Various information needs to be conveyed to persuade the prospective audience: perhaps the story, the performers, or the music will be the draw.

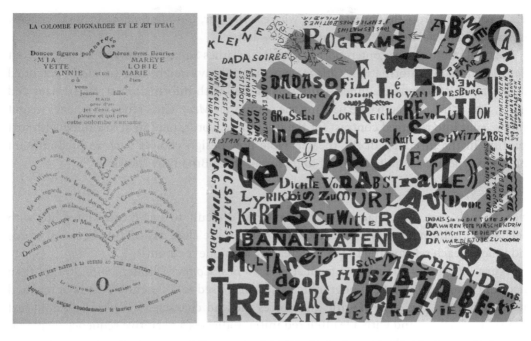

FIGURE 1.19   Expressive text in a Calligramme (1918) and a Dada poster (1923), Centraal Museum.

FIGURE 1.20   Advertisements rely on typography and imagery to convey semantics beyond text.

Far left is a mid-19th century poster with varying type size, typeface, foreground color, background shading, and effects such as polychromatic 3D text to make key information such as the names of stars, venue, and date stand out.

Next is a poster by Jules Chéret for *Casino de Paris* (1891). A fusion of text and imagery, each text block is differentiated from the others using size, color, capitalization, rotation, 3D effect, outlines, and different typefaces – for example, the text *Casino de Paris* is in wide, heavy, rounded, drop-shadowed letters, whereas the star, *Camille Stéfani*, is in tall narrow letters, and *fêtes de nuit* is in extremely narrow letters.

The final photo shows contemporary posters in Times Square Manhattan. Each sets out the title and adds information. *Chicago* has only a heavyweight title (made of extruded 3D letters) and a famous tagline. *Waitress* is packed with information at varied sizes and colors, and a tiny rotated badge naming the composer. *Mean Girls* relies on a heavyweight tagline, split into reversed contrast for the final three words, plus an arrow filled with text pointing in the direction of the theater. Note how design choices such as predominant color and typeface set quite different tones for all three Broadway shows.

1.3.9 Comics

Even though text and imagery may have been difficult to technically integrate with mechanical printing, comics fundamentally rely on the close association between words and images, each reinforcing the other, creating a unique medium.

Figure 1.21 shows an example from *America's Best Comics* (Binder 1945). Rather than encoding quantitative data, typographic variation is used to differentiate parts of text and encode emotion. The large 3D title announces the lead character PYROMAN. Bold text on a yellow background with a leading red initial indicates a narrative sequence. Dialog is set on white speech balloons, with bold for intensity. Exclamations are set off, in a different font evocative of the exclamation, such as the jaggy text **UGH!** Sound effects are set in red text superimposed over the action such as SOK! and POW! Other than the title, almost all

FIGURE 1.21   Comics deeply integrate typographically expressive text and visual imagery.

of the text is nearly uniform in size; the space needs to be shared with the visuals and the text presumably shouldn't be any larger than needed for reading and conveying semantic effects.

Many more techniques are used in expressive text in comics, such as changing fonts to indicate different languages (e.g. *Asterix the Legionary*), lengthening words with added letters (e.g. Aaaaahh!, see Huyghebaert 2017), small-sized text for whispering, and so on.

1.3.10 Post-Modern Text

Post-modernists, starting in the 1980s, challenged the formalities of modernism across many design fields. Using new tools, such as page layout software and digital fonts, they broadly experimented with new ways to convey information in texts and create multiple readings as seen in magazines such as *Emigre, Octavo*, and *Ray Gun* and books such as Avital Ronell's *The Telephone Book* or Johanna Drucker's Letterpress books.

Figure 1.22 (left) is a portion of a page from *Emigre* magazine (VanderLans 1990). Typographic formats shift by word, sentence, and paragraph; the layout splits for a callout; size, word spacing, and line spacing vary significantly; text is superimposed on other text; and more. All issues were highly experimental – breaking with convention to explore new design possibilities and convey different readings of the text.

Figure 1.22 (right) shows sample paragraphs from Ronell's *The Telephone Book* (1989). Deconstructivist Ronell adjusts a wide variety of typographic properties (e.g. tracking, sizing, weight, small caps) and deliberately breaks typographic conventions (e.g. interrupting words with punctuation, adding gaps through text, adjusting layout, setting some text in Morse code) throughout *The Telephone Book* to interrupt readability and convey semantics through typography. Character heights are adjusted to create waves running through

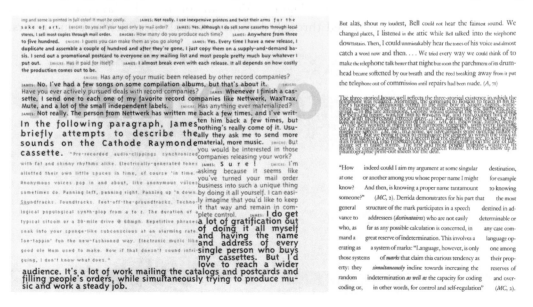

FIGURE 1.22 **Post-modernists disrupt type and layout to create multiple readings of texts. Left, Emigre magazine (1992), right sample paragraphs from Ronell's** *The Telephone Book* **(1989).**

paragraphs; line spacing is tightened to compress text almost to the point of illegibility; and spaces between words align across rows of text to create illusory rivers running vertically through the text.

1.3.11 Data Visualization

There are many charts, visualizations, and dashboards today that use little text within the core plot area of the visualization. However, there are some that extensively use text to directly encode data. Word clouds (Figure 1.8) are a popular text visualization, however, they convey low information as previously discussed. Text visualizations can go further, indicating spatial, temporal, hierarchical, or semantic relationships, such as the many examples at the *Text Visualization Browser* (textvis.lnu.se). *NewsMap*, shown in Figure 1.23, is a treemap of headlines, sized by the number of related articles, with hue indicating topic and brightness indicating recency, with interactive pop-ups, filters, searches, and links to full stories (Weskamp 2004).

Knowledge maps are visualizations used to gain insight into the structure of large-scale information spaces. Many exemplars are curated at scimaps.org. Figure 1.24 shows a small portion of the *Map of Science*, (Boyack, Klavans, and Paley 2009), with the full map shown in the inset bottom right. Fields of science are indicated with large colored labels (e.g. Organic Chemistry, Ecology). Topic words associated with individual nodes are a trail of keywords (e.g. folding rate, quantitative proteomics, peptide ions). An interactive version combined a large, very high-resolution poster, upon which a projector was used to highlight nodes of research focus by user-selected country and field, for example, US research in proteomics.

Real-time visualizations in control centers and trading floors make use of many screens to depict critical information, such as Figure 1.25. Many of these displays are data dense and text heavy. Status is conveyed through dominant visual cues such as color, reverse

FIGURE 1.23   NewsMap conveys data via headline sentence, size, hue, and brightness.

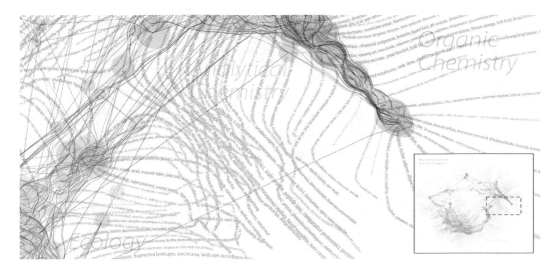

FIGURE 1.24 **Small portion from *Map of Science* showing research fields and detailed topic keywords.**

FIGURE 1.25 Control room visualization of a network with numerous labeled values and entities.

video, or blinking. Secondary information, such as the identity and values associated with each element, is immediately visible as labeled text. The direct labeling is desirable to facilitate the operators' tasks. Operators continuously scan the displays for anomalies, leading indicators, or signals; identify the entity and its values; and then take action to address the situation. These actions may include speaking with adjacent operators, using collaborative tools, and interacting with local displays (e.g. to access detailed data, procedural documentation, tools for analysis and simulation; to modify settings; or to create new tasks).

Infographics may be text dense, such as some visualizations in newspapers, magazines, and posters. A small portion of *Death and Taxes* (Pearlman et al. 2015) is shown in Figure 1.26 (full poster shown in the inset bottom right). It shows a large hierarchy of US government departmental budgets by logo size, and details in sized, colored, and weighted text.

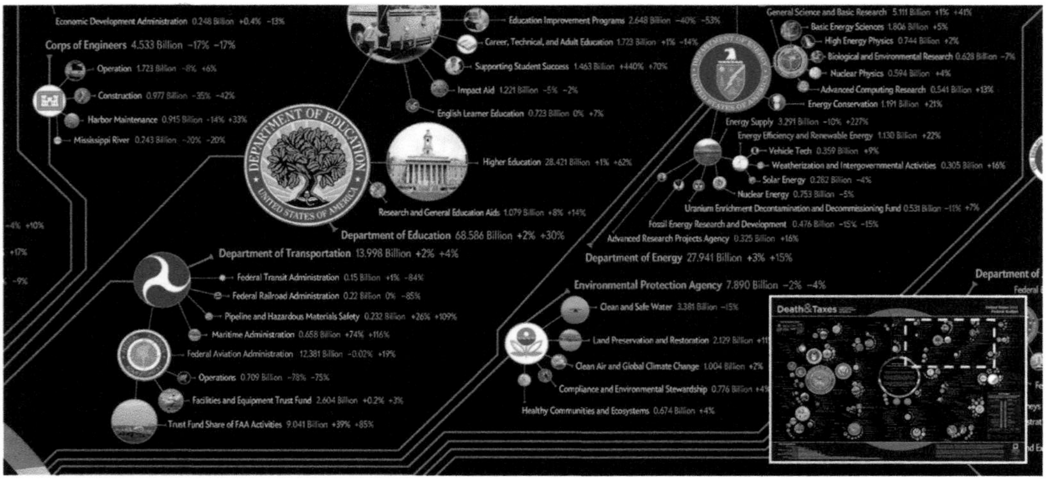

FIGURE 1.26   Small portion from *Death and Taxes* showing the US Discretionary budget.

1.4 FURTHER READING

Historic Visualizations. For the new visualization designer, the books by Edward Tufte and the examples provided by Michael Friendly (e.g. datavis.ca/milestones) provide a good starting point. There are a variety of books on historic visualization people (e.g. Rendgen's *The Minard System*, 2018), data types (e.g. Grafton and Rosenberg's *Cartographies of Time*, 2010), layout types (e.g. Manuel Lima's many collections such as *The Book of Circles*, 2017), inspection of historic techniques and events (e.g. Howard Wainer's many books including *A Gleam in the Mind's Eye*, 2020 with Michael Friendly) or even interactive techniques with paper-based visualizations (e.g. Helfand's *Reinventing the Wheel*, 2006). For further investigation, digitized collections of historic manuscripts, texts, and maps can be found on sites such as archive.org, museums (e.g. britishmuseum.org, getty.edu, digitalcomicmuseum.com), libraries (e.g. bl.uk, digitalcollections.nypl.org), and independent collections (e.g. davidrumsey.com).

Early Modernism and *Post Modernism*. In early modernism, various artists' texts proclaim a rejection of the past and a desire for revolutionary change including simplification, streamlining, and so forth – e.g. see the writings of architects such as Le Corbusier (*Towards an Architecture*, 1923) or typographer Jan Tschichold (*The New Typography*, 1928). For visualization, see Otto Neurath's *International Picture Language: The First Rules of ISOTYPE*, 1936; or *From Hieroglyphics to Isotype: A Visual Autobiography*, 2010. Post-modernism is wonderfully experimental, worth further investigation for challenging assumptions across media, including architecture, fine art, graphic design, and typography. Johanna Drucker has a number of works on type in the arts (e.g. *Letterpress Language* 2008); also consider original periodicals from the 1980s and 90s such as *Octavo, Emigre*, and *Ray Gun*; and modern concrete poetry, such as *The New Concrete: Visual Poetry in the 21st Century* (2015).

Contemporary data visualizations and references will be discussed more in the next chapter.

CHAPTER 2

The Design Space of Visualization with Text

THE PREVIOUS CHAPTER SHOWS text is a key element in a wide range of visualizations. These examples stretch beyond what visualization and infographic designers consider visualizations: sentences in pie wedges; paragraphs interleaved in networks; paragraphs split into hierarchies; tables of codes, numbers, and phrases; graphs with labels on nodes, edges, areas, and notes; typographically expressive posters and comics; software code; and so on.

What is needed is a way to organize these concepts and frame the *design space* of text in visualization. Before systematizing the use of text in visualization, it is necessary consider how visualizations are conceptualized today.

First, is text even a visualization element? Text must be read to be understood. Reading is slow. Reading is the opposite of fast perception of patterns. However, words can be made to visually pop-out. Furthermore, words may be a critical part towards successfully completing visualization tasks.

Then, what are the design choices for encoding data into text within visualizations? The set of all design choices can be described as a *design space*. Defining the design space is important because it organizes the design parameters, which can then be combined in diverse ways to fulfill the viewers' objectives. Different combinations may be more effective for different tasks, different types of data, different display technologies, different interactions, and so forth. Critical evaluation and extension of design spaces is important because it increases the possibilities of what can be solved. Expanded design spaces enabled buildings out of steel instead of stone, or cars that run on electricity. The goal of this chapter is to define the design space for text encoding data in visualizations.

2.1 IS TEXT VISUALIZATION?

Are the prior historic examples visualizations? Before diving into *how* to use text in visualizations, it is worth reconsidering what a visualization is.

2.1.1 Visualization as Visual Patterns

The central concept in many definitions of data visualization is the graphical representation of data to make patterns perceptually visible. Data is encoded into visual attributes (such as size and color) to see trends, outliers, and other patterns (e.g. Ware 2013 or Mackinlay and Winslow 2009). Encoding data into visual attributes, such as those shown in Figure 2.1, enables patterns to be perceived immediately (i.e. preattentively) regardless of the number of elements.

With interactive visualization, these trends and outliers can be explored with simple taps or clicks, such as zooming into a region or identifying a data point using a tooltip. However, not all visualization media are interactive, such as print. Some interactive visualizations are not interactive for all viewers, such as participants in a presentation or viewers of a recorded video. Furthermore, some viewers are not inclined to interact, even when interactions are available. For example, Archie Tse of *The New York Times* (2016) explains: "If you make a tooltip or rollover, assume no one will ever see it. If content is important for readers to see, don't hide it."

Unlike preattentive visual attributes, text must be read. Reading is linear: one-word-at-a-time. Preattention is rapid parallel perceptual processing. Compared to preattention, reading text is slow to comprehend. Further, preattention can immediately detect a red dot amongst many gray dots but finding one word among many is not preattentive. Following this path of logic, text does not fit the criteria for visualization.

However, representing text is not limited to the literal alphanumeric characters. Visual attributes can be applied to text, thereby making outliers and patterns easy to perceive. In addition to common visualization attributes such as position, size, color, etc., additional typographic attributes can be used such as font weight, italic, uppercase, or typeface, as shown in Figure 2.2 (and previously seen in many of the historic examples).

How does this work? With text simply being a jumble of shapes, how can any subset of shapes stand out?

Typographers carefully design letterforms and spacing such that no text stands out. Within a single typeface such as *Helvetica* or *Times*, there is a consistency in the strokes, heights, white space, and so on so that each letter is visually tuned. Figure 2.3 shows some sample letters from the typeface *Franklin Gothic*. At the left, c and d are superimposed over o: note that the letter c is not just an aperture cut into an o, but narrower. The d is narrower and heavily tapered where the circular bowl joins the upright stem. Even a simple lower-case r is modified: the upper portion of the stem is narrower than the lower portion. In the

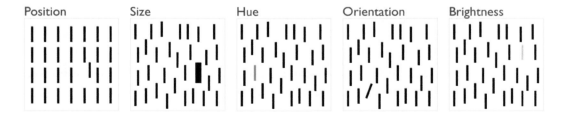

FIGURE 2.1 Preattentive visual attributes. The outlier in each square is fast and easy to perceive.

Position				Size				Hue				Orientation				Brightness			
Odis	Luis	**Alta**	John	Dino	Joey	Trey	Dora	Reta	Lisa	Dara	Theo	Matt	Lacy	Vera	Glen	Jean	Dian	Dick	Tuan
Fern	Neva	Rene	Dora	Nell	Emma	Cary	Kira	Neal	Barb	Gino	Rhea	Kurt	Eula	Rose	June	Cory	Elmo	Burt	Josh
Judy	Ines	Leta	Mose	Cruz	Jodi	Debi	Katy	Rena	Rita	Lila	Tera	Gina	Omer	Cody	Lora	Reva	Lynn	Lacy	Thea
Earl	Nita	Wade	Lacy	Judi	Rita	Elma	John	Gena	Jude	Chas	Joey	Rick	Avis	Milo	Hana	Rick	Leah	Matt	Reva
Judy	Rose	Clay	Tory	Burl	Dean	Kirk	Vern	Burt	Greg	Lino	Doug	Eddy	Beau	Edna	Otto	Tana	Erik	Tory	Jade

Weight				Oblique				Case				Typeface				Underline			
Bess	Kory	**Rita**	Jeff	Rene	Rory	Cari	Mark	Kory	LONG	Elma	Vera	Mary	Jose	Chas	Toby	Gaye	Long	Ines	Etta
Mari	Erin	Hank	Jane	Anne	Jose	*Gena*	Cody	Leif	Alan	Kris	Leon	Lupe	Alan	Reed	Gene	Dona	Lisa	Lacy	Lacy
Cleo	Jame	Tena	Gena	Lupe	Aida	Liza	Hugh	Gwen	Juli	Scot	Abel	Curt	Jude	Ella	Troy	Noel	Lily	Kent	Faye
Avis	Sara	Hugo	Dane	Minh	Jose	Leif	Geri	Vada	Eula	Mary	Mona	Kyla	Jane	Sang	Corp	Cole	<u>Tena</u>	Mack	Kara
Elda	Lupe	Lura	Rita	Dane	Inez	Burl	Tera	Gwen	Nita	Clay	Kira	Jade	Mona	Lynn	Cary	Rory	Ruth	Burt	Gwen

FIGURE 2.2 Visual attributes applied to text. Top row uses the same attributes as the prior figure; lower row uses unique typographic attributes.

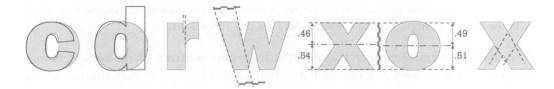

FIGURE 2.3 Type designers carefully tune letterforms to increase legibility and maintain an even weight whether the letter is dense (e.g. w) or sparse (e.g. r).

letter w, many angles come together potentially making for a dark blob: note how the leading stroke significantly tapers down and how thin the next stroke is. The visual centers of the x and o are above the geometric center line so that the letters do not appear top heavy. And, the crossings on the x are offset to increase the whitespace and legibility.

This tuning facilitates reading, as no individual letters distract from the perception of words. The uniformity of ink density across a page is referred to as *typographic color*. A blurred page should have no visible dark spots in a well-designed font. Given a uniform density, then, simply using **bold** creates a deviation that perceptually pops-out following preattentive principles. Similarly, the uniform vertical strokes of letters create a field where some sloped text, such as *oblique*, will visually pop-out. UPPERCASE stands out with wider letters that also significantly stand above the intermediate x-height of lowercase letters. Some typefaces are designed to be highly similar with only minor differences, such as sans serifs. Other typefaces which have greater variance in letterforms, such as 𝖇𝖑𝖆𝖈𝖐𝖑𝖊𝖙𝖙𝖊𝖗 or handletter, are much more likely to be visually distinct from surrounding text. And so on.

Strobelt et al. (2016) conducted a study to show that text formatting can indeed make individual words visually pop-out. Note, however, that the degree of preattention is based on the degree of difference between the target and other items, as shown in Figure 2.4. A bright red target is easier to detect than a dark red target among black items. This applies to all visualizations, not just text. Heavyweight text will be easier to detect among lightweight text than plain text among bold text.

Size

Dion	Leif	Hoyt	Will
Jere	Elba	Alta	Cari
Ella	Adan	Anna	Gale
Cleo	Amos	Eloy	Noel
Theo	Rose	Emil	Enid
Lino	Gena	Omer	Kris
Cara	Olen	Reid	Dale
King	Chet	Juan	Erik
Bill	Lupe	Gena	June
Maya	Iris	Joni	Russ
Marc	Dave	Sean	Aida
Dora	Mari	Robt	Liza
Gino	Pete	Bart	Jame
Pete	Avis	King	Tina
Cruz	Jane	Lesa	Dean

Hue

Jana	Gaye	Herb	Kyle
Toby	Otto	Lyle	Cruz
Otto	Rick	Lisa	Avis
Todd	Yong	Cruz	Robt
Teri	Sean	Cara	Milo
Phil	Chet	Shon	Milo
Rene	Marc	Seth	Flor
Mose	Gwen	Olin	Alex
Rory	Ryan	Ryan	Cruz
Jeri	Maya	Odis	Iola
Stan	Shon	Kurt	Jody
Kyla	Dana	Alma	Lori
Noah	Shad	Aida	Eddy
Curt	Judi	Eloy	Tina
Hope	Rita	Nell	Luke

Weight

Burt	Eddy	Rich	Elva
Omar	Bret	Herb	Jana
Lola	Aron	Levi	Noel
Omar	Jody	Gaye	Dina
Kurt	Todd	Tami	Otha
Tyra	Rhea	Milo	Lane
Dana	Mary	Flor	Thea
Cruz	Soon	Rita	Beth
Greg	John	Kaye	**Cori**
Aura	Noah	Inez	Jung
Bess	Brad	Lura	Thea
Gene	Dara	Leah	Juli
Fred	John	Rich	Hope
Jack	Cleo	Neal	Fred
Tori	Mack	**Cruz**	Noah

Typeface

Nora	Alma	Oren	Gena
Leta	Paul	Hoyt	Elsa
Thad	Lacy	Gaye	Aura
Gina	Eula	Jean	Pete
Jody	Lila	Rick	Floy
Lila	Cleo	Shon	Thea
Ryan	Lola	Ward	Alda
Kent	Abel	Tony	Kari
Minh	Gwen	Gary	Sung
Iola	Lois	Odis	Dawn
Roma	Rick	Clay	Curt
Gene	Shad	Juli	Dana
Evan	Kara	Erna	Cari
Ella	Lacy	Lyle	*Tena*
Opal	Cole	Paul	Edna

Font Width

Minh	Lori	Clay	Tera
Hoyt	Ella	Burl	Rudy
Tori	Ward	Vada	Evan
Owen	Wade	Ruth	Dina
Leah	Lori	Otha	Aida
Rolf	Josh	Erin	Kami
John	Jade	Inez	Enid
Anne	Reta	Sean	Dion
Lina	Sara	Mary	Phil
Noel	Kris	Dale	Gino
Jodi	Alba	Amie	Rena
Rich	Fran	Hugo	Loyd
Zane	Lupe	Dick	Mina
Thad	Olen	Dina	Pete
Dena	Toby	Abby	Cary

FIGURE 2.4 Preattention depends on the degree of difference: anomalous text should be easier to spot in the bottom example of each column where the difference is larger.

The ability to format text such that it can visually pop-out from surrounding text indicates that text can be used as an element in visualizations to perceive patterns, in addition to the literal contents of the text itself.

Using text in this way is consistent with the visualization mantra popularized by Ben Shneiderman (1996): "overview first, zoom and filter, then details on demand." At a macrolevel, the text can be ignored, instead perceiving overall patterns (such as a set of 5 × 3 labels in Figure 2.4) and spotting individual outliers (bright red item, dark black item). Then, with directed attention, the outliers can be read (Pete, Luke, Cruz, Tena, and Zane). Reading the text is a simple shift in attention – which is far faster than interactions such as moving a mouse, waiting for a tooltip, and then reading the contents of the tooltip.

2.1.2 Visualization as Organized Inventory

Not all visualizations are designed for perceiving patterns that perceptually pop-out. The zoological taxonomy in Figure 1.14 is almost entirely made of text and the only visual patterns that pop-out are the relative sizes of branches and classes.

Instead, many text dense visualizations shown in Section 1.3 *organize* a large inventory of related information. A spatial layout provides a unique location for each item and the overall visualization is a comprehensive record of the domain. Relationships are depicted by spatial proximity or connections, aiding access to, and facilitating, visual inferences. While overall structures such as hierarchies and networks may be visible, these visualizations provide incredible detail and are highly useful for exploring and navigating the local topology – e.g. what are the related branches of science (Figure 1.11); which animals are members of the rodent family (Figure 1.14); which atoms have similar characteristics (Figure 1.15); common roadmaps; or the London Underground map (tfl.gov.uk/maps/track/tube).

Modern examples of inventory-oriented visualizations include interactive maps (e.g. Google maps), packed with labels such as street names and landmarks; or knowledge maps structuring a large corpus of information and frequently heavily labeled, such as the *Biochemical Pathways* in Figure 1.16 or *Map of Science* in Figure 1.24. In all cases, interactions aid analysis, such as zoom, adding/removing layers, search, or filtering subsets.

Figure 2.5 is a highly detailed, heavily labeled, interactive system diagram of an electrical grid. It is used for learning the topology of an existing grid, assessing limitations and planning future expansions, and overlaying real-time data for monitoring and operation.

2.1.3 Visualization as Communication

Visualizations are also used for communicating information. An early example is the *Diagram of the Brookes Slave Ship*, a poster from 1787 used to illustrate and explain the harsh conditions of the slave trade and advocate for abolition. The visualization provides a means to express key facts in a form easier to comprehend and recall than text alone.

Figure 2.6 is an information graphic by Nigel Holmes explaining a set of connections between individuals during the 1987 Iran-Contra affair where the core visualization is made almost entirely of text. Instead of colored arrows connecting key individuals, here the links are curved sentences directly showing the witness testimony implicating another individual. Color codes sequence the topics, which facilitates separating the threads of the narrative. Hours of testimony are simplified into a small web of evidence for the viewer to gain an overview of an otherwise complex situation.

2.2 VISUALIZATION DESIGN SPACE TODAY

Fundamentally, in any visualization, data is *encoded* into attributes, such as the size, color, and position of geometrical objects, and then plotted – as shown along the left side of Figure 2.7. There are many design choices to be made for encoding: whether to use color or size; whether to use lines or dots; whether to set out these points on a Cartesian grid, or polar coordinates, or some other layout. This is the *design space* that the designer must consider. This is the primary concern of this chapter: to define the design space of text to encode data in visualizations.

2.2.1 Visualization Anatomy

Once the data is plotted, there are many supporting elements, such as titles, legends, grids, axes, filters, annotations, and explanations surrounding the plot as indicated on the right side of Figure 2.7. These aid the viewer to *decode* the visualization. While many of these elements are literally text, their role is a supporting role and secondary to the definition of the design space.

2.2.2 Visualization Encoding

Jacques Bertin (1967, 1983) deconstructed visualizations to define the design space of visualization. Among other aspects, he identified different *data types* (e.g. categoric, ordered, quantitative); which are represented as *visual attributes* (e.g. hue, size, brightness); then drawn as *marks* (i.e. points, lines, and areas) and composed into a *layout* (e.g. scatterplot, line chart, etc.). This fundamental transformation of data into a visualization can be summarized as a pipeline as shown in Figure 2.8.

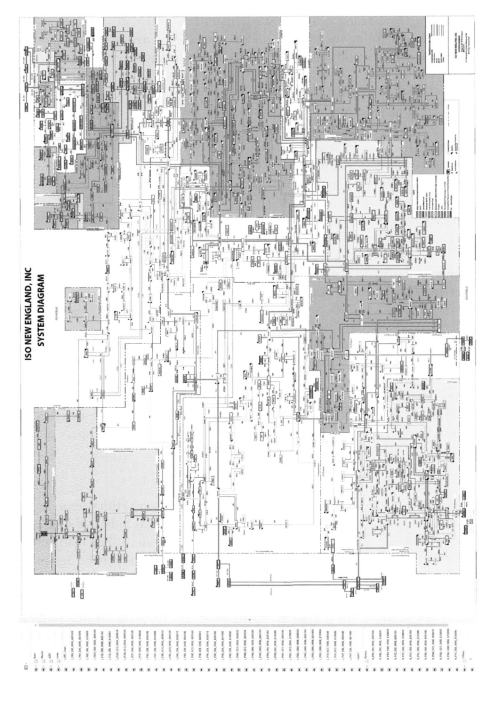

FIGURE 2.5   System diagram of the electrical grid of ISO New England showing topology with many visual attributes and many labels.

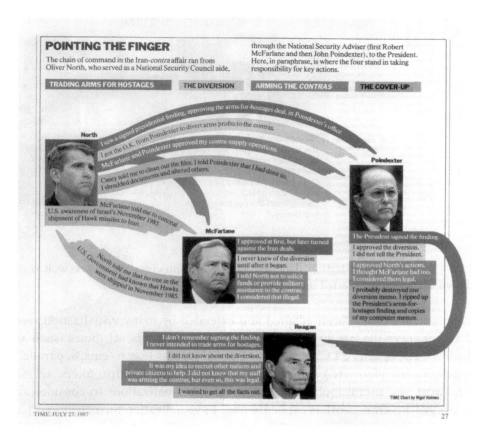

FIGURE 2.6 Connections between key individuals, with testimony, in the Iran-Contra affair by Nigel Holmes for *Time Magazine* in 1987.

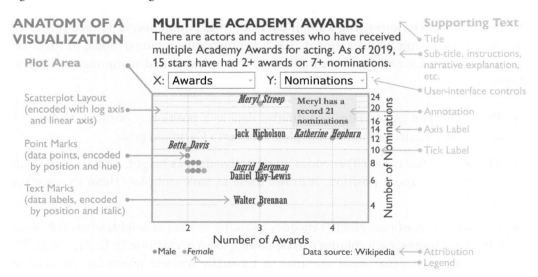

FIGURE 2.7 Data is *encoded* in the plot area as marks and data labels. Surrounding the plot area and overlaid on the plot is text which helps the viewer *decode* and interact with the visualization.

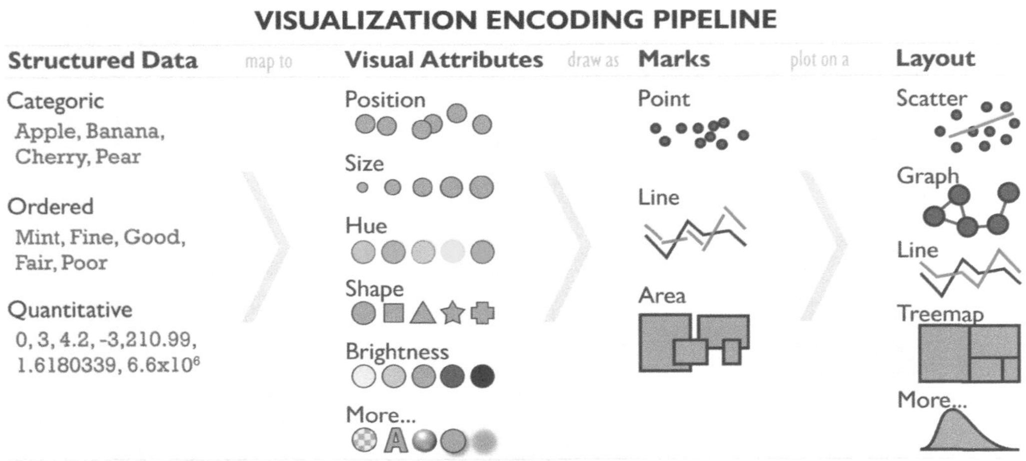

VISUALIZATION ENCODING PIPELINE

FIGURE 2.8   To create a visualization, data (left) is encoded into visual attributes (such as size and color), drawn as marks, and plotted into a layout (right).

This approach has since been adapted and extended by many visualization research-ers and authors over the last 50 years, adding a wide variety of attributes (such as blur, drop-shadows, 3D, opacity); a wide variety of visual layouts (e.g. treemaps, parallel coor-dinate plots, mosaic plots, etc.) and interactions (e.g. zoom, tooltips, filters, animation). This framework is a useful tool to aid the design of visualizations to consider alterna-tive encodings. This framework is explicitly used in visualization formalizations (such as Wilkinson's *Grammar of Graphics*, 2005) and conceptually underpins visualization tools such as Wickham's *ggplot2* and Bostock's *d3.js*.

This pipeline is also a useful tool to explain visualizations and to explore design alternatives. For example, Bertin illustrated this visualization design space by creating 90 different visualizations using a small dataset of the population of France recording three occupations and 90 departments (i.e. administrative regions). Some of these are shown in Figure 2.9 and their configuration can be explained using the pipeline as follows:

- The *bubble plot* (A) encodes quantitative data as x position, y position, and size. It draws these as circular marks and plots them on a Cartesian grid.

- The *stacked bar chart* (B) encodes quantitative data as height, and categoric data as brightness and x position. It draws these as bars and plots them in a stacked layout.

- The *parallel coordinate plot* (C) encodes quantitative data as height, where the layout has four columns, each column corresponding to an occupation (I, II, III, and I). The marks for each department are lines that visually connect where one department occurs in successive columns: for example, following the line for the department at the bottom of column I appears to be at the top of column II and III.

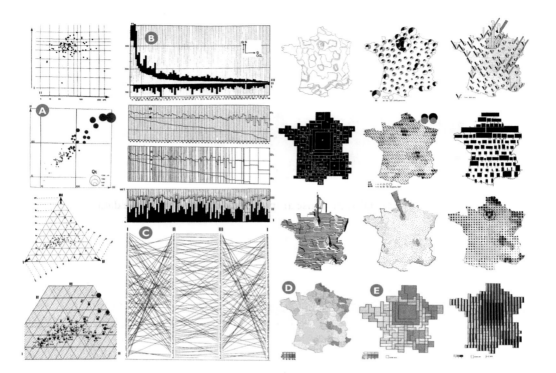

FIGURE 2.9   Some example visualizations from Bertin showing visualization design alternatives.

- The *choropleth map* (D) encodes the quantitative occupation data by the proportion of yellow, magenta, and cyan per department. The departments are drawn as geographic areas which are laid out as a map.

- The *cartogram* (E) encodes with the same color encoding as the choropleth map, plus encodes the population quantity by adjusting the size of the department. Each department is drawn as an area and laid out so that departments retain their relative locations.

- And other examples include scatterplots, ternary plots (triangular scatterplots with three axes), maps that repeat proportions to form textures, small multiples of pie charts set out geographically, contours, dot densities (with 3D for Paris) and more.

This pipeline also explains interactive visualizations. For example, Hans Rosling's famous motion charts (Figure 2.10) represent the quantitative value time as *animation*: the animation steps through time data. The animated playback steps through the data sequence, synchronized with the story-telling. *Filtering* is an interaction which either removes some of the data from the pipeline, or changes the visual attribute of transparency such that filtered data points are shown as transparent while others remain opaque. *Tooltips* are an interaction which typically show additional data attributes as a text pop-over.

Figure 2.11 shows an example of commercial software GeoTime (Eccles et al. 2007), which explicitly encodes latitude, longitude, and time to x,y,z spatial coordinates; additional

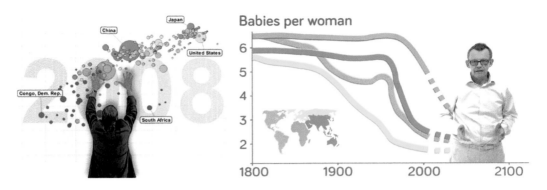

FIGURE 2.10   Gapminder's visualizations use animation to step through time data.

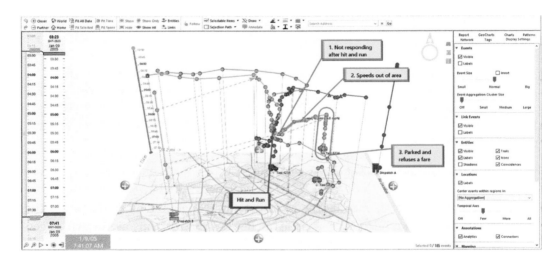

FIGURE 2.11   GeoTime with extensive interactions for data exploration and analysis.

categoric data values as hue and line style. It includes a wide range of interactions for adjusting time range (sliders); spatial extents (pan and zoom); filters to remove subsets of data (checkboxes); tooltips to show additional data attributes; selections to tag and highlight a group of points (red outlines); and user-authored text annotations to record observations (boxes of yellow text).

2.3 PREPROCESSING TEXT FOR THE VISUALIZATION PIPELINE

How can this pipeline be extended for visualizing text?

One simple approach is to add an initial step for natural language processing (NLP) to turn textual data into structured data, such as counts of words, punctuation, structure, or relations between documents. Then, the existing visualization pipeline can be used to re-purpose existing visualizations for text analysis as shown in Figure 2.12.

For example, counts of words can be plotted as a word cloud, where counts are encoded as size (while position and color are arbitrary). Or, connections between documents (such as co-authors) can be plotted as a graph. However, quantifying prose misses much

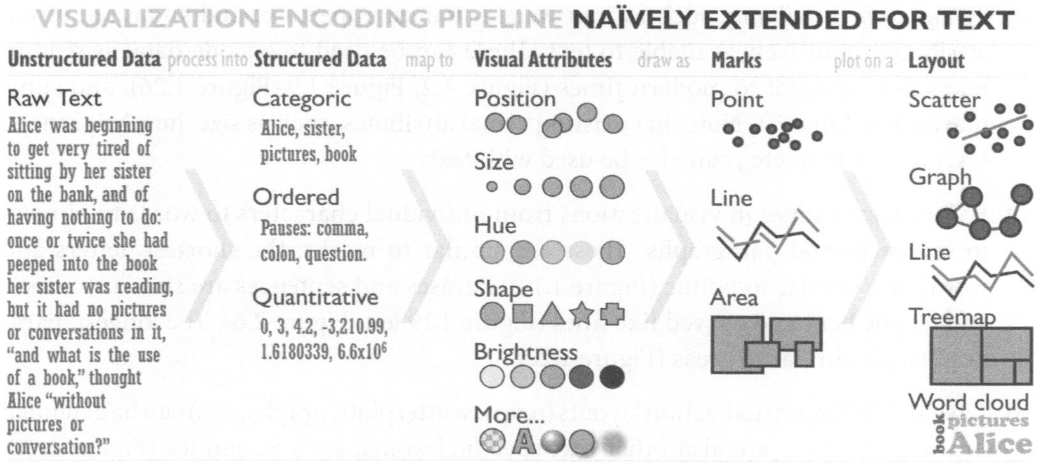

FIGURE 2.12   To visualize text, preprocess the text into structured data and visualize it using all the existing visualization techniques.

informational content. NLP modifies the text as it tokenizes, stems, lemmatizes, tags parts of speech, and removes stop words. The output of some NLP systems are collections of words – which can work well with visualizations that use words as marks. But, word collections lose the semantics of word sequences. For example, in Figure 2.12, Alice refers to books *without* pictures or conversations – *without* negates the following words – should they be counted or subtracted? Negation, irony, and sarcasm may be reversed when text is split apart. Or the meaning of similes, metaphors, aphorisms, and idioms (e.g. "raining cats and dogs") does not correspond to the individual words. Rhetorical devices and stylistic elements impart additional meaning to the text, which is missed when text is reduced to word counts.

Further, a text preprocessor assumes that visualization techniques are constrained to the pipeline as it exists today. As such, the existing visualization pipeline has no adaptations for typographic attributes (e.g. bold, italic, parentheses), long passages of text, or text-based layout techniques. This book is a critical re-examination of the visualization encoding pipeline with respect to text. The resulting pipeline will be extended at every step, weaving text throughout.

2.4 DERIVING A VISUALIZATION PIPELINE FOR TEXT

How can the corresponding visualization ingredients for text be identified and organized? The long history of text and text-based visualizations provide many examples which can be inspected and organized according to the visualization pipeline:

a) *Literal text* is a key data type that should be supported throughout the visualization pipeline. Historic visualizations such as the typographic table of contents (Figure 1.11), the genealogy diagram (Figure 1.12), and the zoological chart (Figure 1.14) are almost entirely non-functional without their literal text.

b) *Typographic attributes*, such as font weight, italics, uppercase, and so on are visual attributes exclusively available to text. These can be used to encode data, as seen in maps from ancient to modern times (Figure 1.2, Figure 1.9–Figure 1.26), and summarized in Table 2.1. Note that existing visual attributes, such as size, hue, brightness, texture, 3D, blur, etc., can also be used with text.

c) *Scope of text* ranges in visualizations from individual characters to words to phrases to sentences and paragraphs. These are similar to marks: the shortest, letters and words, are similar to points (Figure 1.18). Phrases and sentences are similar to lines, and can be bent and curved like lines (Figure 1.19 left, Figure 2.6). The longest, paragraphs, are similar to areas (Figure 1.22).

d) *Layout.* Existing visualization layouts (maps, scatterplots, graphs, etc.) can be extended to use text. There are also other text-specific layouts, such as comics (Figure 1.21), prose (Figure 1.2), lists, tables (Figure 1.13, Figure 1.15), or even superimposed over other text (Figure 1.19 right, Figure 1.22 left).

Incorporating all the above, the extended design space for visualizing with text can be summarized in the diagram shown in Figure 2.13.

Note that Bertin, back in 1967, defined some of these textual aspects in his original *Sémiologie Graphique*, although the pages were in an appendix never translated into English. He includes literal text, some of the typographic attributes, considers scope that varies from letters through words to paragraphs, chapters, and books. He speculates that new kinds of text visualizations might transform catalogs and classifications, but unlike his other work, he does not provide examples. As such, Bertin's work prefigures and confirms this pipeline.

However, all these additions for text to the pipeline above need to be itemized and **characterized**. How is typeface best used? Are symbols the same as alphanumeric glyphs? Are

TABLE 2.1   Typographic Attributes Used in Historic Visualizations

Typographic Attributes in Historic Uses	Medieval	Cartography	Typography	Timetables	Notation	Code Editors	Alphanumeric Charts	Art, Poetry	Graphic Design	Comics	Post Modern Text	Data Visualization
Alphanumerics	X	X	X	X	X	X	X	X	X	X	X	X
Symbols	X	X	X	X	X	X	X	X				
Weight (bold)		X	X	X		X	X	X	X	X	X	
Oblique (and italic)		X	X			X		X		X		X
Underline		X			X	X	X					
Case	X	X	X	X		X	X	X			X	
Width (and spacing)		X						X			X	
Typeface (font)				X	X			X	X			
Baseline (and path)		X	X		X				X	X	X	

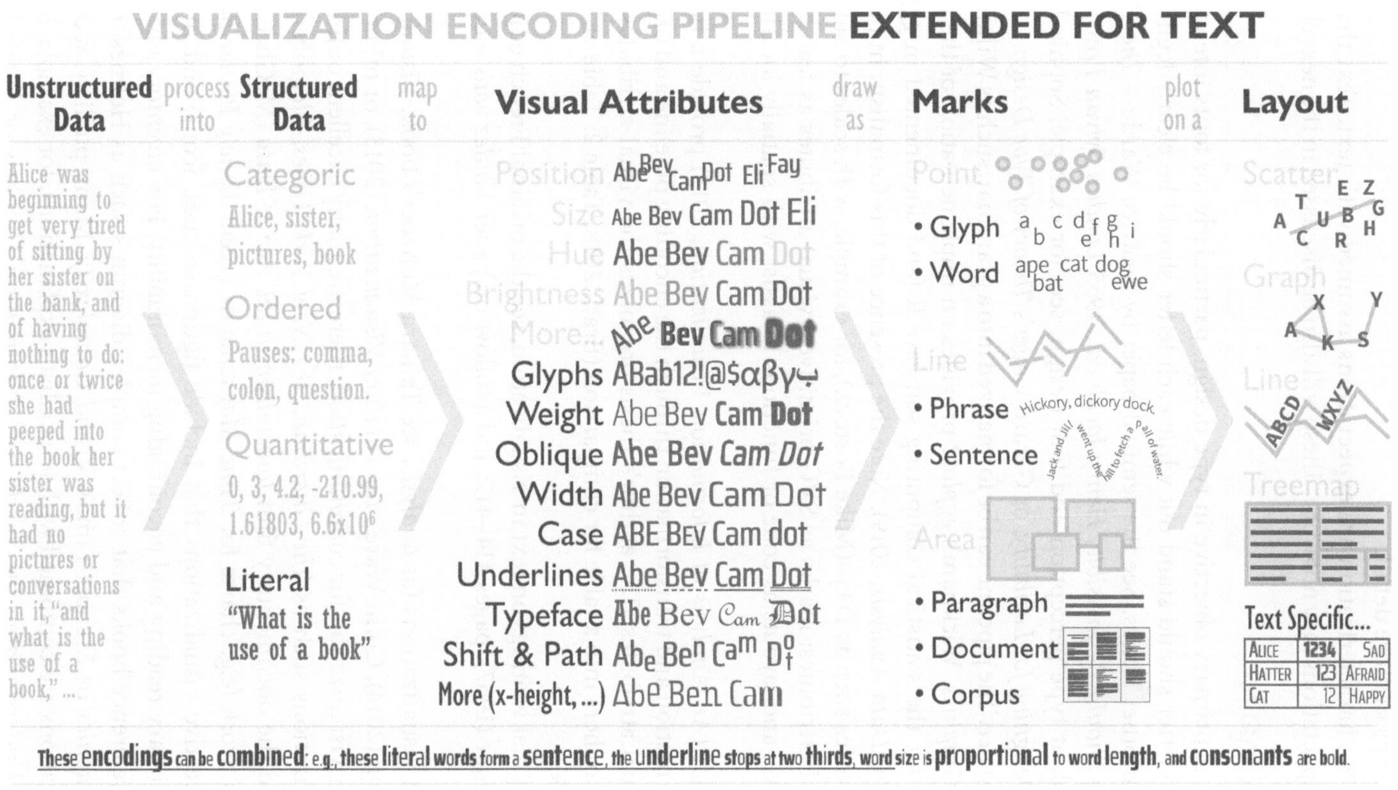

FIGURE 2.13 Extending visualization to text adds: (a) literal data as a base data type; (b) encodes data into text with existing visual attributes and typographic visual attributes; (c) extends marks for different lengths of text; and (d) adds text to existing visualization layouts plus adds text specific layouts.

literal encodings useful if they can't be perceived preattentively? And what caveats are there: do these additions work in other languages? The next task is to characterize each of these textual additions in more detail.

Closely related to characterization are **expectations** assumed with text. Text that does not follow these expectations may not work. These will also be discussed in the next chapter.

2.5 FURTHER READING

Typographic color. A primary objective in type design, particularly for fonts intended for reading, is that no letter should stand out while each letter should be clearly legible and differentiated from other letters. See the seminal paper by Beatrice Warde – *The Crystal Goblet or Printing Should Be Invisible, Henry Jacob ed., 1955 London Sylvan Press.* For a more detailed look at type perception and font design, see, for example, Sophie Beier's *Reading Letters: Designing for Legibility,* or Gerard Unger's *Theory of Type Design.*

Existing design space. The pipeline can be formalized into a grammar, such as Wilkinson's *The Grammar of Graphics.* Wickham's *ggplot2* provides an implementation of the grammar as a package for the statistical computing software R (and documented in *ggplot2, Elegant Graphics for Data Analysis,* 2019). Note the presence of this formalism in popular programming libraries such as D3.js (Mike Bostock); for example, with scales to aid mapping data to visual attributes; marks as SVG primitives; visual attributes as features per each SVG primitive; and layouts as code or functions to assist with spatially locating the marks.

Chen and Floridi (*An Analysis of Information Visualization,* 2013) provide a broader discussion of information and transformation through the encoding pipeline and organize a broad set of visual attributes. The author's thesis organizes the visual attributes itemized by many researchers into a table for comparison (Brath 2018, Table 2: Table of Visual Attributes, page 19).

For Bertin's original writings on text in visualization, see the original French edition of *Sémiologie Graphique* (1967), pages 414–417; and a follow-on paper *Voulez vous jouer avec mon A* (1980).

For more about visualizations for *analysis,* see Tamara Munzner's book, *Visualization Analysis and Design* (2014), Colin Ware's *Information Visualization* (2013), or other excellent textbooks. For visualization for *communication,* there are many excellent online data journalism visualizations such as *The Guardian, The New York Times, Bloomberg,* and *The Economist* and the documentary film *Journalism in the Age of Data* (McGhee 2010). See Nigel Holmes' work (e.g. charts for *Time Magazine* or recent *Lonely Planet Book of Everything*) for creative visualizations that include figurative cues, icons, and imagery reinforcing the primary reading and encouraging memorability. For *inventory* visualizations, see design reference books that collect complex diagrams such as Holmes' *Best in Diagrammatic Graphics* or Manuel Lima's *Visual Complexity.* Many publicly accessible inventory visualizations are combined with journalist's explanations, for example, Sandra Rendgen's books *Understanding the World* and *Information Graphics* or Javier Errea's *Visual Journalism* (2017).

Supporting text: ticks, labels, legends, and annotations. There are many texts that discuss the design and format of supporting text around a visualization, such as tick labels, axes labels, legends, and annotations. For example, see Anders Wallgren et al. (*Graphing Statistics & Data: Creating Better Charts*, 1996) for recommendations originating from statistical graphics; Dona Wong (*Wall Street Journal Guide to Information Graphics*, 2010) from news graphics; or Cynthia Brewer (*Designing Better Maps,* 2005) from cartography.

CHAPTER 3

Characterizing Text

T HERE ARE MANY ASPECTS to text that can be utilized in a visualization as outlined in the pipeline: literal data, typographic attributes, marks, and layouts. Each of these can be characterized in more detail.

3.1 LITERAL DATA

In visualization, literal encoding is rarely discussed; the focus is on the encoding of categoric, ordered, or quantitative data into visual attributes such as size or color. Instead, data can be encoded literally into strings of text and represented directly. Literal encodings are unique to text.

Instead of considering text as a different form of data, some researchers consider text as a visual attribute, similar to shape, size, or color (e.g. Wilkinson 2005, Mazza 2009, Chen and Floridi 2013, Börner 2015), whereas other researchers do not include text. There may be several reasons for non-inclusion of text. Bertin, for example, does not include text as a data type or encoding, however, Bertin narrowly defined his visual attributes as retinal variables, explicitly focusing on low-level visual channels into which data is transformed for fast perception. Bertin *did* discuss text, *only* in an appendix of the original edition of *Sémiologie Graphique* (1967) wherein he states, "The premier property of letters is to be unambiguous," which, in effect, is literal encoding. For the purposes of this book, text is not simply another visual attribute; it is a first-class data type on par with categoric, ordered, or quantitative data.

There are many benefits to literal encoding. These can be itemized by function, perception, cognition, and operation. These benefits can be aligned to a broader visualization pipeline, which encompasses comprehension and interaction in addition to visual encoding, as shown in Figure 3.1.

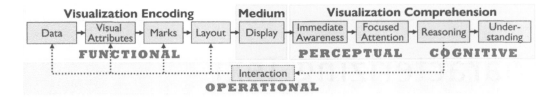

FIGURE 3.1 Visualizations encode data, but also need to be decoded to be understood.

3.1.1 Functional Benefits: The Data Contains Text

Literal text may be effective for some types of visualizations.

Purpose. The goal of a visualization is not necessarily to only analyze patterns by preat-tentive visual attributes, such as a pattern of dots or bright red markers. Tasks such as the identification of specific data points may require text. Visualizations which organize a large amount of information, as discussed in Section 2.1.2, may rely on text. Most of these visualizations could not fulfill their purpose without their text.

Data. Not all text data is categoric data. A few simple repeated labels in a dataset, where the number of unique items is low, may be categoric data. However, text such as proper names, phrases, sentences, and so forth may have hundreds, thousands, or millions of unique values in the dataset.

Subject matter. Some visualizations are primarily about text. Word clouds could not exist without text as an element in the visualization. Similarly, other visualizations related to text analytics and natural language processing (NLP) will have a strong need to explicitly represent literal text, such as extracted entities, topics, keywords, word stems, ontologies, and so forth.

Increased information content. Many of the historic examples have modern interactive visualization equivalents. The zoologic taxonomy (Figure 1.14) is the same as the modern hierarchical pie (aka sunburst) chart with every wedge labeled. Flow charts and networks (e.g. Figure 1.16) are essentially graphs, with larger nodes to accommo-date text to explain process steps. Many historic examples of timelines, such as Pick's *Tableau De L'Histoire Universelle* in Figure 3.2 (or Chapple and Garofalo's *History of Rock N Roll* in Tufte 1990, or the many examples in Rosenberg and Grafton's *Cartographies of Time* 2012) are highly similar to storyline visualizations, with the addition of text. The additional text increases the information content and the context.

3.1.2 Perceptual Benefits: Fast, Efficient Access to Detail

Some visualizations are designed for rapid attention, such as the immediate perception of an outlier (e.g. a red dot). While the literal text is not rapidly perceived, it may use visual attributes, such as bold or color, in order for that text element to gain immediate awareness (visual attributes as applied to text to be discussed in Section 3.2).

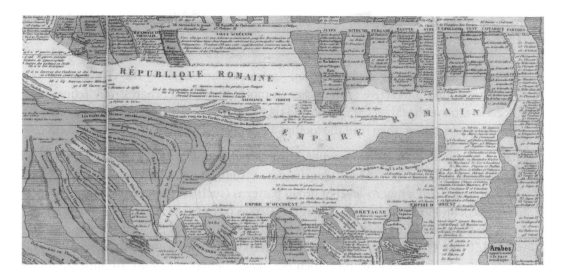

FIGURE 3.2   Chart from 1858 of historic regimes and events – filled with text.

Many real-world tasks require *identification*. In real-time environments, such as air traffic control, factory supervision, electric grid monitoring, or stock trading, it is necessary to identify anomalous entities and access key information quickly. Identification using text labels can be achieved in fractions of a second with a simple shift in attention, such as the control room in Figure 1.25 or the trading watchlist in Figure 3.3. For identification, global

Symbol		Corporate Name	CUSIP No.	Rating	Spread	Change	Date	Volume	Last Headline
BAC 4.5 04/01/22	↗◐▦	Bank of America	19282SAT5	A2/-	132.0	10.0	8/6	5,000	Wells Fargo Is In
GE 3.75 11/14/22	↑◐🖿	General Electric	33684FPT2	Aa2	118.0	23.0	8/3	6,000	Analyst Continue
JPM 3.7 01/20/23	↗○▩	JPMorgan	46505SZG1	Aa3	75.0	4.0	8/5	15,000	JP Morgan Ship
C 6.01 01/15/23	↗◐🖿	Citigroup	70567OLG9	Aa3/-	102.0	2.0	8/4	6,545	Citigroup Expens
GS 6 05/01/22	→◐🖿	Goldman Sachs	89692MKQ1	A1	165.0	-0.2	8/2	23,000	Comparison of T
MS 4.1 01/26/23	↗○▩	Morgan Stanley	88086ZHE8	A2	152.0	1.0	7/28	5,000	Horizon Purchas
BRK 4.85 01/15/23	↓◐■	Berkshire Hathaway	83280ITG2	Aa2		-12.0	8/4	1,000	Warren Buffett's
T 4.85 02/15/22	**↘○■**	**AT&T**	**92153XYD6**	**A2/-**	**65.0**	**-2.0**	**8/6**	**13,375**	**AT&T sued over**
KFT 4.3 02/07/24	↗●▩	Kraft Heinz	44958TOS5	Baa2	85.0	1.0	8/4	11,000	Kraft Heinz: Isn't
TWC 3.5 02/01/23	↘●▩	Warner Media	36393VNX9	Baa2	49.0	-3.0	8/1	1,500	Warner Media ba
UBS 3.8 01/01/23	→●🖿	UBS Group	82682LYX5	Aa3	85.0	n.a.		n.a.	UBS loses role in
WMT 2.8 04/01/23	→○🖿	Walmart	98084PIM3	Aa2		--	8/5	1,000	Walmart's Online
RDSA 3.25 09/15/2	↗●▩	Royal Dutch Shell	74392GNO6	Aa1	15.0	1.0	8/5	1,123	Shell Invests in E
RIO 8.95 05/15/22	→●🖿	Rio Tinto	27092HSP7	A3	80.0	--	8/5	2,650	Deutsche Bank R
VZ 5.55 02/15/24	→●□	Verizon	58504MGP7	A3	80.0	--	8/4	5,000	Verizon sought b
ORCL 5 01/15/24	↑○🖿	Oracle	65527VEZ4	A1	35.0	20.0	8/5	1,000	Oracle Loses Cha
DOW 5.9 02/15/23	↗○▩	DuPont de Nemours	75719OYK6	Baa3	52.0	1.0	8/5	7,850	DuPont may be t

FIGURE 3.3   Color and markers highlight anomalies, plus identity and key information is immediately visible as text in this portion of a bond trading watchlist.

comparison is not needed; access to detail is required. Using literal text for these details offers benefits:

Interaction is slow. Relying on interaction, such as tooltips, is slow. The viewer must first determine their interactive goal, engage in motor skills, and progressively refine those skills to achieve the target data point, and then process the result at the target (i.e. wait for the tooltip to appear, then read the tooltip). Each of these steps requires time and effort.

Micro-readings, not details on demand. Tufte (1983) popularized micro/macro readings of visual displays. That is, high-density data visualizations (e.g. Figures 1.9–1.15) can be understood at a macro-level of broad patterns (such as hierarchal structures, clusters, etc.); and low-level data (such as local areas or individual data points and labels) can be understood by shifting attention. Tufte summarizes this with "to clarify, add detail." This is different from Shneiderman's visual information-seeking mantra: "overview first, zoom and filter, then details on demand" (1996). In Shneiderman's approach, interactivity is used to reveal the detail data whereas Tufte plots it directly. Shneiderman was constrained by low-resolution displays in the 1990s, while Tufte was working with high-resolution print. In effect, Tufte replaces interaction with a direct display of details. These details, such as labels, can be immediately focused on by simply shifting visual attention.

Word recognition is fast. The parallel letter recognition model of words (Rayner and Pollatsek) states letters within a word are recognized simultaneously and the letter information is used to recognize the words. The model shows that word perception is extremely fast (hundreds of milliseconds).

Word recognition is automatic. The Stroop effect (Stroop 1935) is a task where it is difficult to name the color of a word, when the word literally names a different color, such as red or purple. Automatic word recognition theorizes reading is an automatic process which is difficult to voluntarily stop. Automaticity is the ability to perform a well-practiced task with low attentional requirements; the viewer is unaware that the task is occurring, does not need to initiate the task, does not have the ability to stop the process, and the task has low cognitive load (Bargh 1994). This implies that a small number of words will be automatically read and that the cognitive cost of reading the text will be low.

Fast decoding. In any form of visualization the viewer must both perceive the information of interest and then decode it. With text, the viewer can directly decode the literal content (i.e. read it). This is essentially a recognition vs. recall benefit: i.e. seeing text and recognizing text literally (e.g. "Julius Caesar") is faster than seeing some other representation (e.g. red dot) and then requiring an additional step (e.g. such as additionally cross-referencing a legend or using interaction.)

Reduced cognitive load. When a separate legend or interaction is required, additional load is placed on short-term memory. Short-term memory has extremely limited capacity: the viewer can benefit if short-term memory requirements are reduced.

3.1.3 Cognitive Benefits: Reasoning Aid

Once words are acquired, they can be reasoned with and create understanding. A *proposition model* connects common relations across words and sentences (Payne 2007). These relations can be understood through logical inferences, spatialization, temporal sequences, and so on. For example, temporal sequences can be expressed in a sentence or the position of words in a timeline.

At the proposition level, perceptual inferences can be made across collections of labels. For example, columns of times indicate trains in the timetable in Figure 1.13, or the large label stretching across a large portion of a map indicates a larger geographic feature than small labels, such as O D E N W A L D vs. the many smaller labels in Figure 1.10.

The proposition model in turn is enhanced with prior real-world knowledge from memory into a *situation model*. Prior knowledge associated with a label or sentence is available to use. For example, prior knowledge regarding countries may be used when viewing a map or scatterplot to help orient the viewer based on expected relations, potentially predict and confirm where expected data points may occur, and provoke inquiry if there is a mismatch between the expectation and the visualization. For example, in the medieval map of England in Figure 1.2, one may note the significant differences in typography between **NORTHFOLK, DORSET**, and Middlesex implying significant differences, whereas in the mid-20th century they are all equivalent counties.

Labels can aid tasks at the level of the proposition and situation models, such as:

Orientation. Text labels provide named markers which can aid orientation by acting as landmarks (reference points) within a visualization. For example, in the genealogical diagram in Figure 1.12, the viewer may choose among potential landmarks, such as a famous emperor (e.g. Maximillian the Great) as a reference point between ancestors and heirs.

Reduced search. Spatial layout can reduce search effort between related elements. For example, in a flowchart (e.g. Figure 1.16), compounds are shown in molecular notation and metabolic processes are arrows. Together they facilitate a search across steps in the processes.

Local relationships are important in many visualizations. *Tobler's First Law of Geography* states: "Everything is related to everything else, but near things are more related than distant things" (Miller 2004). Many visualization layouts attempt to locate related objects close together (e.g. graph layouts, scatterplots, hierarchical treemaps, etc.). This aids analysis of visual patterns such as clusters, communities, trends, hierarchies, and so forth. Labeling entities facilitates detailed analysis of local relations. For example, in *Tableau De L'Histoire Universelle* in Figure 3.2, for any given empire, left-right are adjacent empires and up-down are the temporal changes in the empire.

Serendipity. Serendipitous discovery is fortuitous unexpected discovery by accident. Related ideas may manifest as different data points that seem acausal but are meaningful. Words and phrases can be recognized, thereby providing different cognitive associations than visual associations alone, by using real-world knowledge. For example, in the periodic table (Figure 1.15) a novice may note that copper, silver, and gold are all in the same column (propositional data) and that these are all precious metals (real-world knowledge).

Moving beyond collections of words, additional semantic content is contained in sentences. Analytic and visualization approaches need to consider uses where a broader context of word sequence is maintained. For example, search user interfaces have evolved significantly beyond simple keywords and document metadata to include contextual titles, phrases, and sentences in search results (i.e. keywords in context (KWIC), see Hearst 2009, Chapter 5).

More broadly, a variety of visualization techniques have evolved in the humanities for close reading, summarized by Jänicke et al. (2015). For close reading, these approaches maintain word sequence and change visual attributes to mark up the text (similar to keyword highlights), superimpose markers and connections on top of words (e.g. like a graph), or increase space between letters and words to add markers such as flows or phonetics. Figure 3.4 shows a WordTree from 1553 showing visually structured text.

3.1.4 Language Constraints

Unlike other visualization encodings, alphanumeric glyphs encode data relative to a specific language. Different languages may have different glyphs or variants. These glyphs are orderable although the order may only be known to a person familiar with the language. Instead of uppercase and lowercase, as in Latin encoded languages, glyphs may vary in other ways, such as position within a word, for example, when used as the lead character or last character in an Arabic word (Figure 3.5 left); or used in combination to form unique ligatures such as Sinhala (Figure 3.5 right). Ligatures, in turn, make it difficult to apply a format to only a subset of letters in a word. There can be multi-level characters and the baseline may not be at the base of a character (e.g. Devanagari). Some joined letters may become very tall in some scripts requiring spacing adjustments in surrounding lines of text.

For some languages, there may be very few fonts available on computer systems (e.g. Cree or Bengali), limiting design choices. In some languages (e.g. Arabic, Hebrew) text is oriented right to left, possibly necessitating reorientation of elements within a visual layout. For eastern languages (e.g. Chinese, Japanese) where a single glyph represents an entire word, characters are denser and word proportions will be more square, potentially

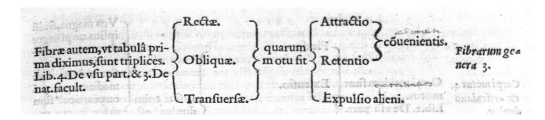

FIGURE 3.4   Branching and merging text in an anatomy book from 1553.

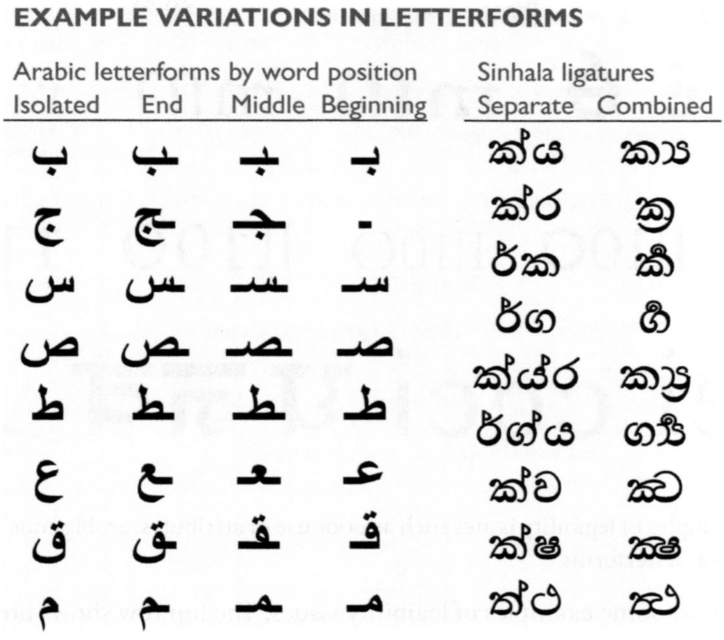

EXAMPLE VARIATIONS IN LETTERFORMS

Arabic letterforms by word position				Sinhala ligatures	
Isolated	End	Middle	Beginning	Separate	Combined
ب	ب	ب	ب	ක්ය	කාා
ج	ج	ج	.	ක්ර	කු
س	س	س	س	ර්ක	කී
ص	ص	ص	ص	ර්ග	ගී
ط	ط	ط	ط	ක්යර	කාු
ع	ع	ع	ع	ර්ග්ය	ගෑ
ق	ق	ق	ق	ක්ව	කව
م	م	م	م	ක්ෂ	කෂ
				ත්ර	කට

FIGURE 3.5 Letterforms can vary in different languages, based on word position or combinations with adjacent letters to form ligatures.

requiring different font sizes and other adjustments to layouts. More generally, each language will have different letterforms (e.g. Greek tends to have more whitespace, Hebrew tends to be squarish and darker) and different character frequencies, resulting in different texture and darkness for a set of text when translated into different languages.

Some other visual attributes have sensitivities of culture (for example, the same hue may have different meanings in different countries). Similarly, certain words may have different meanings to different subcultures within a language. In general, any visualization requiring use across languages should be critically reviewed for language and cultural dependencies.

3.2 TYPOGRAPHIC ATTRIBUTES

Typographic attributes, such as bold, italic, typeface, and letterform, are visual attributes unique to typefaces. These were summarized in Table 2.1. All these attributes are integral to a carefully designed typeface to maintain legibility across any combination of typographic attributes.

Legibility. Legibility is a perception issue concerned with the ability to clearly decipher the individual characters as well as commonalities within a font that increase letter identification (e.g. Sanocki and Dyson 2012). The primary encoding of text is the literal message; text must be legible in order to be understood. Legibility is of paramount concern to typographers, cartographers, and industrial designers; for example, 50 years ago, there were over 200 legibility studies for a wide variety of applications (e.g. summary by Cornog and Rose 1967).

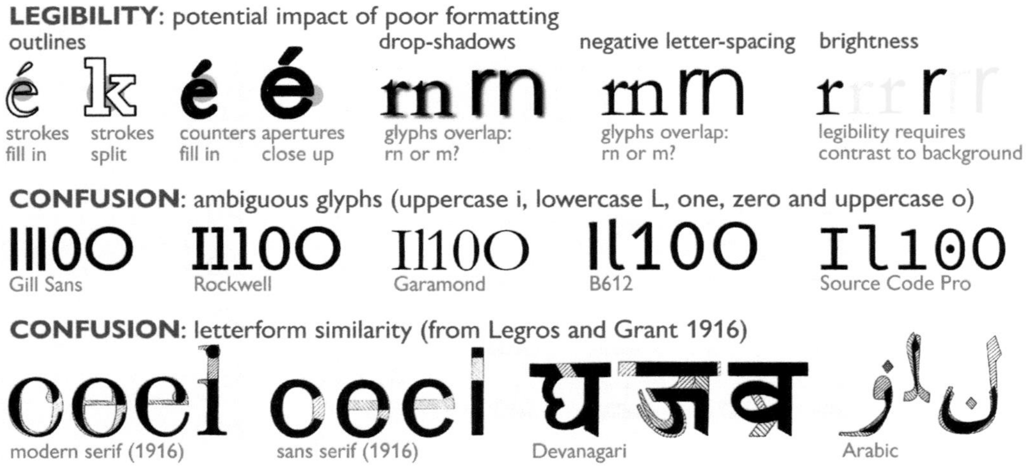

FIGURE 3.6   Examples of legibility issues such as poor use of attributes, ambiguous fonts, and fonts with highly similar letterforms.

Figure 3.6 shows some examples of legibility issues. The top row shows how visual attributes such as outline width, drop-shadows, negative spacing between letters, and brightness reduce legibility. Closely related to legibility is confusability; some letterforms are highly similar. This differentiation is critical in applications such as air traffic and network visualization. In some typefaces, such as Gill Sans, there is a high similarity between some letters and numbers as shown in the middle row of Figure 3.6. There are many analytical approaches to measuring similarity and confusability, such as the superimposed areas of similar letters shown in the final row (e.g. see Beier 2012 for a comprehensive analysis).

Legibility can be severely impacted in visualization by other poor design choices, for example, stretching fonts or poor quality underlines. As such, typefaces should be selected to match the visualization need and use the typographic attributes provided by type designers with care so that legibility is not compromised.

3.2.1 Alphanumeric Glyphs (i.e. Letters and Numbers)

The individual glyphs that make up the letters of the alphabet or a numeric system have several unique properties compared to other types of glyphs such as abstract geometry (such as circle, square, star) or pictographs (e.g. apple, dog, cat).

> *Literal.* Glyphs are combined to form words and words are literal encodings, as discussed in the previous section. There are hundreds of thousands of unique words. It is much more difficult to define a high number of recognizable, uniquely identifiable icons.

> *Other encodings.* In addition to literal encoding, alphanumerics can also be used to encode other kinds of data. For example, the Latin alphabet can encode 26 unique categories (A,B,C) as unambiguous marks, each of similar size and weight. Alphanumerics can be used to encode categories of much higher cardinality, such as element symbols

(Na, Cl, etc.), stock symbols (e.g. AAPL, INTC, MSFT), and so on. Figure 3.7 shows a scatterplot where numerals indicate age brackets (left) and letter codes indicate characters from *Alice in Wonderland* (right).

Ordered sets. Alphanumeric glyphs have defined, well-understood ordering, e.g. A,B,C,…X,Y,Z. Furthermore, there are different sets of ordered glyphs, such as language alphabets, e.g. Latin, Greek, Cyrillic, Arabic, Hebrew, Katakana, etc. (e.g. A,B,C; α,β,γ; а,б,в,г; あ い う え お; د, ح, ﻪ, ﺍ; א,ב,ג), and numeric symbols e.g. Arabic, Roman, Chinese, Devanagari (1,2,3; i,ii,iii,iv; 一二三四五六; ۱۲۳۴۵). Ordering can be useful in many kinds of visualization techniques, for example, ordering a column in a table or ordering items in a parallel coordinate chart alphabetically. Ordering can be used in legends and filters, such as a drop-down menu or as a compact slider bar.

Variants. Note that the same letter can be expressed by different letterforms. For example, there is significant shape variation between a and ɑ; g and ɡ; Q and Q; or 4 and 4. Even the simple letter l has many variants, such as a single sans serif stroke l, a heavily serifed monospace l, a top and tail on a calligraphic *ℓ*, and a full loop on a script *ℓ*. Letter perception is highly automatic; it is unlikely that the reader will be aware of the variant. Thus, letterform variant should not be used to indicate data.

3.2.2 Symbols and Paired Delimiters

Symbols and punctuation marks, such as !@#$%^&*|:?€£§, are conceptually closer to glyphs and shapes than alphanumerics. Punctuation and typographic symbols may be referred to differently in various communities. For example, # may be referred to as hash, pound sign, number sign, sharp sign (in music), or octothorpe – potentially a cause of confusion if used outside the target community. Punctuation and symbols do not have an explicit well-known ordering. Punctuation increases readability but can vary across languages.

Symbols beyond typographic symbols include geometric shapes (e.g. □ △ ○) and representational shapes, also referred to as pictographs or icons (e.g. ☎♛✒🖎📖🏠). These

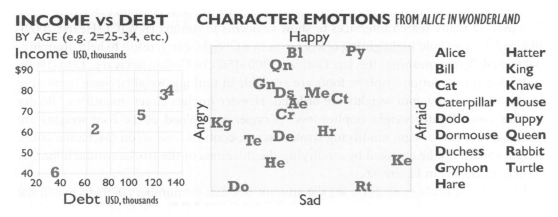

FIGURE 3.7 Alphanumerics can be used directly as marks in a plot. Left: numbers indicate age bracket. Right: letter pairs indicate characters, plotted by emotions extracted via natural language processing.

In this sentence, the mid(point is indicated via a | vertical line and quartiles) shown with parentheses.

Carroll (wrote some | run-on sentences)in *Alice in Wonderland*. The longest sentence, about the puppy, is 178 words long. By comparison, the median sentence is 11 words. If this paragraph represents the longest sentence, then the bar shows the relative length of the median and parentheses indicate quartiles.

FIGURE 3.8   The inserted symbols indicate proportions in relation to the overall string length.

may be combined, such as a background shape and a foreground pictograph, each of which may be adjusted to indicate data, e.g. ⊗⊗⊗⊘⊘⊘ 🖥🖥🖥 ♦ ♦♦♦ ❤❤❤❤❤♡. However, these symbols typically do not have typographic properties, such as bold and italic; are not sequenced into paragraphs; follow different rules of composition; and so forth.

Symmetric delimiters are typographic symbols used to evoke enclosure with mirrored shapes such as (parentheses), [brackets], {braces}, and "quotes." While complete enclosure is not explicit, the Gestalt law of symmetry explains that they are perceived to form a pair; and the Gestalt law of closure explains that concavities enclose (even) (if adjacent).

Punctuation, typographic symbols, and delimiters are designed to be inserted into running text, i.e. with consistent shapes and weights to other glyphs in the typeface, so that these typographic symbols do not visually pop-out from the surrounding text. Dictionaries frequently use these marks, for example, to indicate syllables and stress in a word (e.g. mon′o·nu′cle·o′sis).

With regards to perception, shape is weakly preattentive and thus not a strong cue. From a visualization perspective, symbols can be inserted into a string of text to refer to a quantity or category, as shown by the examples in Figure 3.8. Indicating lengths via inserted symbols or other formats will be discussed in more detail in Chapter 10, Ratios and Quantitative Data.

3.2.3 Weight (and Bold)

Bold is a strong perceptual cue, invented during the industrial revolution (Twyman 1993). It is used in many search interfaces to show *keywords in context* (KWIC) (Hearst 2009). Figure 3.9 shows bold highlighting of key terms in a Google search result to help disambiguate two different meanings (i.e. late Gothic c.1300–1500, or Gothic Revival c. 1750–1900).

With high resolution displays, fonts are available in multiple weights, some up to nine levels. Semantically, font weights are ordered. Heavier implies larger quantities: "Bolder implies more, lighter weight implies less" (Krygier and Wood 2011). Font weights are intrinsic to a font design, modifying strokes, serifs, contrast, and so on (McGuffie 2019); weight should not be changed by modifying the thickness of the stroke around a font, as shown previously in Figure 3.6.

FatFonts (Nacenta et al. 2012) set the amount of black for numbers 0–99 to match the value expressed by that number, e.g. 1 2 3 3 4 5 6 6 7 8 8 9. Grids of these numbers then reveal macro-patterns (by weight) and precise values (0–99).

In visualization, weight can be used to encode ordered data. At a macro-level, increasing weight increases the amount of ink, which increases intensity. At a micro-level, increasing

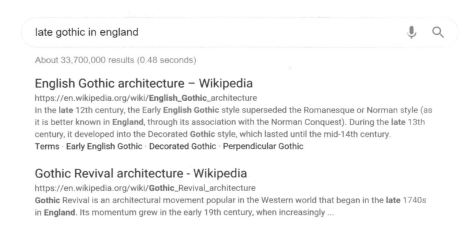

FIGURE 3.9   Keyword in context: bolded search terms in the search results.

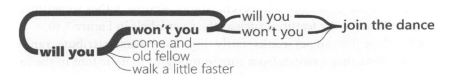

FIGURE 3.10   From *Wonderland*, the phrase *will you* and successive words weighted by frequency.

weight increases the width of the letter stems. Both intensity and width are well-known, strongly preattentive visual cues and thus effective for indicating ordered and quantitative data. At small sizes, such as this text, however, it may be difficult to perceive many levels: between 2–9 levels of weight may be usable depending on size (Figure 3.10).

3.2.4 Oblique Angle (and Italic)

Italics and obliques both refer to sloping text. Oblique text is a sloped font made by geometrically skewing a font (e.g. Arial Figure 3.11 left) while true italics are sloped fonts that have modified letterforms, which may have small variation (e.g. Segoe UI, note f, a, i) or large variation (e.g. Garamond, where every italic letter has modified shapes).

There are no standards for slope angle; most modern usages slope right between 2 and 20 degrees. Historic script may be much steeper, such as the examples shown in Figure 3.12. The right image is a crossed-letter: text superimposed at right angles to save paper and reduce postage costs.

FIGURE 3.11   Arial's sloped font is geometrically skewed while Garamond has completely modified shapes.

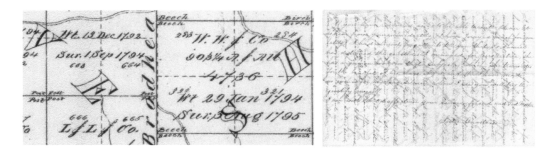

FIGURE 3.12 Steeply sloped italics from the 19th century on a survey and a crossed-letter.

Gryphon, King, Hatter, Hare, Rabbit, Cat, Queen, Alice, *Mock Turtle, Duchess, Puppy*

FIGURE 3.13 Sentiment indicated by slope from negative to positive, per character from *Alice*.

Oblique and italic can also slope left (reverse italic). Reverse italics sometimes occur in cartography to indicate water features, such as the river labels in Figure 1.10.

Perceptually, slope (or angle) ranks fairly high on visual attribute rankings (e.g. Mackinlay 1986). Note that a switch from roman (upright) to italic font in the same typeface maintains consistent font weight so there is no change in the intensity of italicized font. Since oblique slope angle is simply a geometric transformation, a visualization programmer can skew text to create variable slopes associated with quantitative data.

Oblique angle can be effectively used for ordered or quantitative data on a diverging scale with negative values shown in a reverse angle, zero as normal text, and positive values shown with a positive angle. Figure 3.13 shows the net sentiment score per character from *Alice in Wonderland*, ordered most negative to most positive.

3.2.5 Underlines

Underlines are a strong form of emphasis. Underlines are easily drawn on printed texts by readers, such as Figure 3.14. Conventional uses include indicating hyperlinks, wavy (for spelling errors), strikethrough (to indicate deletion), overlines, editor marks (e.g. single for italics, wavy for bold, double for small caps, and dashed to remove formats) and indicating an ordering of labels on some maps (e.g. Figure 1.10).

¶ Liber unus de tranquillitate uitæ ad ſerenum ¶ Liber unus quomodo in ſapientem non cadit iniuria ¶ Liber unus de breuitate uitæ ad paulinum cui continuatur liber unus de conſolatione fratris ad pollibium ſine inſcriptione & internallo ex incuria famuli cōponētis qui incipit ¶ Noſtra compares firma ſunt ¶ Prouerbia Senecæ ¶ Vltimo eiuſdem Epiſtole ad Lucillum Centū uigintiquinq;

Cet index n'existe pas dans une partie des exemplaires de cette première édition de Seneque. à sa place on lit les mots finis registri. Cette différence provient de la nécessité où s'est trouvé l'éditeur d'indiquer l'erreur commise par l'imprimeur,

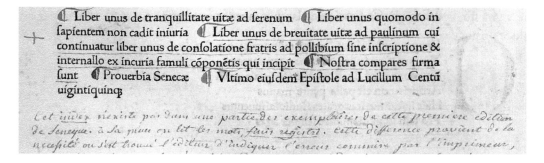

FIGURE 3.14 Underlines added by reader to text and notes.

Quiz jaggy puffs   *Quiz jaggy puffs*
Quiz jaggy puffs   *Quiz jaggy puffs*

FIGURE 3.15   Underlines interfere with descenders on the left, improved with breaks on the right.

Rabbit	47	Mouse	42	Gryphon	55
Hatter	56	Dormouse	40	Mock Turtle	58
Queen	75	Caterpillar	28	King	63
Cat	37	Hare	31	Bill	17

FIGURE 3.16   Character frequency from *Wonderland* shown with underline.

Underlines can be distracting to reading when underlines are heavy. Further, underlines may interfere with the descenders of lowercase letters and punctuation (Figure 3.15 left). The former is addressed using thin or dotted underlines. The latter is addressed in newer web browsers where underlines break around descenders, or can be implemented by the developer. Note that underlines do not change character width whereas bold, italic, and capitalization may. Underlines can span across spaces between words or apply to a fraction of a character.

Underlines are visually separate from the letters. Thus, they can be perceived strongly as an added mark. Further, since they are separate, a viewer can readily attend to an underline independently from other cues – for example, bold, italic, and case are all intrinsic to the letter and require cognitive effort to separate them. As an underline is essentially a line, it can have attributes such as width, length, and style (e.g. dot, dash, single, double, wavy, color, etc.).

Some visualizations use almost-underlines to create labeled bar charts, such as Felton's *2013 Annual Report*. These suggest underlines may encode quantities by their length within text. Figure 3.16 is a compact bar chart created simply using underlines.

3.2.6 Case (Upper, Lower, Small Caps, and Proper)

UPPPERCASE, SMALL CAPS, and lowercase are variations in letterforms used for differentiation and emphasis.

ALL CAPS. "Uppercase letters ask to be noticed," says Wilhide (2010). All caps in email is considered shouting. In news feeds, an all caps headline indicates a breaking story. In some maps, uppercase is used to indicate larger features (e.g. CITY vs. Town). To reduce prescription errors, TALLman lettering is a labeling convention for similar drug names to emphasize the differentiating syllables and reduce prescription errors. Some examples are in Figure 3.17. In some typefaces, all caps is inappropriate as uppercase letters have decorative effects such as swashes or ornament (e.g. some *SCRIPT* and 𝔅𝔏𝔄ℭ𝔎𝔏𝔈𝔗𝔗𝔈ℜ fonts).

Leading Capitals are used to indicate important words, such as proper nouns or uniquely defined words in legal documents. Titles and headings are often set with each

methylPREDNISolone   vinBLAStine hydrOXYzine CARBOplatin
methylTESTOSTERone vinCRIStine hydrALAzine CISplatin

FIGURE 3.17   Pairs of similar drug names differentiated with TALLman lettering.

oh: **DEAR**, MY, I, how, such, it's, won't, she, ever, they'll, 'tis
quite: **FORGOT**, AS, Natural, Out, Tired, Silent, Pleased, Crowd
cry[ed,ing]: **ALICE**, MOUSE, GRYPHON, Mock, Out, Again, come

FIGURE 3.18   Word pair frequencies from *Wonderland*, with leading word on left.

word capitalized. In CamelCase, whitespace between words is removed and a capital is used on the first letter of each word to improve readability.

SMALL CAPS are smaller versions of capitals designed to be used together with lowercase text such that the height and weight match lowercase text. Small caps are used for differentiation with low emphasis, such as lede sentences or acronyms where regular capitals may create too much emphasis (e.g. NATO or NASA).

Note that some languages do not have different cases; some typefaces do not support both upper and lowercase (e.g. COPPERPLATE); and some glyphs do not have case variation (e.g. numbers and punctuation).

In visualization, case can be used to encode ordered data. All uppercase rise to full height and are wider than their lowercase counterparts: uppercase acts as a size cue which is highly preattentive. The difference between small caps and lowercase, however, is limited to shape only, which is a much weaker cue. Thus, a 2–4 level ordering can be created, such as UPPERCASE > SMALL CAPS > Title Case > lowercase.

Figure 3.18 shows some frequent words from *Alice* along the left, with the subsequent word shown in the list along the right. Full caps indicate five or more occurrences, e.g. *oh dear, quite forgot*; small caps indicate three–four, leading cap two, and lowercase only one occurrence.

3.2.7 Width (Condensed/Expanded, Scaling, and Spacing)

The length of text can be adjusted by changing the letter widths and their spacing:

S p a c i n g (referred to as *tracking* for horizontal space between letters) adjusts the size of gaps between letters. Spacing is often used to indicate the extents of an area in cartography, such as a mountain range.

Condensed, expanded, compressed, narrow, and *wide* are variants of a typeface made with different widths but otherwise retain the characteristics of typeface (e.g. Arial Narrow, Roboto Condensed). Condensed type is designed for use in situations where space is tight, such as column headings in tables or map labels.

Scaling text is a geometric transformation which squishes or stretches text horizontally. It is scorned by typographers: "Stretched typefaces lack the integrity of the original

FIGURE 3.19   Left: original text. Center: horizontally scaled to 64%. Right: the condensed typeface.

Items which make Alice smaller include bottles, a fan, cake and the right side of the mushroom; while cake and the left side of the mushroom make Alice larger.

FIGURE 3.20   Font width varies in relation to the action of the items in *Wonderland*.

design and legibility suffers" (Craig et al. 2006); "Correctly condensed fonts retain readability despite a reduction in character width" (Haley et al. 2012); or "fiddling with a [typeface's] scale distorts the line weight of letters, forcing heavy elements to become thin and thin elements to become thick" (Lupton 2010). There are a few fonts that have been explicitly designed to allow for modest horizontal scaling, such as Unger's *Neue Swift* and some variable fonts.

Figure 3.19 shows original text on the left (in *Gill Sans*), scaled text in the center (to 64%), and typographically designed condensed text on the right (*Gill Sans Condensed*). In the scaled version, the *r* has a top-heavy tight hook, *o* has thin sides with a thick top and bottom, and *il* becomes thin and light. In the designed version, the typographer has adjusted thicknesses and shapes to maintain evenness throughout.

Perceptually, width is a quantitative cue, however, variation in letter width is not a commonly used cue and viewers do not attend to word length. For encoding information, a change in width can be used at the level of words or letters. For example, the following city names use extra-condensed letters for letters commonly dropped in contractions, such as highway signs: PHILADELPHIA, BROOKLYN, QUEENS, and WASHINGTON DC. Condensed/expanded can also be used to indicate semantic information, for example Figure 3.20.

3.2.8 Typeface (i.e. Font)

Typeface and font are used interchangeably in common practice to refer to a family of fonts with common characteristics, such as *Garamond*, *Helvetica*, *Comic Sans*, and so on. There are hundreds of thousands of typefaces, many designed for highly specialized applications, such as highway signs (*Interstate*), phone books (*Bell Centennial*), low-resolution screens (*Verdana, Georgia*), aircraft cockpit screens (*B612*), and so on.

Many typefaces are visually similar and may be difficult to differentiate when used at small sizes. For example, Figure 3.21 superimposes a yellow sans serif m over other typefaces in blue: note the similarity between the sans and serif at the far left.

FIGURE 3.21   Differences between some common typefaces, shown by superimposing sample letters.

For the purposes of visualization, differentiation can be created using fonts such as:

- **Plain Sans Serif**, such as **Helvetica, Arial, Roboto,** or Franklin Gothic, tend to have uniform stroke width and a high x-height.

- Serif fonts, such as Times, Garamond, and Century Schoolbook, tend to have variation in horizontal vs. vertical stroke-width (i.e. typographic contrast), which is most pronounced in fonts such as **Bodoni** and Bembo.

- **Slab serifs** have large boxy serifs and uniform stroke width, such as **Rockwell** or **Roboto Slab**.

- Monospace fonts are identifiable by the uniform rhythm of characters (with a wide i and narrow m). Examples include `Courier`, Inconsolata, and `Source Code Pro.`

- 𝕭𝖑𝖆𝖈𝖐𝖑𝖊𝖙𝖙𝖊𝖗 is based on medieval writing styles. Some are ornate (e.g. 𝕺𝖑𝖉 𝕰𝖓𝖌𝖑𝖎𝖘𝖍) while others are simpler (e.g. 𝔉𝔯𝔞𝔨𝔱𝔲𝔯).

- *Script* typefaces imitate handwriting, such as *Lucída Callígraphy*, Monotype Corsiva, and the popular **Comic Sans**.

- Graphic typefaces are designed for thematic purposes such as logos and advertising. Examples include **Cooper Black**, Hobo, ROSEWOOD, and thousands more.

There are several caveats; note that some fonts may intrinsically be much heavier or lighter than the others, meaning that a viewer may notice the difference in weight more than the difference in the shape of the typeface.

Different fonts may be used together to form a *type hierarchy*, such as the different fonts used in this book for the body text, section headings, and chapter headings (in addition to font size). Similarly, many advertisements use typeface variation to separate and differentiate key information as shown previously in Figure 1.20 left.

This differentiation may be used to encode categories into text, such as Haeckl's *Pedigree of Mammals* (1897). As shown in the portion in Figure 3.22, different fonts indicate different classifications. Similarly, some maps, such as *Ordnance Survey*, use typeface to indicate categories of features, such as sans serif for modern features, blackletter for medieval features, and serif for Roman-era ruins.

Note that *all* fonts have semantic associations either accumulated from use over time or created by the designer. Modern fonts also have strong cultural associations, as shown with some of the sample typefaces in Figure 3.23.

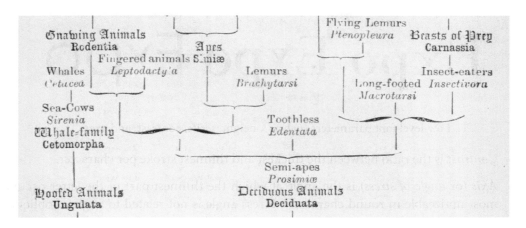

FIGURE 3.22   Haeckl's tree of mammals uses different fonts to indicate different classification schemes.

Industrial Engineering
DIN 1451

Warm and Friendly
Cooper Black

Exclusive Haute Couture
Bodoni

Kindergarten Reader
Century Schoolbook

Basic Commercial Type
Akzidenz-Grotesk

Science Fiction
Eurostile Extended Bold

FIGURE 3.23   Fonts are not neutral and have designed or accumulated cultural associations.

Major characters from Wonderland in order of appearance, indicated as human, animal, fictional creature, or card: Alice, White Rabbit, Mouse, Bill, Caterpillar, Duchess, Cheshire Cat, March Hare, Hatter, Dormouse, Knave, King, Queen, Gryphon and Mock Turtle.

FIGURE 3.24   Major characters from *Wonderland* with types indicated by typeface.

Perceptually, if weights between two typefaces are similar, then the only cue to difference is shape. Shape is a weak perceptual cue, and thus, if differentiation is desired, typefaces which are readily different from each other should be used, such as in Figure 3.24. Shape is not considered an orderable visual cue, although in a highly constrained environment, an order could be created, e.g. a set of fonts ranging from simple to ornate.

3.2.9 Low-Level Font Parameters: X-Height, Contrast, Stress, Serif Types, etc.

Some low-level typographic design parameters are relevant to most alphanumeric glyphs and could be used to create visible differentiation or ordering:

- *X-height* is the intermediate height of lowercase letters. It can vary as seen by the difference between some popular typefaces, as shown in Figure 3.25.

- *Serifs* are short strokes at the end of the letter strokes. Serif shapes and sizes can vary considerably.

X-HEIGHT, SERIFS, CONTRAST AND AXES

Expo Expo Expo

Bodoni   Times Roman   Century Gothic

FIGURE 3.25   Low-level font parameters such as x-height, serifs, contrast, and axes.

- *Contrast* is the ratio between the thickest and thinnest stroke per character.

- *Axis* (or *angle of stress*) is the angle at which the thinnest part of the letter occurs, most noticeable in round characters. Stress angle is not related to angle of obliques or italics.

These typographic design parameters are accessible to the visualization designer using specialized font software such as parametric fonts or variable fonts. Many of these parameters are mutually exclusive; they can be added together in any combination. Figure 3.26 A shows five variants created using parametric fonts, and all the pair-wise combinations.

Some of these parameters have enough variation to create an ordering. Figure 3.26 B shows a parametric font with five ordered levels of x-height and five levels of curviness ordered angular-round-boxy, and all 25 combinations.

Don Knuth claimed with *MetaFont* (1986) that all fonts could be generated with his system of 62 parameters. However, real-world fonts have a vast range of design parameters, difficult to encapsulate in a parametric system. There is incredible variation on serifs and swashes. The underlying skeleton (i.e. stroke path) can be highly varied (e.g. Times Roman vs. Old English). And graffiti shows even more variation is feasible, such as stroke crossings, uneven tops, irregular curvature, and so on, such as the examples catalogued by artist Evan Roth in Figure 3.27.

(A) BINARY	Plain	Boxy	Big Bracket	Wide Serif	Low x-height
Plain	Ferdinand	Charlotte	Cleveland	Rigoberto	Marcelino
Boxy	Millicent	Elizabeth	Cornelius	Magdalena	Georgette
Big Bracket	Dominique	Katherine	Claudette	Kimberlee	Stephanie
Wide Serif	Rosalinda	Christina	Gabrielle	Alejandra	Gwendolyn
Low x-height	Augustine	Josephine	Katharine	Annabelle	Johnathon

(B) ORDER	Curviness 1	Curviness 2	Curviness 3	Curviness 4	Curviness 5
X-height 5	Kristopher	Antionette	Shirleyann	Hermelinda	Margaretta
X-height 4	Bernadette	Fredericka	Florentino	Margarette	Florentina
X-height 3	Antoinette	Evangeline	Georgianna	Marquerite	Clementina
X-height 2	Marguerite	Earnestine	Stanislaus	Hildegarde	Kensington
X-height 1	Jacqueline	Rutherford	Wellington	Sanjuanita	Temperance

FIGURE 3.26   Low-level font parameters and pairwise combinations: (A) binary; (B) ordered.

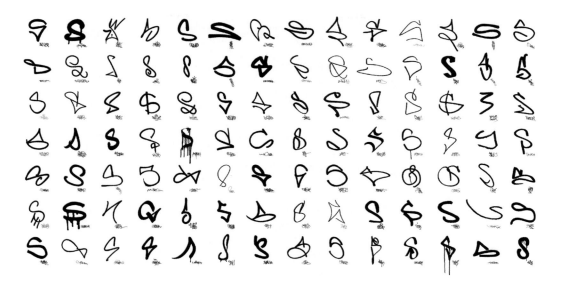

FIGURE 3.27 Diverse graffiti variants of the letter S.

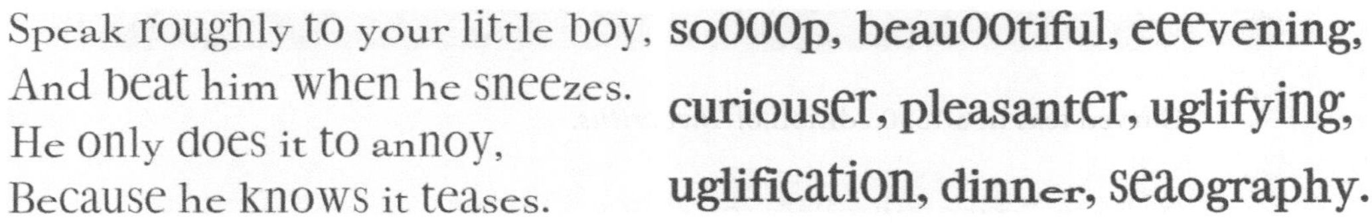

Speak roughly to your little boy,
And beat him when he sneezes.
He only does it to annoy,
Because he knows it teases.

soOOOp, beauOOtiful, eeevening,
curiouser, pleasanter, uglifying,
uglification, dinner, seaography.

FIGURE 3.28 **Variation in x-height. Left: poetic meter unstressed and stressed syllables. Right:** words made by adding or removing letters (taller for added, shorter for removed).

Perceptually, most of these attributes manipulate fine details of letterforms that may not be noticed by a reader. Further, these attributes may not exist in every character (e.g. x-height does not occur in uppercase letters, serifs do not occur on the letter o, etc.) Regardless, these attributes could be effective for specific effects, such as waves embedded in Ronell's post-modern text (Figure 1.22, top right paragraph). A similar effect can be used to indicate poetic meter, such as a verse from *Alice in Wonderland* in Figure 3.28 (left). In Figure 3.28 (right), x-height is used with Carroll's non-dictionary words to indicate added letters (tall x-height) or removed letters (low x-height); a few strategies can be observed, such as added suffixes, modified prefixes, or added vowels to expressively lengthen words.

3.2.10 Shifting Baseline and Text on a Path

As seen in the earlier examples from chemistry and math (e.g. Figure 1.15), subscripts and superscripts are commonly used to express additional information in running text. Similarly, text may be curved to align to a geographic feature (e.g. Figure 1.10), create a shape (e.g. Figure 1.19 left), or create a link between entities (e.g. Figure 2.6). Modifying text to follow curves and shapes is very old; Figure 3.29 is a typeset Greek 1530 edition of

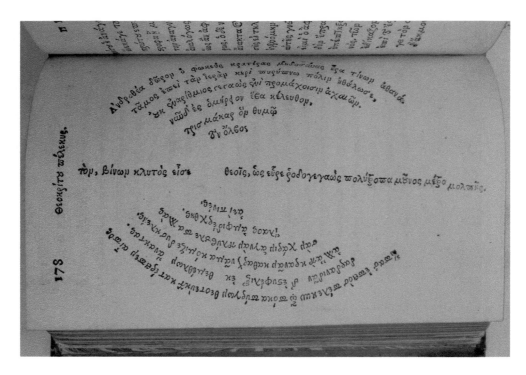

FIGURE 3.29   Curved text in a 1530 edition of *Theocritus*.

only,^{Mouse} timidly,^{Alice} suddenly,^{Rabbit} nearly,^{Gryphon}
dreadfully,^{Hatter} solemnly,^{Dodo} furiously,^{Queen} deeply,^{Turtle}

FIGURE 3.30   Top adverbs from *Wonderland* and the associated character.

Theocritus with a poem set in the shape of an axe, each line curving and length adjusted to fit the target shape.

Typographically, sub- and super-scripts are commonly used at a smaller size than adjacent text to further enhance the separation between the two and reduce the impact on the text flow.

Perceptually, changes in position and size are a strong visual cue. The shifting or curving baseline can be easily perceived. They relate to Gestalt principles of common fate and similarity, which aids the perception of a continuous flow of text.

For a visualization example, *Alice in Wonderland* extensively utilizes adverbs to qualify each characters' dialogue. A list of top adverbs can be extracted, with the top character for each adverb indicated in a superscript (Figure 3.30).

3.3 NON-TYPE VISUAL ATTRIBUTES

In addition to typographic-specific attributes, all the visual attributes used in other visualizations are available to use with text as well, such as: size, fill color, **background color, outline, drop-shadow**, and so on. Some characteristics are as follows.

3.3.1 Size

Size is a strong cue. A wide range in size variation, such as commonly used in word clouds, can result in massive text that dominates the display, leaving less space for other text and adding little additional information. Instead, maps tend to limit the size variation to a narrow range; for example, labels for the largest city are only double the point size of the smallest town on many maps, such as Figure 1.10. Viewers can readily detect small changes in font size without being biased by long vs. short strings (Alexander et al. 2017). Type size in books is also highly constrained; headings, subheadings, body text, and captions may vary by only a few point sizes.

Size also offers the possibility for macro- and micro-readings as seen in many 19th century posters, tickets, and other documents. The railway ticket in Figure 3.31 uses large text to indicate key information: railway line, origin, and destination. Smaller text provides the full context as a sentence. The advertisement uses even greater size variation to create two levels of reading.

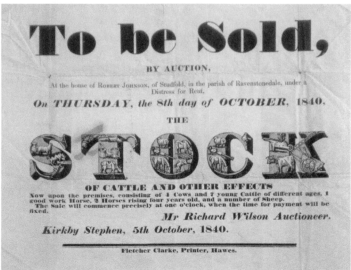

FIGURE 3.31   Railway ticket with key information in a larger size (top). Advertisement with even larger variation (bottom).

3.3.2 Rotation

Text rotation can be used to differentiate text, such as the rotated text in Figure 1.20 middle. Text occurs at normal orientation as well as rotated 90 degrees and 270 degrees in the medieval document in Figure 3.32. The rotated text is easily distinguished but harder to read. Rotation angle could feasibly be used to indicate quantitative data.

3.3.3 Fill Color

Color has been used since medieval times with individual characters or full words. Color can be ordered (medieval ordering is based on color value: black > red > blue > gold) or used for categoric differentiation. Figure 3.33 is an ad from 1900 using colors on initial letters, phrases, and multiple colors on an initial letter. Color can also be used behind text, like a highlighter, such as the initial drop-cap "O."

3.3.4 Outline and Outline Color

Text fill and outline can be separately colored. The text from an 1894 poster in Figure 3.34 has three colors: an outer stroke in a darker shade of the background color, an inner stroke in a saturated highlight color, and a neutral fill. In this example, the inner stroke is slightly offset, creating the illusion of depth as an inner drop-shadow.

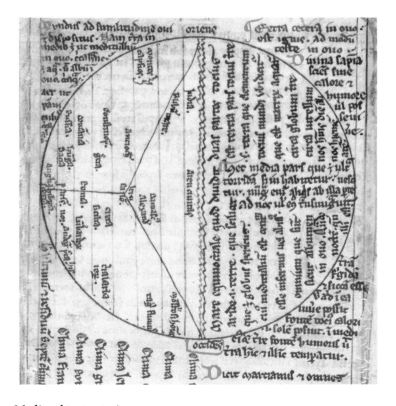

FIGURE 3.32   **Medieval text rotations.**

FIGURE 3.33   Color applied to initial letters, words, and phrases in an ad.

FIGURE 3.34   Multi-color text outlines creating an illusion of floating text.

FIGURE 3.35   Gradient fill and drop-shadow draw attention to the word *sewing*.

3.3.5 Gradients or Drop-Shadows

Text can be filled with gradients, textures, patterns, or imagery. The word SEWING in Figure 3.35 is filled with a bright gradient.

Additionally, the word is visually lifted above the background with a drop-shadow. Drop-shadows can make text illegible, for example, if dark text is used with a dark drop-shadow.

FIGURE 3.36   **Superimposed black text over white text.**

3.3.6 Superimposition and Contrast

In the Dada poster (Figure 1.19) and stamp (Figure 3.36), text is superimposed over other text. The foreground text, in black, is thin and small, while the background text is heavier weight, in a different hue, set at different angles to the foreground text. All these cues aid visual separation. Most important, the contrast between red and white, and between black and red, is sufficient to maintain legibility of each.

3.3.7 Distortion and Extrusion

Letterforms can be bent and manipulated while remaining legible. 3D effects can be added, for example, to extrude letters and create lighting effects such as shading. All these occur in Figure 3.37, with World Almanac pinched in the center and taller at the edges, with 3D extrusions and shadows.

With more extreme distortion, the text becomes more difficult to read, such as 1960s psychedelic posters.

3.3.8 3D Orientation

Text can be oriented in 3D space, as in Figure 3.38. 3D text can convey data by spatial layout, as well as provide context, and aid organization and interaction. Apperley et al. mocked up interactive 3D textual interfaces for email and news in 1982. Muriel Cooper's *Visible Language Workshop* explored interactive 3D typographic visualization workspaces in 1994.

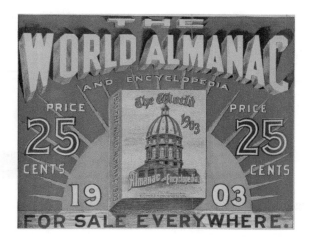

FIGURE 3.37   Text can be distorted and extruded, but requires care to remain legible.

FIGURE 3.38   3D-oriented text is used in ads and modern visualizations.

3.3.9 Motion

Text can move and be readable. Stock market tickers have existed for 150 years. They require literal text to uniquely identify stocks and prices. The speed of scrolling is an indication of the level of activity; faster scrolling means higher trading activity (Figure 3.39).

3.3.10 More: Texture, Blur, Transparency, Etc.

There are other visual attributes that can be used with text, such as texture, blur, line style, or transparency. Figure 3.40 uses transparent red text printed over a light background and a dark figure. Care is required using these attributes to retain the legibility – for example, blurring letters may require increased spacing so that text does not run together.

3.4 MARKS AND TEXT SCOPE

Scope of text ranges from characters, syllables, and words to phrases, sentences, paragraphs, and documents.

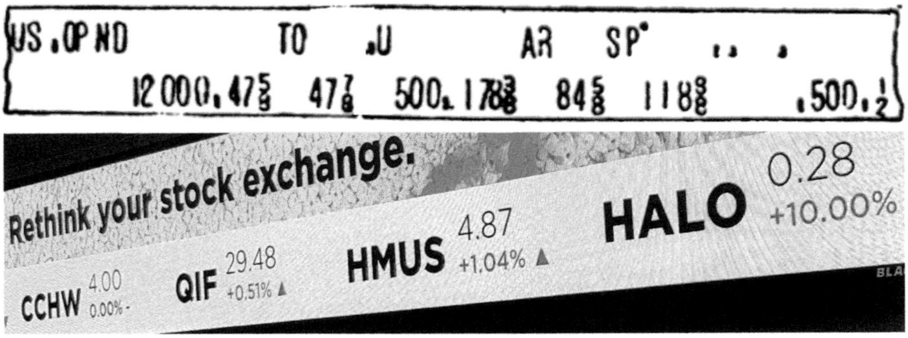

FIGURE 3.39   Scrolling stock tickers use motion to convey activity.

FIGURE 3.40   **Example of legible transparent text over a subtly shaded background.**

3.4.1 Point Marks: Characters, Codes, Syllables, and Words

Characters, codes, syllables, and words correspond to point marks.

High cardinality categories. Characters, codes, and words can be highly effective for encoding categories of high cardinality. Most visual attributes cannot represent many unique categories. For example, hue is difficult to use beyond ten categories; detecting a red dot among 50 other hues, including reddish-orange and reddish-purple, will not be preattentive and will be difficult to discriminate. Abstract shapes can be used, but in practice many visualization systems have a limited number of shapes (e.g. 9 in Excel, 10 in Tableau, and 7 in D3.js). Pictographic icons can be used, but are difficult to design for abstract concepts (e.g. GDP, CPI, or a list of cities); are not intrinsically orderable; and may be ambiguous (e.g. see Clarus the dog-cow, an early Mac icon). Text characters, codes, and words can scale to thousands of unique categories, do not require design effort, and are orderable (alphabetic order).

Individual characters can be used as a point mark to plot data points, as seen in the *market profile* chart in Figure 1.18, where upper and lowercase letters are used to create 48 unique codes. The scatterplot in Figure 3.7 (left) uses single numbers to indicate a numeric range.

Codes can be created from a small number of characters. Many domains use short alphanumeric codes: stock symbols, country codes, state codes, zip codes, industry codes, airline codes, airport codes, train numbers, unit codes, Dewey decimal codes, and so on. All of these are categories of high cardinality. In Figure 3.7 (right), a scatterplot uses two-letter codes to indicate characters in an emotion scatterplot. Structural formulas are schematic visualizations of chemical compounds using line types to indicate structure in addition to codes for groups of atoms, such as the examples in Figure 3.41.

Syllables can be visually manipulated to encode information in subsets of words. The earlier example of TALLman lettering (Figure 3.17) uses capitalization to indicate the differentiating syllable on similar drug names to reduce the risk of prescription errors.

Words can uniquely identify hundreds of thousands of distinct entities such as people, places, organizations, and so on. In the historic examples, proper nouns identify hundreds of geographic features on maps (e.g. Figure 1.9 and Figure 1.10); names of people (e.g. Figure 1.12), and branches in a taxonomy (e.g. Figure 1.14).

3.4.2 Line Marks: Phrases and Sentences

Text is inherently linear, and as such, can be used as line marks. On maps, words may be widely spaced and curved to indicate the range of a geographic area, such as *Odenwald* in Figure 1.10; or longer words such as *Rocky Mountains* on a map of North America.

Phrases and *sentences* are used in *Typographic Maps* and *Smell Maps* (Figure 3.42) to label linear features on maps using continuous text such as "US 101 · HOLLYWOOD FWY" indicating a road (left); or "[I associate coffee to work, friends and Italy, since I only enjoyed it when I lived there]" indicating a contour through a city.

3.4.3 Area Marks: Paragraphs and Chapters

Longer blocks of text typically wrap, forming areas. At a macro-level, these can be used to denote and fill an area; at a micro-level the full text can be read for details. These areas can be simple shapes, such as rectangles or ellipses, or more organic or arbitrary shapes.

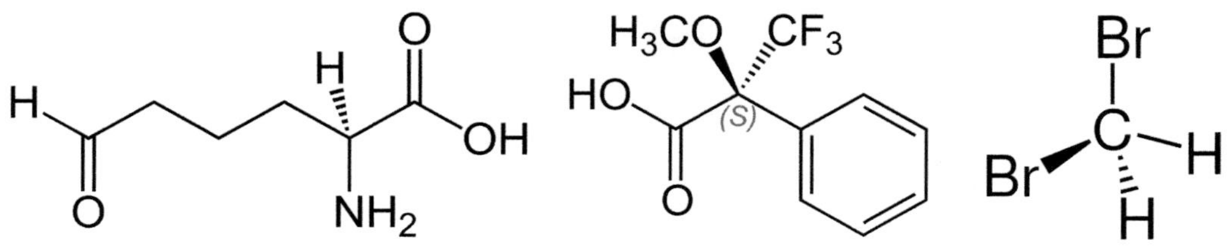

FIGURE 3.41 **Structural formulas combine codes and diagrams.**

Sentences fill areas in the treemap NewsMap.co.jp, indicating the most frequent head-lines, as seen previously in Figure 1.23.

Paragraphs fill elliptical leaves on the *Tree of Knowledge* from the *Encyclopédie* (Roth 1780) in Figure 3.43 (left). In *micrography*, lines of text are curved, aligned, and spaced to fill arbitrary shapes, such as descriptions of constellations in Figure 3.43 (right, Cicero 1100). In Maharik's *Digital Micrography* (2011), algorithms lay out paragraphs to fit arbitrary shapes such as puzzle pieces.

Documents. The text content of documents can be shaped to form areas in visualiza-tions, such as the history of the world in Figure 3.2. The areas formed by the text indicate the geographic expanse and duration of empires. Or, in popular culture, the full text of a book can be set out on a large surface, such as a blanket, with white space used to form representational imagery (e.g. litographs.com).

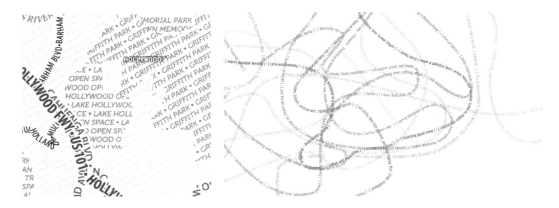

FIGURE 3.42   Typographic maps (left) and smell maps (right) use phrases along linear features.

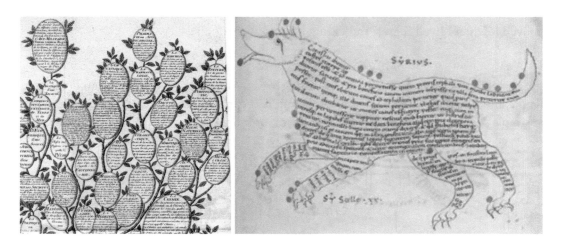

FIGURE 3.43   A small portion from the hierarchy of knowledge from Diderot's *Encyclopedia* (left). Micrography: text aligned and filling arbitrary shapes (right).

3.4.4 Readability of Text

When using longer passages of text, such as lines and areas of text, readability is important. Whereas legibility is a perception issue concerned with unambiguous letter identification (previously discussed at the beginning of Section 3.2), readability is a comprehension issue concerned with ease of reading lines and paragraphs of text. Readability is affected by many factors such as line length, kerning, leading, x-height, font weight, and orientation. Text can be completely legible but difficult to read, as shown in Figure 3.44.

Readability is also related to cultural conventions. Blackletter fonts are difficult to read for modern readers as they are highly unfamiliar. Gerard Unger says:

> Different fonts are not intrinsically more readable: rather it is the readers' familiarity that accounts for legibility and readability. When I designed Swift (typeface) in 1985 it was called hard to read with many angry angles. Now it is the standard used for many newspapers, dictionaries, and other major works.

Some typographers indicate that changes in multiple typographic attributes (e.g. bold, italic, and case) within a line or paragraph of text will be more difficult to read as it does not follow conventional typographic grammar (e.g. Bringhurst 2013), although others suggest such changes can create increased differentiation (e.g. Kane 2011). Further, readability is not as important in uses where the viewer is not continuously reading, such as tables, directories, and dictionaries, where type formats may vary significantly to differentiate across types of information.

3.5 TEXT LAYOUTS: PROSE, TABLES, AND LISTS

A diverse range of visualization layouts have been created to convey data and structure, such as treemaps, parallel coordinates, ternary plots, radar plots, self-organizing maps, networks, and so on. In addition, there are text-specific layouts that can be leveraged to create new types of visualizations. For example:

3.5.1 Prose

The familiar structure of paragraphs running linearly across pages (or columns) is a common layout, particularly for long, linear works such as fiction. The form may vary with document types, for example, line breaks in verse may be based on a set number of syllables. Plays may have more structure, with characters and their associated speaking parts set in blocks, and other descriptive text set off in a different font or italics. Interspersed throughout the text may be organizational text such as chapter and section headings, page numbers, and so forth.

punosun xoq punosun xoq

FIGURE 3.44 Upside down text is legible but difficult to read. Serifs provide a stronger cue of rotation.

Within these forms of running text, there are opportunities for encoding additional information. Medieval documents, such as Figure 3.45, utilize color and decoration to indicate start of sections, sentences, and key words. Color typically has an ordering within medieval documents, such as gold for the most important words, followed by blue, red, and the base color for most of the text such as brown or black.

While color was difficult to use with printing presses, use of italics, spacing, and uppercase to create emphasis started early. These and other forms of emphasis in prose, such as bold, continue through to modern publishing, online publishing, social media, handwritten notes, and so on.

3.5.2 Tables

Tables are pervasive and thus easy to ignore. Tables are a highly flexible form for organizing and visualizing data. *Chronological Tables of Europe* (Parsons 1726), shown in Figure 3.46, is a tiny interactive book. The tables record sovereigns, one century per page, with time running horizontally and countries vertically. Country names and associated sources are indicated as row headers on flaps that fold out from either side. Multiple lines of text fit in cells, some of which span across multiple rows and/or columns and/or text may be rotated 90 degrees to fit narrow columns. Contractions and symbols are extensively used to save space, some of which are shown on the right.

Formats may be used to indicate data. Valerio's *Colloquia* (1576) differentiates language by font, e.g. Flemish in plain serif, Latin in italics, and so on, as shown in Figure 3.47.

Modern tables make extensive use of formats to add information, as shown in the earlier example of the timetable in Figure 1.13. Many screen-based data grids, such as Excel,

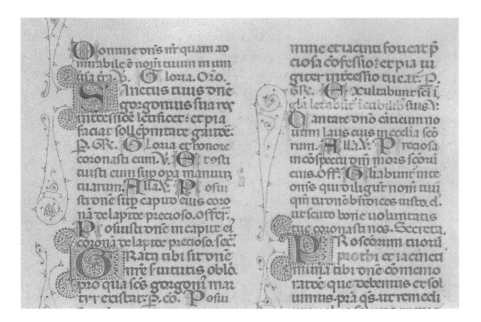

FIGURE 3.45 **Illuminated manuscript from 1400 with full words and initials differentiated and decorated in red or blue from surrounding text.**

FIGURE 3.46   *Chronological Tables of Europe.* A book of tables with interactive flaps from 1726.

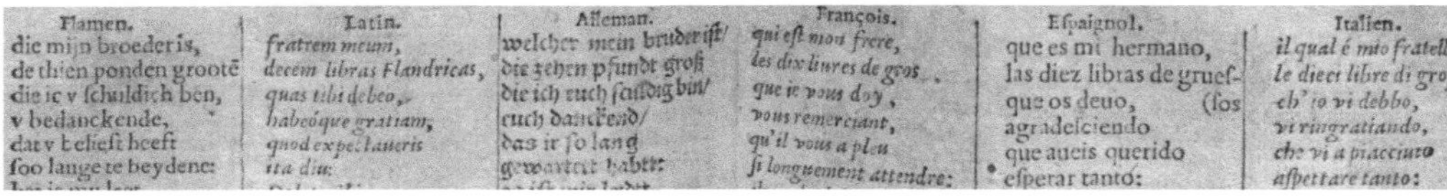

FIGURE 3.47   *Colloquia* (1576) provides tables of translations, using a different font per language.

financial trading watchlists, realtime SCADA systems, and so on use formatting to highlight cells of interest and use interactions such as sorting, grouping, and filtering as in the financial bond watchlist in Figure 3.3. Given the prevalence of highly flexible tables like Excel, spreadsheets in the wild may use combinations of foreground color, background color, bold, italic, underlines, text size, font family, and cell outlines to format content based on data.

3.5.3 Lists and Indices

Reference texts, such as dictionaries, thesauruses, bibliographies, and guidebooks, use formats to differentiate text to facilitate skimming to the text of interest. Figure 3.48 left is a dictionary (Fowler et al. 1912) and Figure 3.48 right is a *Michelin Guide* (1908). Note how both show entries with very heavyweight words (e.g. **rede**, **Coutances**). Then formats such as italics, parentheses, small caps, different typefaces (e.g. **redif**, Stock Michelin, *RN 171*), superscripts, symbols, characters in boxes or circles, and so on, are used to differentiate elements and sub-sections and encode data within each listing. These formats may apply to words, codes, or syllables (e.g. one*self*, **redeem**ABLE).

Online documentation, such as specifications, programming languages, and libraries, are similarly organized and formatted as hierarchical lists, as can be seen in some examples in Figure 3.49.

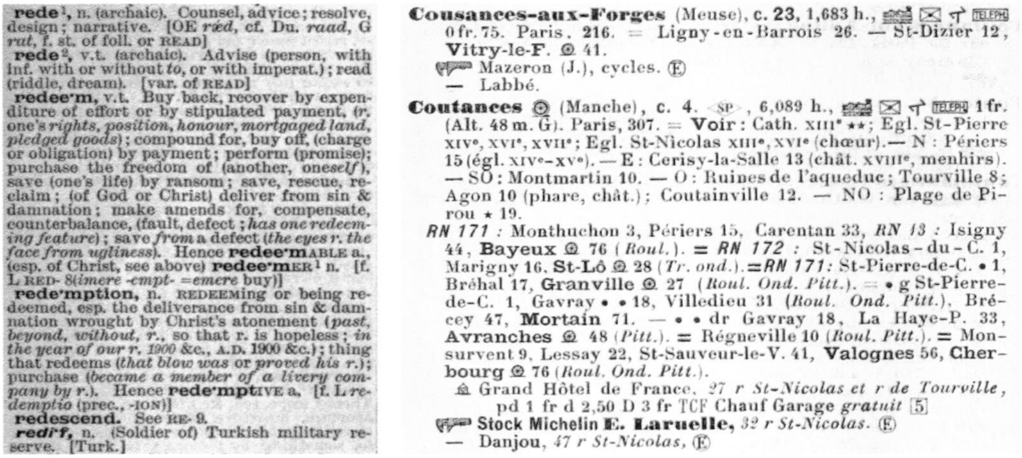

rede¹, n. (archaic). Counsel, advice; resolve, design; narrative. [OE *ræd*, cf. Du. *raad*, G *rat*, f. st. of foll. or READ]
rede², v.t. (archaic). Advise (person, with inf. with or without *to*, or with imperat.); read (riddle, dream). [var. of READ]
redee'm, v.t. Buy back, recover by expenditure of effort or by stipulated payment, (*r. one's rights, position, honour, mortgaged land, pledged goods*); compound for, buy off, (charge or obligation) by payment; perform (promise); purchase the freedom of (another, oneself); save (one's life) by ransom; save, rescue, reclaim; (of God or Christ) deliver from sin & damnation; make amends for, compensate, counterbalance, (fault, defect; *has one redeeming feature*); save *from* a defect (*the eyes r. the face from ugliness*). Hence **redee'm**ABLE a., (esp. of Christ, see above) **redee'm**ER¹ n. [f. L RED- *(i)mere -empt- =emere* buy)]
rede'mption, n. REDEEMING or being redeemed, esp. the deliverance from sin & damnation wrought by Christ's atonement (*past, beyond, without, r.*, so that r. is hopeless; *in the year of our r. 1900* &c., A.D. 1900 &c.); thing that redeems (*that blow was or proved his r.*); purchase (*became a member of a livery company by r.*). Hence **rede'mpt**IVE a. [f. L *redemptio* (prec., -ION)]
redescend. See RE- 9.
redi'f, n. (Soldier of) Turkish military reserve. [Turk.]

Cousances-aux-Forges (Meuse), c. 23, 1,683 h., 0 fr. 75. Paris. 216. — Ligny-en-Barrois 26. — St-Dizier 12, Vitry-le-F. 41.
Mazeron (J.), cycles.
— Labbé.
Coutances (Manche), c. 4. SP, 6,089 h., 1 fr. (Alt. 48 m. G). Paris, 307. — **Voir** : Cath. XIIIe ★★; Egl. St-Pierre XIVe, XVIe, XVIIe; Egl. St-Nicolas XIIIe, XVIe (chœur). — N : Périers 15 (égl. XIVe-XVe). — E : Cerisy-la-Salle 13 (chât. XVIIIe, menhirs). — SO : Montmartin 10. — O : Ruines de l'aqueduc; Tourville 8; Agon 10 (phare, chât.); Coutainville 12. — NO : Plage de Pirou ★ 19.
RN 171 : Monthuchon 3, Périers 15, Carentan 33, *RN 13* : Isigny 44, **Bayeux** 76 (*Roul.*). = *RN 172* : St-Nicolas-du-C. 1, Marigny 16, **St-Lô** 28 (*Tr. ond.*). = *RN 171*: St-Pierre-de-C. • 1, Bréhal 17, **Granville** 27 (*Roul. Ond. Pitt.*). = • g St-Pierre-de-C. 1, Gavray • • 18, Villedieu 31 (*Roul. Ond. Pitt.*), Bré-cey 47, **Mortain** 71. — • • dr Gavray 18, La Haye-P. 33, **Avranches** 48 (*Pitt.*). = Régneville 10 (*Roul. Pitt.*). = Mon-survent 9, Lessay 22, St-Sauveur-le-V. 41, **Valognes** 56, **Cherbourg** 76 (*Roul. Ond. Pitt.*).
Grand Hôtel de France, *27 r St-Nicolas et r de Tourville*, pd 1 fr d 2,50 D 3 fr TCF Chauf Garage *gratuit* 5
Stock Michelin E. Laruelle, *32 r St-Nicolas.*
— Danjou, *47 r St-Nicolas*,

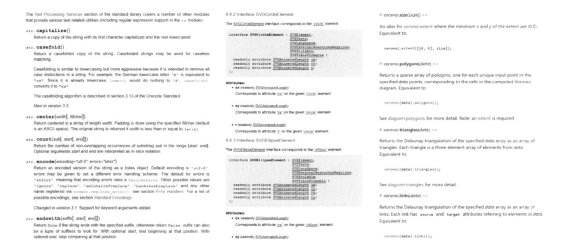

FIGURE 3.48 Reference texts use a variety of formats to differentiate elements in each listing. Left: dictionary; right: *Michelin Guide*.

The Text Processing Services section of the standard library covers a number of other modules that provide various text related utilities (including regular expression support in the re module)

str.capitalize()
Return a copy of the string with its first character capitalized and the rest lowercased.

str.casefold()
Return a casefolded copy of the string. Casefolded strings may be used for caseless matching.
Casefolding is similar to lowercasing but more aggressive because it is intended to remove all case distinctions in a string. For example, the German lowercase letter 'ß' is equivalent to "ss". Since it is already lowercase, lower() would do nothing to 'ß'; casefold() converts it to "ss".
The casefolding algorithm is described in section 3.13 of the Unicode Standard.
New in version 3.3.

str.center(*width*[, *fillchar*])
Return centered in a string of length *width*. Padding is done using the specified *fillchar* (default is an ASCII space). The original string is returned if *width* is less than or equal to len(s).

str.count(*sub*[, *start*[, *end*]])
Return the number of non-overlapping occurrences of substring *sub* in the range [*start*, *end*]. Optional arguments *start* and *end* are interpreted as in slice notation.

str.encode(*encoding="utf-8"*, *errors="strict"*)
Return an encoded version of the string as a bytes object. Default encoding is 'utf-8'. *errors* may be given to set a different error handling scheme. The default for *errors* is 'strict', meaning that encoding errors raise a UnicodeError. Other possible values are 'ignore', 'replace', 'xmlcharrefreplace', 'backslashreplace' and any other name registered via codecs.register_error(), see section Error Handlers. For a list of possible encodings, see section Standard Encodings.
Changed in version 3.1: Support for keyword arguments added.

str.endswith(*suffix*[, *start*[, *end*]])
Return True if the string ends with the specified *suffix*, otherwise return False. *suffix* can also be a tuple of suffixes to look for. With optional *start*, test beginning at that position. With optional *end*, stop comparing at that position.

9.8.2 Interface SVGCircleElement

The SVGCircleElement interface corresponds to the 'circle' element.

```
interface SVGCircleElement : SVGElement,
                             SVGTests,
                             SVGLangSpace,
                             SVGExternalResourcesRequired,
                             SVGStylable,
                             SVGTransformable {
  readonly attribute SVGAnimatedLength cx;
  readonly attribute SVGAnimatedLength cy;
  readonly attribute SVGAnimatedLength r;
};
```

Attributes:
- **cx** (readonly SVGAnimatedLength)
  Corresponds to attribute 'cx' on the given 'circle' element.
- **cy** (readonly SVGAnimatedLength)
  Corresponds to attribute 'cy' on the given 'circle' element.
- **r** (readonly SVGAnimatedLength)
  Corresponds to attribute 'r' on the given 'circle' element.

9.8.3 Interface SVGEllipseElement

The SVGEllipseElement interface corresponds to the 'ellipse' element.

```
interface SVGEllipseElement : SVGElement,
                              SVGTests,
                              SVGLangSpace,
                              SVGExternalResourcesRequired,
                              SVGStylable,
                              SVGTransformable {
  readonly attribute SVGAnimatedLength cx;
  readonly attribute SVGAnimatedLength cy;
  readonly attribute SVGAnimatedLength rx;
  readonly attribute SVGAnimatedLength ry;
};
```

Attributes:
- **cx** (readonly SVGAnimatedLength)
  Corresponds to attribute 'cx' on the given 'ellipse' element.
- **cy** (readonly SVGAnimatedLength)

\# *voronoi*.**size**([*size*]) <>
An alias for *voronoi.extent* where the minimum *x* and *y* of the extent are ⟨0,0⟩. Equivalent to:

```
voronoi.extent([[0, 0], size]);
```

\# *voronoi*.**polygons**(*data*) <>
Returns a sparse array of polygons, one for each unique input point in the specified *data* points, corresponding to the cells in the computed Voronoi diagram. Equivalent to:

```
voronoi(data).polygons();
```

See *diagram*.polygons for more detail. Note: an extent is required.

\# *voronoi*.**triangles**(*data*) <>
Returns the Delaunay triangulation of the specified *data* array as an array of triangles. Each triangle is a three-element array of elements from *data*. Equivalent to:

```
voronoi(data).triangles();
```

See *diagram*.triangles for more detail.

\# *voronoi*.**links**(*data*) <>
Returns the Delaunay triangulation of the specified *data* array as an array of links. Each link has source and target attributes referring to elements in *data*. Equivalent to:

```
voronoi(data).links();
```

FIGURE 3.49 Snippets of online documentation from Python, SVG, and D3.js – formatted with different fonts, weights, italics, and colors – similar to reference works such as dictionaries.

3.6 TEXT INTERACTIONS

As shown in Figure 3.1, an interaction loop in visualization provides operational benefits to visualization. This assumes that the medium used to display the visualization provides interaction, and that the audience can access and use the interaction.

Quantitative data can be transformed via mathematical and statistical operations: sum, percentage, range, min, max, mean, standard deviation, z-score, and so on. These can be applied interactively for filtering, aggregation, zoom, animation, and so on. Similarly, literal text allows for various textual operations which can be used to preprocess text or manipulated interactively to aid tasks.

Ordering. Text can be ordered and sorted (alphabetically), facilitating the viewer's visual search and lookup.

Search. Text can be found by searching with complete or partial strings. Searching text is common across applications, available via semi-standard conventions such as <shortcut key>+F (e.g. desktop) or magnifying glass button (e.g. mobile). As search is now a pervasive interaction paradigm, users may expect a text-centric visualization to offer search interaction. Note that browser-based search is already compatible with browser-based visualization technology such as Scalable Vector Graphics (SVG), thereby providing basic search with any text displayed.

Autocompletion. In text input, autocomplete predicts the word or string the user is typing. Autocompletion, combined with search, can help guide a user to text which exists in the visualization dataset.

Tone, opinion, sentiment, and emotion. Text can be evaluated and assigned quantitative values, for example, for opinion (e.g. ratings), tone (e.g. news tone), sentiment (e.g. score for positive or negative), or emotion (e.g. anger, sadness, joy, or fear).

Categorization, taxonomies, topic analysis, and entity recognition. Many text collections are organized by classification schemes and tagging of topics by subject words; such as general purpose classifications (e.g. Dewey, Library of Congress) and domain-specific classifications (e.g. ACM, IEEE). These topics can be useful for interactive filtering, clustering, etc. Similarly, entity recognition can be used to tag and extract entities such as the names of persons, organizations, and locations, also for interactive filtering.

Faceted search. Extracted categories, topics, entities, keywords, topics, tone, sentiment, and so forth can be used to supplement search interfaces. Faceted search provides a set of criteria, each with top characteristics, which in turn are selected to filter a search. This design pattern is common in shopping websites (such as Amazon) and is applicable to text-analytic visualizations. In the center image of Figure 1.7, a graph visualization is complemented with facets along the right side enabling the user to filter nodes in the graph based on website, geographic location, data source, timestamp, and so on.

Comparison, similarity, and translation. Texts can be compared and assessments made regarding similarity. Tools such as thesauruses, dictionaries, and word embeddings aid in understanding similarity. Translation extends comparative analysis to produce near equivalent meaning in another language.

Summarization. Text can be summarized; longer texts can be reduced to shorter texts while retaining a subset of the original meaning.

Natural Language Processing and Machine Learning. All the above operations are evolving and improving with NLP and machine learning, such as topic extraction, emotion analysis, sentiment detection, machine translation, automated summarization,

Alice was beginning *to* get very **tired** *of* sitting *by* her sister *on the* **bank,** *and of* having *nothing* to do. Once *or* **twice** *she* had **peeped** *into the* book *her* sister was reading, *but it* had *no* **pictures** or **conversations** *in it, "and* what is *the* use *of a* book," thought **Alice,** *"without* **pictures** or **conversations?"**

So *she* was **considering** *in her* own mind *(as* well *as she* could, *for the* day made *her* feel very **sleepy** *and* **stupid),** *whether the* pleasure *of* making *a* **daisy-chain** would be *worth* the trouble *of* getting up *and* **picking** the **daisies,** *when* suddenly *a* White **Rabbit** with **pink** eyes ran close *by her.*

There was *nothing* so very **remarkable** *in that, nor* did **Alice** think *it* so very much out *of the* **way** *to* hear *the* **Rabbit** say to *itself,* **"Oh dear! Oh dear!** *I* shall be too late!" *But* when *the* **Rabbit actually** took *a* watch out *of its* **waistcoat-pocket** *and* looked *at it and* then **hurried** *on,* **Alice** started *to her* feet, *for it* **flashed** *across her* mind *that she* had **never** *before* seen *a* **rabbit** with either *a* **waistcoat-pocket,** *or a* watch *to* take out *of it, and,* **burning** with **curiosity,** *she* ran *across* the field *after it and* was just *in* time *to* see *it* **pop** down *a* large **rabbit-hole,** *under the* **hedge.** *In* another moment, down went **Alice** *after it!*

The **rabbit-hole** went straight *on like a* **tunnel** *for* some *way and* then **dipped** suddenly down, so suddenly *that* **Alice** had not *a* moment *to* think *about* **stopping** *herself before she* found *herself* **falling** down what seemed *to* be *a* very deep well.

FIGURE 3.50   Toggling text to mark uncommon words in heavyweight blue text and show a simplistic two-word summary per paragraph in large orange text underneath the prose.

and so on. NLP can be combined with interactions. For example, in Figure 3.50, words have been toggled to weigh them inverse to their language frequency; and a key character with the most infrequent verb or adjective extracted per paragraph is used as a simplistic summarization.

3.7 TEXT CHARACTERIZATION FOR VISUALIZATION DESIGN SUMMARY

Designing visualizations using text should consider alternatives beyond simple labels, size, and color:

1. **Literal encoding**. Text literally encodes data. Using literal text can increase information content, aid fast identification, reduce search, and facilitate discovery of local relationships. However, text is *language dependent*, requiring translation or adaptation for diverse audiences.

2. **Typographic attributes**. Text can be formatted with a wide variety of visual attributes, such as size, fill color, background color, rotation, 3D, motion, blur, and so on. In addition, typographic attributes such as font weight and typeface are available; each attribute has different characteristics as summarized in the table in Figure 3.51. The column *Pop-out* summarizes whether the attribute is preattentive (as discussed previously in Section 2.1.1). Where an attribute can indicate more than two data types (e.g. continuous changes in weight rather than bold/regular), the estimated number of levels perceivable at *label-size* is indicated (where label-size is expected to be similar to body text in a book).

3. **Text scope**. Text can be manipulated at the level from individual alphanumeric characters through to paragraphs and documents. From a design perspective, a phrase or less text corresponds to a point mark; while phrases and sentences can correspond to

GROUP	FONT ATTRIBUTE	Position	Length/Size	Intensity	Orientation	Shape	Containment	Pop-out*	DATA BEST SUITED FOR (L literal, O ordered, C categoric, Q quantitative, G grouping)	EXAMPLE
Glyphs	Alphanumerics					◆		D	L, O	ape bat 123 d5 داؤد のぞみ
Glyphs	Symbols					◆		D	C	! ? # @ #comment $var
Font Family Attributes	Weight	•	◆					HP	Q 2-9 levels	1.0 2.0 3.0 5.0 **8.0**
	Oblique / Italic				◆			HP	C, Q 2-5 levels	-2.0 -1.0 0.0 *1.0 2.0*
	Underline	◆		•				HP	C, O, Q using length	plain dash single double
	Case & sm caps			•		◆		P	C, O 2-3 levels	BIG Avg. Small tiny
	Width: condensed	◆	•					HP	Q, O 2-4 levels	1200 2000 **3000**
	Width: squished	◆	•					HP	Q not recommended	thin plain wide fat
	Typeface					◆		P	C 2-6 levels	Swiss French German Italian
Sequence	Width: spacing	◆	•					HP	Q, O	tall grand venti
	Path/Superscript	◆	•					HP	C 2 levels	Normal High Low
	Symbols: delimiters						◆	D	G	(but) -and- <or>
Font Design	e.g. x-height, serif length		◆					HP	O, Q few levels	teeny short mid tall lofty
	e.g. contrast, axis					◆		P	O few levels	LOW MED. HIGH

◆ / • indicates primary / secondary visual channel for font attribute (Wolfe & Horowitz 2005) * **HP**: Highly probable, **P**: probable, **D**: doubtful

FIGURE 3.51   Summary of typographic attributes and suitability to data types.

lines; and longer text can correspond to areas. *Readability* is an issue, especially for longer text. Ease of reading must be traded off against additional data being added.

4. **Text layout**. Using text affords different kinds of layouts, including common text layouts such as prose, tables, and lists.

5. **Text Interactions**. Text affords interactions such as ordering, searching, summarizing, and so on. Natural language processing techniques can be used in conjunction with interactions. As *search* and *ordering* are highly common interactions, text-centric visualizations should strongly consider search and ordering interactions.

3.8 FURTHER READING

Much of this chapter covers aspects of typography. For understanding typography in general, consider popular introductory texts in typography, such as Lupton's *Thinking with Type* (2010) or Squire et al.'s *Getting It Right with Type: The Dos and Don'ts of Typography* (2006) or Bringhurst's *The Elements of Typographic Style* (2013). Most undergraduate programs in graphic design have multiple courses on typography; some offer advanced courses for non-typographers (e.g. University of Reading). For *word perception*, see Larson 2004 for an introduction. For a discussion on transpositions and related Internet memes, see Davis 2003. For automaticity, see Bargh 1994. For interaction task decomposition, see Proctor and Vu 2008. TALLman lettering is a convention documented by the FDA and ISMP, e.g. 2010.

For *cognitive benefits* and reasoning aids, start with Larkin and Simon's landmark analysis from 1987, *Why a diagram is (sometimes) worth ten thousand words*. Serendipity is rarely discussed in visualization, see Thudt et al. 2012 for some uncommon visualizations, unique validation, and discussion of serendipity. For search, Hearst 2009 provides a thorough analysis of many different user interface techniques. Jänicke et al. 2015 provide a thorough analysis of close and distant readings of text and associated visualization techniques for the digital humanities.

Typographers have studied *legibility and readability* for more than a century, e.g. Legros and Grant, in 1916, quantitatively measured character similarity for confusability. See Beier's *Reading Letters* (2012) for a comprehensive overview of the many methods to evaluate type legibility. Typographers and psychologists discuss factors at the level of characters (e.g. consistent stroke widths, open counters, wider proportions (Squire et al)), between characters (e.g. risk of identification error, run-together risk, x-height (Beier)), across a series of letters (e.g. predictability across letters, i.e. font-tuning (Gauthier et al. 2006)), and environmental factors such as illumination, contrast, distance and use environment (e.g. roadway signage, cockpits (Grainger et al. 2008)). Also note, studies indicate only a portion of the area of letters are used primarily by observers to identify letters, with letter terminators as the most important cue for letter identification (e.g. Vinot and Athenes 2012).

Parametric fonts are appealing as a way to quantitatively adjust typographic parameters. Typographers have long worked on super-families, e.g. see Bil'ak (2008). Knuth's *Metafont* was an early programmatic parametric font (1986). *Prototypo.io* is a commercially available parametric font generator. *Variable fonts* are a font-standard where the font designer can expose quantitative font properties within a font to be accessed programmatically, such as CSS: see Wikipedia for an overview; developer.mozilla for documentation and v-fonts.com for example fonts, including open source and commercial variants.

Symbols and icons are only briefly discussed here: see Borgo et al. (2013) for a detailed analysis; or Maguire's thesis (2014) for discussion and examples; or Brath (2010) for a discussion regarding some design parameters associated with shapes.

CHAPTER 4

Using the Design Space

UP TO THIS POINT, many historic and existing visualization techniques have been discussed to uncover and define the textual elements used to create visualizations, as summarized in Figure 2.13.

Given a new set of textual design elements, how can they be used to create new visualizations? The goal of this book is not simply to make a better word cloud. In fact, the palette of textual possibilities is so broad, with so many potential permutations, that the full extents of the design space is impossible to cover in the limited space of a book.

For a designer, the design space can act as an aid to consider alternative design choices. There are many frames of references as potential starting points:

- *Structured data.* Text can be used to create variants of existing visualization techniques or create new kinds of visualizations on top of traditional structured data – categoric, ordered, and quantitative data – discussed in Section 4.1.

- *Unstructured data and natural language processing* (NLP). There are many new possibilities for visualizations of unstructured data, such as prose text (Section 4.2).

- *Multiple encoding.* Typography can use many formats simultaneously; this creates opportunities for encoding data into text but also requires caution (Section 4.3).

- *Supporting text.* Outside of the core plot, there are many different supporting roles of text around visualizations and visualization can be applied to this text as well (Section 4.4).

- *Markets.* A very different way to use a design space is to consider business areas and application areas where these new techniques may create new opportunities (Section 4.5).

This chapter has many tiny snapshots of visualizations to visually indicate how the text is used in each design alternative; each of these visual examples will be enlarged and discussed in the remainder of the book, Chapters 5–12.

4.1 STRUCTURED DATA AND BERTIN'S PERMUTATIONS

This text visualization framework as summarized in Figure 2.13 can aid the creation of design alternatives. One reason for the popularity of visualization libraries such as *D3.js* and *ggplot2* is that they provide many example visualizations which can be used as a catalog of ideas, adapted and extended for other uses. A very early example illustrating visualization design alternatives is from *Sémiologie graphique* (1967); Jacques Bertin first creates his visualization framework, then across the next 40 pages (pages 100–138) he creates 90 different visualizations from the same dataset. The dataset is straightforward. It lists 90 French departments (i.e. an administrative region, similar to a state or province), each with nine attributes: the name of the department and its code number, the population employed in three occupations, the proportions for each of those, and the total population. Bertin's visualization examples include bar charts, scatterplots, maps, cartograms, ternary plots, and so on – a small subset were shown in Figure 2.9. Note that text was minimal in Bertin's 90 visualizations. In one example, he labels data points (bottom left of Figure 2.9), but in the other 89 text is restricted to axes and ticks.

Using the *same dataset* as Bertin and the text visualization design framework from Figure 2.13, many extensions and unique visualizations can be created. Fifteen are shown in Figure 4.1. In considering this new design space, it is important not to focus on a narrow subset of possibilities, such as only focusing on labels. A breadth of alternative visualizations can be considered, using some of the dimensions of the design space to organize variants:

- *Data type* is indicated on the vertical axis. At the top are visualizations where marks have been replaced with literal marks (A–D); examples where categoric properties are primarily encoded in marks, such as a set of diagrams (E–F); many examples of ordered data (G–L); and some quantitative encodings (M–O).

- *Mark scope* is indicated on the horizontal axes. Examples range from numeric codes and subsets of words (A,B,G,I) to words (C,E,F,H), sentences (K,M), and paragraphs (L,N).

Compare some of these examples to Figure 2.9. For example, both have bar charts. The bar charts near the top of Figure 4.1 (B–C) are simple extensions to bar charts with the addition of stacked labels to indicate departments. Textual designs can be more innovative too: the examples in the lower right (K–N) are particularly text-dense novel visualizations. Each of these examples represents new approaches to visualizing with text. Each of these will be discussed in more detail in the upcoming chapters.

Chapters 5–7 will focus on using text within existing well-known visualization techniques to overcome limitations in scatterplots, distributions, and line charts by using literal text:

- *Point labels* are the focus of Chapter 5. Specifically, the use of literal text as point markers provides fast access for identification, which also enables perceptual opportunities such as serendipity. Examples include scatterplots, ternary plots (A), and graphs.

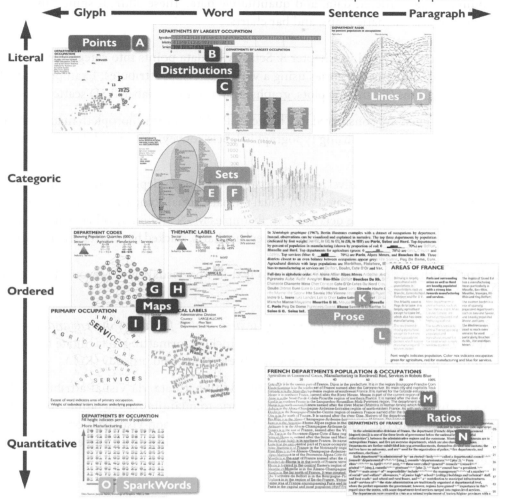

FIGURE 4.1 Fifteen new typographic visualizations, using the same dataset of occupations by departments in France shown in Figure 2.9. The examples include typographic extensions to existing visualizations and new visualizations: (A) ternary plot; (B–C) bar charts; (D) parallel coordinates; (E) Venn diagram; (F) scatterplot; (G–J) thematic maps; (K–L) paragraphs with added ordered data; (M) lines of text; (N) paragraphs with added quantitative data; and (O) SparkWords.

- *Distributions* are the focus of Chapter 6, starting with stem and leaf plots, and extending the approach across text ranging from individual letters to words (such as B and C), and to document summarization.

- *Lines* are covered in Chapter 7. Specifically, a line can be augmented or replaced with a line of microtext. These facilitate identification of lines in data-dense line charts and provides direct access to textual content. Examples include social media and financial data on timeseries charts and parallel coordinate charts (D).

The next three chapters focus on using typographic attributes to represent categoric data (i.e. nominal data), ordered data, and quantitative data. These address some limitations with set diagrams, thematic maps, and bar charts:

- *Set analysis* is covered in Chapter 8. Sets divide data points into categories, and text can represent many categories using a variety of visual attributes. Examples include Venn diagrams (E), mosaic plots, graphs, and a couple of labeled 3D scatterplots (F).

- *Thematic maps* are considered in Chapter 9. Problems with choropleth maps and cartograms are addressed using typographic labels conveying ordered data, such as the examples G–J.

- *Ratios* are the quantitative relation between values. By depicting quantitative values using lengths of text indicated with visual formats, visual comparison of ratios are facilitated while retaining the detailed text. Examples M–N and many others will be shown in Chapter 10, showing some benefits over bar charts, stacked bar charts, and range bars.

Visualizing with text can also add data into text in non-visualization layouts to enhance text or add data to the text:

- *Prose*, or more specifically, *formatting text so that it facilitates understanding of the text*, is the focus of Chapter 11. Techniques include formatting to facilitate text skimming, summarization, pronunciation, abbreviations, and prosody (K–L).

- *SparkWords* are words augmented with additional data via visual attributes. They can range from letters to words and categoric to quantitative encoding. As the data is encoded onto the word, these words can be used in non-visualization layouts such as narratives, lists, or tables. SparkWords will be introduced in Chapter 12, including example O, and many other examples.

4.2 UNSTRUCTURED DATA ANALYSIS AND NLP

Bertin's dataset of occupations is a structured dataset. What about text-centric datasets? In Chapter 3, more than ten examples are illustrated using text extracted from *Alice's Adventures in Wonderland* by Lewis Carroll (1865). Fourteen *Alice* examples from throughout this book are collected here in Figure 4.2.

Given that this new visualization framework is focused on text, it is highly applicable to text analysis and natural language processing whether fictional texts, news, social media, email, legal documents, essays, and so on. Most NLP techniques generate text and associated data, which in turn can be visualized with these new techniques.

In the many NLP techniques, quantitative data is created from the text. Quantities can be plotted along the axes in many visualization techniques, creating scatterplots, line plots, distributions, and so on. Textual variants of these will be seen in Chapters 5–7:

- *Sentiment and emotion* can generate quantitative data, such as the negative to positive sentiment associated with characters from *Alice* set to the text oblique angle in Figure 4.2 J; or the scatterplot showing character emotion (A).

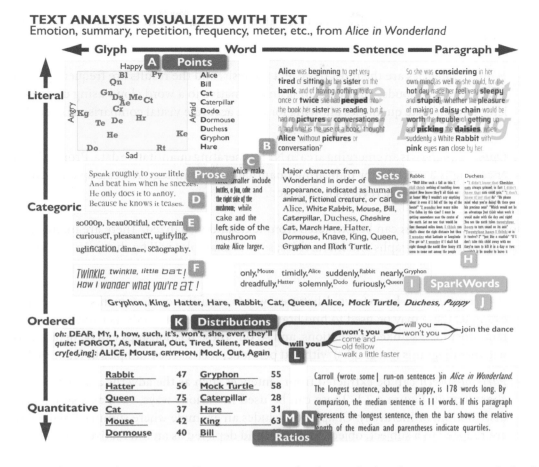

FIGURE 4.2 Visualizing text analysis using examples from *Alice's Adventures in Wonderland*: (A) character emotion; (B) paragraph summarization; (C) entity actions; (D) poetic meter; (E) neologism construction; (F) prosody; (G) character classification; (H) catchphrases; (I) character adverbs; (J) character sentiment; (K) word bigrams; (L) word sequences; (M) character frequency; and (N) sentence analysis.

- *Topics, and their characterization*, create lists of descriptive words, such as the adverbs associated with characters from *Alice* in Figure 4.2 I. These can be stacked to create distributions, or arranged into areas, then plotted so that topics are close to similar topics.

- *Content trends* are timeseries data, and these timeseries can be visualized, for example, as microtext line charts. Examples with Twitter data will be discussed in Chapter 7.

- *Vector spaces.* High-dimensional *vector spaces of text embeddings* (such as Word2Vec) can be created such that the proximity of text in the vector space share common text contexts. Scatterplots (and visually similar dimensional reduction plots resulting from a principal component analysis or t-SNE) are used to assess the results. These plots, in turn, can be facilitated with labeled or annotated plots such as scatterplots (Figure 4.2 A).

- *Bigrams* (and more generally *n-grams*) create pairs and sequences of tokens which can be visualized as distributions (such as the word pair bigrams in K).

Unique approaches to visualize quantities along a string of text will be discussed in Chapter 10:

- *Word frequencies* are the most basic text analysis, and the results are frequently visualized as word clouds. Figure 4.2 M is an alternative to a word cloud using underline length to indicate quantities allowing for more accurate visual comparison of relative magnitude.

- *Opinion analysis* is an emerging area in NLP generating quantitative data. Proportional encoding is a method for indicating quantitative data in text. An example of scored opinions from movie reviews is included.

Graphs and hierarchies can be extracted from texts and visualized. There are many visualization variants for graphs and hierarchies; several examples will be shown in upcoming Chapters 6, 8, and 9:

- *Relationships* can be extracted between words, entities, or documents in NLP. For example, these may be used to find branching sequences of words, networks of sports fans, documents linked by citations, and so on. These relationships can be depicted as network diagrams (i.e. graphs) with text per node, such as the examples in Figure 4.2 L.

- *Parts-of-speech* can be extracted from sentences such as the adverbs associated with characters in Figure 4.2 I. These can be used in various ways, such as a simple list, distribution, or hierarchy. Chapter 6 includes an example where summary sentences are reduced to a subject, object, and verb; and depicted as an interactive hierarchy.

Analysis of text in the context of prose, lists, and tables is the focus of Chapters 11 and 12. Some related text analytic techniques include:

- *Semantic analysis* extracts meaning of words in context. Words of interest can be highlighted inline such as Figure 4.2 B to facilitate skimming. Blocks of text can be extracted, such as dialogue: Figure 4.2 H is an analysis of dialogue between principal characters in *Alice* highlighting sets of repeated words by each speaker, such as "off with her head!" and "are their heads off?"

- *Low-level analysis of letters in words* is required for some NLP tasks. For example, letter frequency analysis is an aspect of language detection in machine translation. Understanding spelling errors can help increase the robustness of NLP, similar to indication of letters added/removed in neologisms in Figure 4.2 E or representation of prosody as in Figure 4.2 F.

- *Text summarization* produces readable summaries of a text. In visualization, aggregation is a form of summarization which can superimpose higher levels of data over top lower levels of data, such as the text superimposed over other text presenting a summary as in Figure 4.2 B.

Classifiers and entity recognition are used in NLP and machine learning, for example, to automatically tag news stories, documents, and emails; and to extract nouns such as the names of people and organizations. Named entities are common throughout many of the examples in the book. Half of the examples in Figure 4.2 display data associated with named characters. Many upcoming examples include countries, parks, people, companies, and so on. Classifiers can generate categoric tags (e.g. Figure 4.2 G) which indicate whether an item is a member of a set; Chapter 8 focuses on set visualization.

4.3 MULTIPLE ATTRIBUTES

Once text represents more than the literal text, multiple encodings are in use. The addition of an attribute, such as red, **bold**, or *italic*, can be used to indicate data and facilitate perceptions of patterns across a field of text. However, when using multiple attributes, care is required, so that the text remains legible and that visual patterns are still apparent.

> *Redundant encoding.* Visual attributes can be configured such that two different visual attributes, say size and color, both indicate the same data attribute. This is typically called redundant encoding, as the same data value is represented with two different visual attributes. Using multiple attributes to encode the same information may be desirable to aid differentiation, for example, if text overlaps. In Figure 4.3 A, country codes are sized and colored based on population. The use of both size and color variation aids in deciphering TOPEFM as TO, PE, and FM. This example will be discussed in Chapter 5. In Figure 4.3 B, a different lightweight font in red italics is superimposed over the silent letters; the many changes help differentiate the superimposed text while still allowing visibility to the underlying text: this example will be discussed in Chapter 11.

> *Conjunction of features.* Visual attributes can also be used such that each attribute conveys different data. This is also known as *visual multiplexing* (Tufte describes this as *multifunctioning graphic elements*). When using multiple simultaneous attributes, the most dominant visual attribute may make patterns in attributes with weaker preattentive perception become less apparent (e.g. italics may be less noticeable when mixed with bold). Furthermore, if a task requires finding a conjunction of attributes, then visual search may be no longer preattentive but slow. Interactive techniques may be useful to toggle on/off attributes of interest, as shown in Figure 4.3 C – a thematic map discussed in Chapter 9.

> *Integral vs. separable dimensions.* When using multiple visual attributes to convey multiple data dimensions, another question is the ease of perceiving and decoding multiple attributes. Using capitalization and italic *TOGETHER* may be noticeable as *different* from the surrounding text, but not as easily decomposed into the component formats (capitalization and italic), as both modify the shape of the letters. Using underline and bold **<u>together</u>** may be noticeable as being *different* as well as easily *decomposable*, as the underline is separate from the weighted text. Figure 4.3 D is a set of SparkWords (Chapter 12) using font weight to indicate data corresponding to

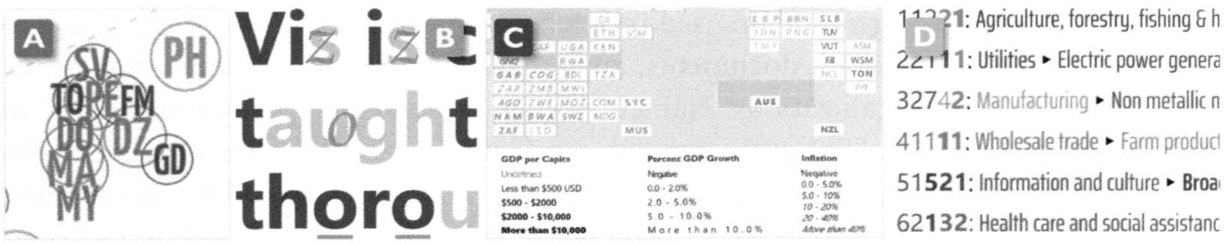

FIGURE 4.3 Multiple attributes on text: (A–B) redundant encoding helps differentiate text; (C–D) multiple data variables are mapped onto visual attributes such as weight, spacing, oblique slope angle, and color.

size, and color to indicate change. Note that the combination of many features, even if not easily decomposable, may be highly useful for *noticing a difference*, discussed in Chapter 8.

4.4 ROLES FOR TEXT IN VISUALIZATIONS

The prior three sections in this chapter follow a data-centric viewpoint, mapping data into text. Examples of structured and unstructured data are processed with literal text and associated typographic attributes directly representing data. This use of text to directly *encode* data is of primary interest in this book.

However, the primary purpose of visualization is to gain insight. To achieve this goal, visualizations need to provide additional support to help the viewer *decode* the visualization, such as titles, axes, and legends. Additionally, text may be used to *guide* the viewer to observations of interest using annotations and explanations. These many different uses of text to facilitate insights, and the potential visual enrichment of the text, are summarized in Figure 4.4. Data (represented by the cylinder on the left) is transformed to create insights (represented by the lightbulb on the right). This can be achieved by transforming data into:

A. *Visualization*. The data is represented visually, and the viewer perceives patterns. In some visualizations there may be very little text, for example, only on interaction.

B. *Text*. The data is transformed into a narrative description of the insights, such as a written research report or presentation. A few supporting data points are embedded into the narrative as facts and summaries, while many of the details may reside elsewhere, such as a separate appendix.

Either visualization or text approaches can be used to gain insight into the underlying data. However, both have issues. With only the visualization (A), there may be *many* patterns visible thereby creating work for the viewer to uncover insights of interest. With only narrative text (B), broader contextual trends and patterns are missing, which, in turn, may provide additional evidence or counter-evidence. For example, a narrative report may indicate that the price of a stock is up 19% over the year, but neglect to mention that it shot up 26%, plateaued, and since lost some of the gains dropping down to 19%, and now appears to be in a downtrend.

FIGURE 4.4 **Techniques for explaining data:** (A) *visualization,* or (B) *text.* Hybrids include: (C) *text-enhanced visualizations* such as text in the plot or enhanced supporting text; (D) *annotated visualizations* add commentary such as call-outs and data comics; (E) *visually enhanced narratives* weave visualization into narratives.

Text and visualization can be combined into hybrids to facilitate understanding as shown by the diagrams C, D, and E in Figure 4.4.

- *Text-enhanced visualizations* extend and enhance well known-visualization techniques, for example, by using text as marks directly in the plot area, or formatting supporting text, such as titles and axes to aid decoding the visualization.

- *Annotated visualizations* bring brief textual insights into the visualization such as call-outs or data comics.

- *Visually enhanced narratives* retain the prose narrative layout and insert visualization into the flow, either sharing the same encoding in the text and the associated visualizations; or dispensing with separate visualizations and encoding data directly into text formats.

These are illustrated with examples in Figure 4.5:

- **Text directly in the core plot** of a visualization, directly encoding data, is the primary intent of this book. This ranges from textual labels in a plot, to individual characters, to sentences and paragraphs in the plot area. All of the examples in Section 1.3 extensively utilize text in the primary plot, as well as all of the examples in Figure 4.1 and Figure 4.2, and almost all the upcoming examples use text as a key element in the plot area.

- **Supporting text**, such as titles, axes, tick labels and legends, is needed in most charts, maps, and visualizations as an aid for the viewer to decode and comprehend the representation (as illustrated previously in Figure 2.7). These elements frame the

TEXT ROLES IN VISUALIZATION
Enhanced text in axes, ticks, annotations and narratives

Text in
Core Plot

**Supporting
Text:** axes,
series &
tick labels

Annotations:
call-outs &
data comics

Narratives:
same encoding
as visualization

no plot area
e.g. prose, list

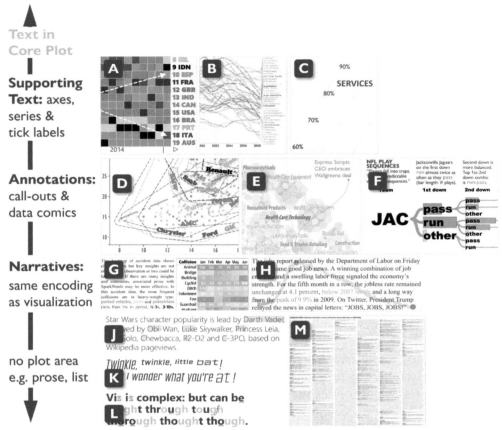

FIGURE 4.5   Examples of additional roles for text in visualization. (A–B) color-coded text at the end of lines; (C) color-coded axis and tick labels; (D) annotations aligned with lines; (E) annotations on leader lines; (F) data comic; (G–H) prose text cross-referencing visualization using color-coded words; (J–M) visualizations made entirely of text.

visualization and are required for essential visual reasoning tasks such as estimating values, identifying categories, locating items, and so on.

In addition, these textual elements facilitate memorability, recognition, and recall. Labels for axes, series, and ticks can be enhanced typographically. For example, the series labels can be formatted consistently with the corresponding data, such as the use of color labels located at the ends of lines on timeseries charts instead of having a separate legend (examples A and B in Figure 4.5), which will occur in a few examples in Chapter 7.

Similarly, axis labels and tick labels can use the same formats as the plot, such as the example axis in Figure 4.5 C which will be discussed in Chapter 5. In effect, the supporting labels act as a legend directly located next to the data, rather than cross-referenced in a separate location.

- **Annotations** indicate insights with snippets of text to augment the visualization. They range from a word or two to a few sentences. They may contain user-generated commentary or system-generated facts and insights (such as summary statistics, indicating outliers or quantifying trends). Annotations may be overlaid or offset from the visualization, such as the following examples, to be covered in Chapter 5:

    i)   *Align* the annotations to added visual elements. For example, a plot may have an added regression line or convex hull and labels can be directly aligned to the added item, such as the labels on the hulls in Figure 4.5 D.

    ii) Use a *leader line* to connect the annotation to the corresponding visual elements, such as the news headline in Figure 4.5 E.

    iii) *Superimpose* the annotation over (or under) the relevant data points. This is seen in the group labels in Figure 4.5 E, spanning across many data points.

    iv) *Interactively access* the annotation. Long annotations may be indicated by a marker and accessed via an interaction such as tooltip, or zoom-in, or linking to another component. Interactive labels based on zoom are used extensively on interactive maps and are also discussed in relation to the interactive scatterplot shown in Figure 4.5 D.

- **Data comics** are a form of narrative integrated with visualization. Successive panels of integrated text and visualization provide for incremental guidance and explanation. For example, Bach et al.'s *Graph Comics* (2016) provides a visual language with elements, connections, transitions, detail, and multiple attributes. The example in Figure 4.5 F is from a data comic describing NFL play sequences, to appear in Chapter 12.

- **Narratives,** such as data journalism, can embed visualizations directly into the text flow. These examples occur in Chapters 11–12:

    The same encoding can be shared between the narrative and the visualization, such as Figure 4.5 G, which shares the same visual encoding of the weight and color of the text in both the narrative and the corresponding heatmap. This shared encoding can be pushed further, such as the example image Figure 4.5 H, where a news paragraph is superimposed directly over the chart which it describes.

    No plot area is necessary. Text with typographic formats can embed data directly (i.e. SparkWords) without the need for any supplementary graphical elements and *no plot area*. These formats can apply to the intrinsic data within the words in their original prose context to indicate, for example, underlays of quantitative data, as in example Figure 4.5 J, pronunciation and prosody in Figure 4.5 K–L, or generalized SparkWords. Figure 4.5 M is an example of a hierarchy of lists visually similar to a treemap or dictionary.

Natural Language Generation is the automated generation of text. NLG is a complement to many of the above roles, as data can be used as an input to NLG processes. For example, data analytics can be used to detect outliers, find facts, and tag insights. These, in turn, can be used to create labels and annotations, and generate narrative paragraphs either inserted directly into the visualization; as an adjunct beside the visualization calling out insights; or replacing the visualization with text and SparkWords.

4.5 VISUALIZATION BUSINESS OPPORTUNITIES

A very different way to use a design space is to compare the new design capabilities, as indicated by the many examples in the earlier sections, to the software industry to identify new potential business opportunities.

Quantitative analysis. There are many software tools in the business intelligence market (such as Tableau and PowerBI), statistical analysis market (such as R and SAS), and related markets for the visual analysis of quantitative data (structured data). The market for these tools is in excess of $4 billion USD per year (e.g. Mordor 2015).

These tools work with well-structured data. This structured data may have fields with individual entities (e.g. named people, organizations, ships, addresses) or categories with many unique entries (e.g. diseases, types of industries, types of food, electronic components, airline routes). Analytic approaches may attempt to cluster these or create a hierarchy, but this organization may be arbitrary. Instead, using text directly in these visualizations may reveal insights otherwise difficult to achieve (such as the many visualization variants of structured data shown in Figure 4.1).

Real-time monitoring. Monitoring of real-time data is growing beyond applications in industrial control (Figure 1.25) and financial markets (Figure 3.3) to operational applications such as log file monitoring for cyber-security and computer network operations; fraud detection; transportation logistics and supply chain visibility; managing ad-words for search engines; and customer call center management. Annual revenues for real-time financial market data alone exceeds $10 billion USD annually. In many of these applications, visual encodings are used to visually depict the current state and highlight anomalies. Responding to any anomaly requires identification of the entity – and these identities are shown directly with text. A broader set of techniques for visualizing text can enable new capabilities in monitoring applications.

Unstructured data. Structured data is data organized in a repository, such as a database or spreadsheet, to facilitate processing and analysis. By contrast, unstructured data is less organized and often text heavy. There are huge amounts of unstructured data; some experts suggest 80% of all data is unstructured (Grimes 2008). Search is a dominant paradigm for working with unstructured data. Advertising associated with Google Search generates almost $100 billion USD annual revenue (2019). Use of text analytics and associated visualization is also applicable to page display (e.g. news readers, email) and composition (e.g. editors, word processors, grammar checking). Industry analysts also predict analytic queries will be migrated to search, natural language, and voice-based interfaces.

Natural Language Processing. NLP is a rapidly growing field extracting information from unstructured documents such as entity recognition and disambiguation, topics, sentiment, emotion, facts, relationships, and so on. NLP is expanding from research into applications such as news and social media analytics; speech recognition (such as Siri); machine translation; and so on. Hundreds of venture-backed NLP startup companies have been created for applications such as legal document analysis; customer service automation; marketing communications; job recruiting; and so on (crunchbase.com). Gartner, Inc., predicts NLP and conversational analytics will increase corporate adoption of analytics by 50% expanding to new uses for front-office workers (Gartner Insight Engines Magic Quadrant, September 2019). New textual visualizations may aid analyses in these new NLP application areas.

Prose markup. Thousands of words per day are consumed by the average adult, via email, web, print, radio, dialogue, and so on. This unstructured data is typically not visually enhanced to convey data other than the text. There is also opportunity for enhancement of text in prose to aid skimming, reveal structure, indicate errors, aid close readings, and so on. Research, intelligence, and competitive analysts; legal, finance, tax, and medical professionals are bombarded with an ever increasing number of text-centric reports. Office workers contend with text-centric email, collaboration, documents, presentations, and forms. Many individuals are highly engaged with text-centric social media. Many of these texts must be read directly; they cannot be summarized or otherwise processed with NLP. There may be new text visualization approaches to aid in the understanding of the many text fragments consumed in daily life.

Augmented Reality (AR) and Virtual Reality (VR). Emerging 3D application areas such as AR and VR need to include some amount of text into the scene. In AR, there is a balance as to how much of the underlying reality can be obscured with augmented graphics. Even simple markers, such as restaurants, stores, and houses for sale, contain a wealth of relevant metadata (e.g. type of cuisine, price point, average review, opening hours, distance, etc.). Therefore, techniques to minimize the amount of text while still conveying metadata are important to convey insight with minimal occlusion of the underlying scene. Consider the panorama in Figure 4.6 from 1914; text is embedded in the scene, where text with each word capitalized typically indicates battle events, rotated text typically indicates topographic features, and so on. Encoding data into the text can increase the information content without adding more and more elements onto the scene.

Knowledge maps are visualizations to gain insights into the structure and evolution of large-scale information spaces. As such, knowledge maps can be large scale, data dense, heavily annotated, highly connected representations, such as the *Death and Taxes* poster (Figure 1.26). Significant effort is required to collect all the content; clearly organize the layout; manage different classes of information to depict; and exercise control over which content to show. For example, there may be very long

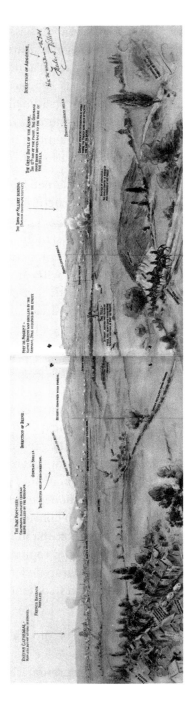

FIGURE 4.6   Terrain panorama from 1914 with key landmarks labeled above and in-scene.

labels that need to be shortened yet remain unambiguous; or there may be too many labels and some subset selected to be represented. The economic value of knowledge mapping is difficult to quantify, yet, the *biochemical pathways* visualization (Figure 1.16) is an invaluable educational tool and reference standard; it has been continuously updated for more than 50 years, with over 700,000 print copies.

4.6 FURTHER READING

Natural Language Processing. NLP is a large research area in computer science with many statistical techniques. For computational techniques to process and analyze text, NLTK and spaCy are easy to use Python programming libraries with online documentation and many explanatory books, such as Bird et al.'s *Natural Language Processing with Python* (2009); or Lane et al.'s *Natural Language Processing in Action* (2016). There are many other NLP textbooks, libraries, and tools, for example, ANNIS3 (Krause and Zeldes 2016) is a point-and-click tool to annotate text for close reading. More broadly, other forms of user-driven text analysis exist in various domains which can be enhanced with visualization techniques – see Jänicke et al.'s *On Close and Distant Reading in Digital Humanities: A Survey and Future Challenges* (2015).

Data journalism is a broad area of visualization focused on communicating findings in data which typically include explanatory infographics, ranging from news stories with charts, to fully featured visualizations with complementary text. For example, watch the documentary *Journalism in the Age of Data* (McGhee 2010), or see Segel and Heer's *Narrative Visualizations: Telling Stories with Data* (2010).

Data comics are an emerging form of narrative visualization. See Bach et al.'s *Telling Stories about Dynamic Networks with Graph Comics* (2016) for a compelling example and an earlier framework extended specifically for communicating insights regarding networks.

Multiple encodings, including redundant encodings, separable and integral dimensions are discussed in Ware's *Information Visualization: Perception for Design* (2013), and various strategies are discussed in Chen et al.'s *Visual Multiplexing* (2014).

II

Labels

Visualizing with Literal Text

CHAPTER 5

Point Labels

M ANY EXAMPLES OF HISTORIC, text-dense visualizations have been shown in prior
chapters. This is the first chapter to explicitly provide detailed examples of how these
textual and typographic ingredients can be combined into new kinds of visualizations. The
next three chapters start simply, by showing how the use of literal text can help with tasks
such as identification and enriched content.

5.1 LABELS AS POINT MARKS

Many traditional visualizations use simple point marks to encode data: such as dots in
a scatterplot, circles on a graph, squares on a heatmap, or shapes. These marks typically
encode data by their position and an additional data variable using a visual attribute such
as color, size, or shape, as shown in Figure 5.1. (Note, these examples are implemented
using D3.js as Observable notebooks by Mike Bostock – observablehq.com/@mbostock.
Many of the examples in this book have been implemented by the author using the D3.js
visualization programming library.)

Instead of simple geometric shapes, data can be encoded literally into strings of text and
represented directly. This can be useful, for example, when there are too many categories
to perceptually distinguish with color, or tasks where a viewer may need to identify individual points, groups of points, and so on.

5.2 READING IS FASTER THAN INTERACTING

As a simple example of points vs. labels consider a plot showing character emotions in
Wonderland in Figure 5.2. On the left (A), dots indicate each character, and on the right
(B), text indicates each character. To identify a point in the dot scatterplot, the viewer must
either cross-reference between the dots and the legends or use an interaction such as a
tooltip. In the text scatterplot, identification can be directly read.

Consider an *identification task*. A simple identification task is "Who is most afraid?"
An identification task can be measured experimentally, or measured using experimentally
derived cognitive modeling methods such as Card et al.'s GOMS model (1983) or Lohse's
UICE (1991).

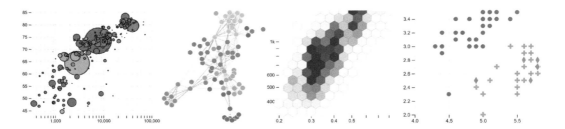

FIGURE 5.1 Examples of point marks in visualizations such as bubbles, dots, hex bins, and shapes.

CHARACTER EMOTIONS FROM *ALICE IN WONDERLAND*

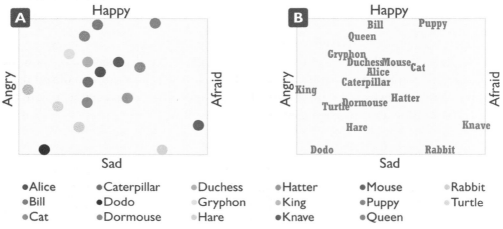

FIGURE 5.2 Emotions of characters from *Alice in Wonderland.* In the left chart (A), colors are used to identify characters as indicated in the legend at the bottom. In the right chart (B), points are displayed as text, literally identifying characters.

- For the text scatterplot, the viewer must do three steps: (1) identify the correct axis; (2) find the rightmost dot; (3) read the text *Knave.* The model predicts the task is approximately 1405 milliseconds.

- For the dot scatterplot, the viewer must also cross-reference between the plot and legend, i.e.: (1) identify the correct axis; (2) find the rightmost dot; (3) commit the dot color blue to short-term memory; (4) scan the legend to find the blue dot; (5) when the correct dot is found, read the name *Knave.* The model predicts the task is approximately 2165 milliseconds.

- For the dot scatterplot using interactive tooltips, the steps are slightly different: (1) identify the correct axis; (2) find the rightmost dot; (3) move hand to mouse, if needed; (4) move mouse to dot; (5) wait for tooltip, as most tooltips have a slight lag; (6) read tooltip. The model predicts the task is approximately 2030 milliseconds.

The label plot has fewer cognitive steps and a shorter time than either the use of a legend or use of interactions. Experimentally, this can also be seen. Perceptual tests of charts go back

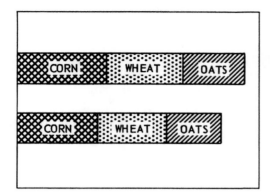 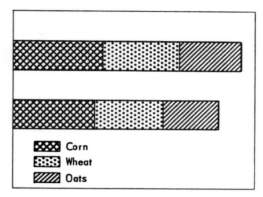

FIGURE 5.3   Sample chart with labels vs. chart with legends tested by Sarbaugh et al. (1961).

at least to 1961 with Sarbaugh et al. concluding that labels are easier to read than legends in a set of 32 comparisons across eight charts, such as the pair in Figure 5.3.

There is a range of identification tasks, such as identifying the highest or lowest value, identifying members within a cluster or group, identifying an outlier, and so on – all of which will similarly outperform legends or interactions.

Text can also benefit other tasks. For example, a *location task* may ask "Where is the Cheshire Cat in the plot – happy or sad, angry or afraid?" Both plots require the viewer to scan through the data points serially to find the targets of interest, which works for small plots but is not efficient in plots with hundreds of points or more. Interactions, such as search or filter, will be more effective with a large number of data points to narrow down the candidates. Text can help disambiguate multiple matches, for example, a search using the term "cat" finds both the Cat and the Caterpillar.

A *proximity task* will also benefit. For example, a proximity task may require the viewer to find: "Who is similar to Alice?" This is a combination of a location task (locate Alice), and an identification task (identify characters nearby). Again, explicit text will aid the performance for the identification subtask.

In general terms, the use of literal text in the plot can reduce reliance on legends and/or interactions. Also, the use of text may reduce load on short-term memory, which is a limited resource. As the identity is externalized, short-term memory is not required to store identity, thereby freeing up memory for other more complex tasks. Presumably the biochemical pathways knowledge map, electric grid map, and financial display (Figure 1.16, Figure 2.5, and Figure 3.3) are all examples where the explicit labels enable the viewer to address more complex reasoning tasks. For example, a viewer of the biochemical pathway map may wish to reason about potential side effects when one biochemical pathway is manipulated. Or the bond trader may need to assess alternative financial instruments in an evolving situation.

5.3 CODES AS LABELS

In Figure 5.4 and Figure 5.5, three variants of a scatterplot are shown; 186 countries are shown as bubbles, codes, or flags. Size (and color) indicate population; and position

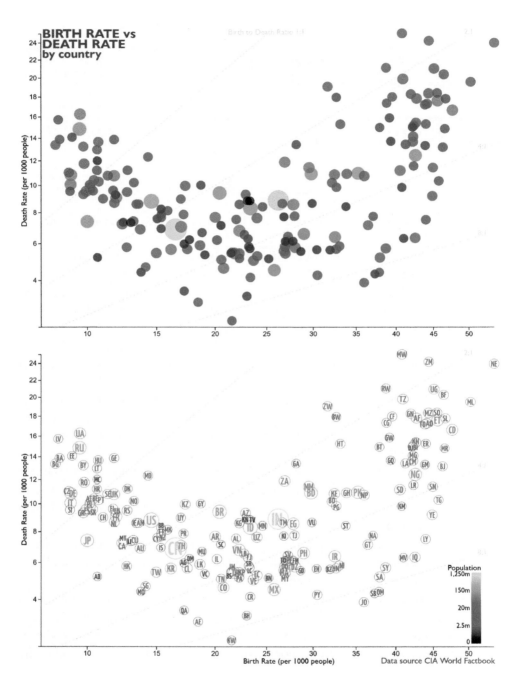

FIGURE 5.4   Two scatterplots of birth rate and death rate per country, each colored by population. The lower scatterplot has the addition of country codes to each dot.

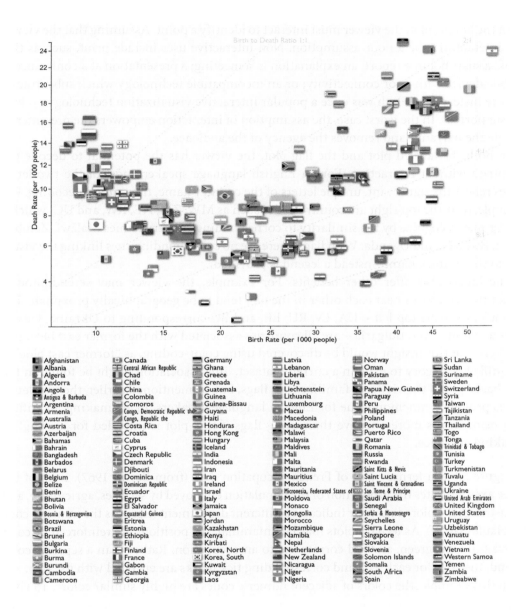

Afghanistan
Albania
Algeria
Andorra
Angola
Antigua & Barbuda
Argentina
Armenia
Australia
Austria
Azerbaijan
Bahamas
Bahrain
Bangladesh
Barbados
Belarus
Belgium
Belize
Benin
Bhutan
Bolivia
Bosnia & Herzegovina
Botswana
Brazil
Brunei
Bulgaria
Burkina
Burma
Burundi
Cambodia
Cameroon

Canada
Central African Republic
Chad
Chile
China
Colombia
Comoros
Congo, Democratic Republic the
Congo, Republic the
Costa Rica
Croatia
Cuba
Cyprus
Czech Republic
Denmark
Djibouti
Dominica
Dominican Republic
Ecuador
Egypt
El Salvador
Equatorial Guinea
Eritrea
Estonia
Ethiopia
Fiji
Finland
France
Gabon
Gambia
Georgia

Germany
Ghana
Greece
Grenada
Guatemala
Guinea
Guinea-Bissau
Guyana
Haiti
Honduras
Hong Kong
Hungary
Iceland
India
Indonesia
Iran
Iraq
Ireland
Israel
Italy
Jamaica
Japan
Jordan
Kazakhstan
Kenya
Kiribati
Korea, North
Korea, South
Kuwait
Kyrgyzstan
Laos

Latvia
Lebanon
Liberia
Libya
Liechtenstein
Lithuania
Luxembourg
Macau
Macedonia
Madagascar
Malawi
Malaysia
Maldives
Mali
Malta
Mauritania
Mauritius
Mexico
Micronesia, Federated States of
Moldova
Monaco
Mongolia
Morocco
Mozambique
Namibia
Nepal
Netherlands
New Zealand
Nicaragua
Niger
Nigeria

Norway
Oman
Pakistan
Panama
Papua New Guinea
Paraguay
Peru
Philippines
Poland
Portugal
Puerto Rico
Qatar
Romania
Russia
Rwanda
Saint Kitts & Nevis
Saint Lucia
Saint Vincent & Grenadines
Sao Tome & Principe
Saudi Arabia
Senegal
Serbia & Montenegro
Seychelles
Sierra Leone
Singapore
Slovakia
Slovenia
Solomon Islands
Somalia
South Africa
Spain

Sri Lanka
Sudan
Suriname
Sweden
Switzerland
Syria
Taiwan
Tajikistan
Tanzania
Thailand
Togo
Tonga
Trinidad & Tobago
Tunisia
Turkey
Turkmenistan
Tuvalu
Uganda
Ukraine
United Arab Emirates
United Kingdom
United States
Uruguay
Uzbekistan
Vanuatu
Venezuela
Vietnam
Western Samoa
Yemen
Zambia
Zimbabwe

FIGURE 5.5   Same scatterplot of birth rates and death rates, using flags instead of dots or labels, with a large legend.

indicates the birth rate and death rate for each country. Top left are countries with more deaths than births. Top right are countries with high birth rates and high death rates.

In the first image, only bubbles are shown. The second is the same as the first, with the addition of standardized two-letter ISO codes per country. These are the same codes used in Internet domain names, e.g. JP for Japan, MX for Mexico. The third version uses flags and is accompanied with a large legend. In all versions, interactive tooltips provide details such as country name and population.

In the bubble plot, the viewer must interact to identify a point. Assuming that the viewer can interact may be a poor assumption. Non-interactive uses include print, such as this book; a snapshot in a report; an explanation in a meeting; a presentation at a conference; a mobile device with poor connectivity; or an incompatible technology which substitutes a picture instead (e.g. Flash was once a popular interactive visualization technology no longer supported). In the worst case, the assumption of interaction empowers the presenter to dictate the narrative and removes the agency of the audience.

In both the labeled plot and the flag plot, the viewer has the potential to decode the countries without interaction. For an English language speaker, most of the two-letter codes reflect the significant, unique letters of the country name, thus aiding decoding. For example, near the top right are country codes such as MW, ZM, NE, RW, and UG, which a viewer may recognize by the similarity to corresponding country names Malawi, Zambia, Niger, Rwanda, and Uganda. With flags, there are no corresponding cues linking the visual flag to the country name: instead a legend is provided.

The labels also offer other benefits. For example, the viewer may serendipitously notice that countries near each other in the plot tend to be geographically proximate. For example, near the top left – UA, LV, RU, EE, and BG corresponding to Ukraine, Latvia, Russia, Estonia, and Bulgaria – are all countries associated with the former east bloc. It is unlikely that this insight would be discovered using color-coding, as "former east bloc" is an unlikely category to exist in a current dataset. This association might be found in the flag-based plot if the viewer is familiar with flags, but, as mentioned earlier, the two-letter codes provide a mnemonic cue for English language speakers, likely making identification using codes more effective than using flags if this plot is intended for an English speaking audience.

Figure 5.6 is a ternary plot of French occupation data (from Bertin 1967). Each of the three axes indicates the proportion of the population employed by services, agriculture, and industry. Each colored number indicates a different department (e.g. 74 is the numeric code for Haute-Savoie). As ternary plots may be unfamiliar, the positions are reinforced by color where full blue, green, and red correspond to an occupation. Rather than a separate color legend, the label for each axis and corresponding tick marks are encoded with its color.

In this example, the colors of adjacent numeric codes are highly similar colors. To visually separate overlapping codes, an extra-bold font with a stroke outline is used. Further, the largest numbers are drawn first, with smaller numbers on top, so that smaller numbers are not occluded.

5.4 FULL LABELS

In many applications, short codes may be unavailable; longer names are required to uniquely identify data points. In Figure 5.7, the full names of U.S. National Parks are used as labels on a scatterplot. Like the previous examples, label deconfliction has been used to nudge apart labels in dense areas of the plot. A narrow font has been used for the labels, as these fonts are designed for use in tight spaces (e.g. Arial Narrow, Gill Sans Extra Condensed, Roboto Condensed, Saira Extra Condensed, etc.).

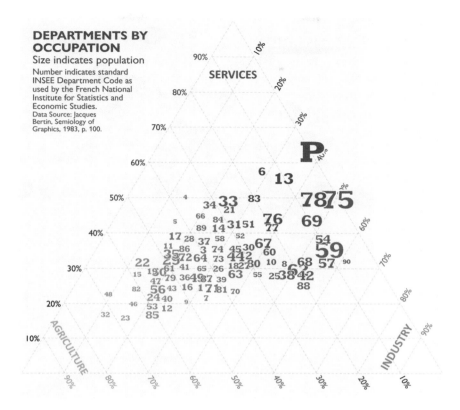

FIGURE 5.6   Ternary plot indicating the proportion of the population in three different occupations. Each corner of the triangle represents 100% of an occupation, e.g. the bottom left corner represents 100% agriculture, the closest department is 32 (Gers) at a little over 70% agriculture. The center point of a ternary plot represents an even proportion of all three axes (33%, 33%, 33%): near the center is department 44 (Loire-Inf.).

Unlike Figure 5.4, filled dots are used instead of outline circles. In Figure 5.4, all labels are consistently two letters. The spatial density of codes is consistent with the spatial density of the plot. Thus, the labels directly act as point markers. And further, where labels partially overlap with other labels, the hue varies, aiding discrimination between the labels.

However, in Figure 5.7 some names are very long (e.g. *Black Canyon of the Gunnison*) while others are very short (e.g. *Zion*). This inconsistency can potentially interfere with the overall macro-patterns of data density in the plot. Therefore, data points are shown with greater prominence as filled dots. Each label has a white halo added to maintain legibility between the label and the underlying circle of the same color.

Maintaining legibility is key so that text can be deciphered. In Figure 5.7, a halo is used. In Figure 5.6, the stroke of the text has been modified to the background color. In Figure 5.4, nothing has been added, as the color difference between adjacent points and background is sufficient. Each has drawbacks, e.g. adding a stroke to characters can reduce legibility by thinning narrow strokes on the letters or filling in counters (i.e. the holes in

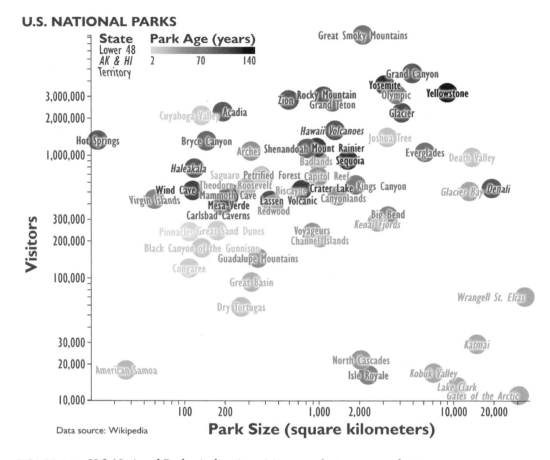

FIGURE 5.7 U.S. National Parks, indicating visitors, park size, age, and state.

letters such as e and a). Or, adding a halo can obscure other text partially behind the halo. Or, relying only on color may be insufficient if the plot is dynamically reconfigurable. The designer must make the appropriate choice based on the data and the use.

5.5 GROUP LABELS AND VERY LONG LABELS

The prior examples show labels for each individual point. Figure 5.8 shows hierarchical labels on a graph of stock market data. This snapshot is from an interactive application where the viewer can choose which levels of labels to display. In each quadrant, different levels of labels are shown; In the top left quadrant, industrial sectors are indicated with large labels, each label positioned relative to a group of connected stocks. In the top right quadrant, a lower level in the hierarchy is shown, with labels indicating specific industries. Bottom right toggles the labels to show only the stock symbols. In the bottom left, all labels are visible.

Some of the industry labels are extremely long, e.g. *Food & Staples Retailing*. Even with a narrow font these labels are long. Various text preprocessing has been done to reduce the length of the longest labels. For example, prepositions and conjunctions are removed or substituted (e.g. *and* has been replaced with *&*). The longest phrases are algorithmically

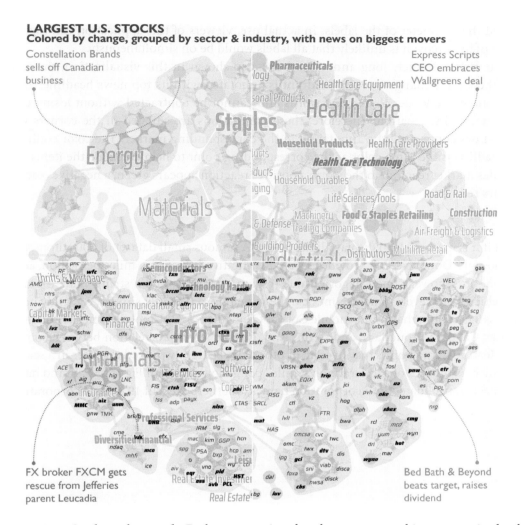

LARGEST U.S. STOCKS
Colored by change, grouped by sector & industry, with news on biggest movers

FIGURE 5.8 Stock market graph. Each company is a dot, dots are grouped into successive levels of a hierarchy. Each quadrant shows different labels toggled on/off; top left shows large industrial sectors labeled; top right has industries; bottom right has stock symbols per dot; bottom left has all labels. The top news headline for the stock with the biggest change is shown per quadrant.

truncated (e.g. *Thrifts & Mortgage Finance* has been reduced to *Thrifts & Mortgage*; *Health Care Equipment & Supplies* to *Health Care Equipment*; and so on). Care must be taken such that the semantics are not altered for the target audience and that labels remain unique: e.g. *Health Care Equipment* and *Health Care Providers* cannot be further truncated. Abbreviations can be used, if the audience is familiar with the abbreviation, for example, *Information Technology* has been reduced to *Info Tech*.

The bottom left shows all labels overlapping; some labels are hard to read. This is somewhat alleviated by having the smallest labels drawn on top of larger labels, thereby ensuring no labels are hidden. However, multiple overlapping labels reduce the contrast of the text to the background thereby reducing legibility. This is alleviated by small white halos around the perimeter of the labels. In actual use, viewers of this application can toggle a subset of hierarchy; it is unlikely that all labels would be on simultaneously.

Note that extremely long annotations are also shown in this visualization; the stock with the largest change in each quadrant is annotated with its top news headline. These annotations are longer than a few words and cannot be contracted without losing critical semantic information. Therefore, these annotations are situated in the corners with leader-lines connecting the annotation to the corresponding marker. The color coding of the headline is the same color as the corresponding point to help associate the items, and provides market reaction to the story; a positive reaction appears green, a negative reaction appears red.

5.6 MANY LABELS AND LONG LABELS

What if it is impossible to display all the labels? A famous small dataset of 400 automobiles (Ramos and Donoho 1983) provides seven quantitative values (e.g. miles per gallon, acceleration, horsepower), one categoric value (region of origin), and a string value (name of the vehicle). However, vehicle names can be very long and highly similar, e.g. Oldsmobile Cutlass Salon Brougham, Oldsmobile Cutlass Ciera (diesel), Oldsmobile Omega Brougham, Pontiac Catalina Brougham, and so on. And, given a strong correlation between some of these features, data points may overlap or otherwise be tightly packed together in a scatterplot, such as the plot of acceleration vs. miles per gallon shown in Figure 5.9. Brand names have been consolidated into corporation names, but there are still 19 unique corporations.

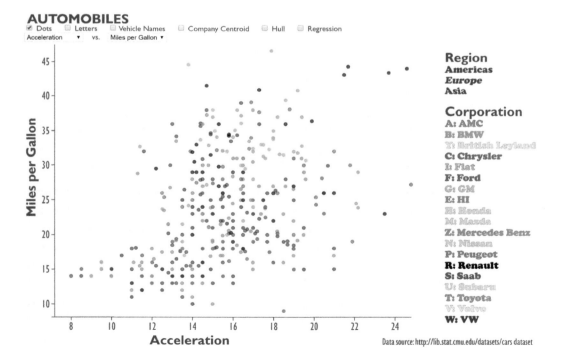

FIGURE 5.9   Four hundred automobiles on a scatterplot: insufficient space to label each automobile.

Attempting to color code these points is problematic as it is not feasible to create 19 perceptually distinguishable colors.

Like the previous stock market example, labels can be applied to the groups of data points. Since each corporation is dispersed across the plot, a visual element is required to associate the data points with a common parent. In Figure 5.10, a convex hull surrounds the data points for each company. There are many overlapping areas making it difficult to visually trace and compare relative areas, particularly for lighter colors with low contrast to the background. Furthermore, using convex hulls, it may be difficult to see if the data points are dispersed across the hull.

Instead of dots, a single letter can be used to identify the corporation. With a small amount of nudging, overlaps can be reduced and most of the letters can be readily identified in Figure 5.11. Outliers are immediately identifiable. For example, the upper outliers – cars with good mileage and slower acceleration – are H (Honda), M (Mazda), and W (Volkswagen). The worst performing vehicle, in terms of mileage, is at the bottom: E (HI, Harvester International). The worst in terms of acceleration – achieving 0–60 miles per hour in 25 seconds – is a P (Peugeot).

While areas of letters are not preattentive, local areas can be scanned for objects of similar color and shape, e.g. Ford (F) and GM (G) dominate the lower half of the display (faster cars with poor mileage), while Volkswagen (W) prevails in the upper right corner (slow cars with great mileage).

The upper middle of this plot is packed with vehicles of many different manufacturers. Exploration of these data points requires much cross-referencing to the legend or the use of

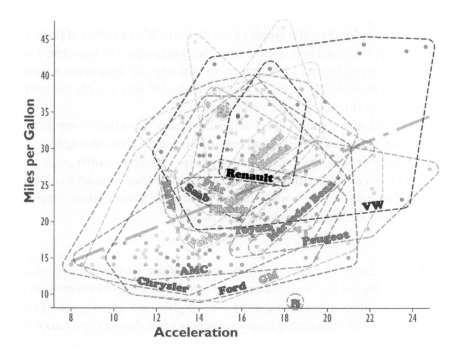

FIGURE 5.10 Convex hulls identify the extents of all the autos per each corporation.

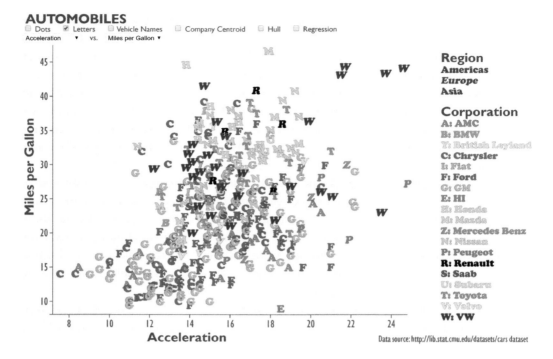

FIGURE 5.11 Letters identify the corporation associated with each auto.

tooltips. Neither cross-referencing nor tooltips are ideal as both rely heavily on short-term memory to store and recall names. This misses the opportunity to directly externalize the vehicle names on the plot.

Another approach to labeling the points in the plot is to label a subset of points such that labels do not overlap. Culling labels is used extensively on maps. For example, a world map with city labels will typically cull labels based on city size and thus show a label for New York City instead of Newark, NJ. This can be complemented with interactive zoom, so that more labels appear the further that the viewer zooms in.

In Figure 5.12 (top), only a small subset of labels appears when the viewer is zoomed out, so that labels (mostly) do not overlap. Outliers are labeled, as there is ample space around them. Dense areas of the plot have some visible labels – thereby identifying at least one of the vehicles in a set of cars with similar mileage and acceleration characteristics. When the viewer zooms in (as shown in the bottom half of Figure 5.12), more labels appear, enabling identification of more vehicles in dense areas of the plot.

5.7 MASSIVE DATA, LABELS, AND ZOOM

Combining label visibility with interactive zoom can work with many large-scale visualization techniques. Figure 5.13 is an example of *graph mapping* of two million tweets by Jonker et al. (2017). Labels are shown for the most highly connected nodes (in gray text); and the most common hashtags in each area (in yellow text). As the viewer zooms in, more labels are made visible. At any time, the viewer can use other interactions, such as tooltips,

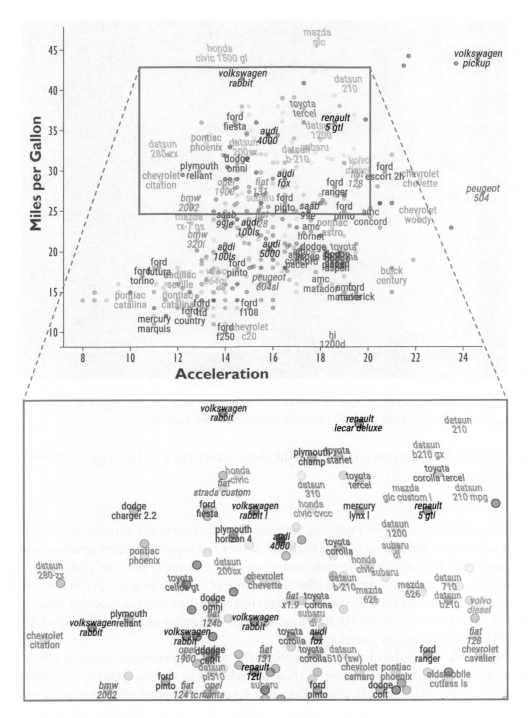

FIGURE 5.12   Labels can be reduced algorithmically, with more labels made visible the further that the viewer zooms in.

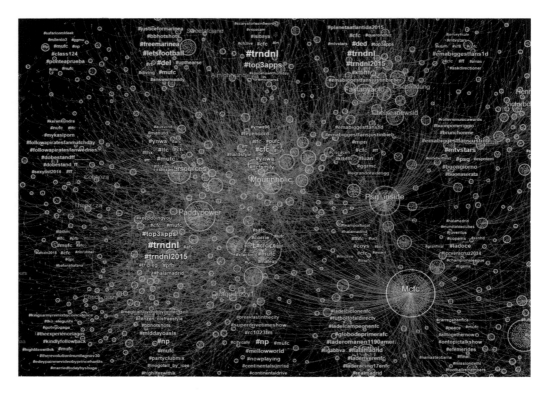

FIGURE 5.13 Massive graph of two million tweets with labels based on the degree of connectivity for nodes, e.g. Mcfc and Mourinholic; plus top hashtags within each area.

to see details for unlabeled nodes, highlight nodes associated with hashtags, click through for Twitter, etc.

5.8 FURTHER READING

Cognitive models. Cognitive modeling methods use experimentally derived times for unit tasks to estimate the amount of time to complete user tasks in a visual user interface – such as search, comparison, identification, and other tasks. As such, they can provide a good means for estimating task time and effort in advance of constructing and performing evaluations. Deviations in times between the experimental values and the modeled values can provide insights into potential design flaws or poor assumptions. See Card et al.'s GOMS model (1983) for more information.

Point labels. Much has been written about the use and placement of point labels on maps, such as labeling cities. Some of these are relevant to visualization: for example, in Figure 5.12, vehicle labels are placed over top dots; whereas map label heuristics would position the labels next to the dots. Furthermore, cartographic heuristics can be used to determine which labels to show or hide in congested areas. For example, see Robinson et al. *Elements of Cartography* (2016), or Tyner's *Principles of Map Design* (2014).

CHAPTER 6

Distributions

BAR CHARTS, TREEMAPS, AND *unit visualizations* (such as the Isotype visualization in Figure 1.6) often show counts of items. A simple alphanumeric extension is to display the text literally as a stem and leaf plot. Visually, most stem and leaf plots are plain-looking alphanumeric charts without the visceral excitement of many other visualizations. Semantically, at a macro-level, they present the same information as a distribution or bar chart.

Figure 6.1 shows a stem and leaf plot of train departures; the stem is the hour of departure, shown vertically, with white text on a deep blue background. The minute of departure within each hour is shown as a horizontal list of minutes (i.e. the leaves). A longer list of leaves means more departures in that hour. At a macro-level, the shape of a distribution emerges, indicating more trains midday and fewer trains in the early morning and late evening. The peak hour on the weekday distribution (left) is early at 7h, while the peak on weekends (right distribution) is late day (17 and 18h).

Even though they may seem boring, stem and leaf plots are used in a wide variety of domains such as statistics, biology, finance, and transit schedules. Why?

a. The construction of a stem and leaf plot is easy, as indicated by Figure 6.2. They can be constructed using a spreadsheet, word processor, statistical analysis software, or easily programmed without requiring knowledge of graphics or visualization libraries. For stacks to be comparable, characters must be placed at regular intervals, which can be easily achieved using a fixed width font.

b. Perceptually, the stack of characters forms a bar, which can be readily perceived. Further, stem and leaf plots retain more detailed information via the text. For example, the hour and minute of train departure times is critical information for a train passenger rushing to board a train. Minimum and maximum values can be read directly from the chart. Individual data points (leaves) can be enhanced with visual attributes to indicate additional data – making stem and leaf plots highly flexible for conveying multi-variate data.

FIGURE 6.1   Train departure schedule, the vertical axis shows hour, the leaves show minutes.

Heights of family members (cm)		Split into Stems and Leaves		Order stems No repeats	Stack leaves
Adam	175	17	5		
Bill	178	17	8	18|7	
Carl	187	18	7	17|258	
Dave	168	16	8	16|85	
Eden	165	16	5	15|2	
Fred	152	15	2		
Gila	172	17	2		

FIGURE 6.2   Process for constructing basic stem and leaf chart.

These inherently text-centric distributions can be enhanced in many ways using the text visualization framework. First, in Section 6.1, statistical measures such as median and quartiles are indicated using formats. Then, leaves can be replaced with literal text to identify specific data points (6.2). Both stems and leaves can use literal text to form a textual bar chart (6.3). Multiple levels of stems can be introduced to allow stem and leaf plots to depict hierarchies (6.4), including the ability to scale to thousands of data points, which were derived from a much larger text corpus.

6.1 HIGHLIGHTING VALUES IN STEM AND LEAF PLOTS

As shown in the train schedules in Figure 6.1, stems and leaves are readily adaptable to enhancement with foreground color, background color, background shape, dots, and so on. However, some combinations can lead to reduced legibility (e.g. red text on an orange background). Instead, font attributes such as bold, italic, and underline can also be used as they have been designed to maintain legibility. Figure 6.3 shows two plots of volcano

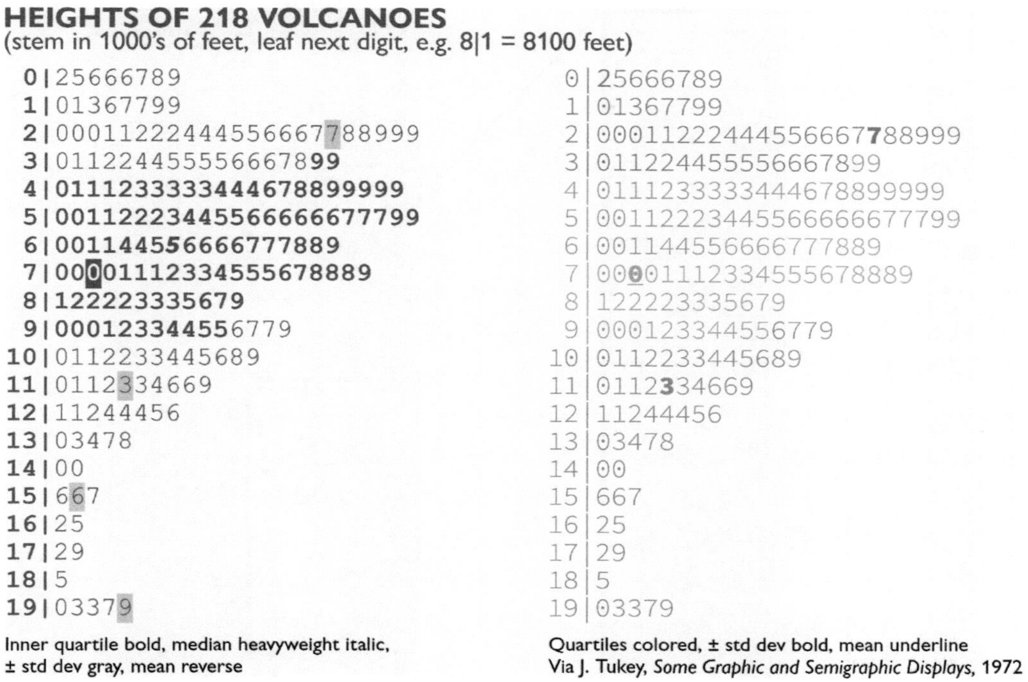

HEIGHTS OF 218 VOLCANOES
(stem in 1000's of feet, leaf next digit, e.g. 8|1 = 8100 feet)

0|25666789	0|25666789
1|01367799	1|01367799
2|000112224445566677**8**8999	2|00011222444556667**88**999
3|011224455556667**899**	3|0112244555566667899
4|0111233333444678899999	4|0111233333444678899999
5|0011222344556666667**7**799	5|00112223445566666677799
6|0011445**56666**777889	6|0011445566666777889
7|00**00**01112334555678889	7|00**0**01112334555678889
8|**122223335679**	8|122223335679
9|0001233445**56**779	9|000123344556779
10|0112233445689	10|0112233445689
11|01123**34669**	11|0112**3**34669
12|11244456	12|11244456
13|03478	13|03478
14|00	14|00
15|66̲7	15|667
16|25	16|25
17|29	17|29
18|5	18|5
19|0337**9**	19|03379

Inner quartile bold, median heavyweight italic, ± std dev gray, mean reverse	Quartiles colored, ± std dev bold, mean underline Via J. Tukey, *Some Graphic and Semigraphic Displays*, 1972

FIGURE 6.3 Two typographically enhanced stem and leaf plots showing quartiles, mean and standard deviation with various visual attributes (weight, reverse, background shading, underline, colors).

heights. Specific values, such as mean and standard deviation, and ranges, such as quartiles, are indicated using visual attributes such as bold, underline, italics, background shading, and foreground color. In the left image, the inner quartile is bold, the median is heavyweight italic, the mean is reversed white text on blue background and standard deviation levels are indicated with a light gray background (e.g. –1, +1, 2, 3 std. dev.) In the right image, each quartile is uniquely colored, standard deviation levels are bold and the mean is underlined.

6.2 LITERAL LEAVES

As shown in market profile charts (Figure 1.18), the leaves in the plot can be alphabetic characters rather than numerical values.

6.2.1 Literal Leaves Showing Alphanumeric Codes

This can be more generally extended to distributions of any quantitative value where the identities of the items are depicted as leaves. Figure 6.4 shows an example stem and leaf plot from a 1930s government publication. The stem represents the quantitative measure (percentage of population receiving relief) and the leaves represent identities of states using a numeric code (two-letter state codes have not been standardized yet). In addition, the textured background indicates the inner quartiles and the arrow indicates the median.

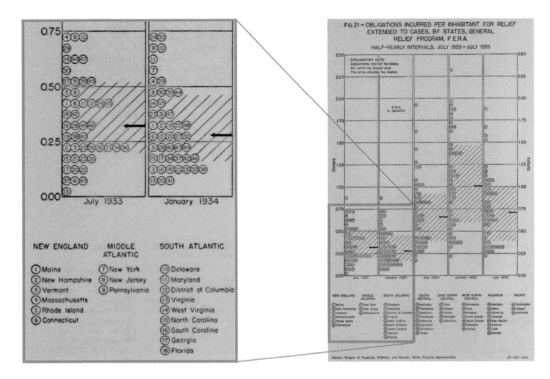

FIGURE 6.4   Percent of population receiving relief per state from the 1930s. Each leaf represents a state as a numeric code.

Similarly, in Figure 6.5 left, the stem represents the quantitative measure (poverty rate) while the leaves represent the identities of states. Font weight and color indicate additional data. Some patterns are visible; e.g. higher gun murder rates (red) are associated with higher poverty rates (upper portion of the plot), but population density (font weight) does not appear to be correlated with either.

In Figure 6.5 right, the stems are oriented horizontally based on a measurement indicating whether a stock market sector is oversold or overbought. Leaves are stacks of four-letter codes corresponding to industrial sectors, e.g. airl = Airlines, aero = Aerospace. Case indicates price volatility. Color indicates one-year change in price; on the left half the color fills a rectangle behind the text, on the right half color fills the letters. Note that slight differences in color are easier to perceive across the larger areas of the background rectangles.

6.2.2 Literal Leaves Showing Words and Phrases

Leaves are typically one or two characters in historic and modern examples. By constraining the leaves, accurate counts are directly represented by stacking characters. If leaves use words, then variable word lengths will result in lower accuracy when creating a line of words. There are a few design alternatives:

Expand and compress. Short words can use a wider font and expanded spacing while longer words and phrases can be compressed, for example, using a condensed font,

U.S. STATE STATISTICS
Poverty, Population Density and Gun Murders

Poverty Rate %   State

20	**DC** MS
18	**LA**
17	NM
16	TX AL
15	AZ **SC TN** AR OK WV
14	**NY GA KY**
13	**CA** MT **NC**
12	RI OR ME KS **MI OH** IN
11	CO IA ND SD **FL IL PA** MO
10	**MA WI WA** WY AK NV
9	**CT** UT NE ID **VA MD DE**
8	HI MN
7	VT
6	**NJ**
5	NH

Font weight by population density (per sq. mile)
   <40   40-100   **100-250**   **>250**
Color by gun murder rate per 100,000 people
   <1.25   1.25-2.75   **2.75-3.50**   **>3.50**
Data via Wikipedia.org

S&P 500 SECTOR DISTRIBUTION
As of June 30, 2012

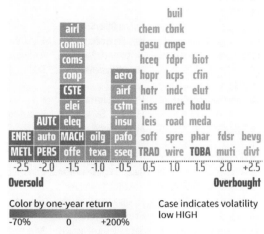

Color by one-year return

-70%   0   +200%

Case indicates volatility
low HIGH

Note: Measure based on current value vs. 20-month simple moving average measured in standard deviations (i.e. Bollinger Bands). As of June 30, 2012. Based on similar technique as Tom Dorsey's Sector Bell Curves (2001).

FIGURE 6.5   Left: Distribution of states by poverty (using state codes). Right: distribution of stock market sectors (using sector codes).

words contracted, condensed intercharacter spacing, strings truncated, and so on. Figure 6.6 shows a distribution of the components in the U.S. Consumer Price Index, the key measurement of inflation. Some component names are short, such as *Pork*, and are set in a wide font and spaced widely. Others are long, such as *Hospital & Related Svcs*, set in a condensed font with narrow spacing, plus contraction of the word *and* into an ampersand and the word *services* into *svcs*. Very long strings are truncated, for example, *Tools, Hardware, Outdoor Equipment & Supplies* is reduced to *Tools, Hardware, Outdoo….* The most important information may be at the end of a label, for example, *Beverage Materials Including Coffee & Tea* is unfortunately truncated to *Beverage Materials Inclu…*, losing critical information; a better natural language processing algorithm for reducing text is desirable.

Vertical stacks. Words can be stacked vertically instead of horizontally. With consistent word height, counts will be accurate, but the number of bins will be constrained given that words are wider than high. Zooming may be required as the text may become very small. Figure 6.7 shows a distribution of large companies, showing individual company names, split into bins based on the financial metric *contribution to return*. In addition, color indicates the industry sector of each company and font weight indicates trading volume.

Average word counts. Alternatively, words can be listed horizontally, without expansion and compression, using estimated word counts based on average word length.

46	Tobacco&SmokingProd...			
20	Hospital&RelatedSvcs			
18	Water&Sewer&TrashCo...			
16	Motor Vehicle Fees			
14	Jewelry&Watches	Tuition,OtherSchoolFee...		
13	Sugar & Sweets	Pets,PetProducts&Svcs	Fats & Oils	
12	Fish & Seafood	MotorVehicleParts&Equ...	ProcessedFruits&Veget...	
10	Postage&DeliverySvcs	MotorVehicleMaintena...	Bakery Products	Cereals&CerealProducts
9	PublicTransportation			
8	MiscellaneousPersona...	Professional Svcs		
7	P o r k	Beef & Veal	HousekeepingSupplies	Other Foods
6	Household Operation...	AlcoholicBeveragesAtH...		
5	P o u l t r y	RecreationalReadingMa...		
4	Personal Care Svcs			
3	BeverageMaterialsInclu...	Owners'EquivalentRen...	Other Recreation Svcs	Juices&NonalcoholicDri... F o o t w e a r
2	Telephone Svcs	New&UsedMotorVehic...		
1	Energy Svcs	PersonalCareProducts	Sporting Goods	
0	Fuel Oil & Other Fuels	Fresh Vegetables		
-1	Motor Fuel	Dairy&RelatedProducts	Men's apparel	
-2	Fresh Fruits	Women's apparel		
-3	Tools,Hardware,Outdoo...			
-4	Photography	Furniture&Bedding		
-5	Video & Audio	Appliances		
-6	LodgingAwayFromHome			
-8	OtherHouseholdEquipm...			
-9	InformationTechnology...			
-10	OtherRecreationalGoods			
-14	Window&FloorCovering...			

U.S. CONSUMER PRICE INDEX
Price percent change per component 2008-2010
Weighted by index weight

Data via bls.gov

FIGURE 6.6 Distribution of price components in the U.S. Consumer Price Index by three-year percent change. Note variable length names, but consistent width cells using expanded and condensed fonts.

6.3 LITERAL STEMS AND LITERAL LEAVES

The prior stem and leaf examples use quantitative values as the basis for the stems: what about literal text as stems? When literal text is used for the stems, the ordering of the stems is no longer based on quantitative values and hence is arbitrary. Each stack of leaves is independent, making the stacks semantically the same as bars in a bar chart.

6.3.1 Literal Stems and Leaves with Codes

A simple example is a bar chart where the fixed length alphanumeric codes are used to create stacks, such as the example shown in Figure 6.8.

In Figure 6.9, the most frequent bigrams in the English language are shown. Bigrams are two-letter sequences of adjacent letters. Frequency of occurrence of bigrams can be used for statistical language identification, prediction for auto-completion, and cryptography. In these two plots, one of the letters in the bigram forms the stem, and the second letter forms the leaves. The length of the stack indicates the frequency of the stem letter in bigrams – for example, bigrams starting with E are most frequent. Similarly, bigrams ending

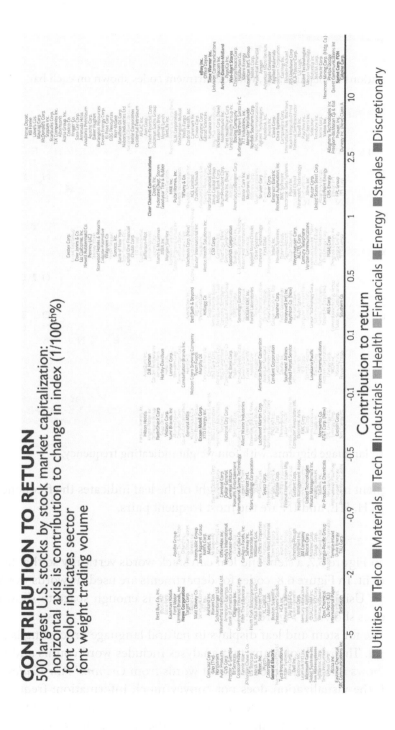

FIGURE 6.7   Distribution of large companies based on financial metrics.

DEPARTMENTS BY LARGEST OCCUPATION

FIGURE 6.8   Occupations by department, with department codes shown on each bar.

ENGLISH BIGRAMS

Starting letter	Second letter		First letter	Ending letter
A	C D I L M N R S T Y		W T S R P N M L H G E D C	A
B	E		S N I E A	C
C	A E H O T		N I E A	D
D	A E I O T		W V T S R P N M L K I H G E D C B	E
E	A C D E F I L M N O P R S T W		O E	F
F	I O T		N	G
G	A E		W T S C	H
H	A E I O		W T S R N M L H F E D A	I
I	C D E L N O R S T		O L I E A	L
K	E		O E A	M
L	A E I L O Y		U O I E A	N
M	A E I O		T S R P N M L I H F E D C	O
N	A C D E G I O S T		E	P
O	F L M N R S T U W		U T P O I E A	R
P	A E O R		U T S R O N I E A	S
R	A E I O S T		U T S R O N I F E D C A	T
S	A C E H I O S T		O	U
T	A E H I O R S T		O E	W
U	N R S T		L A	Y
V	E			
W	A E H I			

Weight by frequency
0.25-0.5 0.5-1.0 **1.0-1.5** **1.5-2.0** **>2.0%**
Data via Wikipedia.org

FIGURE 6.9   English language bigrams, with font weight indicating frequency.

in E are most frequent in English. The font weight of the leaf indicates the frequency of the pair; for example, TH, HE, and IN are the most frequent pairs.

6.3.2 Literal Stems and Leaves with Words

As shown earlier in Figure 6.7, a stem and leaf can stack words vertically so that tall stacks of words can better fit. In Figure 6.8, codes for departments are used, as words would make the chart too wide. Using vertical stacks instead, there is enough space to show the full department names as shown in Figure 6.10.

One potential use for stem and leaf displays in natural language processing is to create a better word cloud. The result of many text analyses includes word counts and frequencies. Figure 6.11 shows a word cloud of frequent words from *Grimms' Fairy Tales*. As previously discussed, the visualization does not convey much information: frequent words can include a variety of words such as descriptive words, for example, thought, saw, away; mixed together with words such as the characters in the stories, for example, king, wife, son, bird, and so on. However, no relationship between the words is depicted.

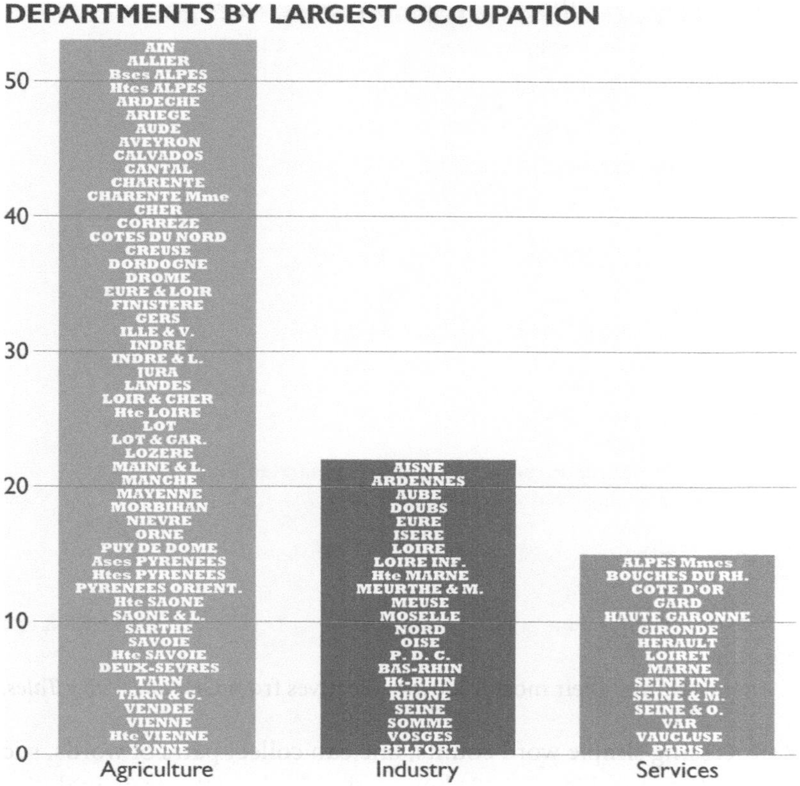

DEPARTMENTS BY LARGEST OCCUPATION

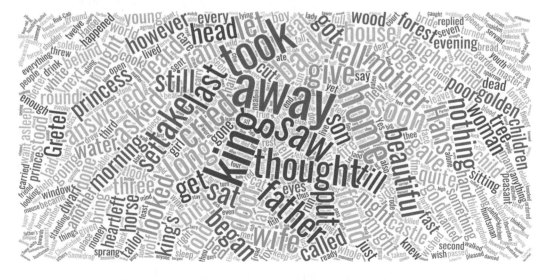

FIGURE 6.10   Occupations by department, with department names shown on each bar.

FIGURE 6.11   **A word cloud based on** *Grimms' Fairy Tales*. Frequent words are identified, but relationships between words are not available.

ADJECTIVES ASSOCIATED WITH GRIMMS' CHARACTERS

Character   List of adjectives, weighted by frequency: 2 3 4-5 **6-9 10+**

bird	**beautiful** splendid open wooden like hanging
cat	little one long
fox	**old** young dead first fast
girl	**little** poor lazy pretty young dead beautiful silly
mouse	little
elsie	**clever**
gretel	little poor good
hans	**ill good** dear
hansel	little like fat
soldier	poor third
cook	**old**
servant	faithful first like
tailor	**little** round
bride	false true first right real
king	**old great one young three** angry beautiful married like third ready sick next round
princess	**beautiful** young last dear enchanted strange true third free
queen	beautiful late little far
wife	standing married next poor two beautiful new one dear true first
witch	**old** wicked

```
0                    5                    10
     Approximate number of unique adjectives          Data via Gutenberg.org
```

FIGURE 6.12   **Characters and their most frequent adjectives from** *Grimms' Fairy Tales.*

Instead of processing simple word counts, one can collect pairs of words, such as adjectives associated with nouns. Figure 6.12 shows a simple character trait analysis of *Grimms' Fairy Tales*, by counting adjectives that occur +/− three words from a character. The stem is the character and the leaves are the descriptors. Adjectives are ordered left to right based on word frequency with font weight indicating the level of frequency.

Thus, the visualization provides descriptions of the characters. For example, birds are often described as beautiful as are princesses, while girls are more likely to be little, poor, and lazy than beautiful or silly. Witches are more frequently old than they are wicked. Not only does the visualization provide insight into the characters, it also provides insight into potential gender biases in folk stories.

This example shows an x-axis indicating approximate number of words, facilitating estimation and comparison of the number of adjectives used to describe characters. However, the semantic analysis of characters is more likely to be meaningful than the number of words.

Similarly, one can extract common word sequences to determine which word pairs appear together. Using *Alice in Wonderland*, some word pairings are shown in Figure 6.13. Some common word pairs from *Alice in Wonderland*, with font weight again indicating frequency: *oh dear, quite forgot,* and *cried Alice* are highly common.

6.3.3 Literal Stems and Leaves with Phrases

Figure 6.14 is a visualization of common phrases repeated in the *Book of Psalms* from The King James Bible (via gutenberg.org). The source text is split on punctuation into phrases. Commonly repeated phrases are shown on the centerline. Phrases immediately prior to the

oh: **dear**, **my**, **I**, how, such, it's, won't, she, ever, they'll, 'tis
quite: **forgot**, **as**, natural, out, tired, silent, pleased, crowd
cry[ed,ing]: **Alice**, **Mouse**, **Gryphon**, Mock, out, again, come

FIGURE 6.13   Some common word pairs from *Alice in Wonderland*.

COMMON PHRASES in the BOOK OF PSALMS
Phrases on the centerline occur at least four times. Phrases above occur immediately prior; phrases below occur immediately after.
Phase frequency: once, twice, three times, **four or more**

	neither chasten me in thy hot displeasure	
	he forgetteth not the cry of the humble	they have done abominable works
	thou hast set my feet in a large room	and have done abominable iniquity
O give thanks unto the Lord	and to him that ordereth his conversation aright will I shew the salvation of God	they are altogether become filthy
for he is good	**Have mercy upon me**	**there is none that doeth good**
for his mercy endureth for ever	**O Lord**	The Lord looked down from heaven upon the children of men
because his mercy endureth for ever		no
		God looked down from heaven upon the children of men
		and not build them up
The earth is the Lords		thou shalt keep them secretly in a pavilion from the strife of tongues
for the world is mine		that the Lord God might dwell among them
let the sea roar	**Oh that men would praise the Lord for his goodness**	Then the proud waters had gone over our soul
and the fulness thereof	**and for his wonderful works to the children of men**	**Blessed be the Lord**
the world	For he satisfieth the longing soul	because he hath heard the voice of my supplications
Will I eat the flesh of bulls	For he hath broken the gates of brass	for he hath shewed me his marvellous kindness in a strong city
Let the field be joyful	And let them sacrifice the sacrifices of thanksgiving	who daily loadeth us with benefits
	Let them exalt him also in the congregation of the people	who hath not given us as a prey to their teeth

FIGURE 6.14   Common phrases in the *Book of Psalms*, with phrases immediately before and after.

common phrase are above the centerline, phrases immediately following are below. Font weight indicates frequency. For example, the phrase "for he is good," is always preceded by "O give thanks unto the Lord." However, "for he is good," is usually followed by "for his mercy endureth for ever," while on one occasion it is followed by "because his mercy endureth for ever"; this may potentially be indicative of a transcription anomaly leading the researcher to investigate prior versions of the document.

6.4 STEMS AND LEAF HIERARCHIES AND GRAPHS

All the prior stem and leaf examples have used only two levels – a *stem* with *leaves*. Essentially this is a two-level hierarchy. Can more levels be depicted? A stem and leaf layout is similar to a tree, where the stem is plotted vertically and the leaves are plotted horizontally. More levels can be added using either a horizontal or vertical orientation for the intermediate stems.

6.4.1 Simple Stems and Leaf Hierarchy

Figure 6.15 shows English trigrams (i.e. most frequent occurrences of three letters) indicated in many small trees. The first character on the left of each tree is the first character in

TOP TRIGRAMS

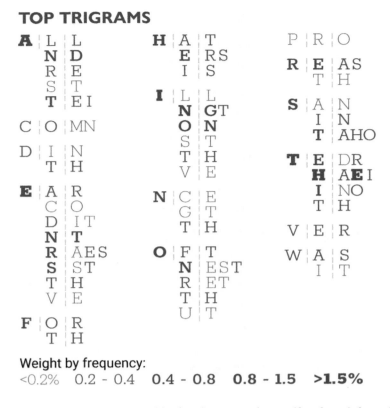

Weight by frequency:
<0.2%   0.2 - 0.4   **0.4 - 0.8**   **0.8 - 1.5**   **>1.5%**

FIGURE 6.15   Top trigrams as a stem and leaf with an initial stem (first letter), branches into multiple second letters (vertical column), which are followed by leaves (third letter in rows).

the trigram. The middle column, oriented vertically, is the second character of the trigram. The third column is the third character of the trigram, oriented horizontally. Weight is frequency. Thus, the tree at the top left indicates the trigrams ALL, **AND**, ARE, AST, ATE, and ATI with **AND** being most frequent.

By allowing changes in the orientation of the stem(s) and leaves, other variations of stem and leaf plots can be constructed. Figure 6.16 shows hierarchies of word roots, with the initial stems rotated 90 degrees, and the leaves set out individually in a vertical column. Intermediate levels in the hierarchy vertically stretch across their leaf words. *Microscope*, *microscopic*, and *microscopy* all share the common five letter root *micro-* and also share the intermediate *microscop-*. This stem and leaf relies on sizing rather than stacking to indicate quantities, conceptually closer to a treemap than a stem and leaf plot.

6.4.2 Stems and Leaf Graph

As these stem and leaf plots add more levels, each level successively stretching out across the screen, the plots are similar to other word hierarchy visualizations including Word Trees (Wattenberg and Viégas 2008) and DocuBurst (Collins et al. 2009). Figure 3.4 shows a graphical sentence from 1553 similar to a Word Tree, with the addition of branches that

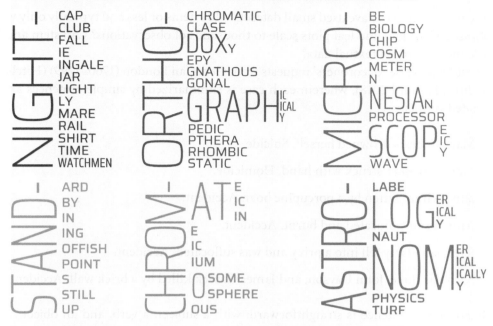

SAMPLE WORDS WITH COMMON FIVE LETTER ROOT WORDS

Extracted from top 36,000 words from https://en.wiktionary.org/wiki/Wiktionary:Frequency_lists/PG/2006/04/1-10000

FIGURE 6.16   Stem and leaf variant showing common word roots as a hierarchy of stems.

rejoin. Figure 6.17 is a similar visualization showing the root phrase "will you" from *Alice in Wonderland*, with branches, joins, and a loop.

Interestingly, text sequence visualizations from the research community, such as WordTrees and DocuBurst, do not contain loops; but older *syntax diagrams* extensively use loops to document the grammar of computer languages. Generalizing graphical depictions of text sequences using loops requires enhancements to the notation; for example, the diagram in Figure 6.17 needs to be constrained to a single loop and only take the upper branch after looping, or else it depicts sentences that Carroll did not write, such as *will you, won't you, will you walk a little faster*; or *will you, won't you, will you, won't you, will you, won't you, won't you join the dance*.

Alternatively, such a diagram could be used to represent a text generator, useful for natural language generation (NLG); or depict text prediction, indicating probabilities of successive words, used, for example, in autocomplete fields in user interfaces and text messaging.

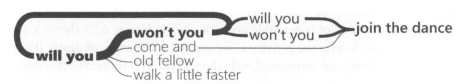

FIGURE 6.17   A directed graph starting at the root phrase "will you" from *Alice in Wonderland*.

6.4.3 Stems and Leaf Hierarchies on a Corpus

All the prior examples have used small datasets – 100 items or less and typically only words or phrases. Can stem and leaf plots scale to thousands of observations? Can stem and leaf handle more nuanced textual data?

Consider a dataset of coroners' inquests from Georgian London (1760–1799) (Hitchcock et al. 2012, Howard 2018), wherein each case is summarized by simple sentences and an associated verdict:

- Mary Roberts drowned herself. Suicide.

- Mary Gardiner struck with hand. Homicide.

- James Grant bitten by a porcupine boar. Accident.

- Ann Fitsall suffocated and burnt. Accident.

- Jeremiah Flarty fell into a privy and was suffocated. Accident.

- Nicholas Bone, John Dayson, and James Cusack killed by a brick wall. Accident.

Each summary sentence is straightforward: with a subject, a verb, and an object. These can be extracted using NLP and counted. For example, the verbs can be extracted (e.g. drowned, fell, suffocated) and counted; then the objects counted (e.g. ladder, hand, wall); then the subject (e.g. Mary Roberts, James Grant) – forming a hierarchy.

Once this hierarchy has been extracted, it can be visualized using any hierarchical visualization technique. Figure 6.18 shows a summary of all 2894 investigations as a treemap (Shneiderman 1992). The size of each box indicates the number of deaths for a verb + object combination; the largest blue box is for drownings where no object has been identified. Color is based on the proportion of men to women, with all-blue indicating only men who died that way, for example, a large blue box near the bottom right is mostly men who shot themselves. The treemap is effective at drawing attention to large boxes and bright colors. Note that treemaps are optimized so that the areas of each box accurately represent the underlying quantities – at the cost of having difficulty fitting labels, skipping labels on small boxes, or otherwise relying on interaction.

Humans are not particularly accurate at area estimation – for example, we perform better at comparison of lengths (e.g. Heer and Bostock 2010). Instead of a treemap, consider a text-based approach using a hierarchal stem and leaf plot as shown in Figure 6.19. Similar to the trigrams (Figure 6.15), multiple columns are used to better fit this tree into the rectangular area of the 4K display.

The entire text of this plot is readable on a 4K screen; Figure 6.20 shows a close up of two columns. The first level is the activity associated with the cause of death. It is shown in bold uppercase, e.g. drowned, emaciated, fell. The second level is the object associated with the cause of death, e.g. ditch, self, banister, barge, cart, etc. It is shown in bold lowercase, nested under the activity. The third level is the subject of the death, that is, the name of the deceased, shown in a lightweight font, color-coded by verdict (i.e. red for homicide, green for suicide, brown for accident, blue for natural causes, and gray for undetermined).

Note that all 2894 names are shown in the same size font as all other text. Even without reducing text size, further data scalability could be achieved, for example, by replacing names with codes M, F, m, f for male adult, female adult, male child, and female child respectively. Using codes would allow this visualization to show more than 20,000 individual data points.

This hierarchical stem and leaf layout is similar to the layout of paper-based dictionaries. Dictionaries also need to create a hierarchy of definitions, first indicating the word to be defined, and then defining different uses of the word. Longer definitions tend to be associated with more common words with many different definitions (e.g. set, to).

In this example of coroner inquests, longer lists indicate a greater number of deaths associated with the cause. For example, in Figure 6.20 there are many people who have drowned themselves (**DROWNED:self** has 12 lines of names) whereas only one person fell into a boat (**FELL:boat** has only a single name in its row). At a macro-level, the height of each entry is indicative of the number of people with that cause of death. Given that columns are consistent widths, comparison of number of deaths is a relative comparison of heights.

Other patterns are visible at a macro-level. All the names listed under **DROWNED:self** are green, indicating all deaths are suicides. Under drownings without cause (**DROWNED:~**), there are a variety of verdicts including accidents (brown), homicides (red), suicides (green), and undetermined (gray). The blue-red background shading indicates a higher proportion of female deaths for drowned self (slightly more red) compared to other drownings (~, which are slightly more blue).

In addition to the strict activity-object-subject hierarchy, there is additional detail in the data that can be directly presented in the visualization without relying on interaction. Deciphering uncommon or unexpected objects is aided by the example text which accompanies each cause of death. For example, **FELL:ceiling** provides the example "fell through joists in ceiling"; **FELL:bed** provides the example "fell on floor when bed collapsed." These indicate some of the unique and potentially fatal hazards in Georgian London.

6.5 STEMS AND LEAF INTERACTIONS

Stem and leaf plots present individual observations which can be directly interacted with. In the prior example of Georgian London, the individual names associated with each case is visible and interactive. A tooltip provides the full summary sentence of the cause of death and verdict. A single click takes the viewer to an online scan of the original handwritten notes of the coroner.

As with many of the example implementations in this book, built-in browser-based searches can be used to find and highlight key terms – for example, many of the coroners' cases involve children or unnamed individuals. A search for *child* immediately highlights all cases where "child" is indicated in the name, revealing common causes of death of children: stillborn, died after birth, suffocated, stabbed, or found dead.

Interaction can also be used to support larger volumes of data. For example, zoom can be used to show more detail or scale to show larger datasets. Filtering can be used to isolate

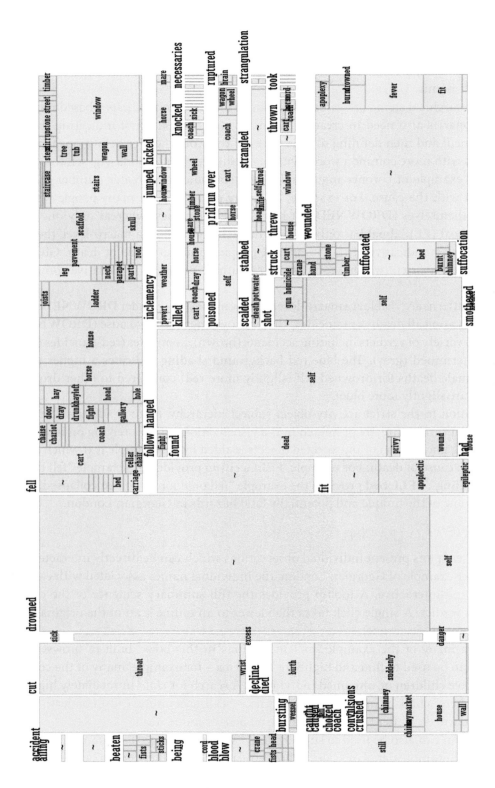

FIGURE 6.18   A treemap representing the causes of death in Georgian London from coroners' inquests.

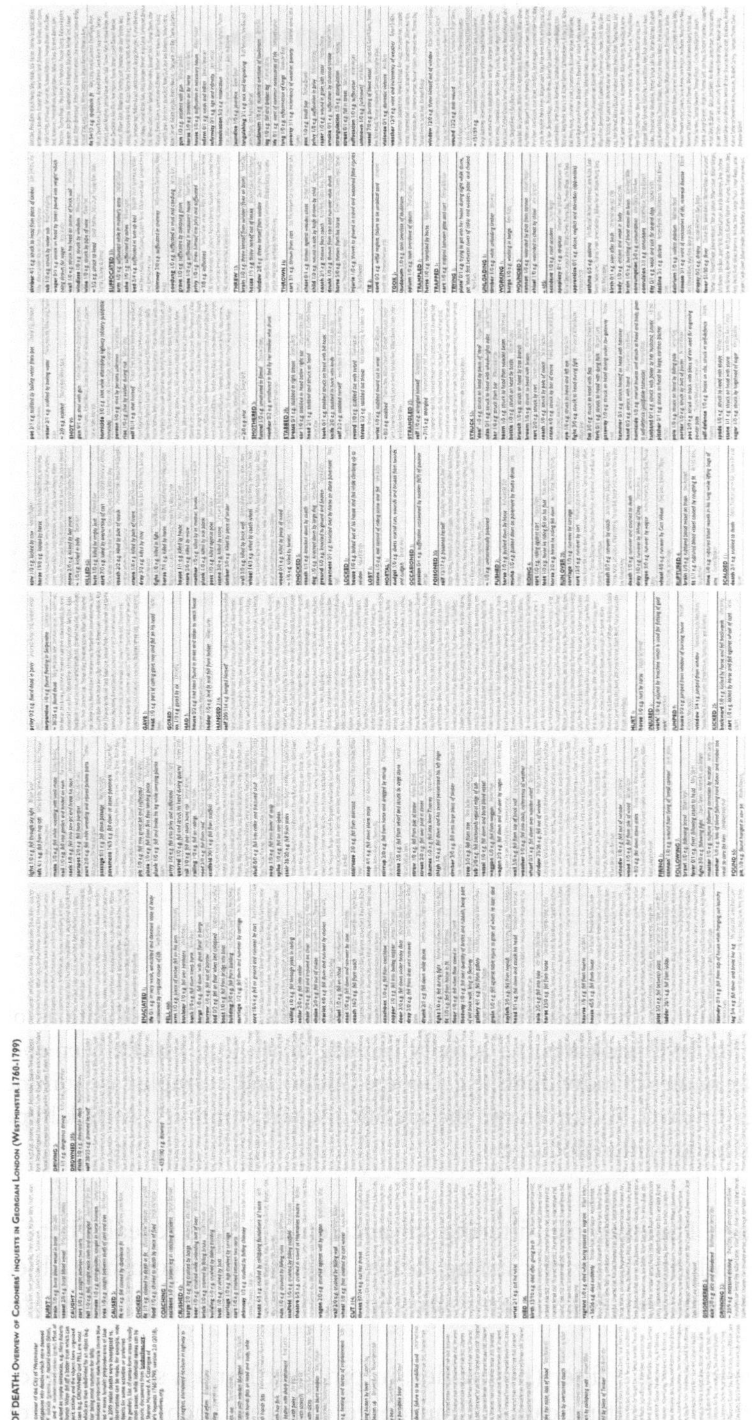

FIGURE 6.19 A stem and leaf variant indicating the activities and objects associated with cause of death, names of deceased, and associated verdict, from Georgian London coroners' inquests.

DROWNED 585:

ditch 1/0 e.g. *drowned in ditch*   Benjamin Ramsey

self 28/23 e.g. *drowned herself*   Unnamed man, Susannah Burton, Elizabeth Mobbes, Thomas Barnes, Elizabeth West, Mary Roberts, John Timbrell, Richard Hurst, Sarah Winter, Unnamed woman, Elizabeth Stone, Joseph Hall, William Parsons, John Coker, Elizabeth Cousings, Grace Hobbins, Thomas Browning, Mary Palmer, Unnamed man, Unnamed woman, Lucy Lincoln, Hugh Perrin, Susanna Sprag, Thomas Gee, Unnamed woman, Mary Clarke, Sarah Payne, Edmund Padbury, John Callockin, Unnamed woman, Jane Longshank, Alexander Anderson, John Berry, Benjamin Allen, Michael Clarkson, Unnamed man, Ann Tindale, Walter Pencutt, Ann Galway, James Lane, Thomas Spiers, Joseph Harris, Sarah Borall, Elizabeth Swaly, Thomas Chalk, Robert Ford, George Dingelear, James Cheetham, James Holt, Margaret Jones, Sarah Molliere

~ 433/100 e.g. *drowned*   John Ryall, Unnamed woman, Unnamed woman, Unnamed man, Samuel Coast, Richard Mills, Unnamed male child, Unnamed man, John Stone, Edward Mulby, Joseph Pargiter, Christian Clipping, George Dewick, Unnamed woman, John Wilkinson, John Webb, John Rowe, George Dodd, Joseph East, Alexander Mearnes, Unnamed man, Katherine Fortescue, Unnamed man, Charles Chamberlain, Unnamed man, Charles Griffin, Sarah Deacon, Unnamed woman, Mary Hill, James Longmire, Elizabeth Lockley, Richard Walker, Henry Curver, Nicholas Moone, Thomas Fou, William Clark, Alexander Lawrence, Elizabeth Every, Charles Lukey, Unnamed woman, Samuel Syar, Unnamed man, Unnamed man, Unnamed man, Adam Horne, William Marshall, James Matthews, Robert Mills, Rebecca Carpenter, Thomas Walker, Elizabeth Hey, Unnamed woman, Unnamed woman, Unnamed woman, Unnamed woman, Thomas Wrightson, Unnamed woman, Frances Gardner, Hester Heedlin, James Jeffreys, Thomas Lloyd, George Oakley, Joseph Wadman, Mary Robinson, William Betts, Unnamed woman, Unnamed male child, George Baggot, Thomas Buck, Thomas Taylor, William Robinson, Unnamed man, Edward Matson, Daniel Stripling, John Ellis, Unnamed man, Unnamed male child, George Giles, William Osborn, Unnamed man, Richard Barret, Frances Clarke, Unnamed woman, Unnamed woman, Joseph Smith, Thomas Birch, Joseph Miller, Thomas Perrin, John Fraser, John Taylor, George Fraizear, Margaret Rouvier, Mary Wall, William Wray, Unnamed woman, Patrick Caffry, Unnamed man, Joseph Bateman, Thomas Green, Thomas Spurrett, Dennis Ould, Dennis Norton, Thomas Core, Barnaby Mitchell, Stephen Rogers, Thomas Price, [...] el Clark, James Elliot, Edward Unnamed man, John Richards, John Robinson, Unnamed woman, William Holden, Hannah Lowrey, Jesse Duckworth, George Bradshaw, William Dunn,

Bailey, John Upton, Unnamed men, Harriet Beard, David Miles, Joseph Whiteman, Mary Marshall, Betty McKenzie, Joseph Gwin, Jane Davis, Joseph Jacques, James Butler, Patience Banfield, Lucy Wilson, Unnamed man, William Grant, - Robinson, Francis Munden, Unnamed man, William Pardoe, George Jackson, Unnamed man, Unnamed man, Unnamed man, Unnamed male child, Edward Giles, Unnamed male child, John Lee, John Kippin, Thomas Barber, Mary Davis, James Elms, John Case, Mary Holland, Unnamed man, Elizabeth Timberlake, Unnamed man, Sarah Stone, Neil Stephenson, Charles Bennett, Alexander Falconer, Augustus Russell, William Wildman, James Cowden, Thomas Bramwell, William Lamb, William Tallet, Elizabeth Parker, John Cook, James Brown, William Duckett, William Blake, Daniel Nibblett, Unnamed woman, John Taylor, Richard Marshall, Samuel Baxtor, George Flower

EMACIATED 1:

life 0/1 e.g. *in very weak, emaciated and diseased state of body occasioned by irregular course of life*
Sarah Downes

FELL 468:

arm 1/0 e.g. *piece of timber fell on his arm*   William Dickety

banister 1/0 e.g. *fell over banisters*   John Holloway

bank 1/0 e.g. *fell down steep bank*   John Martin

barge 1/0 e.g. *fell down 'with great force' in barge*
John Lymm

barrow 1/0 e.g. *fell out of barrow*   James McDougall

bed 0/2 e.g. *fell on floor when bed collapsed*   Elizabeth Bryley, Diana Place

boat 1/0 e.g. *fell from bridge into boat*   James Payne

building 3/0 e.g. *fell from building*   John Rogers, Joseph Barry, Henry Maggs

carriage 1/2 e.g. *fell down and run-over by carriage*
Henry Steadman, Jane Penton, Unnamed woman

cart 18/6 e.g. *fell on ground and run-over by cart*
Mary Macglouson, Jane Price, Eleanor Mathews, Joseph Dell, Malcher George, Edward Atwood, Richard Merry, James Kelly, Isaac Jordison, James Green, James Edwards, John Neale, Mary Evaridge, Letitia Drinkwater, William Thomas, Thomas Stephens, George Gilder, Mary ann Hokes, John

> George Gilder fell off a cart on 1788-09-01: accidental.
> https://www.londonlives.org/browse.jsp?div=WACWIC652280509

ceiling 1/0 e.g. *fell through joists in ceiling*   John White

FIGURE 6.20   A closeup of the prior visualization showing the hierarchy of data associated with each inquest. The top level indicates the activity causing death (e.g. **FELL**); then the associated object (e.g. **cart**); the names of individuals (e.g. George Gilder) and a sample case summary (e.g. fell down and run over by cart). Tooltip shows the specific inquest summary. A click hyperlinks to a scan of the original handwritten document.

categories of values. For example, filtering for accidental deaths reveals that falls are the most common accidental activity causing death, and the most common objects associated with falls are windows, houses, and stairs (presumably there are fewer safeguards on Georgian architecture).

Figure 6.21 shows both a filter (homicides, in pink text) and a search (child, highlight in yellow), thereby highlighting cases of murdered children, such as death from neglect, bleeding, or drowning.

From 1760-1799 the coroner of the City of Westminster performed 2894 investigations into deaths which were deemed ☑ homicide (red) , ☐ suicide (green) , ☐ natural causes (blue), ☐ accident (brown), and ☐ undetermined causes (grey). Most of the deaths are summarized as simple sentences, e.g. *Mary Roberts drowned herself* , or *Thomas Wilton fell off a ladder* from which can be extracted the subject, activity and the object; here organized first by activity in all caps (e.g. DROWNED and FELL are most common activities), which are then subdivided by an object (e.g. window, house and stair being most common for falls). Background shading indicates proportion male/female (more blue = more male, more red = more female): preponderance of blue indicates bias in males: 2099 males deaths were investigated vs. 793 female. Various observations can be made, for example, wide range of associated objects for some activities or preferred methods of suicide (by gender). List of names form areas visually identifying most common causes, while individual names can be clicked for links to historic documents from londonlives.org . Original data is from Sharon Howard, A Catalogue of Westminster Coroner's Inquests 1760-1799, version 2.0 (2018), based on data from londonlives.org.

ABANDONED 1:
highway 1/0 e.g. *wilful neglect, abandoned newborn in highway to die* Unnamed male child

AILING 2:
infirm 0/1 e.g. *ailing and infirm*
~ 1/0 e.g. *weak and ailing*

BEATEN 16:
axe 1/0 e.g. *beaten with axe* Thomas Grimsley
bludgeon 1/0 e.g. *beaten with wooden bludgeon* Nicholas Casson
body 0/1 e.g. *beaten with hands fists on head and body, while pregnant* Hannah Hubbard
fist 2/1 e.g. *beaten with hands fists* Patrick Smith, Jonathan Haleston, Catherine Bull
fork 1/0 e.g. *beaten with hay fork* Thomas Davis
instrument 1/0 e.g. *beaten with sharp instrument* Isaac Layton
poker 1/0 e.g. *beaten with poker* John Bigby
stake 1/0 e.g. *beaten with stake(?)* George Gill
stick 3/0 e.g. *beaten with sticks* Thomas Bull, Frederick Cornman, Henry Newell
weapon 0/1 e.g. *beaten with blunt weapon* Mary Offagan
~ 2/0 e.g. *beaten* Henry Howard, Thomas Hughes

BEATING 1:
imprisonment 1/0 e.g. *beating and duress of imprisonment* John Arthur

BEING 3:
lover 0/1 e.g. *after being beaten by lover*
~ 1/1 e.g. *after being beaten up*

BITTEN 2:
bear 1/0 e.g. *bitten by bear*
boar 1/0 e.g. *bitten by porcupine boar*

BLED 5:
cord 3/2 e.g. *bled to death, failure to tie umbilical cord* Unnamed male child, Unnamed female child, Unnamed male child, Unnamed female child, Unnamed male child

house 6/6 e.g. *crushed by collapsing foundations of house* ....
ruin 1/0 e.g. *crushed by falling ruins*
scaffold 1/0 e.g. *crushed by falling scaffold*
theatre 6/5 e.g. *crushed in crowd at Haymarket theatre* ....
wagon 2/0 e.g. *crushed against wall by wagon*
wall 2/0 e.g. *crushed by falling wall*
wheel 1/0 e.g. *foot crushed by cart wheel*

CUT 114:
throat 87/24 e.g. *cut her throat* ....Elizabeth Briscoe,
....
wrist 2/1 e.g. *cut his wrist* ...

DIED 106:
birth 13/10 e.g. *died after giving birth* ....
vagrant 1/0 e.g. *died while being passed as vagrant*
~ 56/26 e.g. *died suddenly* ....

DISORDERED 2:
sick 2/0 e.g. *sick and disordered*

DRINKING 32:
~ 23/9 e.g. *excessive drinking* ....

DRIVING 2:
~ 1/1 e.g. *dangerous driving* Arthur Leary, Sarah Whitlam

DROWNED 585:
ditch 1/0 e.g. *drowned in ditch*
self 28/23 e.g. *drowned herself* ....
, ,
~ 433/100 e.g. *drowned* ...., Unnamed male child, , Edward Mulby,.....................
.... Unnamed male child ....Unnamed male child, ,
......., Joseph [Unnamed male child drowned on 1767-03-26: homicide. | ....., Unnamed female child, ...
.... https://www.londonlives.org/browse.jsp?div=WACWIC652070184]....Unnamed female child, ...
........................, Unnamed male child,...
.........................., Unnamed male child,.................................Unnamed female child, ...
Elizabeth Carter,...Unnamed female child,.......
....Joseph Heath,....
...., Unnamed male child,..........

EMACIATED 1:
life 0/1 e.g. *in very weak, emaciated and diseased state of body occasioned by irregular course of life*

FELL 468:
arm 1/0 e.g. *piece of timber fell on his arm*
banister 1/0 e.g. *fell over banisters*
bank 1/0 e.g. *fell down steep bank*

FIGURE 6.21   A closeup of Figure 6.19 filtered to only homicides plus a search on the term *child* to identify murdered children.

6.6 FURTHER READING

Stem and leaf plots tend to be under-represented in interactive visualization research. For those interested in alphanumeric charts, a deeper investigation into domains such as statistical and financial charts is recommended. See John Tukey's original paper *Some Graphic and Semigraphic Displays* (1972) for stem and leaf plots and other interesting alphanumeric variants. For financial alphanumeric charts, see *point and figure* charts and *market profile* charts (e.g. DeVilliers and Taylor 1933). With few publications, primary research with end-users is recommended.

Word Clouds. Many visualization experts have issues with word clouds. See Nielsen (2009) or Hearst and Rosner (2008) for critiques. Hearst et al. (*An Evaluation of Semantically Grouped Word Cloud Designs* 2019) provides an approach on better use of word clouds. Many extensions and improvements to word clouds can be found at the *Text Visualization Browser* (textvis.lnu.se). Automated placement of small-scale text and microtext to fill lines and areas has been researched, for example, in Afzal's *Automated Typographic Maps* (2012). For a generalized algorithmic approach to effectively flowing and filling arbitrarily-shaped areas with small-scale text, see Maharik's *Digital Micrography* (2011); or, for algorithmic distortion of letterforms to fit arbitrary shapes, see Xu and Kaplan's *Calligraphic Packing* (2007).

CHAPTER 7

Microtext Lines

Sentences are conceptually similar to lines in visualizations: both are one-dimensional sequences. Therefore, text may be useful in visualizations that extensively utilize lines, such as line charts, parallel coordinate plots, contour maps, network diagrams, and so on.

Consider line charts: Line charts are highly popular and extensively utilized for time-series analysis. A simple line chart with a single line does not require labeling the line: the title can unambiguously identify the line. However, once a few lines are used, a viewer must cross-reference between the lines in the chart and a legend with descriptions. One of the benefits of visualization, as discussed with the labeled scatterplots in Chapter 5, is reduced cross-referencing. That is, identification is faster using labels directly in the visualization as opposed to relying on cross-referencing with a legend or engaging in physical interaction for detailed information.

Figure 7.1 is a line chart showing tweets about hurricanes. Each line is a single tweet, with the x-position indicating time and the y-position indicating the number of retweets. The line is replaced with text, where the text identifies the author and provides the tweet content.

The text can aid insights not feasible with lines. The curvature of the line can be compared to the tweet content. For example, simple factual tweets about the size and category of the storm tend to flatten out (i.e. not retweeted) after midnight. This aligns with intuitive understanding of the situation; the hurricane is changing and the content is outdated. On the other hand, tweets that are comedic, observational, or supportive flatten out at night followed by increased retweets the next morning. Furthermore, the orange tweet (keep people in your prayers) is a more generic message than the blue tweet (which observes a unique numeric pattern in recent events). The orange tweet slope is shallower than the blue tweet after midnight. This suggests that unique content has greater ongoing interest. These are potentially important insights and indicate that tweet longevity is dependent on content, not just authorship.

7.1 TEXT ON PATHS

Text at an angle is more difficult to read than text oriented horizontally. Various chart authors recommend against text at angles, such as axis labels (e.g. see Wallgren et al. 1996).

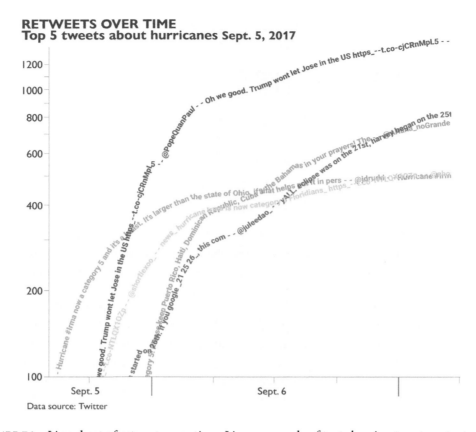

FIGURE 7.1   Line chart of retweets over time. Lines are made of text showing tweet content.

However, path-based text is often a long string of text rather than a short label. There are many historic precedents of text along paths, such as early word balloons used in medieval and renaissance illustrations and paintings such as the example shown in Figure 7.2 by Bruno Carthusianus (1524).

Placing text on paths occurs throughout the history of data visualization. Maps use labels aligned to rivers (as shown earlier in Figure 1.9 and Figure 1.10). These path-oriented labels occur in the earliest data visualizations, as shown in the small portion of a line chart by William Playfair (1824) in Figure 7.3.

An interesting example from the early 1900s embeds tiny text into thick lines in Figure 7.4 (Ayres 1919).

With computers, placing text along lines for visualization becomes easier to implement. For example, Nigel Holmes' infographic explainer for *Time Magazine* (Figure 2.6) is a graph of relationships between individuals with text-on-path pointing out directed claims. Data-driven visualizations, such as Brad Paley's *Map of Science* (Figure 1.24) lays out text along paths; and Ben Fry's *Tendril* (2000) lays out text along 3D cylindrical paths.

7.2 THE NEED TO VISUALIZE MANY TIMESERIES

In financial services, timeseries charts have existed for more than 200 years, going back to William Playfair's charts and Japanese candlestick charts for trading rice. By the early

FIGURE 7.2   Multiple word balloons as scrolls (banderoles) from an early renaissance woodcut.

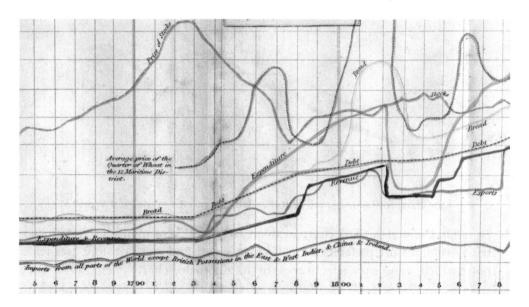

FIGURE 7.3   Labels follow lines on an early line chart by William Playfair from 1824.

1900s, financial organizations maintained many physical paper charts, necessitating *chart libraries* and *chart rooms*. Non-interactive timeseries charts persist today in chart rooms and chart books such as the chart books in Figure 7.5.

Even though interactive financial charts are immediately accessible on many websites, these non-interactive charts appeal to some chart-users because they are:

- *Fast.* Flipping through paper or PDF is considered faster by some users than stepping through a software system that retrieves data and updates charts.

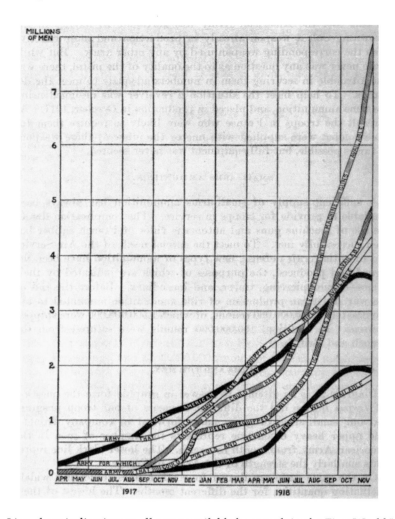

FIGURE 7.4   Line chart indicating small arms available by month in the First World War.

- *Familiar.* Users view these charts regularly (e.g. weekly or monthly). Automated systems may not store preferences, may adjust scales, and may not store user-authored notes which reduces the effectiveness of the automated chart system.

- *Fixed-size.* In paper-based environments, users become familiar with physical sizes, e.g. "a quarter inch represents a 2% change." Interactive features such as zoom, filter, and resizing reduce the effectiveness of recalling physical sizes across multiple charts.

- *High resolution.* Physical charts can be wall-sized at 1200DPI – far higher resolution than 4k screens. Multiple screens have mullions that interrupt the continuity of the timeseries, which is undesirable.

In one financial firm, a sample chart book consists of 262 charts. Although half of the charts display five or fewer timeseries, more than 10% display 11 or more timeseries (31 charts) with the maximum displaying 23 timeseries on a single chart.

FIGURE 7.5   A dozen contemporary chart books, each packed with timeseries charts.

7.2.1 Line Charts with Many Lines

Creating legible and comparable charts with many lines is difficult. There are various challenges when trying to display more than ten timeseries, such as many overlapping lines.

Rank chart. In order to avoid many overlapping observations, data can be ranked at each time interval and then each rank level can be discretely displayed as colored boxes (or as lines in a bump chart). In Figure 7.6, rank of countries over time is indicated by country (color), rank (vertical position), and time (horizontal position). Each square is a unique combination of country + time. Rather than explicitly label each square or provide labels in a separate legend, here the vertical axis identifies each series with country codes. These labels are reinforced with the same color coding as the squares, thereby aiding cross-referencing. This color consistency allows the user to visually follow the colored blocks.

The viewer can also skip from start to finish to match labels of the same color and name to determine the change in rank over time per country. The series with the largest changes are explicitly annotated with overlaid arrows and text callouts along the right side of the chart (e.g. Spain most up (8)). This is an example where text annotation explicitly calls out an insight that would otherwise require significant focused cognitive effort. The visual representation shows each series but the magnitude of the change over the time period is not preattentive. To find the largest changes, the viewer needs to find the start and end point of each series, compare vertical location, mentally calculate the difference, then repeat this across each series to find the minimum and maximum. Instead, automated insights can complement the visual representation to call out patterns of potential interest to the viewer.

COUNTRY RANK

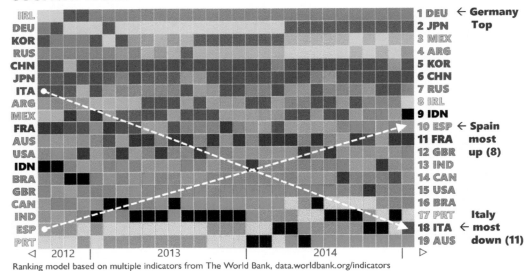

Ranking model based on multiple indicators from The World Bank, data.worldbank.org/indicators

FIGURE 7.6   Ranking of countries on a monthly basis based on economic indicators.

Note that the ranking chart has deficiencies; it is difficult to tell if observations are close or far apart – only rank is shown; and furthermore, even with 19 colors, it is difficult to trace some colors as they are perceptually too close to differentiate.

Differentiated lines. Another possibility is to simply attempt to plot all the lines on the chart. Lines on charts are typically differentiated by color, but it is difficult to display more than ten colors that are perceived as different. Figure 7.7 shows a line chart depicting 40 different timeseries of unemployment rates from 2000–2018. The chart differentiates the lines using color and line style. The chart is still problematic: the colors are not perceptually distinct, and the leader lines are congested, as is the plot area, making it difficult to trace lines back to labels.

Legend. Figure 7.7 uses leader lines to connect the labels to the timeseries lines. Splitting the labels into a separate legend will not solve the problem. There are many lines, many close colors, and a variety of line styles. The viewer will need to cross-reference back and forth between the lines and the legend labels, perhaps multiple times, to disambiguate between lines with similar colors and/or styles. One of the benefits of diagrammatic reasoning is reduced cross-referencing, which is lost if much cross-referencing is required (Larkin and Simon 1987).

Micro charts. Instead of a single chart with crisscrossing lines, each series could be placed into separate charts, such as sparklines, horizon charts, or chart grids. Figure 7.8 (left) shows 16 of the 40 charts from Figure 7.7 as an array of small charts. Each chart has an independent y-axis, making it difficult to compare magnitude across charts. For example, does Belgium or Israel have higher unemployment at the beginning of the time period?

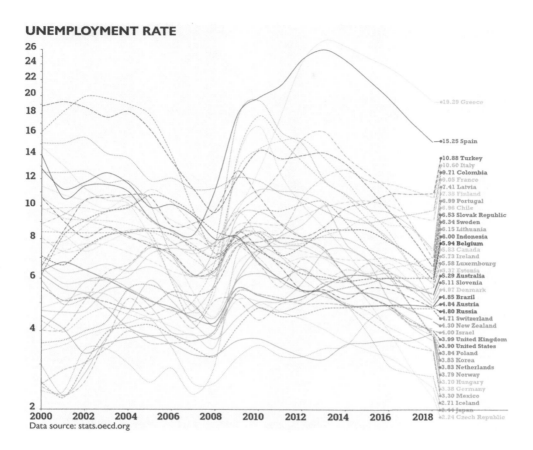

UNEMPLOYMENT RATE

Data source: stats.oecd.org

FIGURE 7.7   A line chart with 40 lines. It is difficult to identify different lines.

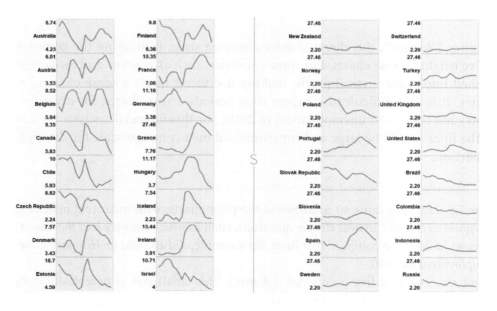

FIGURE 7.8   Left: Comparison of 16 countries' unemployment rate where each chart has a unique y-axis. Right: Comparison of 16 different countries using a consistent vertical scale.

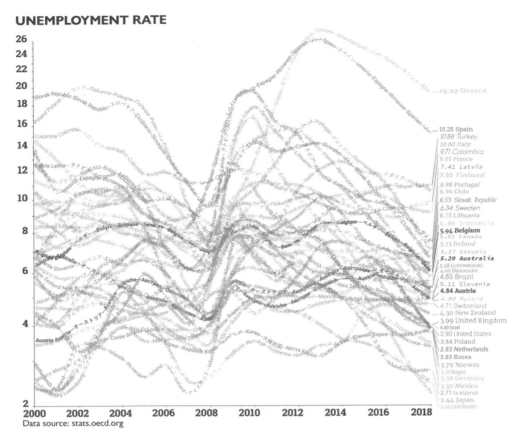

UNEMPLOYMENT RATE

Data source: stats.oecd.org

FIGURE 7.9   Same data as previous charts, here with microtext to facilitate identifying lines and tracing lines through the chart, e.g. Poland. Note different languages along the line.

In Figure 7.8 (right), the charts share a common scale, facilitating the comparison of relative heights across charts. But some countries, such as Norway and Switzerland, are squished into a few vertical pixels, making it difficult to get a sense of trend for that country. It is also difficult to compare time periods across charts; for example, which country has the lowest unemployment in 2010? For this financial analysis use case, ideally the lines should be large and superimposed on a common scale for detailed visual comparison.

7.2.2 Microtext and River Labels with Many Lines

Figure 7.9 shows the same 40 countries as the prior charts, with microtext instead of lines. The viewer can easily answer simple questions, such as *which country had the lowest unemployment in 2004*, or compare two lines, for example, *did Estonia or Hungary have higher unemployment in 2000*.

Font size is a tiny five points (i.e. 1.8 mm). This small size is potentially difficult to read depending on the quality of the print, lighting, and viewer eyesight, although slightly

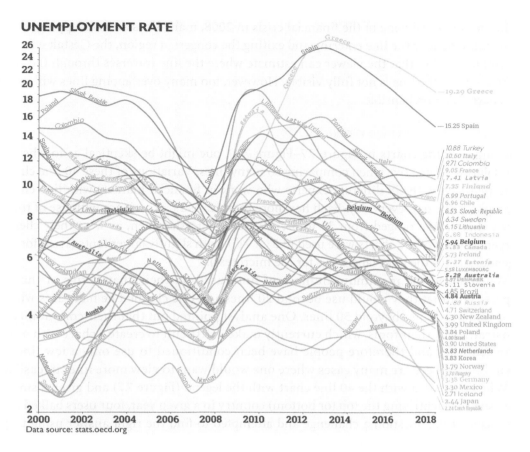

FIGURE 7.10   Same data as previous charts, here with river labels to facilitate identifying lines and tracing along lines, e.g. Poland.

larger than some historic chart and cartography guidelines which set minimum sizes at three or four points. With an interactive version the viewer can adjust the size.

Note that simple labels can be enhanced. In this example, the microtext uses names from various languages (e.g. Greece – ギリシャ– Ελλάδα – Grèce – Греция – Griechenland – اليونان --) creating a chart readable across more nationalities than an English-only chart.

In Figure 7.10, lines are labeled like rivers on maps; two or three labels appear along the length of the line. Labels are marginally larger than the microtext version.

In both the microtext chart and river label chart, type legibility is compromised by overlapping text. Two different strategies are used. For the river labels, an algorithm is used to push apart overlapping text and add a thin halo around the text to separate the text from the background noise, but at the cost of obscuring lines that pass behind the text. With the microtext no halo is used; all the open spaces between letters allow underlying lines to be partially visible, potentially aiding tracing lines across other lines. However, overlapping text is only differentiated by color, and if the contrast is low then the overlapping text is not readable.

In the congested zone of the financial crisis in 2008, many lines are overlapping; if the viewer can identify the line entering and exiting the congested region, the Gestalt effect of continuity implies that the viewer can estimate where the line traverses through the congestion even if the line is not fully visible. However, too many overlapping lines will make the chart incomprehensible.

7.2.3 Do Microtext Lines Work?

Looking over the charts in Figure 7.7–Figure 7.10, one might be skeptical as to whether any solution is effective when comparing so many lines. Variations of these 40 line charts were reviewed with six different experts who work in financial markets with line charts throughout the day, every day. Each has more than 12 years' experience with use of time-series charts. Age ranged from 35 to 65. All were Caucasian men, as were their clients. Larger versions of the charts were used (8.5" × 11"), with slightly larger fonts (8 point for the legend, 7 point for the river labels, 5 point for the microtext).

When asked the maximum number of lines used on their charts, five of the six experts said that they would use beyond 20 lines and one claimed he had cases where he would like to use beyond 50 lines. One analyst pointed out that their community is constrained by their tools, which currently make it difficult to create a chart with more than ten lines and therefore people have been conditioned to use only a few lines – even though there are many cases where one would want to view more lines if feasible.

When presented with the 40 line chart with the legend (Figure 7.7) and given a simple task, such as identifying the top (or bottom) country in a given year, four users balked and two deemed the question a challenge and attempted to find the right answer using their finger to physically trace a line.

When presented with a second 40 line chart with either the microtext or the river labels, the experts responded almost immediately with a visceral response, such as "I really love this," or "Wow, this is exciting!" All six experts completed the task with the second chart, and four of the six completed the tasks with the third chart.

The experts felt compelled to compare the microtext and the river labels. Opinion was divided:

- *Legibility.* The five point microtext font was too small to read for the oldest expert. He preferred the larger river labels and speculated that the microtext lines might be preferable if he could have read them.

- *Microtext lines* were preferred by three of the six experts. One expert found the microtext particularly compelling and referred to it as a very clean layout. He specifically noticed and identified the type variation (weight, case, and typeface) as an effective means for creating differentiation. Another expert was engaged by the multi-lingual microtext and hypothesized that the approach would make his charts more accessible to his global audience. The third explained that the continuous labels could be dynamic based on the underlying data: for example, the text at a high point could be labeled with the high value at that point.

- *River labels* were preferred by two of the six experts. One expert preferred river labels, particularly when river labels were not present in the most congested areas of the chart. Microtext lines were considered distracting by this expert. Another expert hypothesized that river labels would be appealing and easy to understand because of familiarity with them from cartography.

7.2.4 Interactive Microtext Line Charts

While interactions were not reviewed with the experts, there are many possibilities:

- Text search can find and highlight specific terms. For example, during the hurricane season of September 2017, three different hashtags used the term *Irma* (#Irma, #HurricaneIrma, and #HurrcaneIrma). These are highlighted in purple by simply using the built-in browser search functionality in Figure 7.11.

- Text attributes can be manipulated interactively, for example, to adjust text for viewers with poor eyesight, such as adjusting font size.

- Filtering and selection can be used to modify or hide lines, particularly on crowded plots. In Figure 7.12, 82 bond curves are shown, belonging to nine categories. Selecting one category inverts the text color to white on fully saturated lines that are re-ordered to draw on top of other lines, to perceptually differentiate them from the other highly transparent colored lines.

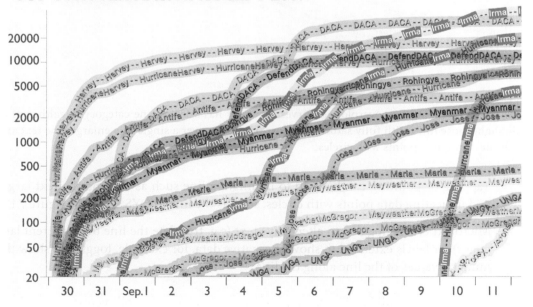

FIGURE 7.11 Microtext lines with search term "Irma" highlighted in three different lines, indicating the hashtags Irma, HurricaneIrma, and HurrcaneIrma.

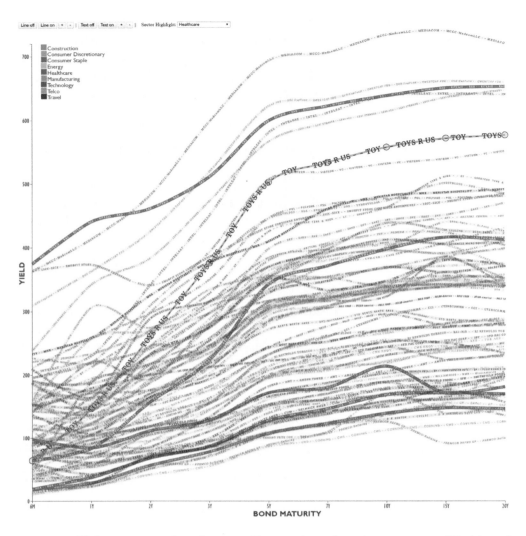

FIGURE 7.12   Eighty-two overplotted curves. The user has selected one category (Healthcare) to highlight those lines with fully saturated colors. Hovering over a single line enlarges the text and indicates key curve points with circles.

- Tapping or pointing can be used to highlight a line such as making the text larger and indicating data points with circles, such as the line "TOYS R US" in Figure 7.12.

- Microtext can be toggled to alternative text (e.g. translate the line to a different language), or labels extended to show alternative data, for example, toggled to show the numeric values of the line along the line.

One feasible but non-validated interaction is the potential use of scrolling text within lines. Similar to scrolling tickers and crawling news headlines, a long line of text can be read within a shorter path when the text scrolls at a rate appropriate for reading. In Figure 7.13,

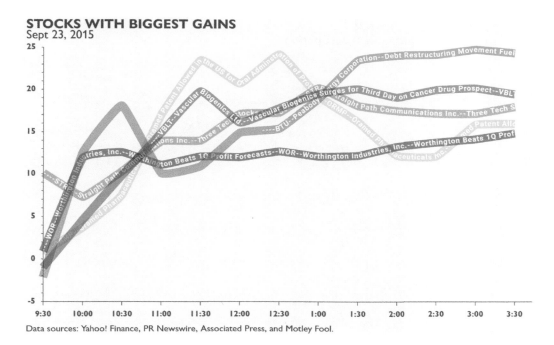

FIGURE 7.13   Scrolling news headlines inside stock price lines: VBLT and BTU are scrolling in progress.

lines indicate the stock price over the course of a day. Inside each line, the most recent headline for the given stock is indicated. Stock prices can be highly sensitive to related news stories, hence a visual representation combining price and news may be desirable. Use of a text crawl may be useful if the chart is congested, thereby enabling reading of the text in an uncongested portion of the chart; text passages longer than the line can be accessible via crawl; or, the arrival of a new headline can be used to trigger a crawl.

7.3   MICROTEXT APPLIED TO OTHER VISUALIZATION LAYOUTS

Microtext can be used in any visualization technique that uses lines, particularly in applications where there are many lines; uses where there is a need to differentiate among the lines; and uses where lines represent complex ideas (such as tweets). This includes contour plots, parallel coordinates, spider charts, edges on graphs (Figure 2.6), subway diagrams, mind maps, bump charts, dendrograms, and so forth. Figure 7.14 shows a parallel coordinates chart of Bertin's occupation by department data (similar to the chart in *Sémiologie Graphique* p. 109) where the lines are replaced with detailed department names. In addition to the broad patterns and individual lines visible in a parallel coordinates chart, each line is immediately identifiable.

Note that lines in some of these visualizations do not need to be straight lines nor of consistent curvature – the line is simply indicating connectivity. As such, the curvature control points can be automatically adjusted to increase the separation between the lines. This aids with the legibility of text.

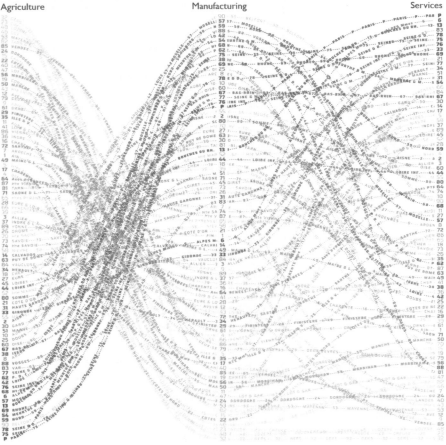

FIGURE 7.14 Parallel coordinates visualization where lines use microtext to indicate department name and number (based on a similar chart with the same data in Bertin's *Sémiologie Graphique*).

7.4 FURTHER READING

Small text, microtext, and minimum font size. How small is too small for microtext? Part of the answer depends on display resolution; text perception requires legible fonts and low-resolution displays such as 72–96 PPI screens limit font sizes to about eight points (3 mm). Printing has supported much higher resolutions for centuries. In cartography, the minimum sizes are given as three or four points; with recommendations for minimum being five or six points. See Cole (1989) or Robinson et al. (2016). Chart authors also permitted small font sizes, e.g. Brinton (1939) recommends four points as a minimum.

Note that there are typefaces specifically designed for use at small sizes and small spaces. A famous example is the font *Bell Centennial* designed by Matthew Carter for printing text at small sizes quickly on poor quality paper for phone books. *Georgia* and *Verdana* (also by Carter) are fonts designed for legibility on poor resolution screens. There are also specific cartographic fonts designed for use at small sizes; National Geographic has many, some of which are described by Valdés (2012). Hernan (2009) outlines the design strategies for increasing legibility of tiny fonts such as adjustments to x-height, connections, and serifs across a number of fonts specifically designed for use at very small sizes, such as *Times 327*, a variation of *Times Roman* which dramatically modifies x-height and other properties to enhance legibility when used at sizes as small as 4¼ points (1.5 mm!).

Text on a Path: There are many examples of text on paths in visualization. For example, Smell Maps by Kate McLean (2014) uses microtext as contour lines (seen earlier in Figure 3.42), or the long thin strands of topic labels as used in the Map of Science (Boyack et al. 2009, see Figure 1.24), or the use of text to form edges between nodes in directed graphs (Wong et al.'s *Dynamic visualization of graphs with extended labels*, 2005).

Formats

Conveying Data with Typographic Attributes

CHAPTER 8

Sets and Categories

T HE PREVIOUS THREE CHAPTERS have focused on the use of text to indicate literal data. The next three chapters focus on enriching text in visualizations to indicate categoric, ordered, and quantitative data.

A categorical variable has a limited number of possible discrete values. Gender (e.g. male, female, non-binary), blood type (e.g. A, B, AB, O), political party affiliation (e.g. democrat, republican, other), country of residence (e.g. Canada, France, etc.,) are examples of categorical variables.

In addition, machine learning clustering algorithms and classification algorithms will generate categorical variables, such as segmenting customers into groups; identifying whether a viewer is likely to purchase a particular item on a website; or automatically tagging streaming data such as news or tweets.

Visualizing categorical data is very common. The number of data points associated with each categorical value can be counted and represented, for example, as bars in a bar chart, wedges in a pie chart, areas in a treemap, or areas on a Venn diagram.

8.1 CHALLENGES VISUALIZING MULTIPLE CATEGORIES

When analyzing multiple sets, visualizations such as stacked bar charts, Venn diagrams, Euler diagrams, and mosaic plots can be used to explore set relationships. However, there are issues with these standard set visualizations:

1. *Underlying elements.* When only summary data is shown, the underlying elements are lost. There are many tasks related to elements in set analysis such as finding elements, characterizing elements, identifying memberships, and so on.

2. *Identifying elements.* While a dot, icon, glyph, or photo can be used to indicate the underlying element, the objective may be to specifically identify the element, such as the names of movies in the Venn diagram of science fiction themes in Figure 8.1 A.

3. *Identifying membership.* The reverse task is also common; given one element, what is its membership? This requires more cognitive effort with more sets. For example, in

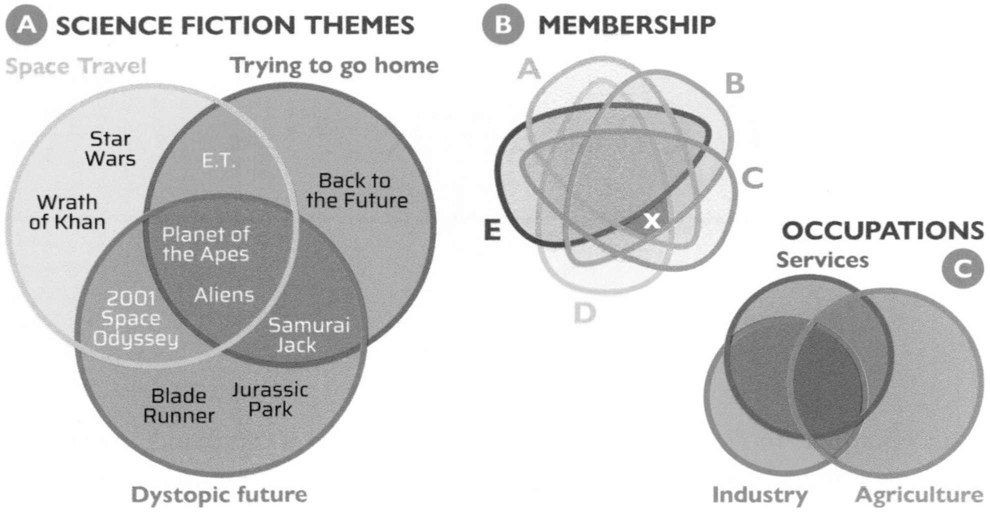

FIGURE 8.1 Venn diagrams. (A) Venn of science fiction themes and example movies. (B) Venn illustrating 32 unique combinations of five sets. (C) Area-proportional Venn of occupations.

a five-way Venn diagram there are 32 possible combinations. To identify the sets corresponding to the pink highlight (x) in Figure 8.1 B requires visually tracing which boundaries it is contained in (in this example, x is in sets A, B, C, and D but not E).

4. *Comparing quantities.* Area-proportional set diagrams are used to indicate the counts of items contained in each set and combination. However, the areas of complex shapes can be difficult to estimate. For example, in Figure 8.1 C, the ratio of departments belonging exclusively to Industry (pure red) versus belonging exclusively to Services (pure blue) requires a visual comparison of the areas of complex curved polygons. Furthermore, it may be geometrically impossible to draw regular shapes, such as circles, where each segment exactly matches its target areas.

Underlying elements can be explicitly represented in Venn diagrams, such as the examples in Figure 8.2.

A) shows TwitterVenn, where matching documents in a search are represented as individual dots colored according to set membership.

B) shows an Euler diagram where elements are indicated with icons. Like Isotype pictograms (discussed earlier in Figure 1.6), the icons can express additional data through attributes such as color or pictographic content. Note that icons can be highly expressive and represent many categories (e.g. Borgo et al. 2013). However, icons do not explicitly encode the identity of the element.

C) shows ComED (Compact Rectangular Euler Diagrams) where elements are explicitly labeled. Labeling all the elements is an effective approach to explain complex

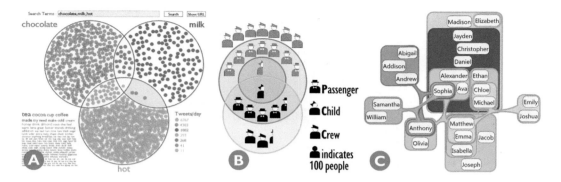

FIGURE 8.2   Representing elements in set diagrams via (A) dots, (B) icons, and (C) labels.

relationships among sets and individual members. For example, *Brexit Explained!* by David McCandless (2019) is an excellent example using country labels in an Euler diagram.

Text labels can go further than simple identification. Categorical properties can be explicitly added to labels using visual attributes such as color, bold, and italic. Using labels and formats can have many benefits over other representations, including:

1. Identification of elements is immediately accessible as literal text (i.e. labels).

2. Visual attributes, such as color, italics, bold, or typeface, can be used to indicate additional data on each label.

3. The visual attributes can be combined so that multiple dimensions of categories can be represented.

4. These combinations can be decoded to assess memberships or simply used for noticing differences between elements indicating different memberships.

5. Groups of labels can indicate macro-level quantities, such as stacks or areas of labels.

6. Formatted text labels can work with a wide variety of existing set visualization techniques.

8.2 INDICATING SET MEMBERSHIP WITH TEXT

In narrative text, there are formatting conventions for indicating members of categories, such as indicating the name of a ship with italics, such as *SS Titanic*; organizational acronyms with small caps, such as NATO; or the presence of hyperlinks with underlines.

Text formats can be combined to indicate multiple categories. Figure 8.3 is an example from an *Ordnance Survey* map and legend from the 1920s. City labels identify the literal names of cities and indicate set membership in four different sets:

- *Case* differentiates between town (uppercase) and village (lowercase).

- *Italics* indicate whether the city is an administrative center or not (i.e. a county town).

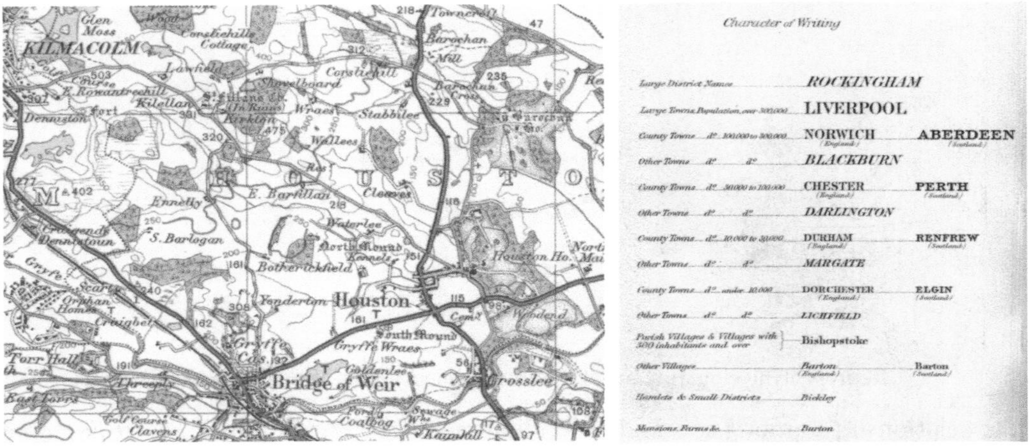

FIGURE 8.3 Ordnance Survey map and legend from the 1920s where labels indicate five different set attributes.

- *Font size* is used to indicate population category.
- *Font family* indicates country: serif for U.K., slab-serif or serif variant for Scotland.

Like the map labels, typographic attributes such as bold and italic can be used to indicate set membership. Furthermore, these attributes are mutually exclusive, and can be combined and still remain decipherable. This is shown in Figure 8.4 where rows, columns, and diagonals have formats applied across all their labels, and all of these formats are readily combined where they intersect.

However, note that many of these visual attributes are not readily perceived as separate (Ware 2013). Barbara is the only unmodified label. Immediately beside Barbara is ANTHONY in capitals, GREGORY in capitals with an underline, and Carolyn set with a sans serif typeface. However, comparing Barbara to the central label ***MARILYN*** requires some cognitive effort to deduce that it varies by capitalization, bold, italics, and use of sans serif font. Like the map labels, these visual attributes are latent cues that can be ignored for simple reading and referred to when needed.

EXAMPLE FONT ATTRIBUTE COMBINATIONS

			sans serif	spacing		
capitals						bold
	ANTHONY	Barbara	Carolyn	Dorothy	**Eleanor**	
	Frances	GREGORY	Heather	**Isabell**	Jeffrey	underline
italic	*Kathryn*	*Loretta*	***MARILYN***	*Norbert*	*Ophelia*	
	Pandora	**Quentin**	Rebecca	SCARLET	Tijuana	condensed
color	**Ulysses**	Vincent	William	Xiomara	YOSHIKO	

FIGURE 8.4 Font attributes in combinations. Note Marilyn in the center: sans serif, italic, bold, all caps.

8.3 TYPOGRAPHIC VENN AND EULER DIAGRAMS

In Chapter 2 (Figure 2.9), Bertin's dataset of occupations across 90 departments was introduced. Each department has a percentage of the population working in three different occupations. Departments where the population in an occupation is high – say greater than 30% – can be assigned to a set for that occupation. For example, the department Ariège has 51% of the population in agriculture-related occupations, and only 27% and 22% employed in industry and services – thus Ariège is a member of the set *Agriculture*. Paris, on the other hand, has 38% employed in industry, 62% employed in services, and zero employed in agriculture – thus Paris is a member of the sets *Industry* and *Services*.

The number of departments in each set can be counted and displayed as a three-way Venn diagram. Figure 8.1 C is an area-proportional Venn diagram of this data, where the size of each circle and each intersection is directly proportional to the number of departments contained within each segment. The area-proportion technique has issues, such as perceptual difficulty for comparing sizes (e.g. Which is larger: exclusive services or exclusive industry?). Moreover, no departments are identifiable (e.g. Where is Côte-d'Or? Which departments belong exclusively to *Services*?).

Instead, Figure 8.5 depicts the same data as the three-set Venn diagram, with labels that indicate set membership. Note: (1) Each department is explicitly depicted literally; the two departments belonging exclusively to *Services* are Alpes-Maritimes and Gironde. (2) Relative heights of text stacks are more easily comparable and more accurately depicted than areas; it is easy to see that there are only two departments belonging exclusively to *Services* versus five departments belonging exclusively to *Industry*. (3) Typographic attributes reinforce the color coding; an underline indicates agriculture, industry in small caps, and services in italic. These attributes can be assembled in any combination; the six departments in the center of the diagram are members of all three occupations, with underlines, small caps, and italics. Like the *Ordnance Survey* labels, population is also shown using font weight to differentiate among four size categories.

The use of typographic attributes can go further. Figure 8.6 shows a four-set typographic Venn diagram indicating each of the 100 members of the U.S. Senate in 2016 by name, with each label indicating seven data attributes:

- *Text* shows the name of each senator.

- *Slope* indicates political party membership. Right-leaning text indicates Republicans, while left-leaning text indicates Democrats. Independents are represented with no leaning at all.

- *Bold* indicates senators who have served more than one term.

- *Underline* indicates senators who have a graduate or professional degree.

- *Hue* indicates gender: blue for male, magenta for female.

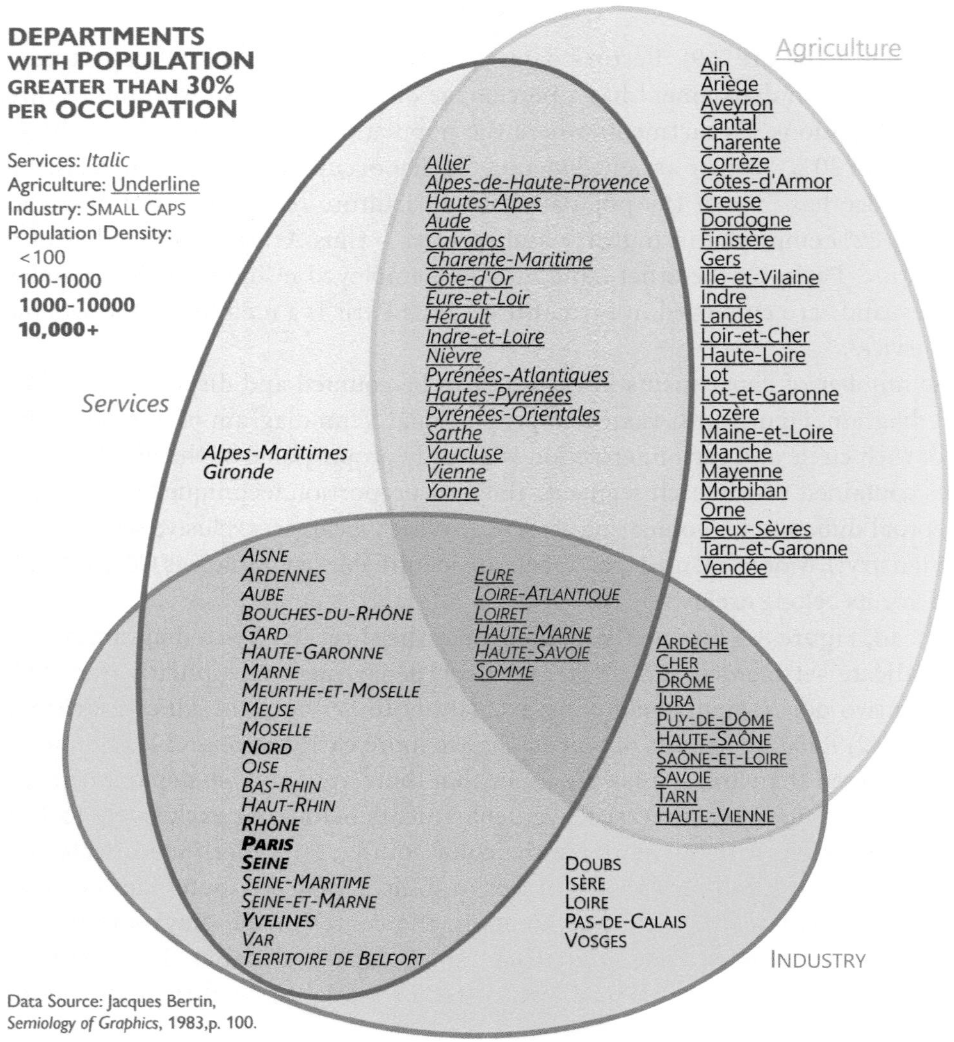

DEPARTMENTS WITH POPULATION GREATER THAN 30% PER OCCUPATION

Services: *Italic*
Agriculture: <u>Underline</u>
Industry: SMALL CAPS
Population Density:
<100
100-1000
1000-10000
10,000+

Services

Agriculture

Ain
Ariège
Aveyron
Cantal
Charente
Corrèze
Côtes-d'Armor
Creuse
Dordogne
Finistère
Gers
Ille-et-Vilaine
Indre
Landes
Loir-et-Cher
Haute-Loire
Lot
Lot-et-Garonne
Lozère
Maine-et-Loire
Manche
Mayenne
Morbihan
Orne
Deux-Sèvres
Tarn-et-Garonne
Vendée

Allier
Alpes-de-Haute-Provence
Hautes-Alpes
Aude
Calvados
Charente-Maritime
Côte-d'Or
Eure-et-Loir
Hérault
Indre-et-Loire
Nièvre
Pyrénées-Atlantiques
Hautes-Pyrénées
Pyrénées-Orientales
Sarthe
Vaucluse
Vienne
Yonne

Alpes-Maritimes
Gironde

AISNE
ARDENNES
AUBE
BOUCHES-DU-RHÔNE
GARD
HAUTE-GARONNE
MARNE
MEURTHE-ET-MOSELLE
MEUSE
MOSELLE
NORD
OISE
BAS-RHIN
HAUT-RHIN
RHÔNE
PARIS
SEINE
SEINE-MARITIME
SEINE-ET-MARNE
YVELINES
VAR
TERRITOIRE DE BELFORT

EURE
LOIRE-ATLANTIQUE
LOIRET
HAUTE-MARNE
HAUTE-SAVOIE
SOMME

ARDÈCHE
CHER
DRÔME
JURA
PUY-DE-DÔME
HAUTE-SAÔNE
SAÔNE-ET-LOIRE
SAVOIE
TARN
HAUTE-VIENNE

DOUBS
ISÈRE
LOIRE
PAS-DE-CALAIS
VOSGES

INDUSTRY

Data Source: Jacques Bertin, *Semiology of Graphics*, 1983, p. 100.

FIGURE 8.5   Venn diagram of Bertin's departments by occupation.

Beyond these five sets, which are also shown by the Venn areas, additional data is encoded:

- *Case* indicates age. Those over 65 are indicated in uppercase.

- *Font family* indicates ethnicity. Most senators are plain Caucasians (in a sans serif font), with a couple of Latinos (in a script-like font), an Asian American (in a serif font), and a couple of African Americans (in a rectangular font).

Note how the mapping of the font attribute to the data variable is based on real-world associations. Republicans are often described as right-leaning and the oblique text leans to the right. Gender stereotypes associate color hues with genders, which are used here. Bold has more weight and represents senators who have spent more time in the senate. Degrees are

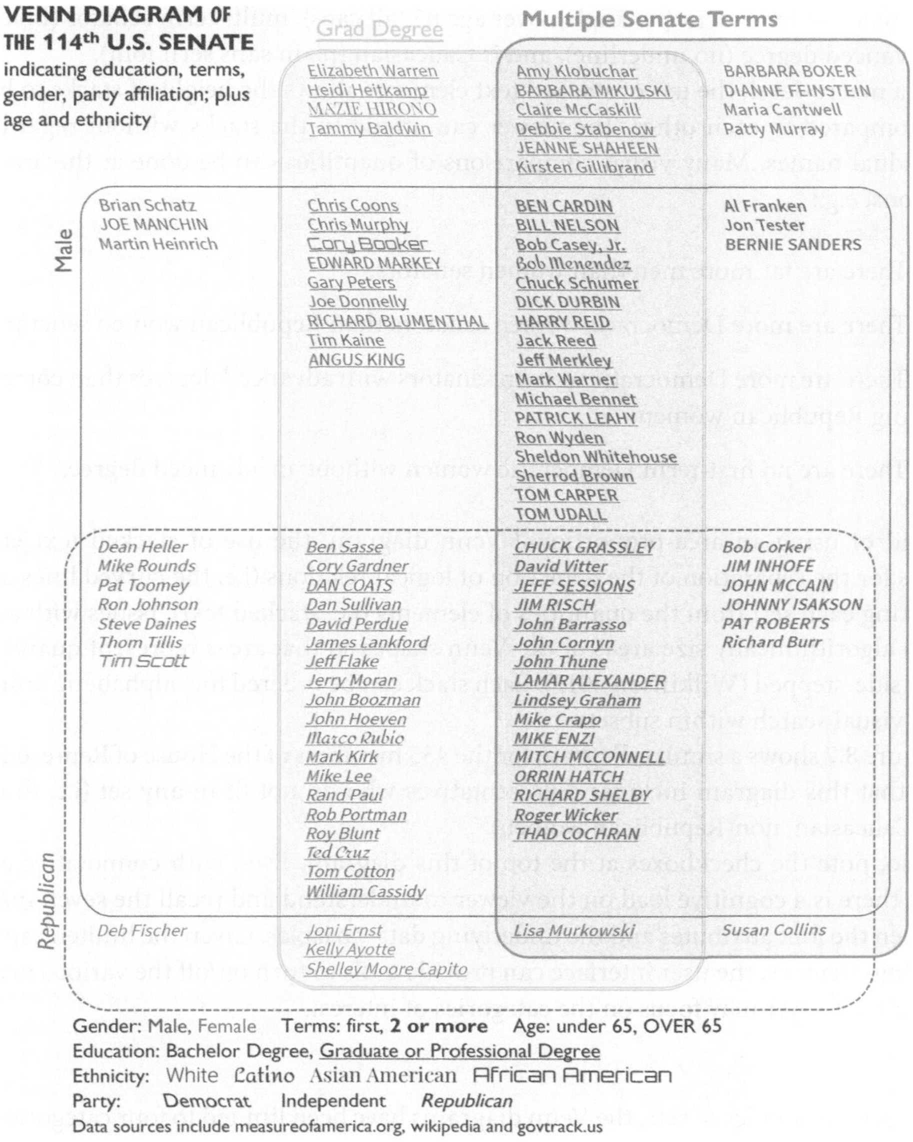

VENN DIAGRAM OF
THE 114ᵗʰ U.S. SENATE

indicating education, terms,
gender, party affiliation; plus
age and ethnicity

Grad Degree

Multiple Senate Terms

Elizabeth Warren
Heidi Heitkamp
MAZIE HIRONO
Tammy Baldwin

Amy Klobuchar
BARBARA MIKULSKI
Claire McCaskill
Debbie Stabenow
JEANNE SHAHEEN
Kirsten Gillibrand

BARBARA BOXER
DIANNE FEINSTEIN
Maria Cantwell
Patty Murray

Male

Brian Schatz
JOE MANCHIN
Martin Heinrich

Chris Coons
Chris Murphy
Cory Booker
EDWARD MARKEY
Gary Peters
Joe Donnelly
RICHARD BLUMENTHAL
Tim Kaine
ANGUS KING

BEN CARDIN
BILL NELSON
Bob Casey, Jr.
Bob Menendez
Chuck Schumer
DICK DURBIN
HARRY REID
Jack Reed
Jeff Merkley
Mark Warner
Michael Bennet
PATRICK LEAHY
Ron Wyden
Sheldon Whitehouse
Sherrod Brown
TOM CARPER
TOM UDALL

Al Franken
Jon Tester
BERNIE SANDERS

Dean Heller
Mike Rounds
Pat Toomey
Ron Johnson
Steve Daines
Thom Tillis
Tim Scott

Ben Sasse
Cory Gardner
DAN COATS
Dan Sullivan
David Perdue
James Lankford
Jeff Flake
Jerry Moran
John Boozman
John Hoeven
Marco Rubio
Mark Kirk
Mike Lee
Rand Paul
Rob Portman
Roy Blunt
Ted Cruz
Tom Cotton
William Cassidy

CHUCK GRASSLEY
David Vitter
JEFF SESSIONS
JIM RISCH
John Barrasso
John Cornyn
John Thune
LAMAR ALEXANDER
Lindsey Graham
Mike Crapo
MIKE ENZI
MITCH MCCONNELL
ORRIN HATCH
RICHARD SHELBY
Roger Wicker
THAD COCHRAN

Bob Corker
JIM INHOFE
JOHN MCCAIN
JOHNNY ISAKSON
PAT ROBERTS
Richard Burr

Republican

Deb Fischer

Joni Ernst
Kelly Ayotte
Shelley Moore Capito

Lisa Murkowski

Susan Collins

Gender: Male, Female   Terms: first, **2 or more**   Age: under 65, OVER 65
Education: Bachelor Degree, Graduate or Professional Degree
Ethnicity: White Latino Asian American African American
Party: Democrat Independent *Republican*
Data sources include measureofamerica.org, wikipedia and govtrack.us

FIGURE 8.6   Venn diagram of the U.S. Senate: both the rounded rectangles and typographic formats indicate which sets each member belongs to.

added over the course of a career and an underline is added onto the name. Use of these connotative associations can potentially help the viewer maintain and decode the mappings in the representation.

At the level of individual elements, the names of individual senators are readable. Set memberships can be seen, either by assessing the containment of elements relative to the set outlines or by the font attributes. For example, MAZIE HIRONO is a female (purple), Democrat (left-leaning oblique), over age 65 (all caps), first term senator (not bold), with an advanced degree (underline), and is an Asian American (serif). **BERNIE SANDERS** is male (blue), independent (no angle), over age 65 (all caps), multi-term senator (bold), with no advanced degree (no underline), and is Caucasian (plain sans serif font).

At a macro-level, the use of stacked text elements allows the height of stacks to be visually compared to each other. The viewer can attend to the stacks without regard to the individual names. Many visual comparisons of quantities can be done at the level of set relations, e.g.:

- There are far more men than women senators.

- There are more Democratic women senators than Republican women senators.

- There are more Democratic women senators with advanced degrees than corresponding Republican women.

- There are no first-term Democratic women without an advanced degree.

Instead of using an area-proportional Venn diagram, the use of stacked text elements allows for the separation of the depiction of logical relations (i.e. the curved lines and fills depicting each set) from the quantities of elements (i.e. stacked text). Issues with attempting to algorithmically size areas of the Venn shapes so that areas represent quantities are easily side-stepped (Wilkinson 2012). Each stack can be ordered too: alphabetic order facilitates visual search within subsets.

Figure 8.7 shows a similar diagram for the 435 members of the House of Representatives. Note that this diagram includes representatives who do not fit in any set (i.e. first term, non-Caucasian, non-Republican women).

Also, note the checkboxes at the top of this diagram. Even with connotative associations, there is a cognitive load on the viewer to understand and recall the seven mappings between the font attributes and the underlying data variables. Given the limited capacity of working-memory, the user interface can provide tools to turn on/off the various mappings so that the viewer may focus on the categories of interest.

8.4 TYPOGRAPHIC GRAPHS

In the prior examples of sets, the Venn diagrams have been limited to four categories. Venn diagrams become more difficult to lay out and require more effort to decode as the number of sets increase. Figure 8.8 A is a seven-set Venn. There are 128 different combinations. It is impossible to use regular shapes (such as circles) to draw the diagram. Plus, it is not feasible to create seven dimensions of color to represent all the combinations; in this example, multiple segments are shaded reddish-brown, each representing distinct set combinations.

Instead, graph-based layouts can be used to represent combinations across a high number of sets. Figure 8.8 B is the same movie dataset previously shown as a Venn diagram in Figure 8.1 A, now shown as a graph. Set names are anchored around the perimeter of the graph. Elements become nodes and are pulled into positions based on the sets that they are connected to using a physics-based layout algorithm (Misue 2006). Element membership is indicated by lines linking nodes back to each set. In this example, element membership is also indicated by the colors of the nodes, e.g. green, being a combination of yellow and blue.

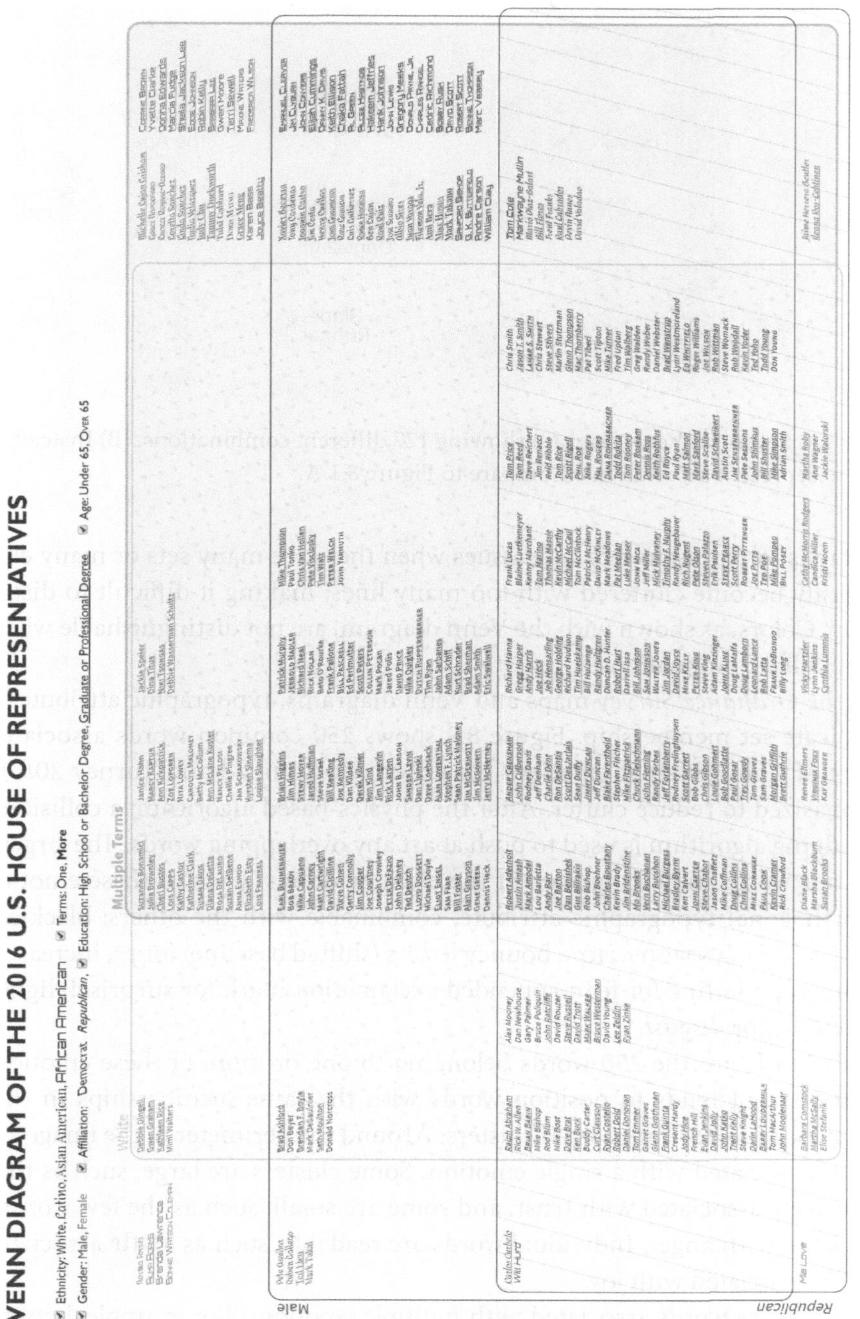

FIGURE 8.7 Venn diagram of U.S. House of Representatives.

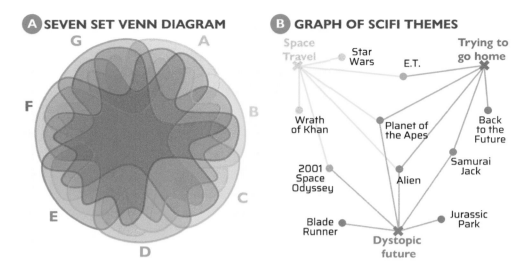

FIGURE 8.8   (A) Seven-set Venn diagram showing 127 different combinations. (B) Instead, a graph can be used to represent set relations. Compare to Figure 8.1 A.

Using graphs to represent sets have issues when there are many sets or many elements. They can easily become cluttered with too many lines, making it difficult to distinguish membership. Colors, as shown with the Venn diagram, are not distinguishable when there are many possible combinations.

As with the *Ordnance Survey* maps and Venn diagrams, typographic attributes can be used to indicate set membership. Figure 8.9 shows 250 common words associated with one or more of eight different emotions (based on Mohammad and Turney 2010). Lines are de-emphasized to reduce clutter. After the physics-based algorithm, a collision detection and nudging algorithm is used to push apart any overlapping words. The larger words are the anchor words indicating each of the eight emotions. Each of these emotions has a unique orthogonal typographic attribute, combinable with the others: blackletter for 𝔞𝔫𝔤𝔢𝔯, small caps for ANTICIPATION, bouncy letters (shifted baseline) for jᵒʸ, increased spacing for t r u s t, underline for fear, appended exclamation mark for surprise!, lightweight for sad, and italic for *disgust*.

The small words are the 250 words belonging to one or more of these emotions. The physics-based layout tends to position words with the same memberships in the same approximate location, forming visual clusters. Around the perimeter of the image are clusters of words associated with a single emotion. Some clusters are large, such as the many words exclusively associated with trust, and some are small, such as the few words exclusively associated with anger. Individual words are readable, such as 𝔟𝔞𝔱𝔱𝔩𝔢 associated with anger, or lᵒᵛᵉ associated with joy.

In the middle are words associated with multiple emotions. For example, between disgust and anger are the words *𝔩𝔶𝔦𝔫𝔤* and *𝔞𝔫𝔤𝔯𝔶*, which are formatted with both blackletter and italics indicating membership in both (and can also be validated that the color of the words is similar to the colors for both anger and disgust but does not match either).

FIGURE 8.9 250 common words associated with one or more of eight different emotions.

Near the center are words that have similar muddy colors but clearly different typographic formats. For example, ESCAPE, WATCH, and ANXIOUS are consistently formatted in small caps and underline indicating fear and anticipation. Close by are ADVANCE! and HIGHEST!, where the formats also include an exclamation and shifted baseline in addition to small caps and underline, thereby indicating membership in surprise, joy, anticipation, and fear. In this case, note that the colors are similar but the difference in formatting provides a cue that these words have different memberships and that the formatting can be decoded.

The graph approach can also be scaled to many more words. Figure 8.10 shows the full 4463 words associated with one or more emotions from Mohammad et al.'s analysis. While the individual words may not be readable within the printed book, they are readable on a 4K monitor (and in the online supplementary website at www.routledge.com/Visualizing-With-Text/Brath/p/book/9780367259266).

In both of these examples, changes in typographic attributes and changes in hue are visual cues to differences between adjacent words; even without decoding the specific difference, these cues aid the viewer in identifying the bounds of a visual cluster to

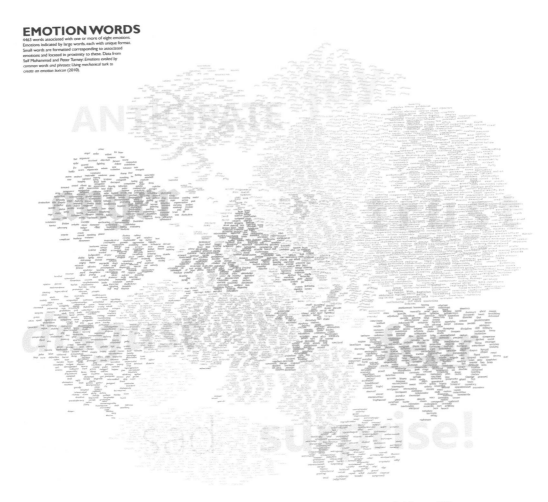

FIGURE 8.10 4463 words associated with one or more emotions. Readable at 4K.

determine which words belong to the same memberships and which words have different memberships.

Then, as a second step, memberships can be decoded using the typographic formats. Again, semantic associations are used. For example, anger words are in a blackletter font, which is sometimes associated with angry heavy metal bands. Surprise adds an exclamation mark, which is a glyph specifically used to indicate astonishment. Joy uses a baseline shift to make a word appear bouncy. In addition, interactive techniques can be used to clearly indicate memberships, such as a mouseover or tap to reveal connections to anchor words, a tooltip to itemize relationships, or a filter to select only elements with the same memberships and their corresponding anchor words.

In the prior Venn examples, the relative heights of stacks of words can be visually compared to accurately compare relative proportions. In the graph, the relative areas of text regions is a less accurate comparison, further compounded by formats that lengthen words (such as the increased spacing of trust words) or change word height (such as the baseline shift for joy, which makes words taller; or the use of small caps for anticipation, which removes descenders making words less tall and allowing more words to be packed vertically). In these typographic graphs, a viewer might be able to perceive that one cluster has more or less words than another, but not accurately estimate the relative magnitude.

8.5 TYPOGRAPHIC SCATTERPLOTS

Note that the typographic graph is highly similar to the scatterplots in Chapter 5; essentially, it is a collection of points represented with labels. More generally, any point-based visualization can represent sets using typographic formats. Using the Bertin dataset of occupations, previously discussed in Figure 2.9 and shown in the Venn diagram in Figure 8.5, the same data can be plotted as a scatterplot. In Figure 8.11, a three-dimensional scatterplot is shown with quantitative values locating points in 3D space, and with membership indicated by the font attributes of the labels: Rockwell for departments that have the highest population employed in manufacturing, Garamond for agriculture, and **Roboto** for services. While such a design variant is *feasible* for the designer to consider, it is likely *not recommended*; text at angles in 3D is more difficult to read (angled and in perspective) and the points in the scatter cloud are difficult to locate (even with leader lines anchoring the points to the base plane).

A more practical example of typographic sets in 3D is Figure 8.12: a mockup of a potential augmented reality view of a housing search application. In augmented reality, text must

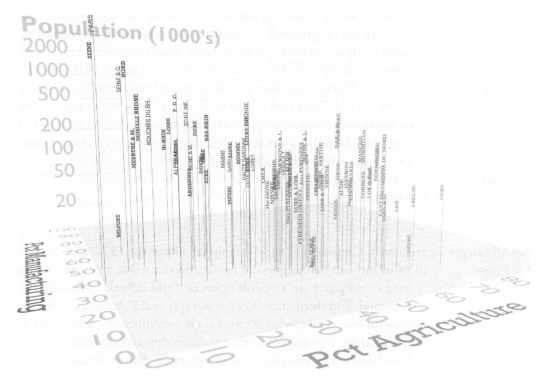

FIGURE 8.11 A 3D scatterplot, with set membership indicated by typeface.

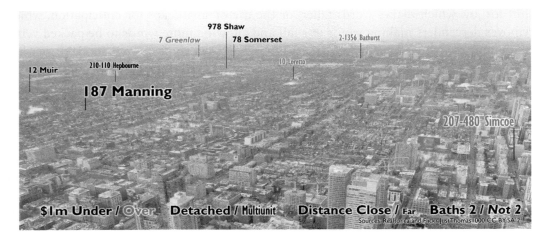

FIGURE 8.12   An augmented reality mockup showing the address of residential real estate listings and search criteria as typographic formats.

be used with care, as it obscures other relevant information behind the text. In a housing search, there may be many potential criteria forming the search, such as this search for a detached house within two miles of downtown Toronto, under $1 million, with three bedrooms and two bathrooms (as of October 2019). Attempting to depict all of the relevant matching information as text would require a lot of space (e.g. 187 Manning, detached, 3 bd, 2 bath, $949k, 1.8 miles), thereby obscuring relevant contextual visual information such as the building scale, density, parks, proximity to built-up commercial areas, and so on.

Instead, the search effectively segments the data into sets, which can then be represented with short text (the address) plus typographic formats (the search criteria). In this mockup, locations meeting all search criteria are shown in a large plain black font. Those that are up to 10% more expensive are red; those that are up to five miles away are in smaller type; those that are part of a multi-unit housing complex are shown in a narrow font; and those that do not have two baths are in italic. Thus, 187 Manning fits the search criteria (black, normal width, large, non-italic), while others shown are in related sets but deviate by one or more set criteria, e.g. 12 Muir and 978 Shaw are further than two miles, while 408 Simcoe is in a multi-unit dwelling and over $1 million.

8.6 TYPOGRAPHIC MOSAIC PLOTS

Not all categories are binary. Consider the survivorship data from the *SS Titanic*. There are 1308 passengers, all of whom can be categorized by age, gender, class, and survivorship. While age is binary (one could purchase an adult ticket or child ticket), there were three distinct classes – first, second, and third class. Venn diagrams and Euler plots only represent categoric variables with two values (whether an item is a member of a set or not), so a different visualization technique is required to show membership among multiple classes in a category. There have been many visualizations of aggregate data of *Titanic* survivorship, such as mosaic plots, treemaps, Venn diagrams, parallel sets, and so on.

Mosaic plots sub-divide the plot area to represent quantities for each class in a category. Multiple categories are represented by successively sub-dividing the area, alternating between horizontal and vertical splits. A simple mosaic plot of *Titanic* passengers is shown in Figure 8.13. Horizontally, the passengers are split into three classes. Then, vertically, passengers are split between deceased (left, reds) and survivors (right, greens). Finally, horizontal class bands are further split to differentiate between men (darker hue variant) vs. women and children (lighter hue variant). Macro patterns are immediately obvious, such as:

- A greater proportion of upper classes survive compared to lower classes;

- Within each class, a greater proportion of women and children survive than men; and

- A greater number of third-class women and children perish than all first-class men who perish.

Statistical summaries aggregate the data but fail to honor the sacrifices of the individuals. It is now common for contemporary monuments of tragedies to name the victims, such as the Vietnam War Memorial or the 9/11 World Trade Center Memorial. Names identify unique individuals, while the collection of all the names provides a summary.

High-resolution displays enable thousands of individuals to be explicitly identified. Figure 8.14 shows a mosaic plot of all 1308 passengers of the *Titanic*. On a HD or 4K display all these names are legible and readable. Macro-patterns are still visible and the detailed names are immediately accessible. Micro-questions can be asked of this dataset, for example, "Did the Astors' survive?" or "To which class did Millvina Dean belong – the last living

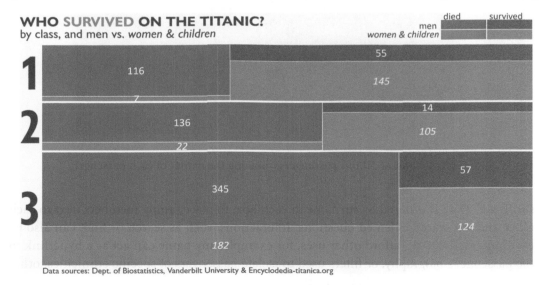

Data sources: Dept. of Biostatistics, Vanderbilt University & Encyclodedia-titanica.org

FIGURE 8.13   Mosaic plot of *Titanic* survivorship.

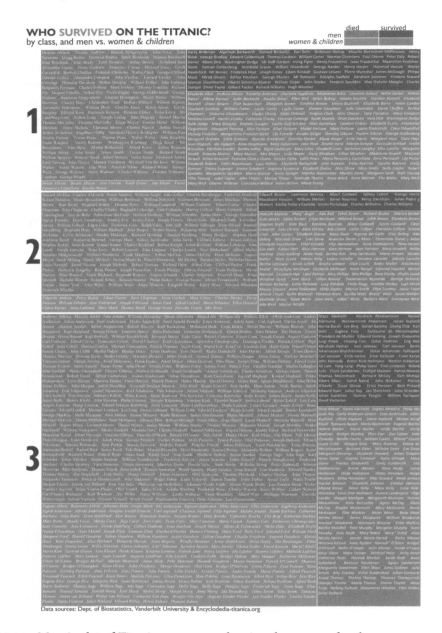

FIGURE 8.14 Mosaic plot of *Titanic* passengers, showing the names of each passenger.

survivor?" Data is ordered by surname in each box, to place family members next to each other and aid search-oriented questions. Interactions, such as search or find, can also be used. Interactions can afford other uses, for example, any name can act as a hyperlink to the passenger's biography, or filters used to isolate passengers of specific ethnicities, other demographic attributes, port of boarding, and so on.

Given the primary intent of a mosaic plot is the depiction of accurate areas, the use of text introduces potential challenges:

Long labels can compromise the use of box sizes to indicate the number of people, if there is a concentration of long labels in one box. For example, the names of surviving first-class women and children are on average 36.7 characters long, whereas deceased third-class men average only 22.0 characters; the former names are 67% longer. In this plot, names have been shortened to a familiar name and a surname. For example, the passenger recorded as *Cardeza, Mrs. James Warburton Martinez (Charlotte Wardle Drake)* is reduced in the visualization to *Charlotte Cardeza*. Similarly, the much shorter name *Miss Ellen Bird* is also reduced to two words: *Ellen Bird*. When passenger names are all reduced to two words, the above two segments average 13.9 and 13.6 characters – only a 2% difference.

Small boxes. The algorithm for this plot nudges rectangle sizes larger to fit text. As a result, there is a margin of error. This is most acute for the smallest boxes. For example, in Figure 8.14 the height of the box corresponding to first-class women and children who died should be 11.5 points tall, however, for both lines of text to fit, the box needs to be 14 points tall to fit two rows of text.

Aspect ratio. Words in horizontally oriented languages are inherently wider than tall. Attempting to fit text into tall narrow boxes results in greater error than text fit into long horizontal boxes. The same mosaic plot is shown in Figure 8.15 with classes oriented horizontally on the left vs. classes vertically on the right. The vertically oriented classes result in tall narrow boxes, which results in greater error when nudged to fit word widths. This error can be quantified as shown in Table 8.1, which shows larger errors with tall thin boxes.

8.7 TYPOGRAPHIC BAR CHARTS WITH STACKED LABELS

Like mosaic plots, stacked bar charts are effective for showing categories with more than two values per category. A typical stacked bar chart shows two sets of categories, one via the categories along the axis and the second by stacking the categories within the bars, usually differentiating these categories by color.

Again, labels can depict individual elements. Figure 8.16 shows top global companies with the horizontal axis indicating six industries, such as energy, industrial, and materials. Vertically, color and typeface indicate in which of the nine regions the company is

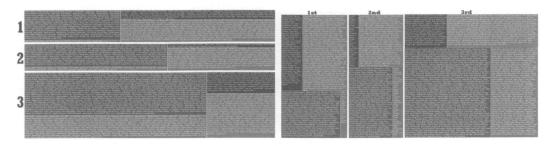

FIGURE 8.15   Two mosaic plot variants of *Titanic* passengers: left with classes oriented horizontally; right with classes oriented vertically.

TABLE 8.1   Area Errors in Mosaic Plot with Sizes Adjusted to Accommodate Text

Original Data		Mosaic: Wide Boxes		Mosaic: Tall Boxes	
Actual Value	% of Total	% of Total	% Difference to Actual	% of Total	% Difference to Actual
116	8.9%	9.1%	2.9%	9.0%	1.8%
7	0.5%	0.6%	20.2%	1.0%	85.6%
55	4.2%	4.6%	9.7%	5.2%	23.7%
145	11.1%	11.1%	0.2%	10.8%	−2.3%
136	10.4%	10.5%	1.4%	10.2%	−2.3%
22	1.7%	1.7%	3.6%	2.4%	42.2%
14	1.1%	1.3%	22.1%	1.8%	63.9%
105	8.0%	7.8%	−2.3%	7.4%	−7.2%
345	26.4%	25.2%	−4.5%	24.9%	−5.5%
182	13.9%	13.4%	−3.5%	13.7%	−1.8%
57	4.4%	4.6%	5.1%	4.5%	3.4%
124	9.5%	9.9%	4.1%	9.7%	2.4%

FIGURE 8.16   Bar chart of companies ordered by size, with color and font indicating region; plus bold indicating whether the company pays dividends, and oblique angle indicating price trend.

located. In stacked bar charts, the colors are contiguous, forming a quantitative length. This is not a stacked bar chart; instead, each company is *ordered* vertically by company size (with largest company by stock market capitalization at the bottom of each stack). This results in an uncommon discontiguous spacing of the categories in the stack. This ordering reduces the accuracy of estimation of the number of companies in a category, e.g. *East Asian Industrials* will be less accurate than if contiguously ordered. On the other hand, questions related to relative rank can be answered directly, e.g. *Exxon* is bigger than *Petrochina*, which, in turn, is bigger than *Royal Dutch Shell*.

Additionally, two other categorical dimensions are indicated. Italics indicate whether the company stock price has been trending up (italic), down (reverse italic), or no trend (no italic). Underlines indicate whether a company pays dividends.

Note that the use of many typefaces complicates the use of additional attributes. It can be challenging to find ten typefaces that are suitably different, yet have consistency in weight, italics, and capitalization. For example, in Figure 8.17, four variants of sans serifs (A) are quite similar in plain weight yet have noticeably different bold weights and different slope angles for their italics. If weight or italics is used to encode additional categorical dimensions, then the inconsistency will make it more difficult to perceive commonality in italics or weights at different levels. To create consistent slopes in Figure 8.16, a skew transformation has been used to generate a consistent oblique angle across all typefaces.

Similarly, in the example serif fonts (Figure 8.17 B), the plain Rockwell appears to be of similar weight to the bold versions of Garamond and Courier, as indicated with red underlines. Uppercase characters can vary greatly in some typefaces such as ornate blackletter fonts (e.g. Old English (C)) or decorative swashes on script fonts. Script and handletter fonts (e.g. Segoe Print (D)) are more casual and may have a slope bias even in their

TYPEFACE CATEGORY	TYPEFACE EXAMPLE	PLAIN	BOLD	ITALIC	UPPERCASE
Geometric Sans	Futura	Sample	**Sample**	*Sample*	SAMPLE
Modern Sans	Arial	Sample	**Sample**	*Sample*	SAMPLE
Utilitarian Sans	Bahnschrift	Sample	**Sample**	*Sample*	SAMPLE
Boxy Sans	Saira	Sample	**Sample**	*Sample*	SAMPLE
Humanist Serif	Garamond	Sample	**Sample**	*Sample*	SAMPLE
Slab Serif	Rockwell	Sample	**Sample**	*Sample*	SAMPLE
Monospace Serif	Courier	Sample	**Sample**	*Sample*	SAMPLE
Monospace	OCR A	Sample	Sample	*Sample*	SAMPLE
Blackletter	Old English	Sample	Sample	Sample	SAMPLE
Blackletter	Simpelgotisch	Sample	**Sample**	*Sample*	SAMPLE
Handletter	Segoe Print	Sample	**Sample**	*Sample*	SAMPLE
Display	Papyrus	Sample	Sample	*Sample*	SAMPLE
Display	Hobo	Sample	Sample	*Sample*	SAMPLE

FIGURE 8.17 Sample typefaces. Variation in bold, italics, and uppercase is not consistent across typefaces.

plain form leading to potential confusion with italics. Finally, the bottom two rows show example Display typefaces. These typefaces are designed for titles, logos, headlines, and other creative uses – as such there is even less consistency in sizes, weights, angles, slopes, descenders, and other typographic parameters. As a rule, typeface can be an effective categorical encoding, but may be difficult to use if additional data needs to be added to the typography of the labels.

If only a few different typefaces are required, note that some professionally designed typeface *superfamilies* are available where consistent weights, slopes, and widths are available across all typefaces within the family. For example, Thesis Pro maintains consistent letterforms, weights, and slopes across serif, sans serif, and slab serif variants. Lucida is a large superfamily primarily designed for legibility at small sizes, as such, weights and slopes are not consistent across all members Lucida.

8.8 HANDLING MANY CATEGORIES

When there are many categories, such as many different sets, it can be difficult to find many different visual attributes which can work together. Two different approaches are considered here: many different attributes (Section 8.8.1) or applying attributes to individual characters (Section 8.8.2).

8.8.1 Many Different Visual Attributes

In Figure 8.9, eight sets are represented, each with a unique typographic attribute (typeface, added exclamation, shifted baseline, spacing, oblique, weight, small caps, and underline). How many different attributes are feasible?

A quick experiment can be made with a typographic graph. There are 151 original Pokémon, each with one or two skill types, such as fire, rock, grass, and water out of 16 total skill types. Figure 8.18 shows the Pokémon as a graph, with a unique visual attribute for each skill type, such dash delimiters around plain type, small caps for fighting, rotation for flying, oblique for poison, and so on. Some unique font variants have been created, including variants with normal letter shapes and boxy letter shapes (for rock); normal x-height and low x-height (for water); normal serifs and bulgy serifs (for grass); a spiky outline (for ice), and so on. Texture is used as an attribute to create stripes in two different orientations (near horizontal for fairy and near vertical for psychic). Color is also used as a redundant encoding of the skills.

Each Pokémon is represented by the combination of attributes corresponding to its skills. Figure 8.19 shows some examples. For example, Gengar is a combination of ghost (outline) and poison (oblique). Mr. Mime is a combination of both orientations of stripes, creating a dot pattern. Note that color cannot uniquely encode the set memberships. For example, Scyther, Kabuto, Poliwrath, and Oddish are all similar shades of brownish-gray. Their skills can be uniquely identified by their attributes: for example, Kabuto has rock and water skills, while Scyther is bug and flying.

Note that while most attributes can be combined, there are some problematic combinations. For example, Poliwrath is a combination water and fighting type, which use low x-height and small caps. But in this font, there is no x-height variation for small caps, so

POKÉMON BY SKILL TYPE

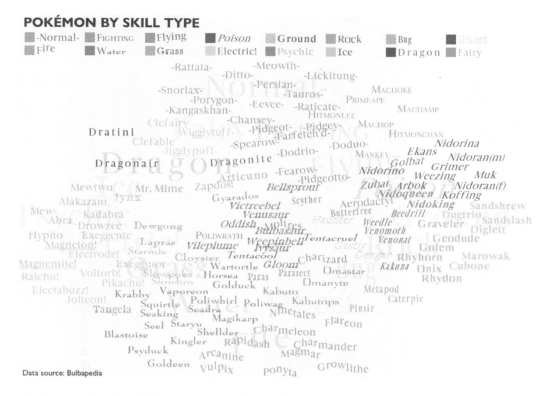

FIGURE 8.18 Graph of Pokémon situated by combinations of 16 skill types. Skill types are also coded with color and typographic attributes such as angle, italic, bold, condensed, outline, etc.

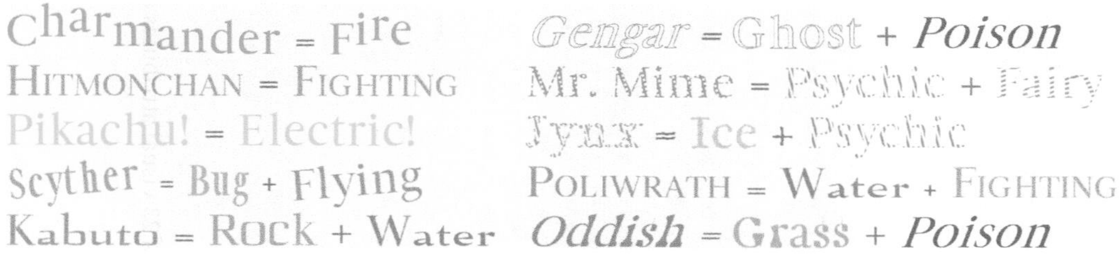

FIGURE 8.19 Sample Pokémon with skills encoded by different attributes.

it is not visible that Poliwrath has fighting capabilities. Or, Jynx, a combination of ice and psychic, is almost illegible between the combination of the stripe texture (which breaks letter forms apart) and the ice spikes (which further disrupts the letter form perimeter).

This approach can extend further. Figure 8.20 shows plain text plus 23 visual attributes and all the pairwise combinations. The first row and column are the plain unmodified text. The next 23 rows and columns each show a different visual attribute. Some of these are straightforward typographic attributes, such as capitalization, baseline shift, spacing, underline, bold, and oblique. A few are low-level typographic attributes, normally only accessible to the type designer, such as the boxy font variant, bulgy brackets, wide serifs, and low x-height. These variants were created procedurally, using the point-and-click

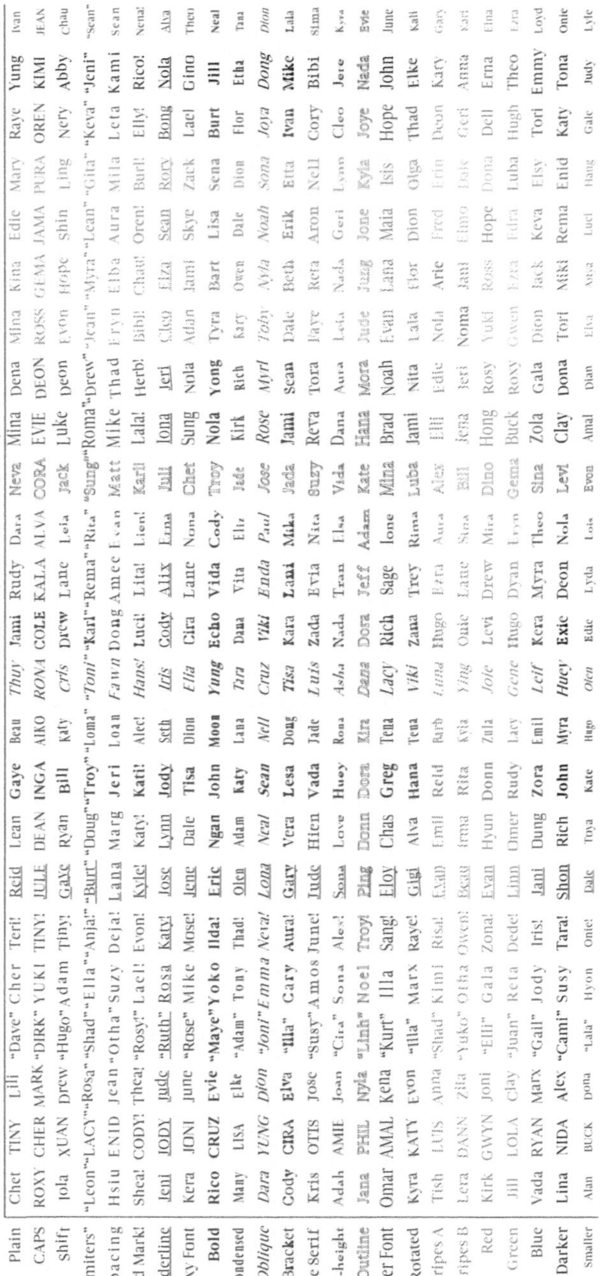

FIGURE 8.20 All pairwise combinations of 23 visual attributes applied to sample text labels.

type-design tool Prototypo.io. Rotation, color, brightness, and size are typical visual attributes used in many visualizations. Textures, in the form of stripes, are also shown. Color, used here as red, green, and blue, can be combined together to form yellow, purple, and cyan. These can be modified to create darker versions as well, but more variants become difficult as color is inherently three dimensional (e.g. red, green, blue; or hue, saturation, and lightness; etc.)

It is questionable how much further this approach can be extended. For example, blur and drop-shadows are visual attributes known to be preattentive but these will reduce text legibility. Motion is a well-known visual attribute, although text in motion may be more difficult to read.

8.8.2 Visual Attributes Applied to Individual Characters

Instead of applying visual attributes across an entire label, each letter in each label can be formatted separately. If labels are constrained to a consistent fixed length (such as three-letter country ISO codes, two-letter state codes, eight-character IP addresses in hex format, etc.,), then a visual attribute applied to the first character can indicate membership in a different set than the same visual attribute applied to the second character, and so on. For example, **N**YC, H**K**G, and LO**N** have bold applied to the first, second, and third letter independently, to indicate membership in three different sets.

Extending this technique across a variety of visual attributes and longer labels implies that many memberships can be encoded into a single label. Figure 8.21 shows data from an intrusion detection system, where eight character IP addresses show 16 different alert types via bold and/or underline per character. An IP address which has few alert types has little formatting, e.g. **5**DBB<u>8</u>EOE or **9**2B9<u>D</u>A93, whereas an IP with many alerts has many formats applied, e.g. **C**0A8**4**E0<u>A</u>. or **55728**44<u>7</u>.

8.8.3 Decoding vs. Noticing a Difference

In both of the high category examples (Figure 8.18 and Figure 8.21) there is presumably significant cognitive effort to remember the encodings. Working memory is typically limited to a half dozen items. Intuitive encodings are feasible (e.g. ice type Pokémon have a

INTRUSION ALARMS
IP addresses indicating 16 alert types by format on character position

					BOLD	POS	UNDERLINE
C0A80A0A	42C7E532	5FA359E2	817922CE	Network Trojan Detected	0	Executable Code Detected
C0A8390A	43C40343	6DEB3188	81794F70	Accessed Vulnerable Web Application	1	Misc. Activity
C0A8380A	43C40345	BCD737B1	8613B092	Attempted Administrator Privilege	2	Misc. Attack
C0A84B0A	43C40346	BCF022CA	8C724343	Attempted Denial of Service	3	Potential Corp Privacy Violation
C0A85A0A	43C40348	2EA69F1E	8E00253C	Attempted Information Leak	4	Potentially Bad Traffic
C0A86A0A	43D2699C	5410E689	8E002D1B	Attempted User Privilege Gain	5	Successful Administrator Privilege
C0A84E0A	44A8DE7A	5BD9995F	904CC064	Detection of Network Scan	6	Successful User Privilege
C0A86D0A	4504E618	5DBB8E0E	904CC065	Detected Non-Standard Protocol	7	Web Application Attack
55728447	4504E619	5E3C7B3A	904CC066			
B212F913	4504E61A	67F760E7	904CC068			
BC28342E	45412A23	68883CE	904CCFE1			
1F073E9A	48A773EC	6B0E2BD2	91647E4A	Priority Class	AAA,	BBB, CCC
6DCEAD80	4A7DE0BB	6B0653AA	92B9DA93			

FIGURE 8.21   Bold and underline *per each letter* indicates set membership.

spiky font, which can be associated with icicles). But these associations are non-obvious for some attributes (e.g. what association does small caps have?). Decoding is difficult, requiring significant cross-referencing to a legend or requiring interaction such as tooltips.

However, there are other benefits for these high-dimensional encodings. The viewer can make integrative perceptual inferences without attending to the specific individual formats:

1. Noticing a difference in typographic attributes indicates that there is a difference in set membership. In a spatial layout where proximity implies similarity (such as graphs and maps), this difference aids visual separation between subsets. For example, in Figure 8.9, *DEATH!*, *darkness*, *terrible*, *sin*, and *broken* are adjacent to each other and similarly colored, but differences in the typographic attributes between words are readily noticeable, indicating that different set memberships are involved.

2. Font attributes can be perceived as few (e.g. plain text) or many (e.g. bold, underline, uncommon typeface, etc.). This indicates whether an element belongs to few or many sets.

Typographers point out that viewers sometimes do not notice a font difference when reading a line of text. That is, viewers attend to words, not fonts, and may miss a difference such as a shift between a common serif and a common sans serif font (e.g. inspect the word *when* in the preceding sentence). It is therefore necessary to use attributes which are noticeable or have a convention to be noticed (e.g. bold, italic, underline, uppercase, red). TALLman lettering, shown in Figure 3.17, is a convention for labeling drugs to deliberately disrupt syllables in look-alike drug names in order to reduce medical errors.

8.8.4 Going Further

If a typographic visualization of many categories is of interest, the visualization designer should consider the users' application and tasks to assess suitability. The designer should consider how or if the visualization adequately addresses the users' ability to (1) notice differences, (2) decode differences, (3) recall the mapping between the data variable and the visual attribute, (4) compare relative areas across categories, (5) legibly perceive the labels, and (6) easily read the labels, especially if many visual attributes are used.

Interactivity can be a useful aid to help with the above tasks. For example, when there are many sets, interaction can turn on/off different set encodings, provide tooltips, visually highlight connections to set labels, visually highlight peers with the same membership, hyperlink to detailed data, and so on.

8.9 FURTHER READING

Set visualization tasks and techniques. Alsallakh et al. (2014) itemize 26 tasks that users do with sets, 14 of which are related to the underlying elements; and provide a comprehensive review of many kinds of unique and interesting set visualizations across various domains. For more information on the set visualization techniques shown, see Clark 2008 for

TwitterVenn, and Riche et al. 2014 for ComEd. See David McCandless' *Brexit Explained!* (2019) for a Venn-like diagram explaining the complexities of Brexit available on YouTube.

Multi-dimensional icons and pictographs. Pictograms, icons, and glyphs can intuitively represent multiple categories of data. In the 1930s, Isotype pioneered the use of pictograms to convey a few dimensions of data (e.g. Neurath 2010). Borgo et al. (2013) define and frame the design space of glyph-based visualization. The multi-dimensional glyph design space is further explored in Maguire's PhD thesis (2014), including procedural glyph generation.

Area estimation. Heer and Bostock (2010) replicate and extend an earlier seminal paper by Cleveland and McGill (1984) where viewers' estimates of relative sizes and areas are compared. While complex curved convex polygons are not included in either study, they do show that estimating lengths is more accurate than estimating sizes of pie wedges (or areas of rectangles, etc.). With regards to accurately drawing regular shapes to create Venn and Euler diagrams, Wilkinson provides the algorithms and code to achieve approximations (Wilkinson 2005).

The *Titanic* has long been a popular dataset for visualization, analytics, and machine learning. See Symanzik, Friendly, and Onder (2019) for many visualization examples of *Titanic* data.

CHAPTER 9

Maps and Ordered Data

O RDERED DATA IS DATA that has an explicit sequence but is not quantitative. The grading of collectables (such as comics, coins, sports cards, stamps, or diamonds) often use an ordering such as poor, fair, good, fine, or mint. Some of these grading systems use numeric grades, but they are not quantitative, e.g. a *near mint* Superman comic graded 9.5 is not twice as good as a *very good* comic graded 4.7.

Quantitative data can be discretized into ordered data, for example, companies can be graded by their stock market capitalization (big cap > $10 billion USD, mid cap $2b–$10b, small cap <$2b). Many customer loyalty programs order their customers by quantitative criteria. For example, airlines split customers into ordered levels such as *standard*, *gold*, and *platinum* based on the distance flown annually.

Scoring algorithms and machine-learning techniques may be used to create probabilities and set thresholds for ordering. For example, in predictive analytics, a propensity-to-purchase model is used to predict the likelihood that a prospective customer will make a buying decision. Credit risk models and credit scores are used to determine the probability that a customer will be unable to pay back a loan. The model results are typically discretized into an ordering, such as a 1–5 scale or letter grades.

Note that some visual attributes cannot express many levels of ordering. For example, there are no color scales that can express quantitative ratios and any color scale will have a limited number of discriminable steps (Ware 2013: 129–133). Therefore, encoding quantitative data into a visual attribute that only supports a few levels of ordering in effect is discretizing quantitative data into ordered data.

Visualizing ordered data is common in many visualizations. Some example representations that might be used on a map or chart include brightness, e.g. ▨▧▨■; hues ordered by perceived brightness, e.g. ▨▨▧■; blur, e.g. ■●●●; transparency, e.g. ▨ ▨ ▨ ▨; and so on. Many typographic attributes are orderable too, such as font weight, e.g. A A **A A**; font width, e.g. A A A A; underline, e.g. A A̲ A̲ A̲; and so on.

9.1 PROBLEMS WITH THEMATIC MAPS

Thematic maps show the spatial variation of one or two variables encoded as ordered visual attributes, such as color and size. They tend to be brightly colored, have minimal text, and are used to present ordered data aggregated to geographic regions such as counties, states, or countries. Figure 9.1 shows three thematic maps of U.S. states. A is a *choropleth map* using color to indicate the unemployment rate. B is a *contiguous cartogram* adjusting state area to indicate electoral votes and color to indicate the political party. C is a *Dorling cartogram* representing states as circles, with size indicating the obese population and color indicating obesity rate.

Thematic maps are popular but have well-known problems:

- Some areas may be too small for color to be discernable (e.g. Singapore on a world map).

- Large regions are more prominent than small regions, but some tasks, such as policy comparison, require that all entities be equally attended to.

- Remote regions are sometimes removed, moved, or displayed at other scales (e.g. note placement or removal of Alaska in Figure 9.1).

- Some viewers are not geographically literate. For example, 63% of young Americans could not locate Iraq on a map of the Middle East in a National Geographic survey.

Instead of color or shapes, labels can be used to show ordered values. Historic maps have many examples where labels encode ordered data values. The map from Stieler's *Atlas* in Figure 1.10 encodes three different orderings in the labels:

- Underlines are ordered to encode the level of administration: double for state capitals (e.g. **Speyer**), single for capitals of administrative districts (***Mosbach***), and dashed for capitals of local government districts (***Sinsheim***).

- Size, caps, and italics are combined to encode an ordering of population of cities: over 100,000 (**MANNHEIM**); over 50,000 (***KARLSRUHE***), over 25,000 (**Heidelberg**), over 5000 (***Mosbach***), and under 5000 (*Hohenbach*).

- Typefaces are ordered to indicate the level of the region: independent country (**FRANKREICH**), state (**BADEN**), counties (**NECKAR KREIS**), and districts (**Odenwald**).

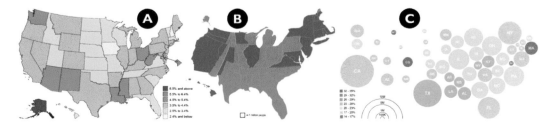

FIGURE 9.1   Sample thematic maps: (A) choropleth, (B) contiguous cartogram, and (C) Dorling cartogram.

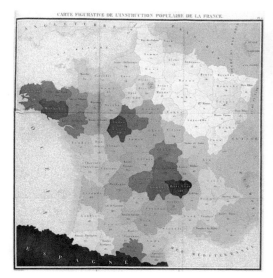 

FIGURE 9.2   Left: the first choropleth map from 1827. Right: an earlier text-based thematic map from 1782.

Why don't modern thematic maps use labels indicating ordered data?

Labeled maps with variation in typography to express data have existed since medieval times (Figure 1.2). Thematic maps are much more recent: the earliest choropleth maps are from Charles Dupin in 1827, as shown in Figure 9.2 left.

A significant influence on Dupin was August Crome, who produced *Neue Carte von Europa* in 1782 (small portion in Figure 9.2 right). Crome starts with a base map that uses the standard labeling conventions of his time, e.g. italics for rivers, all caps for country names, colors for borders. Crome adds on top of this the thematic content using symbols and codes; he cannot differentiate the symbols using color, font size, case, or italics, as those variations are already in use on the base map. Crome cannot use bold, it has not been invented yet. With no variation, the themes do not visually pop-out: that is, the themes are not preattentive. Dupin's genius is to start with a very simple base map, thereby making attributes such as brightness available to indicate thematic data. Dupin also sidesteps many of the issues with choropleth maps: for example, French departments are defined to be of similar sizes. After Dupin, the convention for thematic maps follows his model: geographic polygons with brightness or color to indicate thematic data. Even though a simple base map could support perceptual grouping of labels with visual attributes, using labels to create thematic maps remains uncommon in practice.

9.2 TYPOGRAPHIC THEMATIC MAP WITH A SINGLE ORDERED VARIABLE

Instead of colored polygons and their associated problems, thematic maps can be made where the label is the key element. In Figure 9.3, a sample choropleth map is shown. The same data is shown in Figure 9.4 using three-letter ISO-standard country codes per country. Country codes act as a mnemonic aid to facilitate decoding countries for English

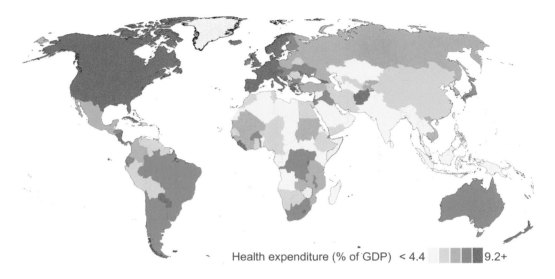

FIGURE 9.3   Choropleth map of health expenditures as % of GDP. Values for small countries are not visible.

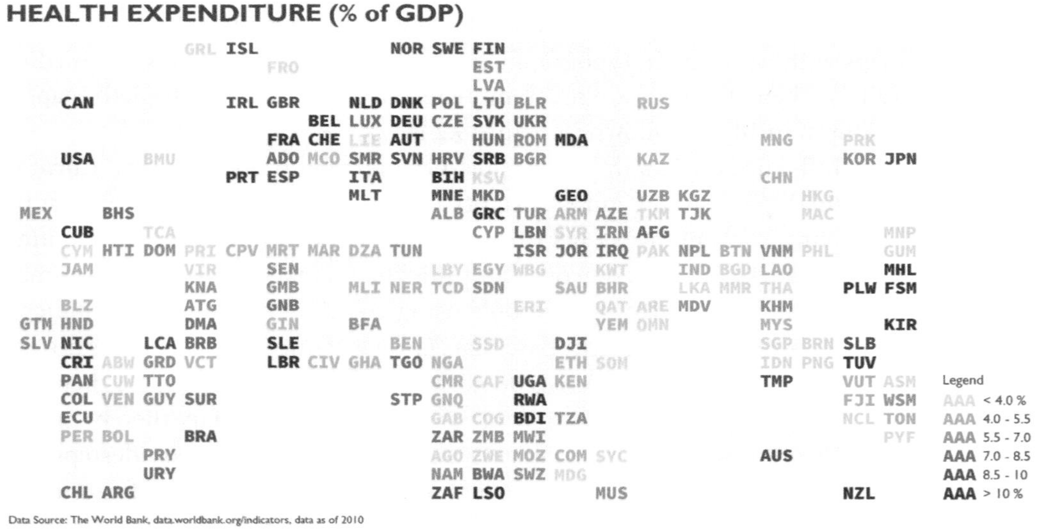

FIGURE 9.4   A typographic cartogram indicating data via text color: small countries are visible.

language speakers, such as CHL for Chile and ARG for Argentina. The layout is a cartogram, where all labels are visible and local adjacencies between elements are maintained.

With both maps, high values and low values are clearly visible, for example, the USA has high health expenditures. In addition, in the cartogram small countries such as Singapore (SGP) and Andorra (ADO) are also visible. Further, countries with large areas, such as Russia (RUS) and Canada (CAN), do not dominate the image with large areas of color.

9.3 MULTI-VARIATE TYPOGRAPHIC THEMATIC MAPS

These labels can be enhanced with a variety of visual attributes and show more than one or two data values. Figure 9.5 shows an economic map of the global economy in 2010. The map depicts three ordered data variables: font weight to encode GDP per capita, font spacing for GDP growth, and font oblique angle for inflation (reverse slope for deflation, e.g. Ireland – IRL). Color shows a fourth variable: region. This representation can be used to answer simple questions of a single variable, for example, *Which countries have negative growth rates?* (Answer: Tightly spaced labels, such as Iceland – ISL, Ireland – IRL, and Greece – GRC). Complex questions across multiple variables can be answered as well, for example, *Which countries have high inflation, high growth and high GDP?* (Answer: steep italics, widely spaced, and heavyweight, such as Gabon – GAB and Argentina – ARG).

Note that font weight is used to indicate sequential ordered data with successively heavier weights indicating successively bigger GDP per capita. However, font oblique angle is used to represent diverging ordered data. That is, oblique angle has a natural zero position (vertical text with no slope in either direction) from which it can represent either positive or negative values using positive and negative slope. Weight does not have a natural zero value and is effective for representing magnitude. GDP growth ranges from negative to positive and is set to font spacing. This is also a diverging scale; here, the zero value is set at normal spacing, with negative values having a tighter spacing and positive values having a wider spacing. Negative spacing can lead to overlapping illegible letters – in this dataset, the negative values are in a very small range and there is only one level of negative spacing to minimize legibility issues.

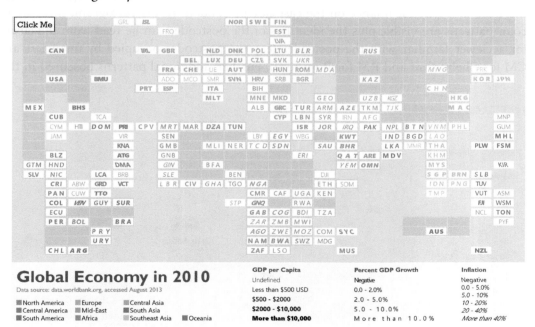

FIGURE 9.5   Multi-variate cartogram indicating data via color, font width, spacing, and oblique slope angle.

9.4 HANDLING LONG LABELS

The prior example used short mnemonic codes. Sometimes only long labels are available. Long labels can be difficult to fit into tight spaces and remain legible. In some cases, long labels have well-known contractions (e.g. DC for Washington D.C.) or can be truncated (e.g. San Fran… for San Francisco). Alternatively, long labels can extend beyond underlying marks as seen previously in Figure 5.7. These underlying marks do not need to be squarish – they can be elongated or based on an underlying grid where the bins are much wider than tall. Figure 9.6 shows a cartogram of Canadian metropolitan areas. Labels are associated with brightly colored fixed size areas. Long labels are not visually dominant; brightly colored fixed size areas are more visually prominent, as are heavyweight labels. For example, short heavyweight labels such as Toronto and Montreal are more prominent than long lightweight labels such as Kitchener-Cambridge-Waterloo or Abbotsford-Mission.

9.5 SCALING TO THOUSANDS OF LABELS

Multi-variate labels can scale up to thousands of labels. Figure 9.7 shows 2269 UK postcode areas plotted with a geographic projection; distances between labels are accurate, but most labels are illegible due to overplotting. Figure 9.8 shows the same data, where labels are pushed apart such that (most) labels are legible and local adjacencies are (mostly) retained.

Codes are comprised of one or two leading letters followed by one or two numbers. The letters are mnemonics for postal code districts (e.g. M for districts in Manchester). Label colors indicate the largest occupation relative to the national average. In both figures, color patterns are visible such as amber for mining in the north-east, green for agriculture in the west, and blue for finance on the east side of London. In the cartogram, these same color patterns are visible plus the identities of the postcodes can be read from the labels for a viewer familiar with the postcodes (e.g. the postcodes occupied by financiers are CM for Chelmsford and RM for Romsford). Further, additional patterns obscured in the

FIGURE 9.6   Long labels extend beyond their underlying markers.

geographic view are visible, for example, there are many transport postcodes on the west side of London (UX for Uxbridge).

Ordered data is shown with additional typographic attributes. Population is indicated via font weight and median age is shown with font oblique angle. For example, central London (EC and WC) has a small population indicated by lightweight codes. This population is also young, indicated by reverse slope, while the ring immediately around London is heavily populated with commuters who also tend to be young. Older populations (sloping to the right) tend to be more remote, such as rural Wales, for example, parts of LL (Llandudno) and SW (Swansea).

To support ever greater labels, interactive techniques such as zoom, or print-based approaches, can be used. Figure 9.9 shows three successive zoom levels starting across New York City (left), midtown Manhattan (middle), and a few blocks around the Rockefeller Center (right) from an interactive visualization by Uncharted Software (unchartedsoftware.github.io/salt-core/demos/taxi-twitter/). Labels are extracted from a few hundred million geo-tagged social media posts. The top hashtags per square are shown, using a *term frequency – inverse document frequency* algorithm (Salton and Buckley, 1988). At the far left, labels indicate large events and neighborhoods such as #nyfw for New York Fashion Week or #queens for the borough of Queens. At the far right, local landmarks occur in tags such as #moma (Museum of Modern Art), or #apple and #bergdorfgoodman for stores on Fifth Avenue.

9.6 NON-DISTORTED TYPOGRAPHIC MAPS

Thematic labels can be used on many types of maps, assuming that labels can be placed so that they remain legible. The next four thematic maps are based on Bertin's dataset of French departments, first introduced in Figure 2.9. In Figure 9.10 (left), a map with thematic labels indicates ordered data with four different visual attributes and set out on a Mercator projection; no cartogram is required as the labels can be set out with only minimal overlap.

Figure 9.10 (right) shows a hierarchy of labels placed on a Mercator projection such that labels align with the corresponding levels of administration. Here label size varies significantly, such that smaller labels can be plotted over top larger labels and the larger labels remain mostly decipherable. Small labels remain legible with the addition of a hairline halo (i.e. white outline) around each character, which aids discriminability if the small label is contained within a letter or two of a larger label (e.g. 44, 53, 85, and 49 overtop Pays de la Loire).

In both maps, the themes are visible, such as the predominance of agriculture in the west (green) or manufacturing in the north-east (red). In both, the automated label layout could be improved. For example, 75, 78, and P obscure some of the letters on Île-de-France in the right map.

9.7 TYPOGRAPHIC SCOPE: PARAGRAPHS AND GLYPHS

Thematic typography can extend to longer passages of text. Figure 9.11 (left) shows a map of France overlaid with paragraphs in nine regions. The color and the weight of the text

UK POSTCODE AREAS: GEOGRAPHIC LAYOUT

■ Agriculture, forestry and fishing
■ Mining and quarrying
■ Manufacturing
■ Electricity, gas, steam and AC supply
■ Water supply, sewerage, and waste management
■ Construction

■ Wholesale, retail and vehicle repair
■ Transport and storage
■ Accommodation and food service
■ Information and communication
■ Financial and insurance
■ Real estate

■ Professional, scientific and technical
■ Administrative and support service
■ Public administration, defence
■ Education
■ Health and social work
■ Other

Data sources: UK Office for National Statistics via nomisweb.co.uk; and postcodepal.com

FIGURE 9.7   UK Postcode areas, plotted with a Mercator projection. Many labels are overplotted. Legend is shared with next figure. *

is based on the underlying data. Each square of text is a data-driven narrative paragraph, with commentary regarding the region including names of some departments and characteristics of the data.

Typographic manipulation to convey data can also be applied to the shape and layout of the word as well as underlying letters. Figure 9.11 (right) shows occupations overlaid across

UK POSTCODE AREAS: CARTOGRAM LAYOUT

Median Age: 20 30 40 *50* *60*

Population (thousands):   <15   15-30   30-45   **45-75**   **75+**

Bedrooms per person: less than 1   GREATER THAN ONE

FIGURE 9.8   Same UK postcode areas, plotted as a cartogram. Labels are legible, local adjacencies remain, more patterns are visible, and individual postcodes can be identified.

the departments where the extents, orientation, and curvature of the label are used to indicate the areas of the primary occupation. Furthermore, the weight of each individual letter is manipulated to indicate the underlying population. For example, note the upper word services is particularly heavyweight for the letters e,r,v corresponding to the underlying region of Paris.

FIGURE 9.9   Localized hashtags from New York City down to a few blocks near Central Park.

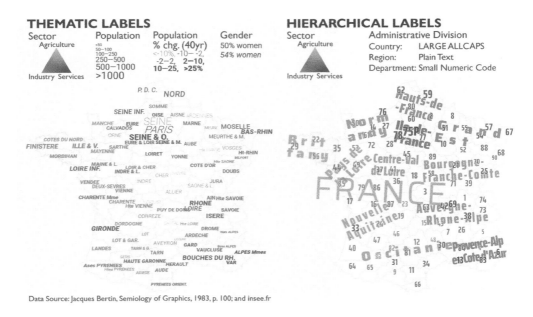

Data Source: Jacques Bertin, Semiology of Graphics, 1983, p. 100; and insee.fr

FIGURE 9.10   Multi-variate thematic maps using only text. Left: color, size, weight, and slope indicate various data variables. Right: administrative hierarchy indicated with typographic attributes.

9.8 DO TYPOGRAPHIC THEMATIC MAPS WORK?

There are many different criteria to consider regarding the effectiveness of label-based thematic maps. Two are considered here:

Information loss. The purpose of the maps in Figure 9.3 and Figure 9.4 is to depict health expenditures per country. Countries can be identified either by the detailed geographic shapes in the choropleth map or the labels on the cartogram. Health expenditures are identified by color. Information loss can be measured in both maps (when constrained to the same resolution). Using the default size of the choropleth map,

AREAS OF FRANCE

Brittany is largely agricultural with populations in departments such as Manche, Cotes du Nord, Finistere and Ille. & V.

Paris and surrounding areas as well as Nord are heavily populated with a strong bias towards manufacturing and services.

The region of Grand Est has a manufacturing focus particularly in Moselle, Bas-Rhin, Meurthe, Voseges, Ht-Rhin and tiny Belfort.

The Atlantic coast is Pays de la Loire. It is largely agricultural except for Loire Inf., which also has some manufacturing.

Most departments in central France, such as Cher, Nievre, Indre, Allier, Creuse, Correze, are sparsely populated and highly agricultural.

The eastern border is a mix of sparsely populated departments such as Jura and Savoie, and heavily populated Rhone and Loire.

The southwest is mostly agricultural, except for the more heavily populated Gironde which is more manufacturing and services based.

The south is similar to central France: sparsely populated and agricultural, except for the coast which is more services oriented.

The Mediterranean coast is much more services focused particularly Bouches du Rh., Var and Alpes Mmes.

Font weight indicates population. Color mix indicates occupation: green for agriculture, red for manufacturing and blue for services.
Data Source: Jacques Bertin, Semiology of Graphics, 1983, p. 100 and insee.fr.

PRIMARY OCCUPATION

Extent of word indicates area of primary occupation.
Weight of individual letters indicates underlying population.

FIGURE 9.11   Left: Data-driven paragraphs positioned relative to an underlying base map, indicating data via color and font weight, as well as narrative text. Right: Data-driven labels where the weight of each character is relative to the geographic location under the character.

44 out of 187 countries are too small for the fill color to be visible in the choropleth map; nearly a quarter of the values are lost. In the corresponding cartogram at the same size, each label is clearly visible and color identifiable with no data loss.

Identification and location tasks. Following the same approach as the National Geographic map literacy survey, simple tasks can be measured for correct responses (GfK 2006). The identification task requires identifying a highlighted country. The location task requires the viewer to indicate the color of a named country. A very small study with 17 participants and the two maps corresponding to Figure 9.3 and Figure 9.4 were tested (Brath and Banissi, *Multivariate label-based thematic maps*, 2017). Each viewer had a set of eight questions evenly split between the two tasks and the two map types for a total of 136 responses. The ISO-code labels outperformed the choropleth map for both tasks, as shown in Table 9.1.

The results indicate that typographic maps should be highly useful in some types of analysis of thematic maps.

TABLE 9.1   Percent of Correct Responses on Tasks for a Choropleth Map and Equivalent ISO-Code Map

Task	Choropleth Map (%)	ISO Code Map (%)	ISO Code Performance Relative to Choropleth
Identify	15	65	4.4×
Locate	53	85	1.6×
Total	34	75	2.2×

9.9 TYPOGRAPHIC ORDERING WITH OTHER ATTRIBUTES AND LAYOUTS

While the examples shown in this chapter have focused exclusively on thematic maps, ordered data has been used in many earlier examples, including:

- *Font weight.* Font weight allows for a few different levels to be perceived. One example is the bar chart of character qualifiers in Figure 6.12, where literal words indicate the qualities of the character while font weight indicates word frequency.

- *Size.* In constrained spaces, a small variation in type size may indicate ordered data, such as the variation in type size in the scatterplot in Figure 5.4. In the root word hierarchy (Figure 6.16), size is used to span across word stems to indicate the number of suffixes.

- *Color.* Variation in color brightness indicates ordered data in many examples. In Figure 6.5 left, colors vary in hue such that brightness is ordered (yellow-orange-red). In Figure 5.8, colors vary in a diverging scale (red-yellow-green) to indicate stock price change. Similarly, in Figure 6.6, the diverging color scale (red-blue-green) indicates price change of goods in the Consumer Price Index.

- *Font oblique angle.* is used in many examples in this chapter to indicate diverging data, for example, deviation from zero (Figure 9.5), from 100 (Figure 9.6) or above/below median (Figure 9.8).

- *Spacing.* In Figure 9.5, a few levels of spacing are used to indicate ordered data.

- *Underlines.* In the historic map in Figure 1.10, an ordering of underlines is used, sequenced dot, dash, thin single underline, thick single underline, thin double underline, and thick double underline.

- *Case.* In Figure 3.18, a sequential ordering of case is created starting from all lowercase to title case (first letter of each word capitalized), to small caps to all uppercase.

- *X-height, letterforms, and font width:* In Figure 3.26, orderings of both x-height and letterforms are shown. In Figure 4.5 K, an ordered x-height per syllable indicates musical pitch and an ordered letter-width indicates duration.

- *Alphanumeric ordering.* While it is feasible to order text alphabetically, such as the stacks of letters in the market profile chart in Figure 1.18, note that letters are arbitrary shapes and not ordered perceptually. That is, alphabetic ordering is not preattentive, whereas visual attributes such as font weight, oblique angle, color brightness, and size have varying degrees of being able to be perceived automatically.

Note that multiple visual attributes can be used to redundantly encode one dimension of ordered data. For example, the scatterplot Figure 5.4 represents population both by text size and color. Similarly, the stock graph Figure 5.8 represents price change using both color and font oblique angle (note the text Health Care Technology and Household Products in the upper right of the figure).

Visual attributes can be used to encode multiple dimensions of ordered data, such as the many examples in this chapter and also the distribution of U.S. State Statistics (Figure 6.5) which uses color and weight to encode two different ordered variables.

9.10 FURTHER READING

Thematic maps. Friendly and Wainer (2020) provide some history on thematic maps. MacEachren (1995) provides a theoretic basis for thematic maps. Dent (2009) provides a useful introduction to the many types and construction of thematic maps.

Geographic literacy. Many visualizations assume some levels of geographic and visual literacy on the part of the viewer. For a survey regarding the low levels of geographic literacy in young Americans, see the study commissioned by National Geographic (GfK 2006).

Cartogram layouts. There are many layout algorithms for creating cartograms. Henriques provides an overview of various algorithms in CARTO-SOM (2005) as well as Nusrat and Kobourov's *The State of the Art in Cartograms* (2016). In the examples shown in this chapter, two approaches are used: (1) A grid-based (or hex-based) approach which successively removes empty rows and columns while maintaining a minimum cell size so that all labels have equal area; and (2) a force-directed approach, which first transforms the data points into a graph using a Delaunay triangulation, followed by force-directed graph layout to adjust positioning while retaining local relationships. For better rectangular approaches than the examples shown in this chapter, consider Heilmann et al.'s *RecMap* (2004), or Cano et al.'s *Mosaic Drawings and Cartograms* (2015).

Parametric fonts and variable fonts can be used to create ordered typographic attributes such as x-height, font width, and so forth. References to parametric fonts were discussed in Section 3.8.

CHAPTER 10

Ratios and Quantitative Data

10.1 QUANTITATIVE DATA

Quantitative data are measured values expressed numerically. In visualizations, quantitative data may be represented using the same encodings as ordered data, such as brightness, blur, transparency, font-weight, and so on. However, these ordered encodings do not enable perceptual comparisons of ratios between adjacent items; perceptually one blue is not twice as blue as another blue. As such, the ordered encodings are limited to showing a few ordered levels rather than enabling perceptual comparisons of quantities.

Length and height are effective for comparing ratios. For example, texts describing steam engine whistles indicate signals with dashes, e.g. "one short whistle (–) is to apply the brakes. Two short blasts (– –) to take them off, … four long blasts (— — — —) call the flagman" (Roberts and Fracker 1875). These added marks can be visually compared.

Without adding dashes, however, length is difficult to indicate with text as word length is determined by spelling. The size of text is often constrained, meaning that labels may only have a few discrete sizes, thereby limiting the size of the text to an ordering with only a few perceptual levels. Word clouds do use size, but often no legend is included, thereby making it ambiguous as to whether the viewer should compare text area or text height.

Instead, consider two novel techniques for encoding quantities along a length of text using visual attributes, such as bold, underline, foreground color, background color, and so on:

- *Proportional encoding* **highlights a subset of text by applying a typographic attribute to a portion of text relative to the quantitative portion represented. For example,** the amount of bold applied to this paragraph indicates the quantitative value of 50%, as the number of characters in this paragraph is 342, of which the first 171 are bold.

- *Positional encoding* indicates a quantitative value by adding a unique format (such as an underline) or inserting a typographically differentiated character (such as a subscript or symbol) at a position relative to the quantitative portion represented. For example, the bold red character indicates the quantitative value of 50%, as the number* of characters in this paragraph is 510 and the 255th character is red. The asterisk indicates the value 2/3, inserted at the end of the word after the 340th character.

10.2 PROPORTIONS ALONG A STRING (BAR CHARTS WITH LONG LABELS)

Proportional encoding can encode quantitative data in text ranging from words to paragraphs. A single value or multiple values can be represented. There are some caveats associated with the type of format used.

10.2.1 Proportions along Words and Phrases

A simple example showing proportions along a string is shown in Chapter 3. It indicates character frequency in *Alice in Wonderland* using underlines (Figure 3.16). For a pragmatic use case, consider using this approach with search queries. Faceted search is a common design pattern for narrowing search results on shopping websites. However, some categories may have very few items, others have many. Providing an underline to indicate the number of search results per facet helps the user understand whether the click will show many or few results, as shown with the underlines on the facets in Figure 10.1 left.

Similarly, search autocomplete provides suggestions for popular queries, but does not differentiate between choices other than order. In Figure 10.1 (right), the top autocomplete suggestions for the search term *peanut* are shown in the order provided by Wikipedia. The background shading indicates the number of page views and the underline indicates the

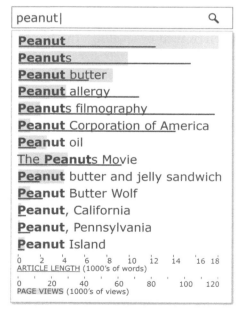

FIGURE 10.1   Mockup of proportional cues indicating quantities in faceted search (left) and search autocomplete (right).

article length: *Peanut* has the most views, *Peanuts filmography* is the longest entry. These visual statistics may help the viewer find the entry of interest.

10.2.2 Proportions along Lines of Text

There are many real-world applications where long phrases or short sentences appear in user interfaces, such as news headlines, search queries, search results, social media (e.g. tweets), titles for books, movies, songs and video games, email subject headings, pull quotes, file names, and so on. With each of these, there is additional data, such as dates, authors, sources, topics, document length, number of views, and so on. Interfaces that list these strings often don't show the metadata or use a grid of text where no data stands out.

Simple charts may not work well with this data; for example, most of the chart area may be used up with the labels, leaving little space for the plot area. Consider the bar chart of best-selling music singles in Figure 10.2. Long labels are necessary to uniquely identify the artist and title of the song. *You're the One That I Want* has been covered by other artists, but the best seller is the recording by John Travolta and Olivia Newton-John. Truncating the text is not a viable solution; neither the artist alone nor the song title alone uniquely identify the single.

Instead, Figure 10.3 shows the same chart where the label also encodes the quantity as indicated by both the length of bold and the length of the background highlight. By superimposing length on the label, both can span the full width of the chart. With the full width, the bars have greater resolution and allow finer comparisons between songs. With the full width, additional text can be added, such as the initial lyrics of the text providing more contextual information.

The added contextual information facilitates additional cognitive processing, such as recognition of lyrics. Furthermore, this added text can be used with interactions, such as highlighting the content of interest. For example, highlighting unique words indicates common keywords associated with top-selling songs as shown in Figure 10.4. In this example, *love* occurs three times in three songs (red highlight), while *Christmas* occurs five times (but in only two songs (green)), and *baby* occurs seven times in four songs (blue).

10.2.3 Proportions to Indicate Ranges

The indicated proportion does not need to start at the baseline: it can indicate ranges, such as used in box plots, range bars, candle sticks, and other plots. Figure 10.5 shows the estimated number of books published by leading authors.

The three charts represent ranges using different visual attributes:

- *Underline*. In the left chart, an underline indicates the range. Underlines can be drawn to a fraction of a character width (drawing the underline separately).

- *Bold*. In the center chart, font weight is used to indicate the range. The extreme difference in weights (using Source Code Pro Thin vs. Source Code Pro Black) makes long ranges visually pop-out (e.g. **ha Christie** and **Shakespeare**) but very short ranges can disappear in the gaps between letters (such as the range for Harold Robbins, which touches only a tiny portion of the letters **o** and **l**).

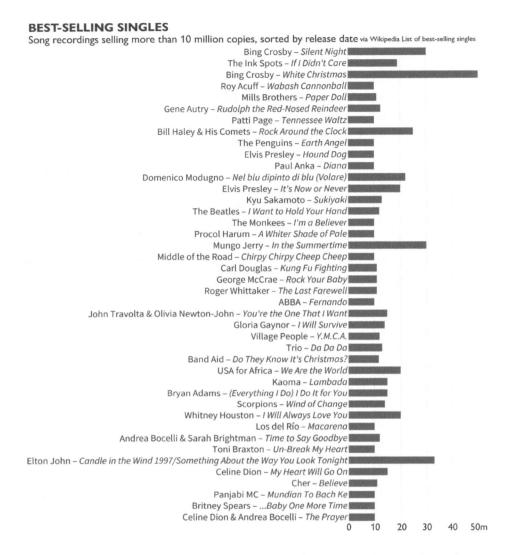

FIGURE 10.2   Bar chart of best-selling singles: the long labels leave little space for the bars.

- *Background color.* In the right chart, a background highlight has been used to indicate the range. Yellow is specifically used as it is familiar (like a highlighter pen) and it maintains high legibility with a high contrast between the dark letterforms and the light highlight.

Note that the extremely narrow ranges for Harold Robbins and J.K. Rowling are not particularly noticeable with any of the representations, suggesting that the technique may be less suitable for narrow ranges or that a minimum range size is required.

10.2.4 Proportions, Distributions, and Areas

Rows can be sorted by their quantitative values. Viewers can then easily find and read the text associated with quantitative values such as minimum, maximum, or median; or assess the overall shape of the distribution.

BEST-SELLING SINGLES
Song recordings selling more than 10 million copies, sorted by release date via Wikipedia List of best-selling singles
Bing Crosby – *Silent Night* ~ Silent night, Holy night, All is calm, All is bright, Round yon virgin mother and chi
The Ink Spots – *If I Didn't Care* ~ If I didn't care more than words can say, If I didn't care, would I feel this way? I
Bing Crosby – *White Christmas* ~ I'm dreaming of a white Christmas, Just like the ones we used to know, Wh
Roy Acuff – *Wabash* Cannonball ~ From the great Atlantic ocean to the wide Pacific shore, From the queen of flo
Mills Brothers – *Paper Doll* ~ I'm gonna buy a paper doll that I can call my own, A doll that other fellows cannot :
Gene Autry – *Rudolph the* Red-Nosed Reindeer ~ You know Dasher and Dancer and Prancer and Vixen, Comet an
Patti Page – *Tennessee* Waltz ~ I was dancing with my darling to the Tennessee Waltz, When an old friend I happ
Bill Haley & His Comets – *Rock Around the Clock* ~ One, two, three o'clock, four o'clock, rock, Five, six, seven o'c
The Penguins – *Earth* Angel ~ Earth angel, earth angel, Will you be mine?, My darling dear, Love you all the time,
Elvis Presley – *Hound* Dog ~ Hey baby I'm here to tell you about yourself, You ain't nothin' but a hound dog, scra
Paul Anka – *Diana* ~ I'm so young and you're so old, This, my darling, I've been told, I don't care just what they s
Domenico Modugno – *Nel blu dipinto di blu (Volare)* ~ Sometimes the world is a valley of heartaches and tears, .
Elvis Presley – *It's Now or Never* ~ It's now or never, Come hold me tight, Kiss me my darling, Be mine tonight, '
Kyu Sakamoto – *Sukiyaki* ~ Let's look up as we walk, so that the tears don't spill, Remembering that spring day,
The Beatles – *I Want to Hold Your Hand* ~ Oh yeah I tell you somethin', I think you'll understand, When I say that
The Monkees – *I'm a* Believer ~ I thought love was only true in fairy tales, Meant for someone else but not for me
Procol Harum – *A Whiter Shade of Pale* ~ We skipped the light fandango, Turned cartwheels 'cross the floor, I wa
Mungo Jerry – *In the Summertime* ~ In the summertime when the weather is hot, You can stretch right up and
Middle of the Road – *Chirpy Chirpy Cheep Cheep* ~ Where's your momma gone, Little baby bird, Where's your mo
Carl Douglas – *Kung Fu* Fighting ~ Now here it is, one to make you move, Something with a funky kung fu groove
George McCrae – *Rock* Your Baby ~ Sexy mama, Woman, take me in your arms, Rock your baby, Woman, take me
Roger Whittaker – *The* Last Farewell ~ There's a ship lies rigged and ready in the harbor, Tomorrow for old engla
ABBA – *Fernando* ~ Can you hear the drums Fernando, I remember long ago another starry night like this, In the
John Travolta & Olivia Newton-John – *You're the One That I Want* ~ I got chills, They're multiplying, And I'm losi
Gloria Gaynor – *I Will Survive* ~ At first I was afraid, I was petrified, Kept thinking I could never live without you b
Village People – *Y.M.C.A.* ~ Young man, there's no need to feel down, I said, young man, pick yourself off the gro
Trio – *Da Da Da* ~ Aha aha aha, Aha, aha, aha, Was ist los mit dir mein Schatz? Aha, Geht es immer nur bergab? A
Band Aid – *Do They Know* It's Christmas? ~ It's Christmas time, there's no need to be afraid, At Christmas time, w
USA for Africa – *We Are the World* ~ There comes a time, When we heed a certain call, When the world must con
Kaoma – *Lambada* ~ Chorando se foi quem um dia so me fez chorar, Chorando se foi quem um dia so me fez ch
Bryan Adams – *(Everything I Do)* I Do It for You ~ Look into my eyes, You will see, what you mean to me, Search y
Scorpions – *Wind of Change* ~ I follow the Moskva, Down to Gorky Park, Listening to the wind of change, An Aug
Whitney Houston – *I Will Always Love You* ~ If I should stay, I'll only be in your way, So I'll go, but I know I'll, Thi
Los del Río – *Macarena* ~ Dale a tu cuerpo alegria Macarena, Que tu cuerpo es pa' darle alegria y cosa buena, Da
Andrea Bocelli & Sarah Brightman – *Time to Say Goodbye* ~ Quando sono sola, Sogno all'orizzonte, E mancan le
Toni Braxton – *Un-Break My Heart ~ Don't leave me in all this pain , Don't leave me out in the rain , Come back a
Elton John – *Candle in the Wind 1997/Something About the Way You Look Tonight ~ Goodbye Norma Jean, Tho
Celine Dion – *My Heart Will Go* On ~ Every night in my dreams, I see you, I feel you, That is how I know you, go or
Cher – *Believe* ~ No matter how hard I try, You keep pushing me aside, And I can't break through, There's no talk
Panjabi MC – *Mundian* To Bach Ke ~ It's the Roc in the building, Calib, Ramel, Tarrell in the house, Mimian to but
Britney Spears – *...Baby One More Time ~ Oh baby, baby, how was I supposed to know, That something wasn't r
Celine Dion & Andrea Bocelli – *The Prayer* ~ I pray you'll be our eyes and watch us where we go, And help us to b

```
0        5       10       15       20       25       30       35       40       45      50m
```

FIGURE 10.3   Proportion of bold and highlight creates bars indicating the number of best-selling singles. The space available permits a portion of the opening lyrics to also be shown.

Consider opinion analysis. Movie reviews contain a narrative opinion and associated metadata such as a rating. When there are hundreds of reviews per movie, it is difficult to assess and compare movies; instead, for many cinema websites, reviews are reduced to an average score. This reduction misses the range of reviews (are there any outliers?) and it misses reviewers' observations (are they objecting to the plot, acting, or other aspect?).

Instead, movie reviews can be depicted together with their scores as proportions. Figure 10.6 is a set of movie reviewers' comments regarding the movie *Frozen* from *rotten-tomatoes.com*. Long comments are truncated, short comments are padded with dots. All reviews have an associated score, which are normalized 1–10. There are over 200 reviews of the movie; the reviews are sorted and sampled at equal intervals to get a representative subset of reviews. The length of bold indicates the movie reviewer score; a low score with almost no bold indicates a poor review, a high score is almost entirely bold. The median is around eight, and range from near zero to near perfect ten. The viewer can immediately

BEST-SELLING SINGLES
Song recordings selling more than 10 million copies, sorted by release date *via Wikipedia List of best-selling singles*
Bing Crosby – _Silent Night_ ~ Silent night, Holy night, All is calm, All is bright, Round yon virgin mother and chi
The Ink Spots – _If I Didn't Care_ ~ If I didn't care more than words can say, If I didn't care, would I feel this way? I
Bing Crosby – _White Christmas_ ~ I'm dreaming of a white Christmas, Just like the ones we used to know, WI
Roy Acuff – _Wabash C_annonball ~ From the great Atlantic ocean to the wide Pacific shore, From the queen of flo
Mills Brothers – _Paper D_oll ~ I'm gonna buy a paper doll that I can call my own, A doll that other fellows cannot
Gene Autry – _Rudolph the_ Red-Nosed Reindeer ~ You know Dasher and Dancer and Prancer and Vixen, Comet ar
Patti Page – _Tennes_see Waltz ~ I was dancing with my darling to the Tennessee Waltz, When an old friend I happ
Bill Haley & His Comets – _Rock Around the Clock_ ~ One, two, three o'clock, four o'clock, rock, Five, six, seven o'
The Penguins – _Earth_ Angel ~ Earth angel, earth angel, Will you be mine?, My darling dear, Love you all the time,
Elvis Presley – _Hound_ Dog ~ Hey baby I'm here to tell you about yourself, You ain't nothin' but a hound dog, scr
Paul Anka – _Diana_ ~ I'm so young and you're so old, This, my darling, I've been told, I don't care just what they s
Domenico Modugno – _Nel blu dipinto di blu (Vo_lare) ~ Sometimes the world is a valley of heartaches and tears,
Elvis Presley – _It's Now or Never_ ~ It's now or never, Come hold me tight, Kiss my my darling, Be mine tonight,
Kyu Sakamoto – _Sukiyaki_ ~ Let's look up as we walk, so that the tears don't spill, Remembering that spring day
The Beatles – _I Want to_ Hold Your Hand ~ Oh yeah I tell you somethin', I think you'll understand, When I say that
The Monkees – _I'm a_ Believer ~ I thought love was only true in fairy tales, Meant for someone else but not for me
Procol Harum – _A Wh_iter Shade of Pale ~ We skipped the light fandango, Turned cartwheels 'cross the floor, I wa
Mungo Jerry – _In the Summertime_ ~ In the summertime when the weather is hot, You can stretch right up and
Middle of the Road – Chirpy Chirpy Cheep Cheep ~ Where's your momma gone, Little baby bird, Where's your mc
Carl Douglas – _Kung Fu_ Fighting ~ Now here it is, one to make you move, Something with a funky kung fu groove
George McCrae – _Rock_ Your Baby ~ Sexy mama, Woman, take me in your arms, Rock your baby, Woman, take m
Roger Whittaker – _The_ Last Farewell ~ There's a ship lies rigged and ready in the harbor, Tomorrow for old engla
ABBA – _Fernando_ ~ Can you hear the drums Fernando, I remember long ago another starry night like this, In the
John Travolta & Olivia Newton-John – You're the One That I Want ~ I got chills, They're multiplying, And I'm losi
Gloria Gaynor – _I Will Survive_ ~ At first I was afraid, I was petrified, Kept thinking I could never live without you t
Village People – _Y.M.C.A._ ~ Young man, there's no need to feel down, I said, young man, pick yourself off the gro
Trio – _Da Da Da_ ~ Aha aha aha, Aha, aha, aha, Was ist los mit dir mein Schatz? Aha, Geht es immer nur bergab? A
Band Aid – _Do They Know_ It's Christmas? ~ It's Christmas time, there's no need to be afraid, At Christmas time, w
USA for Africa – _We Are the World_ ~ There comes a time, When we heed a certain call, When the world must con
Kaoma – _Lambada_ ~ Chorando se foi quem um dia so me fez chorar, Chorando se foi quem um dia so me fez ch
Bryan Adams – _(Everything I Do)_ I Do It for You ~ Look into my eyes, You will see, what you mean to me, Search y
Scorpions – _Wind of Change_ ~ I follow the Moskva, Down to Gorky Park, Listening to the wind of change, An Aug
Whitney Houston – _I Will Always_ Love You ~ If I should stay, I'll only be in your way, So I'll go, but I know I'll, Thir
Los del Río – _Macarena_ ~ Dale a tu cuerpo alegria Macarena, Que tu cuerpo es pa' darle alegria y cosa buena, Da
Andrea Bocelli & Sarah Brightman – Time to Say Goodbye ~ Quando sono sola, Sogno all'orizzonte, E mancan le
Toni Braxton – _Un-B_reak My Heart ~ Don't leave me in all this pain , Don't leave me out in the rain , Come back a
Elton John – _Candle in the Wind 1997/Something About the Way You Lo_ok Tonight ~ Goodbye Norma Jean, Tho
Celine Dion – _My Heart Will Go_ On ~ Every night in my dreams, I see you, I feel you, That is how I know you, go or
Cher – _Believe_ ~ No matter how hard I try, You keep pushing me aside, And I can't break through, There's no tall
Panjabi MC – _Mundia_n To Bach Ke ~ It's the Roc in the building, Calib, Ramel, Tarrell in the house, Mimian to but
Britney Spears – _...Baby_ One More Time ~ Oh baby, baby, how was I supposed to know, That something wasn't r
Celine Dion & Andrea Bocelli – The Prayer ~ I pray you'll be our eyes and watch us where we go, And help us to t
0   5   10   15   20   25   30   35   40   45   50m

FIGURE 10.4   Proportion of bold and underline indicate the number of single song recordings sold, while colored highlights indicate common terms across best-selling songs, such as *love, baby,* and *Christmas.*

read the beginning of the associated text, for example, the lowest score review starts with "Frozen is a glacially stiff, perpetually unamusing animated musical" while the top score review starts with "Frozen is an exhilarating, joyous, human story"

Proportions on opinions can be used to compare multiple movies. The total amount of bold across the set of reviews provides an aggregate of the overall reviews. More bold overall indicates higher scores overall. Figure 10.7 shows the introductory words for 20 reviewers for three popular animated movies. Length of bold is also complemented with background shading corresponding to the score for each line. One can immediately see that *Toy Story 3* has far more blue area than the green area of *Despicable Me 2*. Further, *Despicable Me 2* ranges from a low near one to a high of ten forming a shallow slope along the right edge of the green curve indicating significant divergence in opinion. In comparison, *How to Train Your Dragon* has a steeply sloped curve (right edge of the yellow highlight) indicating a narrow range from five to nine.

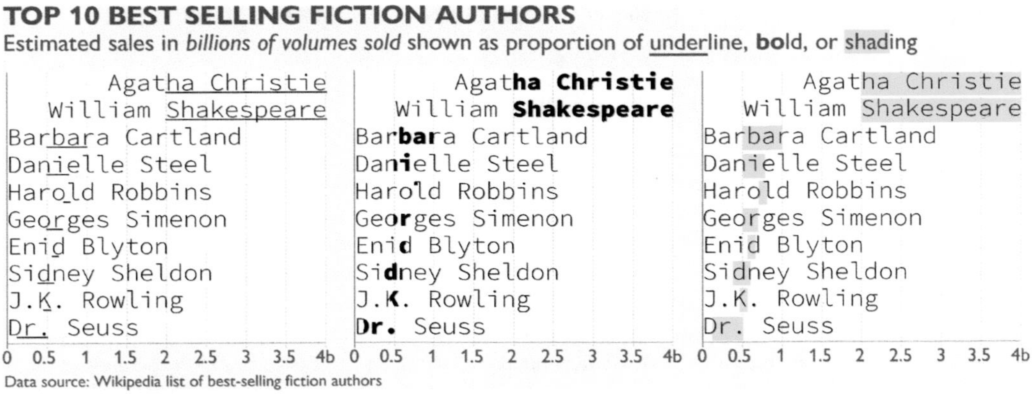
TOP 10 BEST SELLING FICTION AUTHORS
Estimated sales in billions of volumes sold shown as proportion of underline, bold, or shading
Agatha Christie
William Shakespeare
Barbara Cartland
Danielle Steel
Harold Robbins
Georges Simenon
Enid Blyton
Sidney Sheldon
J.K. Rowling
Dr. Seuss
0 0.5 1 1.5 2 2.5 3 3.5 4b
Data source: Wikipedia list of best-selling fiction authors

FIGURE 10.5 Ranges of estimated book sales per author represented with underlines (left), bold (center), and shading (right).

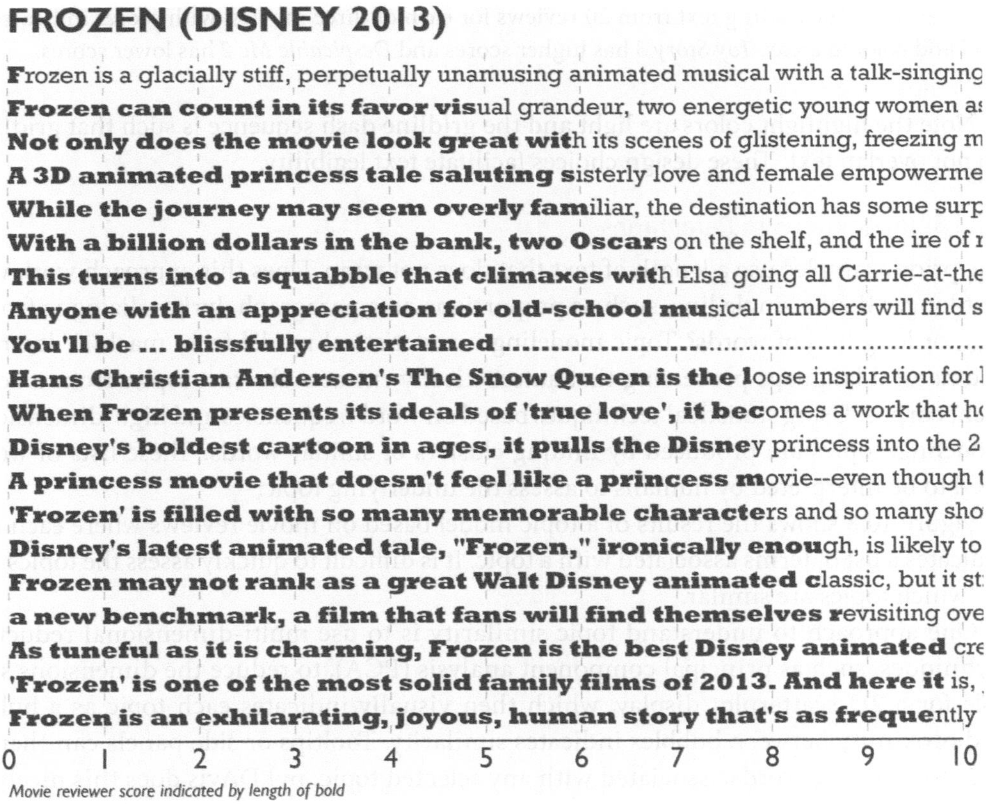
FROZEN (DISNEY 2013)
Frozen is a glacially stiff, perpetually unamusing animated musical with a talk-singing
Frozen can count in its favor visual grandeur, two energetic young women as
Not only does the movie look great with its scenes of glistening, freezing m
A 3D animated princess tale saluting sisterly love and female empowerme
While the journey may seem overly familiar, the destination has some surp
With a billion dollars in the bank, two Oscars on the shelf, and the ire of r
This turns into a squabble that climaxes with Elsa going all Carrie-at-the
Anyone with an appreciation for old-school musical numbers will find s
You'll be ... blissfully entertained ....
Hans Christian Andersen's The Snow Queen is the loose inspiration for
When Frozen presents its ideals of 'true love', it becomes a work that h
Disney's boldest cartoon in ages, it pulls the Disney princess into the 2
A princess movie that doesn't feel like a princess movie--even though t
'Frozen' is filled with so many memorable characters and so many sho
Disney's latest animated tale, "Frozen," ironically enough, is likely to
Frozen may not rank as a great Walt Disney animated classic, but it st
a new benchmark, a film that fans will find themselves revisiting ove
As tuneful as it is charming, Frozen is the best Disney animated cre
'Frozen' is one of the most solid family films of 2013. And here it is,
Frozen is an exhilarating, joyous, human story that's as frequently
0 1 2 3 4 5 6 7 8 9 10
Movie reviewer score indicated by length of bold

FIGURE 10.6 Twenty representative movie reviews for *Frozen*. Length of bold indicates review score.

DESPICABLE ME 2

I guess it shouldn't be a surprise that
The script's jumble of plot asides and
The beautiful digital animation is sta
Given the outlandish premise, you'll v
The original had something equally i
How do you tell a story about a bad
Neither directors Pierre Coffin and (
You can wish for a tighter plot, yet
If Despicable Me 2 feels like little m
It's all about The Minions................
[It's] fun. It's cheerful. It's lollipop (
While Despicable Me 2 isn't the mo
this movie never quite reaches the
Exactly what a cartoon should be. /
Despicable Me 2 feels like a opportu
Not only a fun cartoon but - that i
Dreamworks' Madagascar and Shre
Simply works because the filmmak
What language do the Minions, th
The pratfalls, gizmos and Loony '

0 1 2 3 4 5 6 7 8 9 10

HOW TO TRAIN YOUR DRAGON

Everything from the angle of the sh(
A visually stimulating, but slightly i
While the 3D-animated experiences :
The 3D is justified, mostly by flying
The 3-D throughout How to Train Y
The swarming dragon attacks may
It is, quite simply, a good story tol
The production's magnificent vibe
Three cheers to DreamWorks for zi
Each time I go to the movies, I'm
Beautifully animated, genuinely to
Beautifully animated and superbly
It's a flick full of adrenaline, and :
Kids will absolutely adore and thri
The dragon designs are wonderful,
One of the pleasures in this wise,
Sanders and DeBlois have given D
The film truly starts to soar when
How To Train Your Dragon may l
With its messages about acceptan

0 1 2 3 4 5 6 7 8 9 10

TOY STORY 3

[VIDEO ESSAY] An obvious split betw
"Toy Story 3" is a bit on the safe s
Good but not great.......................
I expect its target audience will lov
The glow of originality may have
After all is said and done, Toy Stol
Can we put Pixar in charge of eve
Pixar has done it again, extending
The film succeeds mostly because
Toy Story is a funny, touching and
A brief flashback sequence filled v
Locating a winsome blend of pepj
I tried stuffing paper into my no:
It makes sense that the film was
This is another home run for Pix
The eternal questions that the fir
In execution, entertainment value
How does Pixar keep doing it? I t
How the animation wizards at Pi:
On a scale of one to ten, Toy Stol

0 1 2 3 4 5 6 7 8 9 10

Movie reviewer score indicated by length of bold. Area of highlight indicates aggregate opinion.

FIGURE 10.7 The leading text from 20 reviews for each of three movies, with scores indicated by bold and colored areas. *Toy Story 3* has higher scores and *Despicable Me 2* has lower scores.

Note the highlight colors are light and the gridline dash sequence is such that gridlines do not overlap text. These design choices facilitate text legibility.

10.2.5 Proportions in Paragraphs

The prior examples use a length of text that does not wrap. Does this approach work with text longer than a single line, such as proportions on a paragraph, lyrics, dialogue from a play, or long lists of words? Topic modeling is a statistical model from machine learning and natural language processing that automatically extracts abstract topics from a document corpus. Using statistical techniques based on word frequencies and high-dimensional modeling, topics are produced by finding clusters of similar words. These lists of words need to be interpreted by humans to assess the underlying topic.

Figure 10.8 shows the results of a topic model based on movie reviews where each row indicates a list of terms associated with a topic. It is difficult to quickly assess the topics and see which topics are similar.

One approach to understand topic similarity is to use multi-dimensional reduction techniques, such as principal component analysis (PCA), to reduce the dimensions suitable for a 2D scatterplot display, which then visually indicates each topic as a bubble and proximity between bubbles indicates similarity. Tooltips or side panels can then be used to show the words associated with any selected topic. pyLDAvis does this nicely, as shown in Figure 10.9. However, only one topic at a time can be inspected, thereby relying on the user to remember and recall words as they move between topics, which increases cognitive load.

Topic	Word list (ordered by frequency in topic)
1	film, movie, time, good, characters, character, films, story, make, people, scenes, director, scene, great, doesnt, plot, end, work, n
2	life, world, story, city, dark, sense, young, man, death, human, power, true, place, god, art, visual, society, white, message, mr, el
3	movie, bad, good, dont, movies, im, guy, thing, plot, time, hes, worst, funny, people, youre, stupid, minutes, big, doesnt, theyre,
4	love, family, life, mother, father, woman, son, romantic, home, husband, comedy, daughter, man, wife, parents, married, children,
5	action, crime, cop, thriller, police, murder, killer, de, jackie, prison, carter, fiction, tarantino, pulp, cops, brown, willis, agent, part
6	alien, aliens, science, effects, star, space, planet, earth, fi, mars, sci, fiction, trek, special, computer, series, action, human, mission
7	funny, comedy, jokes, humor, movie, show, laughs, truman, allen, carrey, hes, woody, hilarious, jim, gags, laugh, joke, comic, brot
8	war, men, american, battle, army, black, political, soldiers, ryan, spielberg, private, history, action, president, military, leader, stat
9	disney, animated, animation, wars, story, voice, star, tarzan, lucas, menace, phantom, mulan, jedi, family, special, young, effects, c
10	school, high, sex, comedy, sam, things, max, chris, football, funny, student, teacher, girl, pie, bill, wild, friends, kevin, american, t
11	horror, film, vampire, original, effects, version, special, house, vampires, book, witch, video, blair, scary, spawn, dvd, blade, films,
12	ship, effects, godzilla, deep, special, disaster, action, giant, apes, summer, joe, crew, monster, impact, big, island, harry, water, tea
13	sex, julia, comedy, wedding, drug, joe, roberts, party, vegas, writer, drugs, singer, 54, porn, romantic, las, hollywood, disco, studic
14	action, jackie, chan, fight, hong, van, kong, chinese, bond, arts, martial, plot, films, damme, master, scenes, fu, sequences, kung,
15	scream, horror, killer, smith, summer, 2, kevin, julie, slasher, sequel, wild, urban, movie, jay, west, bob, movies, death, 3, teen, g
16	10, music, love, 7, titanic, 8, musical, rock, story, songs, flynt, 5, band, jack, cameron, annie, show, critique, rose, great, dicaprio
17	murphy, john, hes, eddie, funny, brooks, nights, boogie, dog, jack, comedy, melvin, anderson, bulworth, cusack, cast, bobby, beatt
18	good, williams, dr, lawyer, case, evil, patch, character, courtroom, austin, powers, death, scene, hes, wife, young, adams, hunting,
19	batman, robin, arnold, harry, cage, mr, devil, schwarzenegger, george, wife, schumacher, joel, action, lebowski, dude, hes, welles, l
20	files, ryan, movie, tom, series, nbsp, hanks, sixth, oscar, boy, christmas, sense, ghost, show, meg, cole, television, mulder, dog, du

dataset via Pang and Lee, 2004; processed with pyLDAvis by Ben Mabey, ported from LDAvis by Sievert and Shirley 2014

FIGURE 10.8 Twenty topics each with more than 20 terms. No individual terms or categories stand out.

Instead of accessing topic word lists one at a time, these word lists can be shown directly in the plot by enlarging each bubble on the plot into a rectangle and shifting the layout so that adjacent relationships are maintained, similar to the cartograms previously shown in Chapter 9. Then, all the words for all the topics can be displayed explicitly in each rectangle, making it easy to compare words between adjacent (similar) topics. And proportional formats can be used to indicate quantitative data associated with the topics and the words.

Figure 10.10 shows the same movie review topics as in the prior two images. Underline length spans across multiple words and lines, indicating the prevalence of the topic across all documents. In this example, topic #1 corresponds to about half of the corpus, and the words indicate generic terms likely occurring in almost every review.

The yellow bar behind each word indicates the frequency of that word within the topic. For example, *alien* and *aliens* are the most relevant frequent terms associated with topic #6 at the top of the figure.

Word weight indicates the ratio of the word frequency within the topic to overall word frequency; words that are highly unique to a topic will be heavyweight, while words occurring in other topics will be lighter weight. Thus, attending to the heavyweight words in a topic visually filters to the words that make the topic unique. For example, at the top, #6 is a topic about *aliens, space, mars, trek,* and *starships*. Immediately below is topic #11, about *vampires* and *witches*, while topic #12, to the left, are monster movies, with words such as *godzilla, apes, armageddon, monsters,* and *snakes*. The similarity of the topics at the top (conveying aspects of adventure) can be contrasted with topics at the

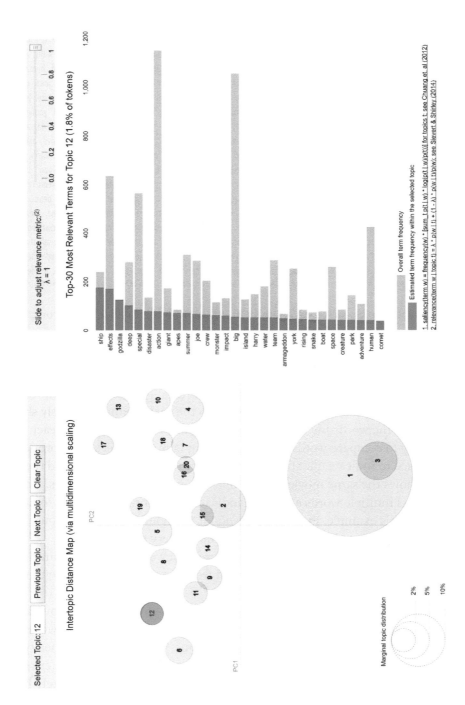

FIGURE 10.9   Twenty topics using a scatterplot to indicate similarity by distance, with details for selected topic.

MOVIE TOPICS
Topic adjacency, terms, frequency & uniqueness

#6. alien aliens
science effects star
space planet earth fi
mars sci fiction trek
special **computer** series
action human mission
film **species troopers**
starship

#12. ship effects
godzilla deep special
disaster action **giant**
apes summer joe crew
monster impact big
island harry water team
armageddon york **rising**
snake

#11. horror film
vampire original
effects version special
house **vampires** book
witch video **blair scary**
spawn dvd blade films
blood comic **hollow**
woods **haunting**

#9. disney animated
animation wars story
voice star **tarzan lucas**
menace phantom mulan
jedi family special
young effects original
kids **disneys** king
computer **bugs**

#8. war men american
battle **army** black
political **soldiers** ryan
spielberg private
history action
president **military**
leader states country
soldier saving **united**

#14. action **jackie chan**
fight **hong** van **kong**
chinese bond **arts**
martial plot films
damme master scenes **fu**
sequences **kung**
wrestling king **li**
american

#5. action **crime cop**
thriller police murder
killer de jackie prison
carter fiction
tarantino pulp cops
brown willis agent
partner plot **criminal**
fbi lee

#15. scream horror
killer smith summer 2
kevin **julie slasher**
sequel wild **urban** movie
jay west bob movies
death 3 teen genre
legend williamson

#2. life world story
city **dark** sense young
man death human **power**
true place **god art**
visual **society** white
message mr effective
images emotional

#1. film movie time
good characters
character films story
make people scenes
director scene great
doesnt plot end work
makes man made movies
back

#19. batman robin
arnold harry cage mr
devil schwarzenegger
george wife **schumacher**
joel action **lebowski**
dude hes **welles** big **8mm**
clooney money plot **noir**

#16. 10 music love **7**
titanic 8 musical rock
story songs **flynt 5**
band jack **cameron annie**
show **critique** rose
great **dicaprio larry**
chris

#20. files ryan movie
tom series **nbsp hanks**
sixth oscar boy
christmas sense **ghost**
show **meg cole**
television **mulder** dog
duchovny poker beloved
bob

#3. movie bad good dont
movies im guy thing
plot time hes **worst**
funny people youre
stupid minutes big
doesnt theyre didnt
scene pretty

#17. murphy john hes
eddie funny **brooks**
nights boogie dog jack
comedy **melvin anderson**
bulworth cusack cast
bobby beatty political
rick james **bowfinger**
campaign

#18. good **williams** dr
lawyer case evil **patch**
character **courtroom**
austin powers death
scene hes wife young
adams hunting robin
hopkins pitt bill
relationship

#7. funny comedy **jokes**
humor movie show **laughs**
truman allen carrey hes
woody hilarious jim
gags laugh **joke** comic
brothers big 2 girls tv

#13. sex **julia** comedy
wedding drug joe
roberts party **vegas**
writer **drugs singer 54**
porn romantic **las**
hollywood **disco** studio
lucy lynch mike friends

#10. school high sex
comedy **sam** things **max**
chris **football** funny
student teacher girl
pie bill **wild** friends
kevin american teen
girls van **bacon**

#4. love family life
mother father woman **son**
romantic home **husband**
comedy **daughter** man
wife **parents married**
children relationship
story year town day
young

Rectangles are topics. Underline indicates prevalence of topic across all docs. Weight indicates uniqueness of word to topic. Yellow bar indicates term frequency in topic.
Based on pyLDAvis demo, trained on LDA model in R, using a corpus of 2000 movie reviews by Pang and Lee, ACL, 2004.

FIGURE 10.10 Each box shows terms associated with movie topics. Similar topics are closer together. Underline indicates prevalence of the topic across all documents, font weight indicates most unique terms, and the yellow bar indicates the frequency of the word in the topic. The top topic (#6) is about aliens, immediately below is about vampires (#11), to the left are monster movies (#12).

bottom, such as #13, #10, and #11 with terms such as *julia, wedding, vegas, porn, school, football, romantic, husband,* and *married* (conveying aspects of romance and relationships). Light words tend to occur across many topics and thus are less likely to uniquely identify the topic, for example, the term *comedy* is lightweight and occurs in five of the six topics at the bottom of the image, or the term *funny* occurs in four topics (#3,7,10,17). Any term can be highlighted to see where it occurs across topics by using a browser-based find functionality or point and click highlighting.

10.2.6 Stacked Proportions

Much like a stacked bar chart, proportions can also be stacked. A salient categorical attribute should be used to differentiate each level in the stack. In Figure 10.11, Bertin's occupation dataset is shown, with each department represented as a single row. Instead of the simple department name, the start of the initial paragraph from Wikipedia is shown for each department. Portions of the text are differentiated using color and typeface to indicate proportions of occupation in each department as indicated by the axis along the top of the chart. The rows are sorted by proportion of population employed in agriculture.

In the top third of this chart, only typeface is used to differentiate categories: an old humanist font with a low x-height for agriculture (Garamond), a chunky slab-serif with a medium x-height for industry (Rockwell), and a modern simple sans serif with a high x-height for services (Roboto). Note that the normal weight for Rockwell is heavier than the normal weight for the other two. Overall, the different fonts have a significant difference in x-height, weight, and letterform, thereby making the three categories readily perceivable.

In the central third of this chart, only color is used to differentiate categories. Green is used for agriculture, which leverages a semantically meaningful color association to the category, that is, green is commonly associated with vegetation. Red is used for manufacturing, a color associated with heat and activity. Blue is used for services, a calmer, more passive color. In all cases, the colors used are not fully bright, so that the text maintains a strong contrast against the background. Again, the three colors are readily perceivable, if the viewer does not have any deficiencies in color perception, such as red-green color blindness.

In the bottom third of the chart, the three categories are dually encoded using both color and font (redundant encoding was introduced in Section 4.3). As such, the dual encoding increases the visual differentiation between the categories and aids perception if the viewer does not perceive one of the encodings. The semantic associations also aid in decoding, making the viewer less likely to need to cross-reference the legend.

A second variable is also encoded in each line of text. The length of the underline represents the total population in each department, as indicated by the axis at the bottom of the visualization.

As with the previous example, the viewer can attend to macro patterns, such as a relatively consistent portion of the population employed in services across all departments (with a few outliers). The viewer can also read the department name, as well as the introductory sentence(s) from Wikipedia, which typically indicates where the department is located in France, the origin of the name of the department, and potentially the associated prefecture (the administrative city associated with the department).

10.2.7 Multiple Proportions

The previous example encoded two different metrics per row of text: occupation with color and font; and population with underline. Can this be extended further; can more quantitative values be represented on a row of text?

FRENCH DEPARTMENTS POPULATION & OCCUPATIONS
Agriculture in Garamond Green, **Manufacturing in Rockwell Red**, Services in Roboto Blue

| 0 | 20 | 40 | 60 | 80 | 100% |

The Gers is in the Languedoc-Roussillon-Midi-Pyrenees region in the south**west of France** named after the Gers F
Creuse is in central France named after the river Creuse. Gueret is the **prefecture. It is** in the region Nouvelle-Aqui
Lozere is in the region of Languedoc-Roussillon-Midi-Pyrenees in sou**thern France** near the Massif Central. It is r
Lot is in the southwest of France named after the Lot River. Caho**rs is the prefec**ture. It is in the region Occitanie
Mayenne is in northwest France named after the Mayenne River. **Mayenne is part** of the current region of Pays c
Tarn-et-Garonne is in the southwest of France. It is traversed by **the Rivers Tar**n and Garonne, from which it tak
The Vendee is in the Pays-de-la-Loire region in west-central France, **on the Atlan**tic Ocean. The name Vendee is
Dordogne is in southwestern France, with its prefecture in Peri**gueux. The dep**artment is located in the region o
Cantal is in south-central France, with its capital at Aurillac. Its **residents are** known as Cantalians (French: Cant
Cotes-d'Armor formerly named Cotes-du-Nord, is in the nort**h of Brittany, i**n northwestern France. Saint-Brieuc
Landes is in southwestern France. Mont-de-Marsan is the pre**fecture. It is in** the region Nouvelle-Aquitaine
Lot-et-Garonne is in the southwest of France named after the **Lot and Garonne** rivers. Agen is the prefecture. It i
Morbihan is in Brittany, situated in the northwest of France. **It is named after** the Morbihan (small sea in Breton
Correze is in south-western France, named after the river **Correze. The de**partment are called
Manche is in Normandy (Normandie), named for the Eng**lish Channel, which** is known as La Manche, literally "
Haute-Loire is in south-central France named after the Loi**re River. Haute-Loire** is part of the current region of ,
Aveyron is located in the north of the Languedoc-Roussi**llon-Midi-Pyrenees regi**on of southern France named
Deux-Sevres is. Deux-Sevres literally means "two Sevres": **the Sevre Nantaise** and the Sevre Niortaise are two ri
Ariege is in the Languedoc-Roussillon-Midi-Pyrenees **region of southwestern France** named after the Ariege Ri
Orne is in the northwest of France, named after the ri**ver Orne. Alencon is** the prefecture. It is in the region Nor
Finistere is of France in the extreme west of Brittany. **Quimper is the prefec**ture. It is in the region Brittany
Ille-et-Vilaine is of France, located in the region of **Brittany in the north**west of the country. Rennes is the prefe
Aude is in south-central France named after the river **Aude. The** local council also calls the department "Cathar
Loir-et-Cher is a department in the Centre-Val de **Loire region, France.** Its name is originated from two rivers
Vienne is in the French region of Nouvelle-Aquita**ine. It takes its name** from the river Vienne. Poitiers is the pre
Indre is in the centre of France named after the ri**ver Indre. The inhabitants** of the department are called Indrie
Charente is in southwestern France, in the Nou**velle-Aquitaine region,** named after the Charente River, the mo
Sarthe is situated in the Grand-Ouest of the coun**try. It is named after the** River Sarthe, which flows from east (
Ardeche is in the Auvergne-Rhone-Alpes region of **south-central France.** It is named after the River Ardeche. F
Ain is named after the Ain River on the eastern edge of France. Being part of the region Auvergne-Rhone-Alpes and b
Maine-et-Loire is in west-central France, in the Pays de la Loire region. Angers is the prefecture. It is in the region Pays
Hautes-Alpes is in southeastern France named after the Alps mountain range. Gap is the prefecture. It is in the region
Charente-Maritime is on the southwestern coast of France named after the Charente River. La Rochelle is the prefectur
Alpes-de-Haute-Provence is in the south of France, it was formerly part of the province of Provence. Its inhabitants ar
Pyrenees-Atlantiques is in the region of Nouvelle-Aquitaine, in southwestern France. It takes its name from the Pyrene
Haute-Vienne is named after the river Vienne. It is one of the 12 departments that together constitute the French regio
Tarn is located in the Languedoc-Roussillon-Midi-Pyrenees region in the southwest of France named after the Tarn riv
Saone-et-Loire is, named after the Saone and the Loire rivers between which it lies. Macon is the prefecture. It is in the
Hautes-Pyrenees (Gascon: Nauts Pirenèus / Hauts Pireneus; Spanish: Altos Pirineos) is in southwestern France. It is pa
Eure-et-Loir is, named after the Eure and Loir rivers. Chartres is the prefecture. It is in the region Centre-Val de Loire
Pyrenees-Orientales is of southern France adjacent to the northern Spanish frontier and the Mediterranean Sea. It also
Jura is in the east of France named after the Jura mountains. Lons-le-Saunier is the prefecture. It is in the region Bourg
Allier is located in the Auvergne-Rhone-Alpes region of central France named after the river Allier. Moulins is the prefe
Indre-et-Loire is in west-central France named after the Indre and the Loire rivers. Tours is the prefecture. It is in the re
Yonne is named after the river Yonne. It is one of the eight constituent departments of Bourgogne-Franche-Comte and
Drome is in southeastern France named after the Drome River. Valence is the prefecture. It is in the region Auvergne-l
Haute-Saone is of the Bourgogne-Franche-Comte region named after the Saone River. Vesoul is the prefecture. It is in
Savoie is in the Auvergne-Rhone-Alpes region of the French Alps. Together with the Haute-Savoie, Savoie is one of the
Haute-Savoie is in the Auvergne-Rhone-Alpes region of eastern France, bordering both Switzerland and Italy. Its capit
Nievre is in the region of Bourgogne-Franche-Comte in the centre of France named after the River Nievre. Nevers is th
Calvados is in the Normandy region in northwestern France. It takes its name from a cluster of rocks off the English C
Puy-de-Dome is in the centre of France named after the famous dormant volcano, the Puy de Dome.Inhabitants were a
The Vaucluse is in the southeast of France, named after the famous spring, the Fontaine-de-Vaucluse. The name Vauch
Herault is in southern France named after the Herault river. It is part of the Languedoc-Roussillon-Midi-Pyrenees regic
Cher is in the Centre-Val de Loire region of France. It is named after the Cher River. Bourges is the prefecture. It is in
Eure is in the north of France named after the river Eure. Evreux is the prefecture. It is in the region Normandy
Loiret is in north-central France. The department is named after the river Loiret, a tributary of the Loire, and which is l
Loire-Atlantique is on the west coast of France named after the Loire River and the Atlantic Ocean. Nantes is the prefe
Haute-Marne is in the northeast of France named after the Marne River. Chaumont is the prefecture. It is in the region
Somme is of France, located in the north of the country and named after the Somme river. It is part of the Hauts-de-Fr
Cote-d'Or is in the eastern part of **France. Dijon is the prefec**ture. It is in the region Bourgogne-Franche-Com
Haute-Garonne is in the south**west of France named after the** Garonne river. Its main city and capital is Toul
Gironde is in the Nouvelle**-Aquitaine region of southwest** France. It is named for the Gironde estuary, a majo
Meuse is in northeast France, **named after the River Meuse. Meuse** is part of the current region of Alsace-Ch
Aisne is in the Nord-Pas-de-Ca**lais-Picardie region of northern** France. It is named after the river Aisne. Lao
Gard is in southern France in **the Languedoc-Roussillon-Midi-Pyrenees** region. The department is named a
Marne is in north-eastern **France named after the river Marne** (Matrona in Roman times) which flows throu
Aube is in the Alsace-Champ**agne-Ardenne-Lorraine region of** north-eastern France. As with sixty departm
Doubs is in the Bourgogne-**Franche-Comte region of eastern France** named after the Doubs River. Besanc
Oise is in the north of France. **It is named after the river Oise.** Natives of the department are called Isarien
Bas-Rhin is in the Alsace-C**hampagne-Ardenne-Lorraine region of** France. The name means "Lower Rhine"
Isere is in the Auvergne-**Rhone-Alpes region in the east of France** named after the river Isere. Grenoble is t
Ardennes is in the Alsace-**Champagne-Ardenne-Lorraine region of** northeastern France named after the A
Vosges is in the east of **France, named after the Vosges Mountains. The** department consists of 17 cantor
The Var is in the Provence-**Alpes-Cote d'Azur region in** Provence in southeastern France. It takes its name
Seine-et-Marne is, **named after the Seine and Marne rivers,** and located in the Ile-de-France region. Melun i
Pas-de-Calais kalɛ]) **is in northern France.** Its name is also used in French to refer to the Strait of Dover, wh
Loire is in the east-**central part of France** occupying the River Loire's upper reaches. Saint-Etienne is the p
Seine-Maritime is of **France in the Normandy region** of northern France. It is situated on the northern coas
Haut-Rhin is in the **Alsace-Champagne-Ardenne-Lorraine region** of eastern France, named after the Rhine river.
Alpes-Maritimes is of the **Provence-Alpes-Cote d'Azur region** in the extreme southeast corner of France. Th
Moselle is in the east of France named after the river Moselle. Metz is the prefecture. It is in the region Gr
Bouches-du-**Rhone is in the south** of France named after the mouth of the Rhone River. It is the most popu
Rhone is located in the central Eastern region of Auvergne-Rhone-Alpes. It is named after the river Rhon
Meurthe-et-Moselle is in the Alsace-Champagne-Ardenne-Lorraine region of France, named after the Me
Nord is in the far north of France. It was created from the western halves of the historical counties of Fla
The Territoire de Belfort is in the Bourgogne-Franche-Comte region of eastern France. Belfort is the pr
Yvelines is in the region of Ile-de-France. Versailles is the prefecture. It is in the region Ile-de-France
Seine was of France encompassing Paris and its immediate suburbs. Its capital was Paris and its official
Paris is the capital and most populous cityof France, with an administrative-limits area of 105 square kilo

| 0 | 500 | 1000 | 1500 |

Underline length indicates population (in 1000's)

FIGURE 10.11 **Each row describes one department in France. The proportion of font and/or color indicate the population employed in the occupations of agriculture, manufacturing, and services. The length of the underline indicates the population per department.**

Figure 10.12 shows Wikipedia's daily English *Featured Article* for the month of August 2019. The opening sentence of each article is shown on each row. Wikipedia collects many statistics per article, six of which are shown represented as proportions along the rows, each using a unique format:

- *Page views* are indicated with length of **bold** characters: the most viewed article is about *Taylor Swift*, with 191,606 views (as indicated by the legend in the bottom right corner).

- *Page length* is indicated by the length of red characters, i.e. the number of words in the article. The longest article is about *Hillary Clinton*.

- *Total edits* is indicated by the length of underline. *Clinton* has been most edited.

FIGURE 10.12 Six statistics associated with Wikipedia featured articles, each represented with a unique format. Taylor Swift has the most views (longest bold), Hillary Clinton has the most edits (longest underline), and both are on many watchlists (long yellow shading).

- *Years wait*, from the date the page was nominated to the date the page was displayed, is indicated in *italic*. Both *"Touch Me I'm Sick"* and *Bernard Fanning* articles waited more than 11 years before appearing on the front page of English Wikipedia.

- *Article age* is indicated by a font change from `Source Code Pro` to `Courier`. *Clinton* is the oldest, over 18 years, with *Stephen* and *Analog Science Fiction and Fact* also over 18 years.

- *Number of watchlists* that the given page is on is indicated with the shaded bar. *Clinton* and *Swift* are on many watchlists.

With the multiple metrics per bar, it is possible to see some multi-variate patterns. For example, both *Clinton* and *Swift* are among the highest for many metrics: page length, edits, article age, and watchers. However, in terms of views, *Swift* is the most popular, followed by *Vesna Vulović* and the *Marchioness disaster*. Otherwise, *Vulović* and *Marchioness* have very few edits, are short, and have few watchers. *The Gadsen Purchase half dollar* has short page length and few edits, like many other articles, however, it quickly changes font and italics after the initial "The," indicating that the page is relatively new with a short wait before becoming a featured article.

Note that some of the format changes are not easy to visually detect in this image. All six attributes are turned on simultaneously. Some formats interfere with perception of other formats: strongly preattentive cues such as bold and color dominate, making it difficult to see attributes such as italic or a change in typeface. Also, with many simultaneously depicted formats, it is difficult to keep track of the encodings in the viewer's short-term memory. In practice, the viewer can turn on/off the metrics of interest to focus on only a subset of metrics, using the buttons at the top of the chart.

Also note that even though the source data is from English Wikipedia, the actual text contains Cyrillic, Japanese, Latin accents, and phonetic symbols, all of which need to be drawn.

10.2.8 Semantic Proportions and Expressive Text

All prior examples modify the formatting around the text, but do not modify the spelling or otherwise modify the text. Instead, conversational cues (e.g. O'Connor 2013 or Bamman et al. 2014) can be represented by modifying text with techniques such as expressive lengthening (e.g. heyyy), repeated punctuation (!!!), repeated modifiers (e.g. very, very big), and sound cues (e.g. ah, hmm, grr, um). While expressive text may be prevalent in modern social media, it has been used for more than a century. It is commonly used in comic book lettering. And earlier, in 1865, Carroll used lengthened vowels in *Wonderland* shown in Figure 3.28, such as soooop, beauootiful, and eeevening.

These cues can be used together with text to modify string lengths to expressively convey quantities. For example, the word *long* is stretched in the following sentence to indicate one bridge is 1.5x times longer than the other: The Golden Gate Bridge is long, but Akashi-Kaikyo Bridge is longgg.

This can be combined with formatting such as a shaded bar, so that the word sequence and spelling can indicate the magnitude by expressive text while the bar highlights the

CANADIAN CANNABIS SURVEY 2019
Responses about use, opinions and knowledge related to cannabis

- A quarter of respondents used cannabis at least once in the last 12 months (25%).
- Just over a third of respondents indicated knowledge of harms related to cannabis increased somewhat (36%).
- Almost half of respondents indicate social acceptance of cannabis use (44%).
- A bit more than half respondents aged 20 to 24 reported cannabis use (51%).
- Waaaay more than half of respondents reported cannabis smoke can be harmful (76%)
- A verrrrry large majority of respondents (85%) think that cannabis use affects driving.
- An extreeemely large majority of respondents (90%) think using cannabis could be habit forming.

Length of green indicates proportion of respondents. Data from Health Canada's Canadian Cannabis Survey 2019 - Summary

FIGURE 10.13 Expressive lengthening of text can be used to indicate quantities, visually rein-forced with corresponding quantitative bars.

visual comparison. For example: Elephants are tall, but the dinosaur Sauroposeidon was verrry muuuch tallerrr.

Expressive text can be used to create a bar chart indicating data by both bar length and expressively lengthened text, such as the example in Figure 10.13 (inspired by Duncan and Zapponi 2016).

10.3 POSITIONS ALONG A STRING

Rather than highlighting a length of a string, another approach is to simply mark the place along the string that corresponds to the length of interest. A simple example was previously shown indicating statistics regarding sentence length in *Alice in Wonderland* in Figure 3.8. In Figure 10.14, lengths are marked with symbols such as a vertical bar and parentheses to indicate quantitative values as measured from the start of the string. While this approach is feasible, it interrupts words with added symbols reducing readability, while not creating visual patterns that visibly pop-out.

The same data can be shown with proportional range bars underneath as shown in Figure 10.15, which is less disruptive than splitting words apart.

Alphanumeric symbols and text can be used to represent many values. In Figure 10.16, four paragraphs of introductory text regarding departments of France (from Wikipedia) are shown. Within this text are red superscripts uniquely identifying the proportion of residents in each department employed in services. Quantitative values are represented across the length of the four paragraphs – 2870 characters long. Superscripts are inserted after full words so that words are not split apart and thus follow the typical convention for use of superscripts in prose. An axis along the right edge identifies the cumulative propor-tion of text from the start.

At a micro-level, individual departments are identifiable by their department codes. At a macro-level, the viewer can attend to red marks, which are largely concentrated at the beginning of the second paragraph, indicating that the typical proportion of services is approximately 21–35%; and the overall range approximately 18–65%. At an interaction-level, one can point at any code to get the full name of the department and a higher level of accuracy for the quantitative value.

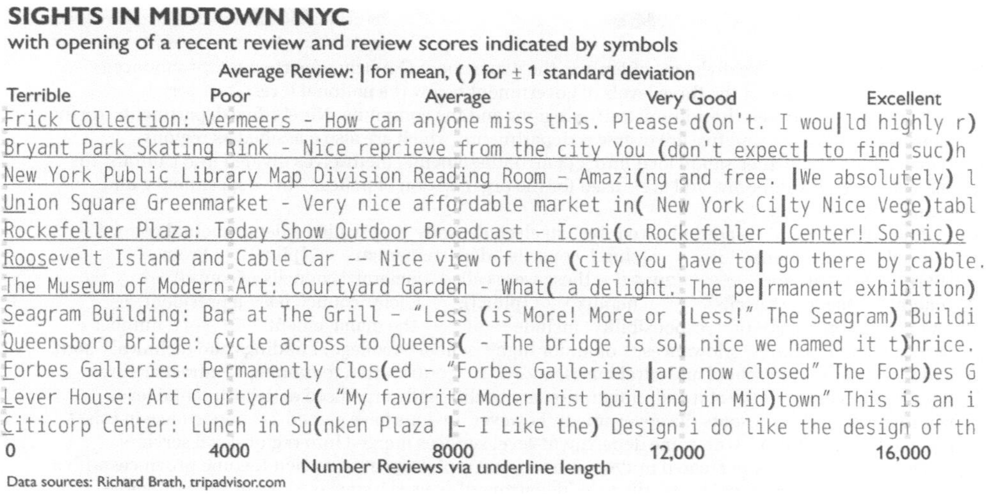

SIGHTS IN MIDTOWN NYC
with opening of a recent review and review scores indicated by symbols

Average Review: | for mean, ( ) for ± 1 standard deviation

Terrible	Poor	Average	Very Good	Excellent

Frick Collection: Vermeers - How can anyone miss this. Please d(on't. I wou|ld highly r)
Bryant Park Skating Rink - Nice reprieve from the city You (don't expect| to find suc)h
New York Public Library Map Division Reading Room - Amazi(ng and free. |We absolutely) l
Union Square Greenmarket - Very nice affordable market in(New York Ci|ty Nice Vege)tabl
Rockefeller Plaza: Today Show Outdoor Broadcast - Iconi(c Rockefeller |Center! So nic)e
Roosevelt Island and Cable Car -- Nice view of the (city You have to| go there by ca)ble.
The Museum of Modern Art: Courtyard Garden - What(a delight. The pe|rmanent exhibition)
Seagram Building: Bar at The Grill - "Less (is More! More or |Less!" The Seagram) Buildi
Queensboro Bridge: Cycle across to Queens(- The bridge is so| nice we named it t)hrice.
Forbes Galleries: Permanently Clos(ed - "Forbes Galleries |are now closed" The Forb)es G
Lever House: Art Courtyard -("My favorite Moder|nist building in Mid)town" This is an i
Citicorp Center: Lunch in Su(nken Plaza |- I Like the) Design i do like the design of th

0	4000	8000	12,000	16,000

Number Reviews via underline length

Data sources: Richard Brath, tripadvisor.com

FIGURE 10.14   Sights in midtown Manhattan with average review score indicated via a vertical bar | and ± one standard deviation indicated via parentheses.

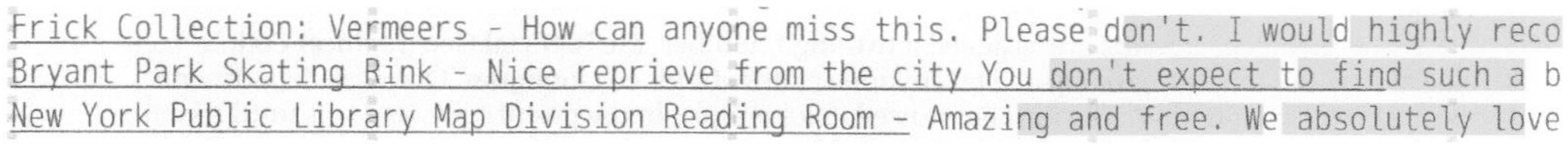

Frick Collection: Vermeers - How can anyone miss this. Please don't. I would highly reco
Bryant Park Skating Rink - Nice reprieve from the city You don't expect to find such a b
New York Public Library Map Division Reading Room - Amazing and free. We absolutely love

FIGURE 10.15   Sights in midtown Manhattan with average review score indicated via range bars.

The axis can be removed if the magnitude is made explicit in the text. Figure 10.17 is a single sentence regarding illiteracy and gender. In this example, superscripts are mnemonic three letter country ISO codes, with a legend in the footer. The explanation of the representation and the overall length are described directly in the text, meaning that the sentence can stand-alone without axes, ticks, and titles; for example, as a descriptive element in a dashboard, as a call out in a report, or as a poster.

10.4 CAVEATS, ISSUES, AND LIMITATIONS

Different approaches can be used to implement proportions along a string:

- Using a *fixed width font*, such as in Figure 10.12, is easy to implement as formats can be applied to the count the number of characters in proportion to the value represented. The accuracy is limited to the number of characters, e.g. for a string 100 characters long the accuracy will be 1%.

- In a *proportional font* each letter has a different width. Subsets of string can be measured, and the closest character used. Variable width fonts tend to have more characters per line, increasing the resolution. This approach may result in some un-evenness in lengths, as seen in Figure 10.7, where the lines are ordered by value, but sometimes a slightly longer format will appear above a slightly shorter format. This approach

DEPARTMENTS OF FRANCE

Percent of population employed in services, indicated by department code superscript: 0%

In the administrative divisions of France, the department (French: département, pronounced [depaʁt(ə)mã]) is one of the three levels of government below the national level ("territorial collectivities"), between the administrative regions and the commune. Ninety-five departments are in metropolitan France, and five are overseas departments, which are also classified as regions. Departments are further subdivided into 334 arrondissements, themselves divided into cantons; the last two have no autonomy, and are[32] used for the organisation of police,[23] fire departments, and sometimes, elections.[48]

—17

Each department[85] is administered[9] by[12] an elected[53] body[43,40,24] called a departmental council[7,46,82] (conseil[47] départemental[81,88,56,79,19] [sing.], conseils[15] départementaux[70,50] [plur.]).[71,1] From 1800[61,39,29,16,22] to April[25,42,36,38] 2015,[41,49] these were called[63] general[87] councils[62] (conseil[35,26] général[73,18] [sing.], conseils[65,86,72] généraux[8,57,27] [plur.]).[11,68] Each[90] council has[10] a president.[74,64] Their[80,55] main areas[44] of[60] responsibility[3] include[2,4,59,28,52,45] the management[89,37,58,5] of a number[17,14] of social[30] and welfare[67] allowances,[84] of junior high[66] school[54] (collège) buildings and technical[31] staff, and local roads[51] and school and rural buses, and[34,77] a[21] contribution to municipal infrastructures. Local[69] services of[33,76] the state administration are traditionally organised at departmental level, where the prefect represents the government; however, regions have gained[75,78] importance in this[83] regard since the 2000s, with some department-level services merged into region-level services.

—21

—26

—31

—37

—43

—50

The departments were created in 1790 as a rational replacement of Ancien Régime provinces with a view to strengthen national unity; the title "department" is used to mean a part of a larger whole. Almost all of them were named[13] after physical geographical features (rivers, mountains,[6] or coasts), rather than after historical or cultural territories which could have their own loyalties. The division of France into departments[P] was a project particularly identified with the French revolutionary leader the Abbé Sieyès, although it had already been frequently discussed and written about by many politicians and thinkers. The earliest known suggestion of it is from 1764 in the writings of d'Argenson. They have inspired similar divisions in many countries, some of them former French colonies.

—57

—64

—71

Most French departments are assigned a two-digit number, the "Official Geographical Code", allocated by the Institut national de la statistique et des études économiques. Overseas departments have a three-digit number. The number is used, for example, in the postal code, and was until recently used for all vehicle registration plates. While residents commonly use the numbers to refer to their own department or a neighbouring one, more distant departments are generally referred to by their names, as few people know the numbers of all the departments. For example, inhabitants of Loiret might refer to their department as "the 45".

—100

FIGURE 10.16 Departments of France. Descriptive text with embedded department codes in red superscript to indicate quantitative values.

COUNTRIES WITH THE HIGHEST POPULATIONS OF ILLITERACY AMONG WOMEN
Data indicated by position from start of sentence

More[MEX] than[BRA] [IDN]5[ZAR]0[EGY]0 million women[ETH] in[BGD] the[NGA] world are[PAK] il[CHN]literate: the superscripts on this sentence indicate the number of illiterate women per country with sentence start indicating zero and sentence end indicating three hundred million illiterate [IND]women.

Data sources: UNESCO, World Bank, Wikipedia, 2013.
MEX: Mexico. BRA: Brazil. IDN: Indonesia. ZAR: Democratic Republic of Congo. EGY: Egypt. BGD: Bangladesh. NGA: Nigeria. PAK: Pakistan. CHN: China. IND: India.

FIGURE 10.17 Population of illiterate women per country indicated by the position of superscripts from the start of a sentence. A significant number of women in the world still do not have access to literacy education.

also allows for fonts of different widths to be used with the formats, as shown in Figure 10.6, to increase the differentiation in the text.

- *Sub-character formats* are feasible. As shown in Figure 10.5, the ranges are indicated with formats that start/stop mid-character. Underlines and background shading behind text are straightforward to implement, but cropping other formats requires more programmatic effort.

Further caveats include the choice of attribute to use. For example, underlines and background shading behind text span across spaces and can clearly distinguish when a space is included in the value represented. Attributes such as bold, italic, and typeface only apply to characters; are not visible for spaces; and may be difficult to detect for punctuation (e.g. a period or comma does not substantially change with a change in bold, italic, or typeface). Thus, typographic formats encode quantitative data at a lower resolution than underlines or background shading.

Furthermore, some visual attributes are more salient than others, as previously discussed in Section 3.7. As can be seen in Figure 10.12, it is easy to identify the rows with the longest red color, background shading, underline, and weight. Identifying the row with the longest italic or longest typeface requires much slower inspection. However, changes in typeface in Figure 10.11 are much easier to distinguish than changes in typeface in Figure 10.12; the degree of difference between formats is important to ease perception. In all these examples with multiple encoding, interaction can be used to turn on and off the formats of interest.

For further reading, these techniques of proportional and positional encoding are untested. Inspiration may be found in original documents created by concrete poets (e.g. *The New Concrete: Visual Poetry in the 21st Century*, Bean et al. 2015) and post-modern typographers in magazines such as *Emigre*, *Octavo*, and *Ray Gun* and books such as Avital Ronell's *The Telephone Book*, or Johanna Drucker's Letterpress books.

IV

Text Layouts

Manipulating Text in Text Layouts

CHAPTER 11

Prose and Prosody

I N THE PRIOR CHAPTERS, text is used in common visualization layouts to enhance functionality, particularly within the plot area of the visualization. These prior examples
assume that the text is placed within a visualization layout.

In the next two chapters, visualization leaves the plot area and the data becomes embedded in the words directly in textual layouts such as prose, tables, and lists. In this chapter, the focus is on formatting text so that it facilitates understanding of the text. That is,
additional data is embedded into formats, and the data is about the words and their context. The following chapter generalizes the use to embed any kind of additional data into
SparkWords.

11.1 ENHANCED READING

There are many ways that a reader may approach text. A mechanic may need to quickly
skim an instruction manual to find the relevant portion to a given task. A student learning
a second language may have issues with pronunciation. A more advanced student, focused
on spelling, may need to attend to portions of words. A reader may be unaware of melodies
associated with rhymes and could benefit from enhanced cues. A corporate brand manager
may be interested in emotion and sentiment in social media. And so on.

All these use cases can benefit from enhancements to the text to facilitate the target task.
And, in many of these cases, algorithmic techniques from natural language processing can
be used to automatically tag subsets of text to enhance.

Historically, there are many examples of typographically enhanced texts to facilitate
reading, to call out keywords, to order text importance, and so on. Medieval documents,
such as the example seen in Chapter 3 (Figure 3.45), use color for leading initials and words
ordered brown/black, red, blue, or gold.

Figure 11.1 left is a mathematics textbook (Ward 1724) where most text is set in italics,
with newly introduced keywords set in heavyweight **blackletter** and previously defined
text in a plain roman font. In Figure 11.1 right, a railway employee's instruction manual
(Broughton 1879) uses an ordering of all caps bold > bold > plain to indicate the priority
of keywords. Presumably this guides attention and aids skimming for the novice employee.

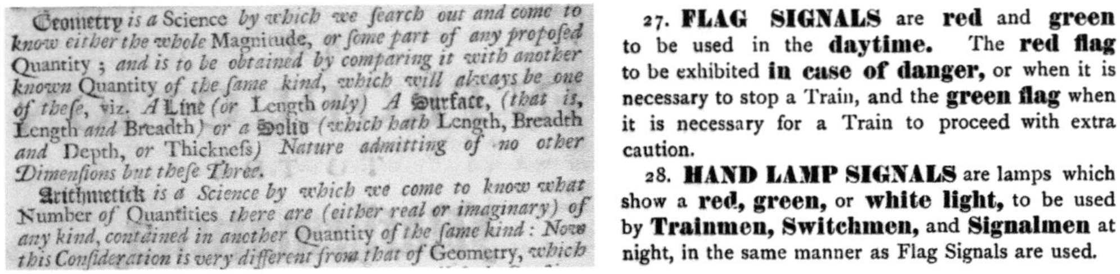

(a) (b)

FIGURE 11.1 Left: Mathematics text from 1724 mostly in italic with keywords in blackletter or plain roman. Right: Instruction manual from 1879 with text ordered all-caps bold, bold, or plain.

Manipulating text in advertisements to make particular words stand out from their context was seen in the theater posters in Figure 1.20 – such as the use of color, size, rotation, or different typefaces. Similarly, prose in advertising may use typographic variation to make specific words more prominent to highlight key messages as shown in Figure 11.2, whether aimed at adults (left, from Good 1890) or children (right, from comic book *Billy the Kid* 1958).

Modern examples include TALLman lettering to draw attention to specific syllables in drug names (Figure 3.17); and highlighting keywords in context to facilitate skimming search results (KWIC – Figure 3.9).

11.2 SKIM FORMATTING

Reading every word in a document is slow. Text skimming is a reading technique of rapid eye movement across a large amount of text to acquire key ideas and content overview. At

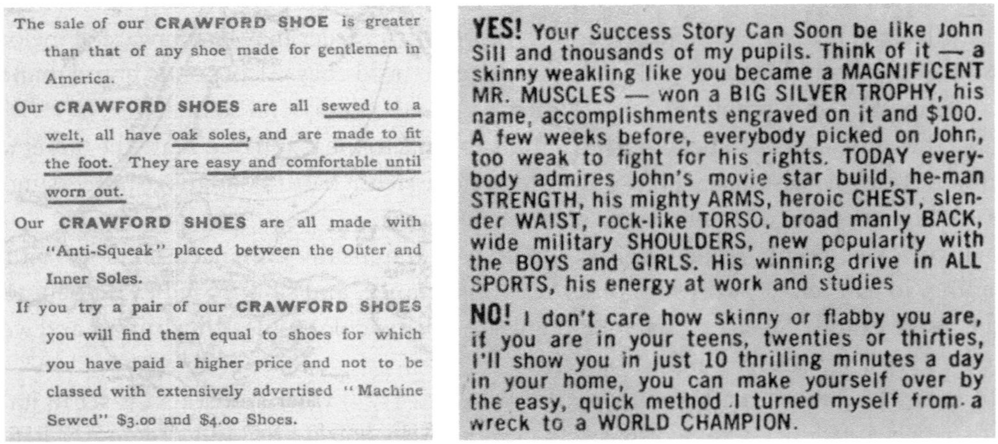

(a) (b)

FIGURE 11.2 Left: Portion of ad for shoes from 1890. Right: Portion of ad for physical training from a 1958 comic book. In both cases the advertisers emphasize text with formats such as weight, underline, and capitalization.

a high level, this reading strategy includes reading titles, headers, and captions, and at a lower-level, this requires the reader to dip into the text for words such as proper nouns, unusual words, and enumerations. The historic examples in Figure 11.1 and 11.2 use formatting to facilitate skimming in prose text.

The salient text can be visually enhanced to make the most salient words pop-out while retaining the context of the surrounding text. This first example is from Verne's *Around the World in Eighty Days*, where the proper nouns and cardinal numbers are set in larger text, with other text wrapped in between:

Mr. Phileas Fogg lived, in 1872, at No. 7, Saville Row, Burlington Gardens, the house in which Sheridan died in 1814. He was one of the most noticeable members of the Reform Club, though he seemed always to avoid attracting attention; an enigmatical personage, about whom little was known, except that he was a polished man of the world. People said that he resembled Byron — at least that his head was Byronic; but he was a bearded, tranquil Byron, who might live on a thousand years without growing old.

Certainly an Englishman, it was more doubtful whether Phileas Fogg was a Londoner. He was never seen on Change, nor at the Bank, nor in the counting-rooms of the City; no ships ever came into London docks of which he was the owner; he had no public employment; he had never been entered at any of the Inns of Court, either at the Temple, or Lincoln's Inn, or Gray's Inn; nor had his voice ever resounded in the Court of

When this example was shown to some typographers, the response was negative. The alternating type sizes with multiple line wraps per row are not easy to read. In general, the frequent change in type size and flow is considered highly disruptive to reading.

Instead, other typographic variations, such as weight, width, and underline, are visually salient without changing font size. The following paragraphs are the first three paragraphs from Robert Louis Stevenson's *Treasure Island*, where the least frequent words in English are formatted most heavily. Bold words such as **Treasure**, **Admiral Benbow inn**, **sabre**, **sea-man**, **sea-chest**, and **sea-song** indicate that this story is about more than an island:

SQUIRE **TRELAWNEY,** Dr. **Livesey,** and the rest of these **gentlemen** having asked me to write down the whole **particulars** about **Treasure** Island, from the beginning to the end, **keeping** nothing back but the **bearings** of the island, and that only because there is still **treasure** not yet **lifted,** I take up my **pen** in the year of **grace seventeen-** and go back to the time when my father kept the **Admiral Benbow** inn and the brown old **seaman** with the **sabre** cut first took up his **lodging** under our roof.

I remember him as if it were **yesterday,** as he came **plodding** to the inn door, his **sea-chest** following behind him in a **hand-barrow -** a tall, strong, heavy, **nut-brown** man, his tarry **pigtail** falling over the shoulder of his soiled blue **coat,** his hands **ragged** and **scarred,** with black, broken nails, and the **sabre** cut across one **cheek,** a dirty, livid white. I remember him looking round the **cover** and **whistling** to himself as he did so, and then **breaking** out in that old **sea-song** that he **sang** so often afterwards:

Fifteen men on the dead **man's** chest- **Yo-ho-ho,** and a bottle of rum!

While there are many algorithmic approaches to tagging text, this example (and the following examples) uses the skimming recommendation of identifying unusual words. The *term frequency – inverse document frequency* algorithm (TF-IDF) establishes a baseline for a corpus, then scores words in a document based on their inverse frequency compared to the baseline. Effectively, TF-IDF scores the uncommon words in the document most highly. (The collection baseline in these examples use the Wiktionary word frequency lists from Project Gutenberg.)

Once the words are scored, any combination of formats can be used to create an ordering from the most unusual to the most common. In this next example, the introductory paragraph for the Wright brothers' *The Early History of the Airplane* uses both width and weight so that the most unusual words dominate (e.g. **fluttered**, **helicoptere**, and **torsion**) while function words (e.g. prepositions, pronouns, and articles) recede as narrow lightweight oblique words:

Though *the* subject *of* **aerial navigation** *is generally considered* new, *it has* **occupied** *the* **minds** *of men more or* less *from the* **earliest ages**. *Our* **personal** interest *in it* **dates** *from our* **childhood** days. *Late in the* **autumn** *of* **1878** *our* father came *into the* house *one* evening *with some* object **partly concealed** *in his* hands, *and before we could see what it was, he* **tossed** *it into the* air. *Instead of* **falling** *to the* **floor**, *as we* **expected**, *it* **flew** across *the* room, till *it* **struck** *the* **ceiling**, where *it* **fluttered** awhile, *and* **finally sank** *to the* **floor**. *It was a little* **toy**, known *to* **scientists** *as a* **'helicoptere**,*" but which we, with* **sublime disregard** *for* **science**, *at* once **dubbed** *a "***bat.*"* *It was a* light **frame** *of* **cork** *and* **bamboo**, covered *with* **paper**, *which* formed *two* **screws**, **driven** *in* **opposite directions** *by* **rubber bands** under **torsion**. *A* **toy** *so* **delicate lasted** *only a* short *time in the* hands *of* small **boys**, *but its* **memory** *was* **abiding**.

Or, the text can be formatted using fonts relevant to semantics of text. The next example from Austen's *Emma* is formatted with a period serif font and uses now uncommon ligatures on the most unusual words to draw attention to words such as disposition, distress, youngest, mistress, and affection:

Emma Woodhouse, **handsome**, **clever**, *and rich, with a* **comfortable** *home and happy* **disposition**, *seemed to* **unite** *some of the best* **blessings** *of* **existence**; *and had lived nearly* **twenty**-one *years in the world with very little to* **distress** *or* **vex** *her.*

She was the **youngest** *of the two* **daughters** *of a most* **affectionate**, **indulgent** *father; and had, in* **consequence** *of her* **sister's** *marriage, been* **mistress** *of his house from a very early period. Her mother had* **died** *too long ago for her to have more than an* **indistinct remembrance** *of her* **caresses**; *and her place had been* **supplied** *by an* **excellent** *woman as* **governess**, *who had* **fallen** *little short of a mother in* **affection**.

Several strong responses resulted from a survey using some of the above examples. Responses were highly polarized, with some respondents indicating a strong preference for skim formatting, such as "Can you install this on my iPad now?" or "I can see using this immediately." Some respondents indicated an *intense* dislike. Comments from the negative responders indicated that (1) font weight interferes with linear reading thereby potentially introducing a different reading of the text; (2) other formats may be less obtrusive; and (3) the formatting focuses attention on individual words rather than sentences.

Interestingly, weight variation to support skimming already exists in Japanese texts. Eiichi Kono (*Computers and Typography 2*) explains that Japanese writing is a mix of Kanji pictographic/ideographic glyphs which are visually dense; plus Kana glyphs which are visually sparse. Kanji is used for core words while Kana are usually used for inflection, suffixes, prepositions, and conjunctions. The resulting text is 30% Kanji and 70% Kana. Japanese is easy to read partially because the Kanji core text stands out as a much darker tone against a larger background of phonetic Kana, as shown in this sample text from a Japanese Wikipedia article:

> 任天堂はハードウェアとソフトウェアの開発を共に手がけるビジネスを展開している。
>
> ハードウェアに関しては、堅牢性と耐久性を重視している。かつてハードウェア開発責任者を務めていた竹田玄洋によると、それは子供ユーザーに配慮したものであり、ゲーム機が壊れてしまった時に「僕が壊した」ではなく「勝手に壊れた」となってしまう事態を見越した上での設計文化が出来上がっているのだという。
>
> 任天堂名義の外部向けの開発は行っていないが、電通との合併で外部向けの開発を専業とした子会社である「株式会社マリオ」を設立したことがあり、任天堂の開発スタッフをそのまま利用している。サンリオグループのゲーム会社であるキャラクターソフトの『ハローキティワールド』と、『サンリオカーニバル2』の開発を行っていた。

While Japanese readers may be familiar with reading across changing densities, these changes may be distracting for western readers. Interaction is an easy means to toggle the algorithms on/off. The following examples show the first paragraphs of Marx and Engel's *Communist Manifesto*, on the left with no formatting, center with uncommon words weighted and right with lead sentences indicated in bold small caps. Note the choice of fonts are such that lines wrap (nearly) consistently regardless of the formatting. A reader can switch between modes and maintain reading position.

A spectre is haunting Europe - the spectre of Communism. All the Powers of old Europe have entered into a holy alliance to exorcise this spectre: Pope and Czar, Metternich and Guizot, French Radicals and German police-spies.
Where is the party in opposition that has not been decried as Communistic by its opponents in power? Where is the Opposition that has not hurled back the branding reproach of Communism, against the more advanced opposition parties, as well as against its reactionary adversaries?

A **spectre** is **haunting** Europe - the **spectre** of **Communism.** All the **Powers** of old Europe have entered into a **holy alliance** to **exorcise** this **spectre:** **Pope** and **Czar, Metternich** and **Guizot,** French **Radicals** and German **police-spies.**
Where is the party in **opposition** that has not been **decried** as **Communistic** by its **opponents** in power? Where is the **Opposition** that has not **hurled** back the **branding** reproach of **Communism,** against the more **advanced opposition parties,** as well as against its **reactionary adversaries?**

A SPECTRE IS HAUNTING EUROPE - THE SPECTRE OF COMMUNISM. All the Powers of old Europe have entered into a holy alliance to exorcise this spectre: Pope and Czar, Metternich and Guizot, French Radicals and German police-spies.
WHERE IS THE PARTY IN OPPOSITION THAT HAS NOT BEEN DECRIED AS COMMUNISTIC BY ITS OPPONENTS IN POWER? Where is the Opposition that has not hurled back the branding reproach of Communism, against the more advanced opposition parties, as well as against its reactionary adversaries?

Other natural language processing algorithms could be applied, for example, to focus on emotion or sentiment; to extract summaries; to order qualified facts, unsubstantiated claims and opinions; to encode confidence in term processing during automatic translation or speech-based interfaces; or other analytics.

Other techniques may be more relevant to other tasks. For example, the task may be to navigate around a document. The objective is to quickly locate the section of interest. Finding a paragraph of interest is challenging on a mobile device as only a couple of paragraphs may be visible and other landmarks, such as section headings, may be off screen. A visually accessible summary per paragraph could aid navigation.

In Figure 11.3, the plot from the movie *Blade Runner* is superimposed over a simplistic summary of each paragraph. The two-word summary indicates the most unique character and first associated verb in the paragraph. A viewer quickly scrolling through many paragraphs can attend to the large text to locate their position. Then the detailed text, superimposed in front, can be skimmed and read as needed. Note that the large text is an intermediate brightness such that both the foreground text and background text have sufficient contrast for legibility. Also, the foreground text has a light halo added to further separate it from the underlying text.

This separation of foreground and background text can be further enhanced with interactive techniques. Large text can fade in/out on scroll. Or motion parallax can be used to create perceptual separation: for example, on iOS devices, the foreground icons and background wallpaper move at different rates based on the tilt so that the icons appear to float in front of the background. Stereoscopic images create the illusion of depth by providing two offset images separately to the right and left eye of the viewer, and are used in modern 3D movies, virtual reality, and augmented reality devices. Figure 11.4 is a historic stereo image of overlapping text, easier to read when viewed through the stereo device.

In Los Angeles in November 2019, ex-police officer **Rick Deckard** is detained by officer *Gaff* and brought to his former supervisor, BRYANT. **Deckard**, whose job as a "*Blade Runner*" was to track down bioengineered beings known as replicants and "retire" (a euphemism for killing) them, is informed that four have come to Earth illegally. As Tyrell Corporation *Nexus-6* models, they have only a four-year lifespan and may have come to Earth to try to extend their lives.

Deckard watches a video of a *Blade Runner* named *Holden* administering the "*Voight-Kampff*" test designed to distinguish replicants from humans based on their emotional response to questions. The test subject, **Leon**, shoots *Holden* after *Holden* asks about **Leon**'s mother. BRYANT wants **Deckard** to retire **Leon** and the other three replicants: **Roy Batty, Zhora, and Pris**. **Deckard** initially refuses, but after BRYANT ambiguously threatens him, he reluctantly agrees.

Deckard begins his investigation at the Tyrell Corporation to ensure that the test works on *Nexus-6* models. While there, he discovers that Dr. Eldon Tyrell's assistant **Rachael** is an experimental replicant who believes herself to be human. **Rachael** has been given false memories to provide an "emotional cushion". As a result, a more extensive test is required to determine whether she is a replicant.

Events are then set into motion that pit **Deckard**'s search for the replicants against their search for Tyrell to force him to extend their lives. **Roy** and **Leon** investigate a replicant eye-manufacturing laboratory and learn of J. F. Sebastian, a gifted genetic designer who works closely with Tyrell. **Rachael** visits **Deckard** at his apartment to prove her humanity by showing him a family photo, but after **Deckard** reveals that her memories are implants from Tyrell's niece, she leaves his apartment in tears. Meanwhile, **Pris** locates Sebastian and manipulates him to gain his trust.

While searching **Leon**'s hotel room, **Deckard** finds a photo of **Zhora** and a synthetic snake scale that leads him to a strip club where **Zhora** works. **Deckard** kills **Zhora** and shortly after is told by BRYANT to also retire **Rachael**, who has disappeared from the Tyrell Corporation. After **Deckard** spots **Rachael** in a crowd, he is attacked by **Leon**, but **Rachael** kills **Leon** using **Deckard**'s dropped pistol. The two return to **Deckard**'s apartment, and during an intimate discussion, he promises not to hunt her; as she abruptly tries to leave, **Deckard** physically restrains her, forcing her to kiss him.

Arriving at Sebastian's apartment, **Roy** tells **Pris** the others are dead. Sympathetic to their plight, Sebastian reveals that because of "*Methuselah Syndrome*", a genetic premature aging disorder, his life will also be cut short. Sebastian and **Roy** gain entrance into Tyrell's secure penthouse, where **Roy** demands more life from his maker. Tyrell tells him that it is impossible. **Roy** confesses that he has done *questionable things* which Tyrell dismisses, praising **Roy**'s advanced design and accomplishments in his short life. **Roy** kisses Tyrell, then kills him. Sebastian runs for the elevator followed by **Roy**, who then rides the elevator down alone. Though not shown, it is implied by BRYANT via police radio that **Roy** also kills Sebastian.

Upon entering Sebastian's apartment, **Deckard** is ambushed by **Pris**, but he manages to kill her just as **Roy** returns. As **Roy** starts to die, he chases **Deckard** through the building, ending up on the roof. **Deckard** tries to jump to an adjacent roof, but misses and is left hanging precariously between buildings. **Roy** makes the jump with ease, and as **Deckard**'s grip loosens, **Roy** hoists him onto the roof, saving him. As **Roy**'s life runs out, he delivers a monologue about how his memories *will be lost in time, like tears in rain*; **Roy** dies in front of **Deckard**, who watches silently.

Gaff arrives and shouts across to **Deckard**, "It's too bad she won't live, but then again, who does?" **Deckard** returns to his apartment and finds the door ajar, but **Rachael** is safe, asleep in his bed. As they leave, **Deckard** notices a small tin-foil origami unicorn on the floor, a familiar calling card that brings back to him *Gaff*'s final words. **Deckard** and **Rachael** quickly leave the apartment block.

FIGURE 11.3 Large paragraph synopses are added behind narrative text to facilitate locating paragraphs, for example, scrolling on a mobile device.

FIGURE 11.4   Stereoscopic image pair filled with overlapping text.

11.3 FORMATTING LETTERS FOR PRONUNCIATION, SPELLING, AND PROSODY

Pronunciation is a challenge for many learners of English. Inconsistencies in spelling make it difficult to determine pronunciation based on letters. Reference works such as dictionaries may accurately record pronunciation using the *International Phonetic Alphabet*, but this alphabet uses different glyphs and diacritic marks which completely transform the spelling of the word and may be unrecognizable (e.g. dʒæm, ˈæktʃuəl, ˈhæpi, fɜː(r), əˈbaʊt, /tʃeɪn). Instead, visual attributes can be used. The following sentences indicate long vowels with an underline, silent letters in a light shade, and superimposed letters for a different sound:

> ## Viz iz complex: but can be taught through tough thorough thought though. Ph haz different soundz, e.g. shepherd, diphthong, hyphen, Stephen, Stephen.

Spelling English words are also difficult due to these same inconsistencies. Visual attributes can be used to indicate the frequency of misspelled letters, aiding the reader to focus on the parts of the word prone to error, as indicated in the following paragraph:

> This example uses x-height to indicate frequency of misspelled letters: government, occasionally, restaurant, and caterpillar. X-height is the intermediate height of lowercase letters. A low x-height indicates no error, (such as the letter *g* in government), and a high x-height indicates the most frequent misspelt letter (such as the *n* in government).

X-height can represent ordered data as shown in the example above, however, x-height is unreliable across all letters; there is no variation in x-height for uppercase letters, numbers, and the letter l. There is the potential for confusion between a h and n when an n has a high x-height. Alternatively, an attribute such as color could be used:

> This example uses color to indicate frequency of misspelled letters: government, available, publisher, and occasionally. Colors are ordered purple through amber (■ ■ ■ ■), where purple indicates no error, (such as the letter *o* in occasionally), and bright amber indicates the most frequent misspelt letter (such as the *i* in occasionally).

Contractions and abbreviations can also be represented with manipulation of individual letters. Contractions and abbreviations may be desirable in applications when space is constrained, such as signage, column headers in tables, or labels in visualization plots:

> Shimabukuro (2017) abbreviates text based on a crowd-sourced survey. Letter size is used to indicate the most important letters, such as atmₒsphₑrᵢc or cₒngrₑsswₒmₐn. Width could be used instead, for example, atmospheric, automotive, circumstance, dealerships or electrical. Width-variation may be less noticeable and easier to read while still reducing word length.

Song in prose is often minimally differentiated from other text, for example, by putting the text in italics. However, this doesn't convey the *prosodic* qualities such as note pitch, note duration, and intensity. Traditional music notation could be used, but this would interrupt the flow of the text, require a lot of space, and require that the reader be familiar with and capable of sight-reading music notation.

There are many possible encodings to embed prosody into text. For example, below is a short snippet of prose with an embedded song from Carroll's *Alice's Adventures in Wonderland*. In the left version, baseline shift is used for note pitch, and spacing used for note duration. To make the shift visible, a dotted underline has been added to make the baseline visible.

The Hatter shook his head mournfully. "Not I!" he replied. "We quarrelled last March – just before HE went mad, you know –" (pointing with his teaspoon at the March Hare,) "– it was at the great concert given by the Queen of Hearts, and I had to sing:

Twinkle, twinkle, little b a t !
How I wonder what you're a t !

You know the song, perhaps?"
"I've heard something like it," said Alice.

The Hatter shook his head mournfully. "Not I!" he replied. "We quarrelled last March – just before HE went mad, you know –" (pointing with his teaspoon at the March Hare,) "– it was at the great concert given by the Queen of Hearts, and I had to sing:

TWINKLE, twinkle, little bat!
How I wonder what you're at !

You know the song, perhaps?"
"I've heard something like it," said Alice.

In the right example, letter width indicates note duration; the double-width letters for *bat* and *at* indicate notes that have double the duration as the prior syllables. Note that pitch is encoded in the letter x-height and a high baseline. Tall words starting from a low base are a deep pitch, while short words starting from a high base are high pitch.

No visible baseline is required, as the consistent x-height provides a consistent reference line across all the words. A reference line across the top of the letters may be unfamiliar in western languages. However, the letterforms in Devanagari use a consistent horizontal line near the top of each glyph and letter height can vary:

अनुच्छेद 1 (एक) – सभी मनुष्यों को गौरव और अधिकारों के विषय में जन्मजात स्वतन्त्रता और समानता प्राप्त है ।

The above examples are highly experimental. None follow familiar conventions. X-height and baseline shifts seem intuitive as the positions can be quantitatively defined and perceived, but readability will be impacted. Variable letter colors within words may be distracting and not easy to decode. Variation in letter width interrupts the expected cadence of letters. Superimposition interferes with legibility. And so on.

On the other hand, these variations suggest interesting creative approaches for solving new kinds of problems previously not explored in data visualization.

11.4 FURTHER READING

Text skimming is advocated by organizations such as colleges (e.g. Anne Arundel College 2007, Butte College, etc.) and skills development programs (e.g. BBC: *Reading, Skimming and Scanning*, 2015). This can be evaluated in eye tracking or comprehension tests, e.g. see Duggan and Payne, *Skim Reading by Satisficing: Evidence from Eye Tracking* (2011); Yang et al., *HiText: Test Reading with Dynamic Salience Marking* (2017); or Chi et al. *ScentHighlights: Highlighting Conceptually-Related Sentences during Reading* (2005).

There is a long history of highlighting keywords in context to emphasize a word or two in a short snippet of text as shown in Hearst's book *Search User Interfaces*. Many visualization systems include variations of keywords in context combined with other user interface elements to create analytic systems, such as Don et al.'s *FeatureLens* (2007), which highlights multiple words in context. Sultanum et al. (2018) shows full medical records, with multiple formats for various search criteria in *Doccurate*. Lee et al. (2016) introduce *Spotlights*, an interactive skimming technique that extracts keywords for static overlays while scrolling through long text documents. In addition to manipulating formats, *Poemage* by McCurdy et al. (2015) automates overlaid marks overtop text and adjusts visibility of words.

Regarding formatting and manipulating individual letters within words, there are use cases for language learning and other types of visualizations of prosody. For example, see Patel and Furr, *ReadN'Karaoke* (2011) or Hailpern et al., *VocSyl* (2010). Abdul-Rahman et al. (2013) map words to visually enhanced phonetic glyphs and icons.

CHAPTER 12

SparkWords

THE PRIOR CHAPTER FORMATTED text to facilitate skimming, pronunciation, spelling, and contractions. The text is manipulated to facilitate the understanding of that text.

Instead, running text can be enhanced with extrinsic data – facts about the words from other contexts and sources. Visualization of this extrinsic data can be embedded directly in the words, in-line, or in running text such as narrative or lists, as shown in the following sentence:

> Canada's largest cities, from west to east, weighted by population <500k, 500-1m, **1-2**, **2-5**, **>5m**, are: **Vancouver**, **Calgary**, **Edmonton**, Saskatoon, Winnipeg, **Toronto**, Ottawa, **Montréal**, Québec, Halifax.

In this example, ordered data is represented using the font weight of the city names. This is similar to city names encoded with data in maps. More generally, SparkWords can encode any categoric, ordered, or quantitative data; applied to words, syllables, or even letters in running text. In this respect, SparkWords are an encapsulation of many of the techniques discussed in this book.

12.1 HISTORIC PRECEDENT FOR SPARKWORDS

The earlier historic images show several examples of SparkWords. For example, the dictionary and *Michelin Guide* in Figure 3.48 use formatting to indicate different categories of information. The medieval illuminated manuscript calls out specific words via color and illumination of initial letters in Figure 3.45.

Contemporary examples include use such as *code editors* (Figure 1.17), drug labels using *TALLman lettering* (Figure 3.17), or in some *information retrieval* applications where multiple different types of attributes are highlighted (e.g. Sultanum et al.'s *Doccurate* 2018).

Post-modernists, discussed previously in Figure 1.22, also manipulated the formatting of letters, words, phrases, and paragraphs to convey additional semantics beyond the literal text. Beyond simple differentiation or ordering, post-modernists push formatting effects further, such as the creation of waves running through text in the example by Ronell.

Most of these historic examples use visual attributes to create differentiation or identify categories of information. Can SparkWords go further? Can they be generalized for categoric, ordered, and quantitative data? And work at the level of letters, syllables, or words?

12.2 SPARKWORDS DEFINED

What are SparkWords?

- *Words.* SparkWords encode data into words, not charts.

- *Layout.* SparkWords are embedded in text layouts, such as prose, lists, or tables.

- *Scope.* The format can apply to a word or two, or a syllable or a character.

- *Data type.* The encodings support categoric, ordered, and quantitative data.

- *Visual attributes.* SparkWords can use many different visual attributes, whether traditional visual attributes (such as hue, see Section 3.3) or typographic attributes (such as weight and italic, see Section 3.2).

- *Multiple attributes.* Attributes can be combined.

  - *Redundant.* Multiple attributes can encode the same data, such as the use of word weight and width, to represent inverse frequency as shown in the previous chapter with the *Wright Brothers* example, e.g. known *to scientists as a* "helicoptere."

  - *Multiplex.* Multiple different data attributes can be encoded into multiple different visual attributes, such as the example of politician names encoding political affiliation, gender, terms in office, and so on, as seen in the set visualization examples in Chapter 8.

Because text is unlike simple marks such as dots and triangles, there are some constraints:

- *Not size.* As shown in the earlier *Verne* example at the beginning of Section 1.1, large variation in size should not be used.

- *Readability.* More generally, the degree of text formatting should not be overly disruptive. For example, 𝔟𝔩𝔞𝔠𝔨𝔩𝔢𝔱𝔱𝔢𝔯 𝔦𝔰 𝔩𝔢𝔤𝔦𝔟𝔩𝔢 𝔟𝔲𝔱 𝔪𝔞𝔶 𝔟𝔢 𝔡𝔦𝔣𝔣𝔦𝔠𝔲𝔩𝔱 𝔣𝔬𝔯 𝔞 𝔪𝔬𝔡𝔢𝔯𝔫 𝔞𝔲𝔡𝔦𝔢𝔫𝔠𝔢 𝔱𝔬 𝔯𝔢𝔞𝔡.

- *Legibility.* Encodings should not reduce legibility. For example, too much variation in brightness reduces contrast, reducing legibility. Blur and drop-shadows reduce the clarity of letterforms, reducing legibility. And so on.

12.3 SPARKWORDS IN NARRATIVE

Since SparkWords are applicable to a range of data types, text scope, and attributes, many examples are considered.

12.3.1 Categoric SparkWords

The earlier example of character types in *Wonderland* uses typeface to indicate categories (Figure 3.24). As previously shown in Chapter 8 regarding sets, SparkWords should be well suited to indicate multiple categoric data points.

Data associated with entities, such as persons, places, organizations, and things, can be directly presented in the narrative context. Named Entity Recognition (NER) is a task in Natural Language Processing – once entities are recognized, additional data can be encoded:

> Shipwrecks from January 2019 include: **London**, *Ou Ya Leng 6*, *Kalebi*, *Cavalier XV*, **Jie Hai 189**, *Forever Lucky*, **NV-8836**, *Tom Bussler*, **Volgo-Balt 214**, **Mary B II**, *KMP Sangke Palangga*, *Star Centurion*, *Rix Emerald*, **Tour 2**, *Wardeh*, *Priboy*, **Zhongxing689**, **Kandy**, **Maestro**, *Oriental Nadehiko*, *Sea Frontier*, and *Kados*. Color indicates vessel type (cargo, fishing, passenger, tanker, tug, other) and **bold** indicates loss of life.

Furthermore, categorical encodings can be used to create a visual cross-reference between data points in a chart and words in a corresponding text. Consider the following example of unemployment data widely reported in March 2018. Text color corresponds to data points in the timeseries, facilitating cross-referencing between the text and the graphic:

> The jobs report released by the Department of Labor on Friday offered some good job news. A winning combination of job creation and a swelling labor force signaled the economy's strength. For the fifth month in a row, the jobless rate remained unchanged at 4.1 percent, below 2007 levels and a long way from the peak of 9.9% in 2009. On Twitter, President Trump relayed the news in capital letters: "JOBS, JOBS, JOBS!"

This experimental example also breaks other conventions. No horizontal or vertical axis is provided as the narrative text explicitly identifies the start time, end time, minimum, and maximum value. Further, the text is superimposed over the chart, rather than separating the chart from the text, such as a sparkline or otherwise visually located in a separate block.

12.3.2 Ordered SparkWords

Many visual attributes provide a few levels of ordering, such as hue, brightness, font weight, or font width as discussed in the introduction to Chapter 9. The examples of skim formatting in Chapter 11 use typographic attributes to indicate a few levels of word frequency, such as weight, width, and small caps. The first example in this section uses a single ordered value to indicate population via font weight. The viewer can read the text sequentially, or visually skip to the heaviest weight fonts for the largest cities, such as **Vancouver**, **Toronto**, and **Montréal**.

The following example indicates four ordered data values using attributes of weight, red, green, and blue:

In *Sémiologie Graphique* (1967), Bertin visualizes a dataset of occupations. Here the data is visualized – *and explained* – in narrative. The most populated departments are **Paris**, **Seine** & **Nord** (shown by font weight: 34k-102, to 130, **to 173**, **to 236**, **to 1517**). Top departments for manufacturing are Belfort, **Moselle** & **Nord** (proportion of red). Agriculture are Gers, Creuse & Lozere (green). Services are **Paris**, **Alpes Mmes** & **Bouches Du Rh** (blue).

This paragraph can be further enhanced by adding inline histograms to indicate the data range and distribution per variable:

The top three departments by population (indicated by font weight: 34k-102, to 130, **to 173**, **to 236**, **to 1517**) are **Paris**, **Seine** and **Nord**. Top departments by percent of population in manufacturing (shown by proportion of red: 0 ▬▬▬ 70%) are Belfort, **Moselle** and **Nord**. Top departments for agriculture (green: 0 ▬▬▬ 70%) are Gers, Creuse and Lozere. Top services (blue: 0 ▬▬▬ 70%) are **Paris**, **Alpes Mmes**, and **Bouches Du Rh**. Three districts closest to an even balance between occupations appear grey: Hte Saone, **Puy De Dome**, Eure. Agricultural districts with large populations are **Morbihan**, **Finistere** and **Ille & V.** Small departments with bias to manufacturing or services are Belfort, Doubs, Cote D'Or and Var.

Full data in alphabetic order: Ain, **Aisne**, Allier, **Alpes Mmes**, Ardeche, Ardennes, Ariege, **Ases Pyrenees**, Aube, Aude, Aveyron, **Bas-Rhin**, Belfort, **Bouches Du Rh.**, Bses Alpes, **Calvados**, Cantal, Charente, **Charente Mme**, Cher, Correze, **Cote D'Or**, **Cotes Du Nord**, Creuse, Deux-Sevres, **Dordogne**, Doubs, Drome, **Eure**, Eure & Loir, **Finistere**, Gard, Gers, **Gironde**, **Haute Garonne**, **Herault**, Hte Loire, Hte Marne, Hte Saone, **Hte Savoie**, **Hte Vienne**, Htes Alpes, Htes Pyrenees, **Ht-Rhin**, **Ille & V.**, Indre, Indre & L., **Isere**, Jura, Landes, Loir & Cher, **Loire**, **Loire Inf.**, Loiret, Lot, Lot & Gar., Lozere, **Maine & L.**, **Manche**, Marne, Mayenne, **Meurthe & M.**, Meuse, **Morbihan**, **Moselle**, Nievre, **Nord**, Oise, Orne, **P. D. C.**, **Paris**, Puy De Dome, Pyrenees Orient., **Rhone**, Saone & L., Sarthe, Savoie, **Seine**, Seine & M., **Seine & O.**, **Seine Inf.**, Somme, Tarn, Tarn & G., Var, Vaucluse, **Vendee**, Vienne, **Vosges** and Yonne.

The second paragraph lists all the departments in alphabetic order. Ordered lists are useful with SparkWords as the viewer can (a) read the list sequentially; (b) find named departments using the ordering to facilitate search; or (c) focus on a visual attribute (e.g.

blue or heavyweight) to identify departments with that characteristic. Further, in an inter-active environment, lists can be re-sorted by other criteria, for example, by population, proportion of the population in an occupation, or any other data variable.

Word lists organized geographically. Rather than using SparkWords in narrative text or sequential lists, SparkWords can be organized into a spatial list. The next example shows top hashtags in New York City. Weight indicates the frequency of the hashtag, and they are ordered such that each geolocation indicates the top hashtag with the highest frequency in that area.

automotive bbb shoppingwithbeth howtogetawaywithmurder coloring **broncos ci225 northbergen** g2b juventus womenswear lhhatl **gh** teamkristian peopleschoice leo followmeaaron shawnfollowme highlights thebachelor giantschat mlg5k nblalinavoto healthy tweetconfection **amnh museum 2030now** 1stavecitycuts mtvstars finalbattle14 **jgto600k met themet** justkeepswimming supersoulsunday life **lincolncenter 99conf jeffkoons** momconf bratty weehawken adhds2014 **nyfw mbfw centralpark** snow browns astoria jersey **jovani books columbuscircle apple** rwya 8daysforexpelledmovie **airjordans** lincolntunnel pachanyc **moma art rainroom giveaway win** follow smashbash tessanne **nycc nyias timessquare** latism13 rooseveltisland marionightlife hoboken **tcdisrupt bryantpark camfollowme** penthouse808 crossfitbell gustokolangnamanay **nyr msg empirestatebuilding csw58** salute aerospace gigaomlive **highline** marcovando motatakeover lic **longislandcity** arganoil nowwatching **smwnyc flatiron** cantstopwontstop skilledtrade longislandmedium impactlab 7on7htc parsons **unionsquare ferguson** fffweek latex **americafirst** hudsonriver **westvillage drag websterhall** eastriver indiefilm sdny graveyard **westgay nyu nytm nyuef eastvillage** szoldplace **unitedxxvi** paintingexchange sushiazabu **soho cronut** davidwright sammywilkfollowspree mahps hashtagwars pier26 **tribeca littleitaly les** williamsburg brooklynbowl boulevardtavernbrooklyn tff2013 **clerical it finance karawalkerdomino** knittingfactory locallybrewed **wtc neverforget socialmedia** scny hiring peterluger the100dayproject **makeup wallstreet brooklynbridge** dmargeniis_x3 soberanopalpoeta followmeaustin megafest statueofliberty pixiemarketgirl blogwell **dumbo** tsod sod factorystudios **bushwick**

Instead of variably sized words placed overtop a map (i.e. a word cloud), these consistently sized SparkWords offer:

- *Locality sensitivity.* Every word is highly local, e.g. *BrooklynBridge* and *MOMA* are extremely close to their actual locations.

- *Word sequence.* Words form lines facilitating reading word sequences, for example, *MOMA* is next to *art* and *WallStreet* is next to *BrooklynBridge*.

- *Thematic patterns.* Weight is a strong visual cue. As weight indicates tweet frequency, it is a proxy for the density of people. Note that the heavyweight text largely corresponds to the densely populated island of Manhattan.

Word formats linking values in narrative and visualization. Narrative explanations accompanying visualizations are common in data journalism, such as *The New York Times* or *The Guardian.* Cross-referencing between the narrative and the visualization is typically expressed literally, such as indicating the line color that a viewer should attend to.

In the next example, shared formatting between the visualization and words in a narrative paragraph are used to facilitate cross-referencing. This can also reduce learning effort as both the visualization and the narrative explanation use the same encoding. Figure 12.1 pairs a heatmap with a narrative paragraph where the SparkWords use the same weight and hue as the corresponding cells in the heat map.

Rather than full paragraphs spatially separated from the visualization, data comics use a sequence of panels to incrementally advance the explanation in step with the visualization (see Bach et al. 2016 regarding data comics). The narrative in the panels aids with how to interpret the visualization, calls out specific data points, and describes analytic comparisons. This literal narrative text acts as an introductory tutorial for the viewer providing concrete examples of analytical tasks that can be done visually.

Figure 12.2 shows play sequences from the U.S. National Football League in 2011. In the core visualization, a tree diagram indicates play combinations across each down in sequence. Within each down, the play is indicated by a labeled, colored bar. Bar length indicates number of plays, bar color indicates the number of yards gained (or lost), and label indicates the play type, of which there are only three (pass, run, and other). While the labels are not unique, it is the sequence of plays that are of interest. The play sequence is

This heatmap of accident data shows clear patterns but key insights are not obvious. An observation or two could be highlighted. If there are many insights and comments, associated prose with SparkWords may be more effective. In this accident data, the most frequent collisions are in heavy-weight type: parked vehicles, posts and pedestrians (less than ½% in period, ½-3%, 3-10%, 10+%). Animals, cyclists, ditches and trees are also quite frequent. Severity of injury varies from none to non-incapacitating to fatal. Worst injuries result from collisions with pedestrians and cyclists. The least injurious accidents are fires and animals. Collisions with trains, buildings and roll-overs are also injurious, but infrequent.

Collision	Jan	Feb	Mar	Apr	May	Jun	Jul	Aug	Sep	Oct	Nov	Dec
Animal	106	66	70	75	99	95	65	60	56	139	240	169
Bridge	26	17	25	12	8	18	15	14	12	14	14	18
Building	16	10	9	4	8	5	8	11	7	12	15	9
Cyclist	63	63	60	101	139	168	211	157	105	48	53	100
Ditch	135	120	103	93	72	91	111	100	85	131	120	95
Embankment	89	61	52	51	48	50	49	54	48	62	68	58
Fire	5			3		9	4	7	4	3	5	3
Guardrail	126	84	90	60	64	68	87	75	77	127	111	77
Hydrant	9	13	10	2	11	8	6	6	4	11	4	4
Jackknife	20	20	14	10	10	8	10	18	15	20	17	11
Parked vehicle	167	177	169	163	171	166	155	174	143	164	160	143
Pedestrian	149	118	124	156	160	152	132	131	145	124	134	150
Post	172	178	183	126	119	126	126	140	136	177	167	137
Rollover	137	104	115	126	136	137	153	168	104	150	133	144
Train	3	6	4	3	2	2	4	2	2	2	5	4
Tree	140	132	125	85	83	97	104	98	102	141	135	107
Wall	27	21	18	14	8	11	22	10	9	21	20	15

FIGURE 12.1 **Number of vehicle accidents by month, colored by severity and weighted by frequency, in both the text and the visualization.**

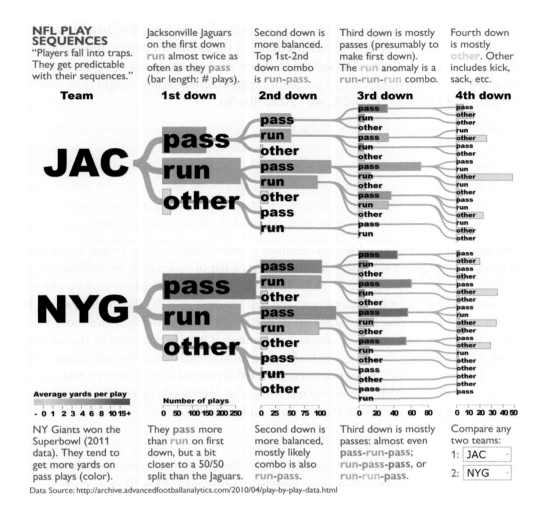

NFL PLAY SEQUENCES
"Players fall into traps. They get predictable with their sequences."

Jacksonville Jaguars on the first down run almost twice as often as they pass (bar length: # plays).

Second down is more balanced. Top 1st-2nd down combo is run-pass.

Third down is mostly passes (presumably to make first down). The run anomaly is a run-run-run combo.

Fourth down is mostly other. Other includes kick, sack, etc.

| Team | 1st down | 2nd down | 3rd down | 4th down |

Average yards per play
- 0 1 2 3 4 6 8 10 15+

Number of plays
0 50 100 150 200 250

0 25 50 75 100

0 20 40 60 80

0 10 20 30 40 50

NY Giants won the Superbowl (2011 data). They tend to get more yards on pass plays (color).

They pass more than run on first down, but a bit closer to a 50/50 split than the Jaguars.

Second down is more balanced, mostly likely combo is also run-pass.

Third down is mostly passes: almost even pass-run-pass; run-pass-pass, or run-run-pass.

Compare any two teams:
1: JAC
2: NYG

Data Source: http://archive.advancedfootballanalytics.com/2010/04/play-by-play-data.html

FIGURE 12.2   National Football League play sequences for Jacksonville Jaguars and NY Giants.

indicated by left to right connectivity, for example, the Jacksonville Jaguars are most likely to do a *run-pass-pass-other* combination. The words in the narrative share the same color as their corresponding bar in the visualization. This consistency in color coding aids cross-referencing between the two.

Formats and hierarchies. Ordered encodings can be applied to syllables or characters. Some examples shown earlier include contractions and spelling in Section 11.3. Ordered encodings are highly applicable to codes. Coded hierarchies are frequently used by experts, such as labeling equipment in a computer network or an electrical grid; product codes in the consumer price index; industry codes in financial markets; aircraft flight numbers; Dewey decimal codes for organizing books; and so on.

NAICS, the *North American Industry Classification System*, is used by national statistical agencies, economists, and financial professionals. As industry data is updated monthly, these subject matter experts need to quickly assess where the biggest changes are and what the underlying drivers are. NAICS is a numeric hierarchy; for example, 11 indicates all agriculture, 112 is animal production, 1123 is poultry, 11234 is poultry hatcheries. 11 can be encoded to indicate the change in agriculture, 2 the change in animal production, 3 for poultry, and 4 for hatcheries. The following shows the biggest changes per sector via color (bright red for big decreases, bright green for biggest increases) and weight (size relative to peers at that level: <10%, 10–40%, **40–90%**, 90+%):

11221: Agriculture, forestry, fishing & hunting ► Animal production and aquaculture ► Hog & pig farming ► **Raising hogs and pigs**

22111: Utilities ► Electric power generation, transmission & distribution ► **Electric power generation** ► Hydro-electric power generation

32742: Manufacturing ► **Non metallic mineral products** ► Lime and gypsum products ► Gypsum product manufacturing

41111: Wholesale trade ► Farm products merchant wholesaler ► **Farm products merchant wholesaler** ► Live animal merchant wholesaler

51521: Information and culture ► **Broadcasting (except Internet)** ► **Pay and specialty media** ► Pay and specialty television

62132: Health care and social assistance ► **Ambulatory health care services** ► Other health practitioners ► Optometrists

For the non-expert, the added text enables decoding the numeric codes. However, the text labels are long and verbose – for the expert, a list of codes may be sufficient: 11221, 22111, 32742, 41111, 51521, 62132. These 30 numeric characters convey the same information as the prior 637 characters. The first example, 11221, shows that raising hogs has significantly decreased (as indicated by the bright red trailing 21), and more broadly agriculture and animals have also decreased somewhat less (as indicated by the darker red leading 11) – meaning that hogs are leading a general trend across the agriculture sector. The last example, 62132, shows optometrists have decreased somewhat in a mid-red (32); whereas the overall health care sector has somewhat increased (green 62) – meaning that optometrists are divergent from the general trend in health care.

12.3.3 Quantitative SparkWords

Visual attributes such as brightness, hue, and font weight in practice can only represent a few ordered levels of data at typical reading size. Length is a more accurate visual attribute for perceiving and comparing quantities. Length can be encoded into a word or two using proportional encoding, i.e. by varying the length of a visual attribute across a subset of the word, with consistent sizing used for all words in the paragraph. For example:

> Star Wars character popularity can be measured by Wikipedia page reads. Darth Vader is most popular at 16,714,958 page views as indicated by the length of underline. Obi-Wan, Luke and Leia lag behind, the sum of their views lower than Vader. Han, Chewbacca and R2-D2 are all nearly tied, with C-3PO the least read of major characters at only 1,453,936.

Underlines are subtle. A bright, filled box behind the text can be used for a stronger visual impact:

Star Wars character popularity is lead by Darth Vader, followed by Obi-Wan, Luke Skywalker, Princess Leia, Han Solo, Chewbacca, R2-D2 and C-3PO, based on Wikipedia pageviews.

The same approach can be used at an alphanumeric level. Consider spark bar charts. Small spark bar charts are used in sports to summarize the results of a series of games, such as examples seen in Tufte's *Beautiful Evidence* (2006) or this example summarizing the New York Yankee's 2018 season (from baseball-reference.com):

The chart shows the win/loss sequence (green/red) and the score differential (bar height). The opposing team is not indicated but could be important; for example, a win against the leading team is different than a win against a weak team.

Opposing teams can be shown using team codes. All teams have mnemonic three-letter codes, e.g. NYY for the New York Yankees. Further, baseball games are typically played in a series of two to four games per opponent. Each letter in the code can be used to represent each successive game in a series. For example, the Yankees started 2018 with a four game series versus Toronto: TOR4, where the outline color indicates win/loss (green/red), and the score differential is indicated by the proportion of the fill (a low fill is a loss by one run, a full fill is a loss by 10 or more runs). The full season, then, can be represented as a paragraph of codes:

TOR4 TBR BAL4 BOS DET MIA TOR4 MIN4 LAA HOU4 CLE BOS OAK WSN KCR TEX LAA HOU BAL DET TOR NYM WSN TBR4 WSN SEA TBR PHI BOS ATL TOR BAL4 CLE4 NYM TBR KCR4 BAL BOS4 CHW TEX4 NYM TBR TOR MIA BAL4 CHW DET4 OAK SEA MIN TOR BOS BAL TBR4 BOS

Within the list of codes, there are visibly many wins early in the season (top line) with complete sweeps against Tampa Bay, Minnesota, Los Angeles, and Cleveland. One particularly poor series stands out in the second half of the season when the Yankees lost four straight games against their archrival Boston (all red BOS4).

Attempting to embed quantities as fills in letters is highly experimental. In the above example, a game series that is four games long needs to append an extra numeral 4 so that there is a fourth letter to fill in. All letters need to have the same height to represent the data range.

Rather than filling the letter, a separate box behind each letter could be used, where the box height is the score differential. Using the old technique of *reverse video*, high contrast can be maintained between the letter and background by having a white letter over a box, and a filled letter when it is over the background. This very high contrast can be useful in bright environments, such as full sun in the stadium of an afternoon baseball game.

TOR TBR BAL BOS DET MIA TOR MIN LAA HOU CLE BOS OAK WSN KCR TEX LAA
HOU BAL DET TOR NYM WSN TBR WSN SEA TBR PHL BOS ATL TOR BAL CLE NYM TBR
KCR BAL BOS CHW TEX NYM TBR TOR MIA BAL CHW DET OAK SEA MIN TOR BOS
BAL TBR BOS

The simplest variant is shaded boxes using light colors to maintain legibility of the text. This also allows for more compact letters to be used and is easy to implement:

TOR TBR BAL BOS DET MIA TOR MIN LAA HOU CLE BOS OAK WSN KCR TEX LAA HOU BAL DET TOR NYM WSN
TBR WSN SEA TBR PHL BOS ATL TOR BAL CLE NYM TBR KCR BAL BOS CHW TEX NYM TBR TOR MIA BAL CHW
DET OAK SEA MIN TOR BOS BAL TBR BOS

12.4 SPARKWORDS IN LISTS

Lists of words are common in prose and represent an ideal opportunity to represent data related to each item directly in the words without needing a separate visualization. The use of SparkWords on lists have occurred in many prior examples, such as:

- *Alice in Wonderland* examples with enriched lists include character sentiment (Figure 3.13), word pair frequencies (Figure 3.18), major character types (Figure 3.24), word spelling modifications (Figure 3.28 right), and top adverb per character (Figure 3.30).

- *Distributions* in Chapter 6 contain many examples where the leaves are essentially lists of codes or words typographically enhanced to indicate additional data, such as lists of states (Figure 6.5), categories of purchases (Figure 6.6), adjectives associated with characters (Figure 6.12), and the hierarchy of lists indicating causes of death in Georgian London (Figure 6.19).

- The prior section on *prose* (Section 12.3) has many examples where paragraphs list a few items, such as the example of shipwrecks, departments in France, Star Wars characters, and baseball game series.

12.5 SPARKWORDS IN TABLES

SparkWords are versatile and can be used to enhance both numeric tables and tables of text.

12.5.1 Orders of Magnitude

In the visualization of quantities, typically a linear mapping between the numeric value and the graphical representation is used, for example, bars on a bar chart. Sometimes areas are used, for example, boxes on a treemap. These techniques work well when the variance in the data is one or two orders of magnitude. However, some datasets have many orders of magnitude between the largest and smallest values. Figure 12.3 shows a small subset of country data in a table and in Figure 12.4 the same data is shown as bar charts.

With as many as six orders of magnitude between the largest and smallest values, this data is difficult to visualize with quantitative graphics. It is difficult to tell from the bars whether Tuvalu or the UAE have more roads, even though the UAE has 500 times more. Even area-based visualizations, such as a treemap, are difficult to use with this wide variation. If the roads in the United States were represented by the size of this page, then the roads in Tuvalu would be a fraction of a period.

Furthermore, some analytical tasks require more accuracy than can be depicted graphically with bars or areas. A financial analyst may be interested in a few digits of accuracy in a report. For example, a fraction of a change in nominal GDP may not be visible as bars but have significant economic impact. Or a small variation in file size indicates a change in file contents. The author has previously worked on a visualization where users were adamant in visibly depicting items that ranged across six orders of magnitude to at least 3 significant digits.

Figure 12.3 does show accurate quantities as long numbers. These long numbers take up a lot of screen space. Furthermore, long strings of zeros require focused attention to mentally parse (is the GDP of the UK billions or trillions?). Some tabular software will automatically format these values such that the scale is encoded after the number (e.g. T for trillions, B for billions, etc.), as shown in Figure 12.5. These aid accurate reading of the quantitative values to at least a few significant digits; provides immediate, unambiguous indication of the order of magnitude; and it significantly reduces the width of the table,

Country	Area(km2)	Population	GDP (USD)	Roads (km)	PopDensity (people/km2)	GDP per capita (USD)
Tuvalu	26	11,147	42,000,000	8.0	428.7	3,768
Uganda	241,038	40,853,749	89,190,000,000	20,544.0	169.5	2,183
Ukraine	603,550	43,952,299	369,600,000,000	169,694.0	72.8	8,409
United Arab Emirates	83,600	9,701,315	696,000,000,000	4,080.0	116.0	71,743
United Kingdom	243,610	65,105,246	2,925,000,000,000	394,428.0	267.3	44,927
United States	9,833,517	329,256,465	19,490,000,000,000	6,586,610.0	33.5	59,194

FIGURE 12.3   Portion of a table of country data. Note many orders of magnitude in most columns.

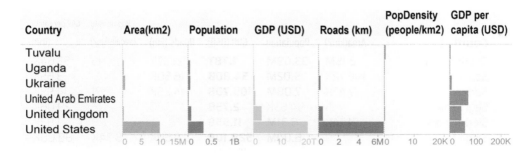

FIGURE 12.4   Same table, shown with multiple bar charts. Given the wide range of the data, many bars are too small to discern.

Country	Area(km2)	Population	GDP (USD)	Roads (km)	PopDensity (people/km2)	GDP per capita (USD)
Saudi Arabia	2.15M	33.09M	1.78T	221.37K	15	53.64K
Senegal	196.72K	15.02M	54.80B	16.50K	76	3.65K
Serbia	77.47K	7.08M	105.70B	44.25K	91	14.93K
Seychelles	455	94.63K	2.75B	526	208	29.06K
Sierra Leone	71.74K	6.31M	11.55B	-	88	1.83K
Singapore	719	6.00M	528.10B	3.50K	8.34K	88.08K
Sint Maarten	34	42.68K	365.80M	53	1.26K	8.57K

FIGURE 12.5   Country data where trailing letter indicates order of magnitude for each number. While accurate and space-efficient, outliers and distributions are not easily detected.

which is important for many applications, such as financial trading screens or directory listings showing computer file statistics.

However, once the numbers are formatted to indicate order of magnitude via a letter, it becomes difficult to scan the numbers to find the large values or the small values; or even to get an overview of the most common sizes. For example, the GDP of Saudi Arabia is significantly larger than Serbia, but Serbia's GDP is more visually prominent at six characters rather than Saudi Arabia's four characters. And although GDP is most frequently indicated in billions, there are also instances of millions and trillions in the column – a careful reading is required to get a gist of the sizes.

Instead, a highly salient format, such as font weight or color, could be used to create an ordering through trillions, billions, millions, and thousands as shown in Figure 12.6. In this table, the ordering of magnitude is explicit. For example, between Figure 12.5 and Figure 12.6, it is easier to see in the latter that Saudi Arabia has a larger land area and GDP than the other visible countries; while the Seychelles and Sint Maarten have small populations; and that Singapore and Sint Maarten have high population densities.

This can also be effective with interactions such as sorting, for example, to see if large values in one column corresponds to large values in adjacent columns. In Figure 12.7, where the data is sorted based on the quantity of roads, it appears from the top seven observations that GDP may be a better predictor of the quantity of roads in a country than the area of the country.

Country	Area(km2)	Population	GDP (USD)	Roads (km)	Pop Density (people/km2)	GDP per capita (USD)
Saudi Arabia	2.15M	33.09M	**1.78T**	221.37K	15	53.64K
Senegal	196.72K	15.02M	**54.80B**	16.50K	76	3.65K
Serbia	77.47K	7.08M	**105.70B**	44.25K	91	14.93K
Seychelles	455	94.63K	**2.75B**	526	208	29.06K
Sierra Leone	71.74K	6.31M	**11.55B**	-	88	1.83K
Singapore	719	6.00M	**528.10B**	3.50K	8.34K	88.08K
Sint Maarten	34	42.68K	365.80M	53	1.26K	8.57K

FIGURE 12.6   Table where font weight indicates the order of magnitude in addition to trailing character. Common sizes and outliers are more apparent.

Country	Area(km2)	Population	GDP (USD)	Roads (km)	Pop Density (people/km2)	GDP per capita (USD)
United States	9.83M	329.26M	**19.49T**	6.59M	33	59.19K
China	9.60M	1.38B	**23.21T**	4.77M	144	16.76K
India	3.29M	1.30B	**9.47T**	4.70M	395	7.31K
Russia	17.10M	142.12M	**4.02T**	1.28M	8	28.26K
Japan	377.92K	126.17M	**5.44T**	1.22M	334	43.14K
France	643.80K	67.36M	**2.86T**	1.05M	105	42.40K
Canada	9.98M	35.88M	**1.77T**	1.04M	4	49.44K

FIGURE 12.7   Country table sorted by quantity of roads.

As only font-weight is used to indicate the order of magnitude, all the other formatting techniques associated with text can be used, such as foreground color and background color, italics, added icons, font width, and so on. As such, this approach is highly compatible with other table needs and can also be extended to other chart types and dashboards where totals and quantities are shown, such as donut charts.

12.5.2 Tables with Data Added into Typographic Formats

Tables of text are also common. The tiny table in Figure 3.46 is a grid packed with sovereign rulers. Any of these words could be enhanced with visual attributes, such as the duration of the reign, number of heirs, number of siblings, and so on.

The table in Figure 12.8 shows the players for Major League Baseball organized by team and position. Each cell identifies a player and formats indicate data. *Batting average* is represented by font width, varying from highly compressed for the lowest quartile to wide for the top quartile, so that players that hit more frequently are more visually prominent. *On base percentage* is indicated by font weight, lightweight for those below 0.300, heavyweight for those above 0.400, so that players who reach base after they hit are more prominent. Color indicates *slugging percentage*, ranging from light orange for the lowest to deep blue for the highest, again, so that players that achieve the most bases on their hits are most prominent.

The combinations tend to reinforce each other as someone who tends to bat well tends to get on base more, and those that manage to get on base tend to get more bases. The combinations can be read holistically: for example, Mike Trout and Yordan Alvarez visually pop-out across all the variables. Brock Holt and Jorge Polanco are heavyweight (get on base) but lighter hues (don't get as many bases). Miguel Cabrera is wide (bats well) but not heavyweight (doesn't get on base as much). And so on. In a single view, three hitting statistics for 255 named players across the league are visible with various visual patterns.

Cells can be shorter than a word. Figure 12.9 is a table where the cells contain numeric codes for the departments of France. The cells are organized with increasing manufacturing vertically and increasing agriculture horizontally. The corresponding values for each department are represented by the proportion of fill in each department code: green fill for agriculture on the first digit; and red fill for manufacturing on the second digit.

2019 MLB BATTING STATISTICS

Team	Catcher	1st base	2nd base	Short stop	3rd base	Left field	Center field	Right Field	Designated Hitter
New York Yankees	Gary Sanchez	**Luke Voit**	**DJ LeMahieu**	Didi Gregorius	**Gio Urshela**	**Mike Tauchman**	Brett Gardner	**Aaron Judge**	Edwin Encarnacion
Tampa Bay Rays	Mike Zunino	**Ji-Man Choi**	Brandon Lowe	Willy Adames	Yandy Diaz	**Tommy Pham**	Kevin Kiermaier	Avisail Garcia	**Austin Meadows**
Boston Red Sox	Christian Vazquez	Mitch Moreland	**Brock Holt**	**Xander Bogaerts**	**Rafael Devers**	Andrew Benintendi	Jackie Bradley Jr.	**Mookie Betts**	**J.D. Martinez**
Toronto Blue Jays	Danny Jansen	Justin Smoak	**Cavan Biggio**	Freddy Galvis	Vladimir Guerrero Jr.	Lourdes Gurriel Jr.	Teoscar Hernandez	Randal Grichuk	Rowdy Tellez
Baltimore Orioles	Pedro Severino	Chris Davis	Jonathan Villar	Richie Martin	Rio Ruiz	Dwight Smith Jr.	Stevie Wilkerson	**Trey Mancini**	Renato Nunez
Minnesota Twins	**Mitch Garver**	C.J. Cron	Jonathan Schoop	**Jorge Polanco**	Miguel Sano	Eddie Rosario	Byron Buxton	Max Kepler	**Nelson Cruz**
Cleveland Indians	Roberto Perez	**Carlos Santana**	Jason Kipnis	**Francisco Lindor**	Jose Ramirez	Jake Bauers	Oscar Mercado	**Tyler Naquin**	Franmil Reyes
Chicago White Sox	James McCann	**Jose Abreu**	Yolmer Sanchez	**Tim Anderson**	**Yoan Moncada**	Eloy Jimenez	Adam Engel	Ryan Cordell	Yonder Alonso
Kansas City Royals	Martin Maldonado	Ryan O'Hearn	**Whit Merrifield**	Adalberto Mondesi	**Hunter Dozier**	Alex Gordon	Billy Hamilton	Bubba Starling	**Jorge Soler**
Detroit Tigers	Grayson Greiner	Brandon Dixon	Gordon Beckham	Jordy Mercer	Dawel Lugo	Christin Stewart	JaCoby Jones	Nicholas Castellanos	Miguel Cabrera
Houston Astros	**Robinson Chirinos**	**Yuli Gurriel**	**Jose Altuve**	**Carlos Correa**	**Alex Bregman**	**Michael Brantley**	Jake Marisnick	Josh Reddick	**Yordan Alvarez**
Oakland Athletics	Josh Phegley	**Matt Olson**	Jurickson Profar	**Marcus Semien**	**Matt Chapman**	Robbie Grossman	**Ramon Laureano**	Stephen Piscotty	Khris Davis
Texas Rangers	Jeff Mathis	Ronald Guzman	Rougned Odor	Elvis Andrus	Asdrubal Cabrera	Willie Calhoun	Delino DeShields	Nomar Mazara	**Shin-Soo Choo**
Los Angeles Angels	Jonathan Lucroy	Albert Pujols	Luis Rengifo	Andrelton Simmons	**David Fletcher**	**Brian Goodwin**	**Mike Trout**	Kole Calhoun	**Shohei Ohtani**
Seattle Mariners	**Omar Narvaez**	Austin Nola	Dee Gordon	J.P. Crawford	Kyle Seager	Domingo Santana	Mallex Smith	Mitch Haniger	Daniel Vogelbach
Atlanta Braves	Tyler Flowers	**Freddie Freeman**	**Ozzie Albies**	Dansby Swanson	**Josh Donaldson**	Austin Riley	**Ronald Acuna Jr.**	**Nick Markakis**	
Washington Nationals	Yan Gomes	Matt Adams	Brian Dozier	**Trea Turner**	**Anthony Rendon**	**Juan Soto**	Victor Robles	**Adam Eaton**	
New York Mets	**Wilson Ramos**	**Pete Alonso**	Robinson Cano	Amed Rosario	Todd Frazier	**J.D. Davis**	Juan Lagares	**Michael Conforto**	
Philadelphia Phillies	**J.T. Realmuto**	**Rhys Hoskins**	Cesar Hernandez	Jean Segura	Maikel Franco	**Andrew McCutchen**	Scott Kingery	**Bryce Harper**	
Miami Marlins	Jorge Alfaro	**Garrett Cooper**	Starlin Castro	Miguel Rojas	**Brian Anderson**	Curtis Granderson	Lewis Brinson	Harold Ramirez	
St. Louis Cardinals	Yadier Molina	**Paul Goldschmidt**	**Kolten Wong**	Paul DeJong	Matt Carpenter	Marcell Ozuna	Harrison Bader	Dexter Fowler	
Milwaukee Brewers	**Yasmani Grandal**	Eric Thames	**Keston Hiura**	Orlando Arcia	Mike Moustakas	**Ryan Braun**	Lorenzo Cain	**Christian Yelich**	
Chicago Cubs	**Willson Contreras**	**Anthony Rizzo**	Addison Russell	Javier Baez	**Kris Bryant**	**Kyle Schwarber**	Albert Almora	Jason Heyward	
Cincinnati Reds	Tucker Barnhart	Joey Votto	Jose Peraza	Jose Iglesias	**Eugenio Suarez**	**Jesse Winker**	Nick Senzel	Yasiel Puig	
Pittsburgh Pirates	Elias Diaz	**Josh Bell**	Adam Frazier	**Kevin Newman**	Colin Moran	**Bryan Reynolds**	**Starling Marte**	Melky Cabrera	
Los Angeles Dodgers	Austin Barnes	**Max Muncy**	Enrique Hernandez	**Corey Seager**	**Justin Turner**	Joc Pederson	**A.J. Pollock**	**Cody Bellinger**	
Arizona Diamondbacks	Carson Kelly	Christian Walker	**Wilmer Flores**	Nick Ahmed	Eduardo Escobar	David Peralta	**Ketel Marte**	Adam Jones	
San Francisco Giants	Buster Posey	Brandon Belt	Joe Panik	Brandon Crawford	Evan Longoria	Mike Yastrzemski	Kevin Pillar	Austin Slater	
Colorado Rockies	Tony Wolters	Daniel Murphy	Ryan McMahon	**Trevor Story**	**Nolan Arenado**	Raimel Tapia	Ian Desmond	**Charlie Blackmon**	
San Diego Padres	Austin Hedges	Eric Hosmer	Ian Kinsler	Fernando Tatis Jr.	Manny Machado	Wil Myers	Manuel Margot	Franmil Reyes	

Batting Average: < 0.240ᵃ · 0.260 – 0.280ᵃ above   On Base Percentage: < .300 – .325 – .350 – .400 **above**   Slugging Percentage: 0.244 – 0.398 – 0.454 – 0.513 – 0.670   Source: baseball-reference.com

FIGURE 12.8   Table of baseball players by team and position, with statistics by width, weight, and color.

DEPARTMENTS BY OCCUPATION
Fill height indicates percent of population

More Manufacturing

```
90 59 75 57 54 78 69 PA 13
68 42 88 62 76 08 77 83 06
38 25 67 60 10 02 55 30 51
80 27 52 44 31 18 45 21 33
63 70 73 26 74 58 14 84 34
39 81 71 65 89 03 37 28 66
87 07 01 49 64 04 72 05 17
16 36 09 41 86 29 61 35 11
12 43 79 19 50 40 56 47 22
85 24 15 82 53 46 48 23 32
```

More Agriculture

Data Source: Jacques Bertin, Semiology of Graphics, 1983, p. 100.

FIGURE 12.9   Table of departments indicating data by proportion of fill and position.

Cell contents can extend to sentences and paragraphs. An *adjacency matrix* can be used to indicate dialogue between characters, such as Figure 12.10. This matrix can be greatly enhanced with text, as shown in Figure 12.11. Cells indicate text spoken from the character on the left to the character named in the column. The height of each row is proportional to the total dialogue of the character. Cells are expanded to the next column, if the next column is otherwise empty. Within each cell are the first few sentences of dialogue.

The dialogue can be enhanced with additional information depicted as SparkWords, for example, highlighting literary devices, such as alliteration, oxymorons, metaphors, irony, puns, and so on. One can automatically mark up the text to find patterns that may provide deeper insight into a single character, or the relationship between characters. In this example, commonly repeated sets of spoken words per character are highlighted. Repeated word sets are bolded and underlined, with a unique color for each set per character. The repeated

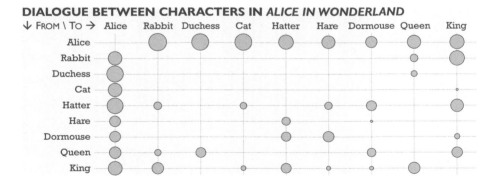

FIGURE 12.10   Adjacency matrix indicating quantity of dialogue between characters in *Wonderland*.

DIALOGUE FROM ONE CHARACTER TO ANOTHER IN ALICE IN WONDERLAND

↓ From \ To →

	Alice	Rabbit	Duchess	Cat	Hatter	Hare	Dormouse	Queen	King
Alice									
Rabbit									
Duchess									
Cat									
Hatter									
Hare									
Dormouse									
Queen									
King									

FIGURE 12.11 Matrix indicating dialogue between characters in *Alice in Wonderland*, with repeated sets of words per character highlighted.

word sets can be exact matching sequences, such as the Duchess frequently repeating to Alice: "and the moral of that is," shown in orange text in the cell corresponding to the Duchess speaking to Alice. The same sequence with an added word or two are also highlighted, such as the Rabbit anxiously repeating: "Oh dear, oh dear," and a few sentences later, "Oh my dear." This set-based analysis also highlights sequences where words have been transposed, thereby highlighting some of Carroll's popular logical inversions, such as the Hatter saying "'I see what I eat,' [is the same thing as] 'I eat what I see.'" This approach also highlights sequences such as the Queen's catchphrase: "Off with his/her head," and many variants thereof: "Are their heads off?" "[Your] head must be off," and "[just take] his head off." Alice frequently repeats "I think," "I know," "I wonder," and "I don't know," all related to a central theme throughout Wonderland questioning knowledge.

Questioning knowledge is a fitting final example: questioning the definition of visualization and the role of text is the focus of this book.

12.6 FURTHER READING

SparkWords. The term SparkWords is derived from Edward Tufte's *sparklines*, word-sized charts embedded inline in running text. These word-size graphics were first introduced in *The Visual Display of Quantitative Information* (1983) and expanded in *Beautiful Evidence* (2006). Many extensions since then have been collected by Goffin et al. in *An exploratory study of word scale graphics in data rich text documents* (2017), which provides an overview of many techniques and associated interaction techniques.

Tables cross many domains and various texts discuss table design. For example, Marchese (2011) explores historic tables; Few (2004) discusses tables of numbers; and Gratzl et al. (2013) present a visualization technique for ranking tables. For timetables, see articles such as Barman's *Timetable Typography* (1938) or Barry Kitt's *Printed Time* (1986).

Note that there are fonts specifically designed for use at small sizes. *Optical sizing* refers to adjustments made by typographers so that thin strokes on letters do not become too thin and visually break apart when the text is used at small sizes. In general, *book fonts* are designed for use at small sizes (e.g. Times Roman, Georgia, Verdana and Source Sans Pro); whereas *display fonts* are designed for large sizes (e.g. fonts with fine details such as Bodoni, intricate fonts such as Rosewood, and typically fonts designed for signage). When working with long labels in a table, a narrow, condensed, or extra condensed font may be desirable, such as Rockwell Condensed, Arial Narrow, Roboto Condensed, or Gill Sans Extra Condensed. Furthermore, note that there are fonts specifically designed for very small sizes, for example, see Hernan's *Compact Typography* (2009).

CHAPTER 13

Opportunity and Checklist

T HIS BOOK PROVIDES A breadth of example visualizations, using text in many ways to embed data into visualizations. A wide variety of design variants are feasible. The next two-page figure (Figure 13.1) collects 80 small snapshots of the new visualizations with text created in this book, organized into one diagram. Vertically, the snapshots are organized by the chapter themes. Scanning through the examples, one can see many common visualization types extended with text such as scatterplots, distributions, bar charts, line charts, set diagrams, graphs, mosaic plots, cartograms, maps, box plots, and cumulative distributions – indicated with orange labels. And one can see visualization embedded into words in prose, lists, tables, and so on.

Furthermore, there are new opportunities for visualizing text together with natural language processing (NLP) and generation. The purple labels indicate relevance to text analytics and NLP. The examples suggest many potential applications, such as text summarization, common sequences (potentially useful for speech interfaces), characterization (potentially useful for fake news), indicating difficult text (for language learners), identifying uncommon clauses (in legal documents), uncovering repeated word sets (from robots), tracking emotion and sentiment (from trolls), revealing topics (to identify phishing emails), and so on.

But text offers more to visualization than just literal sequences, typographic enhancements, and NLP. Literal encoding adds information that cannot be ignored and triggers association with pre-existing linguistic knowledge. It shifts visualization from preattentive perception and pattern analysis into opportunities for simultaneous, multi-level macro/micro patterns where the viewer can shift attention up and down levels of detail instantly for multi-layered interpretation. In addition to the cognitive modality of the visual, text-rich visualizations enable the cognitive modality of language to be used simultaneously, thereby allowing for new ways of comprehending and reasoning about information in visualizations. The foundations of this work offer new opportunities for applications across domains such as psychology, perception, linguistics, philosophy, design, typography, cartography, statistics, natural language processing, human computer interaction, and visualization.

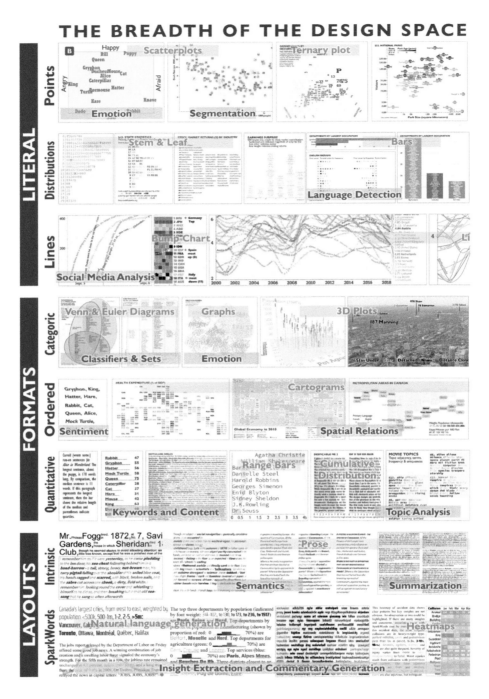

FIGURE 13.1   80+ visualizations using text by the author, organized by type and annotated with visualization type (orange overlay) and text analyses (purple overlay).

FOR VISUALIZING WITH TEXT

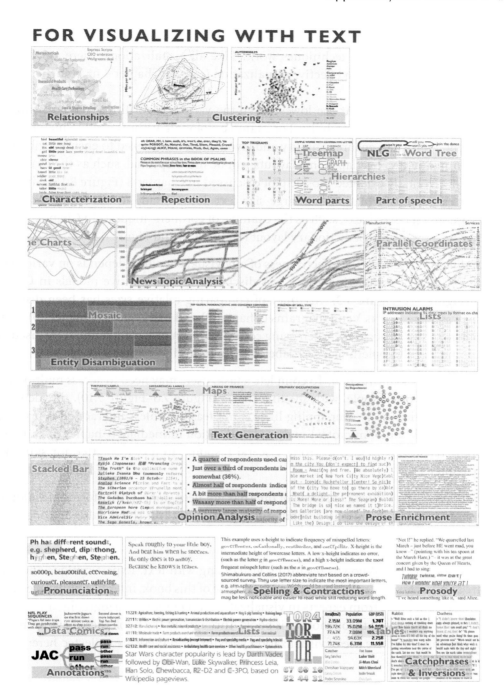

FIGURE 13.1 (Continued)

13.1 VALIDATION

Do these text visualization techniques work? Like all visualizations, there are different levels to consider to make an effective visualization (e.g. see Chapter 4 in Munzner 2014).

Algorithm effectiveness. At the lowest level, the various algorithms manipulating text need to maintain text legibility. For example, color algorithms need to maintain sufficient contrast to ensure legibility and layout algorithms need to ensure legibility by minimizing text overlap. Some layouts will be more optimal, such as the example of the horizontally oriented mosaic plot discussed in Chapter 8 (Figure 8.15). Similarly, text can add information, but large-size text does not add as much information as more smaller-sized text, such as the example of coroners' inquests in Chapter 6, comparing a treemap to a dictionary layout (Figure 6.18 and Figure 6.19).

Encoding effectiveness. The effectiveness of any visual encoding depends on various factors. *Speed* of completing a task was discussed using cognitive models in Chapter 5 (Figure 5.2–Figure 5.3). *Accuracy* of comparing relative sizes has been discussed many times such as Venn diagrams (Chapter 8) and bar lengths (Chapter 10), or the potential loss of accuracy when using codes. *Errors* in task completion were discussed comparing choropleth maps vs. labeled cartograms in Chapter 9 (Table 9.1).

Appropriate task abstraction. To complete a task, users may need to access multiple data variables. For example, with the line charts (Figure 7.6–Figure 7.10), the identification task with many overlapping lines is not feasible unless interaction is provided, but the addition of microtext makes identification immediate (Chapter 6). Similarly, some readers expressed a strong visceral response to text formatted for skimming (Chapter 11).

Validation over an extended period of time has not been done. Other forms of validation for other tasks, encodings, combinations, and algorithms should also be done.

13.2 CHECKLIST

There are still many unknowns regarding visualizing with text. Expert critique and guidance are another form of validation. Over the course of this book, interdisciplinary feedback has provided guidance from experts in visualization, typography, cartography, and graphic design and incorporated throughout this book. Throughout the book there have been comments regarding effective use of visualization with text and these are collected here:

13.2.1 Language

Access. Using text within a visualization binds the visualization to the language(s) represented. Accessibility is reduced or unavailable to those who do not speak the language, have low literacy, or poor eyesight. Further, some organizations (e.g. United Nations) and some countries (e.g. Canada, Switzerland, and Belgium) have multiple official languages, therefore visualizations may need to support multiple languages, for example, provide an interactive toggle between languages or multilingual labels. While automated translation may be used, note that average word lengths and type density may change across languages, requiring testing in each supported language.

Typographic constraints. Some typographic formats may not work across languages, for example, case may not be available, or fonts supporting different widths, or there may be very few typefaces available, for example in endangered languages. The direction of text and the aspect ratios of text change with different languages.

13.2.2 Legibility

Literal text can increase information content, aid fast identification, reduce search, and facilitate discovery of local relationships. *But,* text only works if the characters are legible! The following factors should be considered:

- *Minimum size.* Map guidelines recommend a minimum of 5 or 6 points, and many of the examples use 6 points (1/12" or 2.2 mm). Contrast and illumination affect legibility, for example, situations such as glare require larger text. Older people typically require larger text.

- *Contrast.* A greater difference in brightness between text and background will increase legibility. Black on white is high contrast, yellow on white will be too low. If the contrast is too low, consider adjusting the text color; using a different attribute (e.g. font weight instead of color); adding a halo (e.g. Figure 5.7); using a thin outline (Figure 7.6); or using a thin drop-shadow (e.g. Figure 7.11).

- *Drop-shadows, outlines, and negative spacing.* Should be used with caution, as text may run together, break apart, or cause letters to fill in – which reduces legibility.

- *Separation.* Text over other text or graphics can be difficult to visually parse. Legibility can be improved by adjusting text position to reduce overlap. There are many possible techniques including accepting some amount of overlap (e.g. Figure 9.10 right, note smaller labels are on top of larger labels); automation to detect overlap with small nudges to reduce overlap (Figure 9.10 left); use of leader-lines to position labels nearby congested areas (e.g. Figure 5.8); and modifying the layout of the plots to maintain local relations but shift elements to make labels legible (such as the cartogram in Figure 9.8).

- *Superimposition.* If text must be placed over other text and graphics, legibility can be improved using contrast techniques mentioned earlier, or by varying visual attributes to increase the difference between text – for example Figure 5.4 varies size and color of labels to help visually distinguish one code from another, or Figure 7.9 uses variation in typeface, weight, color, and italic to distinguish lines.

- Use *fonts and typographic attributes* as intended by the type designer. Do not squish fonts not designed to be squished; do not use font outline thickness to create bold, and so on; these abuses reduce legibility (e.g. see *Type Crimes* in Lupton 2010).

13.2.3 Alphanumeric Codes

If codes are being used in a visualization, then:

- *Are codes familiar to users?* If unfamiliar, an explicit legend should be provided. Consider a coding scheme that is easier to decode such as a mnemonic. For example, in Figure 5.11, the first letter of large company names are used, for example, C for Chrysler, F for Ford, and G for GM.

- *Not Helvetica.* Do the codes mix alphabetic characters and numeric characters? Use a font with clear differentiation between uppercase, lowercase, and numbers, for example: 0 and O; I, 1 and l; and so on.

13.2.4 Formats

Encoding data with formats, such as color, font weight, typeface, and so on, enables text to convey additional data beyond the literal words. However:

- *Typographic color* is the consistency in weight, slope, etc., so that no text stands out in a large portion of text (Section 2.1.1). Type color is leveraged by the visualization designer, using bold, color, italic, etc., to make some text stand out. The designer must ensure that use of attributes do not interfere with each other – for example, the use of a blackletter font may appear as dark as bold in another font, confounding the perception of bold.

- Some typographic attributes are only perceived in a *sequence* of characters, such as spacing or a baseline shift, therefore the designer must ensure that these attributes are not used inadvertently with single-letter words or codes do not use these attributes.

- Some typographic attributes only work with a *subset of characters*. For example, capitalization only applies to characters and languages that support capitalization (e.g. numbers can't be capitalized); or x-height is only applicable to lowercase alphabetic characters.

Redundant encoding, wherein one data value is represented with multiple formats (such as both color and font weight), may aid perceptual differentiation among data points. Redundant encoding can help where one attribute may not be easily perceived, such as a color-blind viewer (Figure 10.11), or, can help disambiguate overlapping labels by also encoding with label color (Figure 5.4).

Multiple encoding. When a piece of text indicates multiple data values, each with a different format, consider the tasks. These combinations may be effective if the user task is to notice a difference (Figure 8.9). If the task is to find a subset of values or specific combination of features, additional interactions such as selection, highlighting, and filtering may aid the task (Figure 10.12).

Intuitive encoding (font semantics, font affect, expressive text). Decoding a format is easier if the designer has chosen a format that is semantically related to the data value. For example, in Figure 8.6, the names of Democrats and Republicans slope in the same direction as they are described in political commentary (lean left, lean right). Font weight is effective for indicating (non-zero positive) magnitude such as income, counts, and company size (e.g. Figure 6.5, Figure 12.1) – more ink implies bigger data values. Expressive lengthening manipulates word length and spelling to indicate relative sizes (e.g. Figure 10.13). Note that typefaces are not neutral; fonts have semantic associations (Figure 3.23). Further, there are additional semantic associations in other domains only touched on in this book, such as comic book lettering conventions (Figure 1.21).

Readability is the ease of reading text, which is impacted by many factors such as choice of typeface, kerning, line length, x-height, and so on. For example, for multi-line labels the spacing between the lines within a label should be tighter than the spacing to adjacent labels, so that the correct text is perceptually grouped together (e.g. Figure 5.12). Furthermore, many changes to formats can disrupt readability. Figure 10.12 uses six different formats – for a task focused on reading comprehension, these additional formats are disruptive and should be turned off.

13.2.5 Long Labels

Long labels can create problems, such as being difficult to fit into a small space, or potentially creating bias when some labels are very short and others are very long. There are possibilities to shorten strings of text:

- *Use codes*. Sometimes short codes, known to the users, can be used instead of labels, e.g. country codes, stock symbol codes, etc.

- *Truncate*. Sometimes long labels can be shortened to a set number of characters, e.g. 20 characters; although care must be taken so that salient information remains.

- *Contract and abbreviate*. Some words may have familiar contractions within a domain. E.g. information technology is often abbreviated IT, telecommunications is telco, etc. Or some intermediate words can be dropped (e.g. middle names and titles of *Titanic* passengers are dropped in Figure 8.14).

- *Use narrow font*. Font designers have created narrow, condensed, and extra condensed fonts specifically designed to reduce width.

- *Wrap text*. A long string can be wrapped into a multi-line label.

Alternatively, long strings can be used with other approaches to offset the effect of the length:

- *No adjustment*. Familiarity with maps implies that viewers can readily detect small changes in font size, without being biased by long vs. short strings. The emotion word visualization in Figure 8.9 plots each word as-is with its formats.

- *Underlying mark*. The underlying mark can be made visually dominant and the text can run longer than the mark (e.g. park names are longer than the dots in Figure 5.7).

- *Mean reversion*. If using text in a sequence of words or clusters, a large number of words will tend to revert to the average word length (e.g. average word length is used as the axis for the adjective list in Figure 6.12).

- *Padding*. String lengths can be adjusted so that they are all of similar width, for example by using a condensed font for a long string and an extended font for a short string and/ or adjusting spacing between letters (Figure 6.6); adding additional contextual text to short strings (e.g. Figure 10.3); adding padding to short strings such as a set of dots (Figure 10.6); or creating an underlying container of consistent width with text inside.

- *Stacking*. Instead of relying on text width, use consistent height of text to create comparable stacks, such as Figure 8.6 or Figure 6.7.

13.2.6 Layout Challenges

Many visualization algorithms assume that marks are square or have been optimized to create equal distances in x and y, such as squarified treemaps or default collision detection algorithms. However, text is not square; for example, strings in Western languages are wide. This may necessitate tweaking visualization layout algorithms to create marks and areas that are wider (e.g. Figure 8.15).

Visualization algorithms may overplot points or push apart points so that marks do not overlap. However, these algorithms may not consider associated text labels, and an additional computational pass may be required to reduce overlap on the labels (e.g. Figure 5.4).

13.2.7 Typeface

There are hundreds of thousands of fonts to choose from. In general, choose fonts that are designed to work well at smaller sizes (i.e. book fonts) rather than flamboyant fonts that are typically created for signage (i.e. display fonts).

Codes. If alphabetic characters are mixed with numeric characters, use a font that clearly differentiates between them. Verify that confusable characters, such as O and 0; or l, 1, and I; 5 and S; B and 8; and so on are easily distinguishable. Consider fonts such as Century Schoolbook, Garamond, Georgia, Verdana, B612, and Source Code Pro.

Consistent length. Some uses may need strings to have consistent length. Be aware that heavier weights are wider in most proportional-spaced fonts (e.g. Thesis Pro is an exception). Fixed width fonts are consistent across weights (e.g. Courier, Consolas, Source Code Pro, and Roboto Mono).

Pop-out. Perception of one word or character visually popping-out against a background of other text depends in part on the use of a high-quality font where letter shapes have been tweaked, kerning and font-hinting have been designed so that no letters pop-out. Then the degree of differentiation must be considered (Figure 2.4).

Mixing typefaces. When mixing and matching fonts, it is unlikely that weights, widths, and other properties will align, e.g. bold in one font may be much heavier than bold in another font. The visualization designer is required to experiment to find a combination that works well together. Note that there are *superfamilies* of fonts where variants such as sans serif, serif, and fixed-width are all available (e.g. Roboto, Roboto Slab, and Roboto Mono). However, font variants within a superfamily share the same underlying skeleton and are designed to be harmonious, which may not meet the visualization designer's requirements. If the design needs differentiation across the fonts, such as encoding categoric data, then the designer will be required to mix different fonts.

13.2.8 Interactions

If creating a visualization in an interactive medium, consider adding interactions to facilitate common tasks.

Search/find are highly common interactions in most text documents (such as the example highlighting tags in Figure 7.11), therefore text-centric visualizations should strongly consider search interactions. Autocomplete is commonly associated with search and can be used to trigger visually enhanced suggestions (Figure 10.1 right).

Interactive *ordering*, such as column sort, is a common interaction with alphanumerics in lists or tables, whether sorting by alphabetic order or by a quantitative value (e.g. Figure 12.6 and Figure 12.7).

Mouse-over and *click* are useful, for example, to increase the size of the text under the cursor (Figure 7.12), show a contextual sentence (Figure 6.20), and then hyperlink to navigate to a source document (also Figure 6.20).

Toggles and filters. When working with many different data variables, encoding all simultaneously may be overwhelming; these can be easily toggled on/off (Figure 8.7). Similarly, these formats may be disruptive to reading, and can similarly be toggled off, or toggled to show different analytics, such as *The Communist Manifesto* in Chapter 11.

Zoom. With large-scale data, zoom can be used to show more labels, such as Figure 5.12 (with a few hundred labels) or Figure 9.9 (with hundreds of thousands of labels).

Layers. Additional information can be added as toggleable layers, such as labels, text summaries (Figure 3.50), or bars behind text (e.g. many examples in Chapter 10).

Layouts. Layouts can be dynamic; many of the maps in Chapter 9 can animate between a standard map projection and a cartogram, such as the "Click me" button in Figure 9.5.

13.2.9 More

The reader is also encouraged to look carefully at the examples; many design decisions have been made per visualization, for example, to enhance legibility. Not all small design decisions are explained. Further, not all examples are perfect: some have incomplete legends or may be missing references. Technology improves: for example, variable fonts are fairly new at the time of publishing and are not used in any of the examples. See links on the publisher's website: https://www.routledge.com/Visualizing-with-Text/Brath/p/book/9780367259266 or the author's blog richardbrath.wordpress.com for high resolution images, sample code, and other notes.

Moreover, the reader is encouraged to look at all typography more critically. Rather than being invisible, consider the choice of type, the layout, the text, and their coordination with graphics in any composition. This book is only a hint of what is feasible; the design space is vast, the application areas are extremely broad, the emerging algorithms from machine learning and AI promise even more analytic possibilities, and the needs for critical analysis of text are increasing.

CHAPTER 14

References

T HE DESIGN SPACE OF text and visualization is vast, informed by prior examples (see the list of figures), as well as consultation with many experts and review of research detailed below.

14.1 ACKNOWLEDGMENTS

Much of this research has been aided by my thesis supervisor, Ebad Banissi. Over the course of the research, many experts from across disciplines have provided excellent feedback and guidance including typographers, cartographers, visualization experts, machine learning experts, financial analysts, industrial engineers, industrial designers, and graphic designers. The author is highly grateful for all the feedback from these experts over the last seven years. Uncharted Software, the author's employer, has been highly supportive throughout the process. Major museums, research libraries, national libraries, and public libraries have increasingly been making their collections available as high quality scans and open source licenses. Most of the example visualizations were created using open source software, typically NLTK for NLP and D3.js for visualization.

14.2 PEER-REVIEWED RESEARCH

This book is based on a PhD thesis and 20 peer-reviewed research papers and peer-reviewed presentations by the author and co-authors. They are listed here in time-order, with italics indicating journal articles and underline indicating article length.

"**The Design Space of Typeface**," at VisWeek, 2014 (Paris 2014). Co-authored with Ebad Banissi.

This poster itemizes typographic attributes to preattentively encode data.

"**Using Font Attributes in Knowledge Maps and Information Retrieval**," at First Workshop on Knowledge Maps and Information Retrieval, 2014 (London 2014). Co-authored with Ebad Banissi.

This paper shows new visualization techniques based on typographic attributes relevant to knowledge maps.

"Evaluating Lossiness and Fidelity in Information Visualization," at SPIE 2015 (San Francisco 2015). Co-authored with Ebad Banissi.

This paper provides a quantitative scoring model for comparing information loss between text and non-text visualizations.

"Using Text in Visualizations for Micro/Macro Readings," at TextVis Workshop 2015 (Atlanta 2015). Co-authored with Ebad Banissi.

This paper considers literal encoding as separate from other preattentive encodings enabling micro and macro readings of text visualizations and novel word-based stem and leaf plot.

"Using Type to Add Data to Data Visualizations," at TypeCon 2015 (Denver 2015). Co-authored with Ebad Banissi.

This presentation provided a historic review of the font attribute design space with several applications including a novel glyph-based technique.

"High Category Glyphs in Industry," at IEEE Vis 2015, Practitioner Session (Chicago 2015). No co-authors.

This poster and short paper provided a review of industrial visualizations that required encoding categoric data where many different discrete categories needed to be represented.

"Font Attributes Enrich Knowledge Maps and Information Retrieval," in _International Journal on Digital Libraries_, 2016. Co-authored with Ebad Banissi.

This journal article reviews font attributes and applies them to tasks relevant to knowledge maps (document overviews) and information retrieval (search), including text analytic tasks (i.e. natural language processing) such as skimming, opinion analysis, character analysis, topic modeling, and sentiment analysis.

"Using Typography to Expand the Design Space of Data Visualization," in _She Ji: The Journal of Design, Economics, and Innovation_ vol. 2, no. 1 (Spring 2016): 59–87. Co-authored with Ebad Banissi.

This journal article summarizes the cross-disciplinary research approach engaging visualization researchers, cartographers and typographers to (1) identify the gaps in visualization theory, (2) review adjacent fields to comprehensively assess techniques, (3) extend a common existing visualization framework with separation between type attributes, typographic scope, and data type, (4) illustrate many potential applications from this framework, and (5) broad evaluation including critiques across domains.

"Typographic Sets: Labelled Set Elements with Font Attributes," at International Workshop on Set Visualization and Reasoning 2016 (Philadelphia 2016). Co-authored with Ebad Banissi.

This paper shows how many visualization techniques indicating members in sets can be extended using typographic attributes, with unique contributes including identification of membership in up to ten sets and scalability to thousands of elements.

"Evaluation of Visualization by Critiques," at Beyond Time and Errors: Novel Evaluation Methods for Visualization (BELIV) (Baltimore 2016). Co-authored with Ebad Banissi.

This position paper extends design critiques as a form of evaluation, different than pre-existing "evaluation by inspection" techniques, uniquely providing broader scope and context.

"***Multivariate Label-based Thematic Maps***," in *International Journal of Cartography*, 23 Mar 2017. Co-authored with Ebad Banissi.

This journal article focuses on thematic maps where traditionally colored shapes are used to indicate data instead use labels, which can indicate more than one or two variables; and provides solutions to issues of representation of strings of differing lengths and label occlusion.

"**Beyond Technical Analysis: Using Data Visualization to Understand Market Data, Fundamentals, Technicals, Models, News and More**," at Market Technicians Association Annual Symposium (New York, 2017). No co-authors.

This financial industry presentation covered a wide variety of visualization techniques, including typographic economic maps, microtext line charts of economic data, and stem and leaf distributions of companies.

"**Stem & Leaf Plots Extended for Text Visualizations**," at 14th International Conference Computer Graphics, Imaging and Visualization (CGiV) 2017 (Marrakech, 2017). Co-authored with Ebad Banissi.

This short paper extends the visualization technique of "stem and leaf plots" using font attributes and tokens of different scope (single character, word, phrase).

"**Text Analytics and New Visualization Techniques**," at a peer-review industry conference Strata Data Conference: Make Data Work (New York, 2017). Co-authored with Scott Langevin with research assistance from Craig Hagerman.

This presentation to an industry audience provided an overview of research techniques and some applications to big data from industry. Slides online at: conferences.oreilly.com /strata/strata-ny-2017/public/schedule/detail/61248 Video online at: uncharted.software/ research/#talks

"**Microtext Line Charts**," at Information Visualization 2017 (IV2017) (London 2017). Co-authored with Ebad Banissi.

This paper brings together microtext and path dependent cartographic text to embed text directly into lines on line charts, making it easier to identify lines and enabling additional data to be displayed.

"**Text in Visualization**," PhD dissertation. London South Bank University, 2018. No co-authors.

The PhD thesis organizes all the research co-authored with Ebad Banissi into a dissertation. The dissertation provides more extensive references than shown here, more details regarding some underlying issues and inconsistencies with the foundations of visualization, more discussion regarding typography, more details regarding evaluations of individual techniques as well as two forms of evaluation (critique and information density) used across many of the text visualizations. (283 pages.)

"Automated Annotations," at Visualization for Communication Workshop (VisComm, Berlin 2018). Co-authored with Martin Matusiak.

This poster itemizes automated types of automated insights, including text, which can be automatically placed within a visualization.

"Techniques for Adding Diverse Contextual Data into Visualizations," at Information+ 2018 (Berlin 2018). No co-authors.

This presentation considered a variety of historic visualizations that use techniques to add data into visualization, including textually oriented visualizations such as timetables and genealogical diagrams.

"*Bertin's forgotten typographic variables and new typographic visualization*," in Computer and Geographic Information Systems (CaGIS). Journal special issue on 50th anniversary of Jacques Bertin (Nov 2018). Co-authored with Ebad Banissi.

Shows how the text framework can be used to create a dozen new visualizations using Bertin's same data, including two new visualization techniques.

"The Design Space of Sparkwords," at Eurovis 2019: 21st EG/VGTC Conference on Visualization (Porto, June 2019). Co-authored with Ebad Banissi.

This paper generalizes text formatted with typographic attributes representing data for use in textually-oriented layouts such as running prose, lists, and tables.

BIBLIOGRAPHY

Abdul-Rahman, Alfie, Julie Lein, Katherine Coles, Eamonn Maguire, Miriah Meyer, Martin Wynne, Chris R. Johnson, Anne Trefethen, and Min Chen. "Rule-based visual mappings – with a case study on poetry visualization." *Computer Graphics Forum* 32, no. 3pt4. 2013: 381–390. Blackwell Publishing Ltd, Oxford, UK.

Afzal, Shehzad, Ross Maciejewski, Yun Jang, Niklas Elmqvist, and David S. Ebert. "Spatial text visualization using automatic typographic maps." *IEEE Transactions on Visualization and Computer Graphics* 18, no. 12. 2012: 2556–2564.

Alexander, Eric, Chih-Ching Chang, Mariana Shimabukuro, Steven Franconeri, Christopher Collins, and Michael Gleicher. "Perceptual biases in font size as a data encoding." *IEEE TVCG* 24, no. 8. 2017: 2397–2410.

Alsallakh, Bilal, Luana Micallef, Wolfgang Aigner, Helwig Hauser, Silvia Miksch, and Peter Rodgers. "Visualizing sets and set-typed data: State-of-the-art and future challenges." In *Eurographics State of the Art Reports*. 2014, pp. 1–21.

Anne Arundel College. "Skimming and scanning," October 27, 2007. www.aacc.edu/tutoring/file/skimming.pdf.

Apollinaire, Guillaume. *Calligrammes*, Mercure De France, Paris. 1918. archive.org/stream/calligrammespo00apol.

Apperley, M.D., I. Tzavaras, and R. Spence. "A bifocal display technique for data presentation." In *Proceedings of Eurographics*. 1982. See also: youtube.com/watch?v=JmzsltNbM_M.

Ayres, Leonard Porter. *The War with Germany: A Statistical Summary*, Government Printing Office, Washington, DC. 1919.

Bach, Benjamin, Natalie Kerracher, Kyle Wm Hall, Sheelagh Carpendale, Jessie Kennedy, and Nathalie Henry Riche. "Telling stories about dynamic networks with graph comics." In *Proceedings of the 2016 CHI Conference*, 2016, pp. 3670–3682.

Baecker, Ron and Aaron Marcus. *Human Factors and Typography for More Readable Programs*, ACM Press, New York. 1989.

Bamman, David, Jacob Eisenstein, and Tyler Schnoebelen. "Gender identity and lexical variation in social media." *Journal of Sociolinguistics* 18, no. 2. 2014: 135–160.

Bargagli, Scipione. *La prima parte dell'imprese di Scipion Bargagli: dove, doppo tutte l'opere cosi a penna, come a stampa, ch' egli ha potuto vedere di coloro, che della materia dell'imprese hanno parlato, della vera natura di quelle si ragiona*, Appresso Francesco de'Franceschi, Venice. 1589.

Bargh, John A. "The four horsemen of automaticity: Awareness, intention, efficiency, and control in social cognition." In *Handbook of Social Cognition*. R. Wyer and T. Srull, eds. Lawrence Erlbaum Associates, Hillsdale, NJ, 1994, pp. 1–40.

Barman, Christian. "Timetable typography." In *Typography: 5*. Robert Harling, ed., Shenval Press, London. 1938, pp. 9–17.

BBC. "Skimming and scanning," 2015. www.bbc.co.uk/teach/skillswise/skimming-and-scanning /zd39f4j.

Bean, Victoria and Chris McCabe. *The New Concrete: Visual Poetry in the 21st Century*, Hayward Publishing, London. 2015.

Beier, Sophie. *Reading Letters: Designing for Legibility*, BIS Publishers, Amsterdam. 2012.

Bertin, Jacques. *Sémiologie graphique*, Gauthier-Villars, Paris. 1967.

Bertin, Jacques. "Classification typographique: Voulez vous jouer avec mon A." In *Communication et langages*, n°45, 1er trimestre. 1980, pp. 70–75. doi: 10.3406/colan.1980.1369. http://www .persee.fr/doc/colan_0336 1500_1980_num_45_1_1369.

Bertin, Jacques. *Semiology of Graphics*, trans. William Berg, University of Wisconsin Press, Madison, Wisconsin. 1983.

Bil'ak, Peter. "Family planning or how type families work." In *Font, The Sourcebook*, Nadine Käthe Monem, ed., Black Dog Publishing, London. 2008. www.typotheque.com/articles/type_fa milies

Billy the Kid, vol. 1, no. 13. Charlton Comics Group, Connecticut, September 1958, p. 2.

Binder, Jack. "Pyroman." In *America's Best Comics*, N. L. Pines, ed., Nedor Publishing Company, New York. 1945, pp. 27–35.

Bird, Steven, Ewan Klein, and Edward Loper. *Natural Language Processing with Python: Analyzing Text with the Natural Language Toolkit*, O'Reilly Media. 2009.

Blaeu, Willem Janzoon. *Terra Sancta quae in Sacris Terra Promissionis olim Palestina*. Willem Janzoon Blaeu, Amsterdam. 1629.

Borgo, R., J. Kehrer, D.H.S. Chung, E. Maguire, R.S. Laramee, H. Hauser, M. Ward, and M. Chen, "Glyph-based visualization: Foundations, design guidelines, techniques and applications." In *Eurographics State of the Art Reports*. EG STARs, Eurographics Association. 2013, pp. 39–63.

Börner, Katy. *Atlas of Knowledge: Anyone Can Map*, MIT Press, Cambridge, MA. 2015.

Bostock, Michael, Vadim Ogievetsky, and Jeffrey Heer. "D³ data-driven documents." *IEEE TVCG* 17, no. 12. 2011: 2301–2309.

Boyack, Kevin, Dick Klavans and W. Bradford Paley. *Map of Science*. Research and node layout by Kevin Boyack (Principal Member of Technical Staff, Sandia National Laboratories) and Dick Klavans (President, SciTech Strategies, Inc.); data from Thompson ISI; graphics & typography by W. Bradford Paley (Adjunct Associate Professor, Columbia University; Director Information Esthetics). 2009.

Bradshaw's Railway and Steamship Timetables for the United Kingdom of Great Britain and Ireland, Henry Blacklock & Co., London. 1906. archive.org/stream/Bradshaw1906/Bradshaw%2019 06.

Brant, Sebastian. *Stultifera nauis: Narragonice p[ro]fectio[n]is nunq[uam] satis laudata nauis. Imp[re]ssu[m] ... ac vrbe libera Arge[n]tina: per Magistru[m] Ioanne[m] Gruninge[r]*, Basel. 1497.

Brath, Richard. "Multiple shape attributes in information visualization: Guidance from prior art and experiments." In *2010 14th International Conference Information Visualisation*. IEEE. 2010.

Brath, Richard, and Ebad Banissi. "Multivariate label-based thematic maps." *International Journal of Cartography* 3, no. 1. 2017, pp. 45–60.

Brath, Richard. *Text in Visualization*. PhD dissertation. London South Bank University. 2018.

Brath, Richard. See also List of Author's Papers and Presentations in Section 14.2: Peer-Reviewed Research.

Brewer, Cynthia A. *Designing Better Maps: A Guide for GIS Users*, ESRI Press. 2005.

Bringhurst, Robert. *The Elements of Typographic Style*, Hartley & Marks. 2013.

Brinton, Willard C. *Graphic Methods for Presenting Facts*, The Engineering Magazine, New York. 1919.

Brinton, Willard C. *Graphic Presentation*, Brinton Associates, New York. 1939.

Broughton, F. *Rules & Regulations for the Conduct of the Traffic and for the Guidance of the Officers & Servants in the Employment of the Great Western Railway Co.*, Advertisers Steam Presses, London, ON, Canada. 1879.

Burke, Christopher, Eric Kindel, and Sue Walker. *Isotype: Design and Contexts 1925 – 1971*, Hyphen Press, London. 2014.

Cano, Rafael G., Kevin Buchin, Thom Castermans, Astrid Pieterse, Willem Sonke, and Bettina Speckmann. "Mosaic drawings and cartograms." *Computer Graphics Forum* 34, no. 3. 2015: 361–370.

Card, Stuart K., Thomas P. Moran, and Allen Newell. *The Psychology of Human-Computer Interaction*. Laurence Erlbaum Assoc., Mahwah, NJ. 1983.

Card, Stuart K., Jock D. Mackinlay, and Ben Shneiderman (eds.). *Readings in Information Visualization: Using Vision to Think*. Morgan Kaufman, San Francisco. 1999.

Carey, Mathew and M. Lavoisne. *A Complete Genealogical, Historical, Chronological, and Geographical Atlas*, M. Carey and Son, Philadelphia, PA. 1820. David Rumsey Map Collection. www.davidrumsey.com/luna/servlet/s/5c7166.

Carthusianus, Bruno. *Brunonis Carthusianorum Patriarche sanctissimi, theologi Parisiensis Scholae doctissimi: & Remensis ecclesiae canonici moratissimi*, Venundatur Jodoco Badio Ascensio, Paris. 1524.

Chambers, Ephraim. *Cyclopaedia, or An Universal Dictionary of Arts and Sciences*. 1st edition. Printed for James and John Knapton (and others), London. 1728.

Chen, Min, and Luciano Floridi. "An analysis of information visualisation." *Synthese* 190, no. 16. 2013: 3421–3438.

Chen, Min, Simon Walton, Kai Berger, Jeyarajan Thiyagalingam, Brian Duffy, Hui Fang, Cameron Holloway, and Anne E. Trefethen. "Visual multiplexing." *Computer Graphics Forum* 33, no. 3. 2014: 241–250.

Chi, Ed H., Lichan Hong, Michelle Gumbrecht, and Stuart K. Card. "ScentHighlights: Highlighting conceptually-related sentences during reading." In *Proceedings of Intelligent User Interfaces*. 2005. pp. 272–274.

Cicero, *Aratea*. Benedictine Abbey of St Peter, St Paul and St Andrew, Peterborough. 1100. British Library shelfmark Cotton MS Tiberius C 1. www.bl.uk/collection-items/cicero-aratea-with-scholia.

Clark, Jeff. *Twitter Venn*. 2008. www.neoformix.com/2008/TwitterVenn.html.

Clarkson, Thomas. "Drawing of the slave ship 'Brookes.'" In *The History of the Rise, Progress, and Accomplishment of the Abolition of the African Slave-Trade by British Parliament.* Longman & Co., London. 1808. British Library shelfmark G:16302. www.bl.uk/restoration-18th-century-literature/articles/britains-involvement-with-new-world-slavery-and-the-transatlantic-slave-trade

Cleveland, William S., and Robert McGill. "Graphical perception: Theory, experimentation, and application to the development of graphical methods." *Journal of the American Statistical Association* 79, no. 387. 1984: 531–554.

Cole, Daniel. "Cartography for the scientific illustrator." In *The Guild Handbook of Scientific Illustration*. Hodges, E. R. S., ed. Van Nostrad Reinhold, New York. 1989, pp. 461–484.

Collins, Christopher, Sheelagh Carpendale, and Gerald Penn. "Docuburst: Visualizing document content using language structure." *Computer Graphics Forum* 28, no. 3. 2009: 1039–1046, Blackwell Publishing Ltd, Oxford, UK.

Cooper, Muriel. "Information Landscapes" at *TED5 Conference*. 1994. youtube.com/watch?v= BhrZHkdc2rU.

Cornog, D.Y. and F.C. Rose. "Legibility of Alphanumeric Characters and Other Symbols." Technical report, National Bureau of Standards, Institute for Applied Technology, Washington, DC. 1967.

Craig, James, Irene Korol Scala, and William Bevington. *Designing with Type: The Essential Guide to Typography*, 5th edition, Watson-Guptill Publications, New York. 2006.

Crome, August. *Neue Carte von Europa*. F. A. Pingeling, Hamburg. 1782.

Davis, Matt. "Aoccdrnig to a rscheearch at Cmabrigde…," Blog post 30/10/03. www.mrc-cbu.cam. ac.uk/people/matt.davis/Cmabrigde/.

Dent, Borden. *Cartography: Thematic Map Design*, 6th edition, McGraw Hill. 2009.

DeVilliers, Victor and Owen Taylor. *Point and Figure Charting*. Stock Market Publications, New York. 1933.

Diderot, Denis, Jean Le Rond d'Alembert, and Pierre Mouchon. *Encyclopédie, ou dictionnaire raisonné des sciences, des arts, et métiers*. Suite du recueil de planches, sur les sciences et les arts, Paris. 1777.

Don, Anthony, Elena Zheleva, Machon Gregory, Sureyya Tarkan, Loretta Auvil, Tanya Clement, Ben Shneiderman, and Catherine Plaisant. "Discovering interesting usage patterns in text collections: Integrating text mining with visualization." In *Proceedings of ACM Conference on Information and Knowledge Management*. 2007, pp. 213–222.

Dorsey, Thomas J. *Tom Dorsey's Trading Tips*. Bloomberg Press, New York. 2001.

Drucker, Johanna. "Letterpress Language: Typography as a Medium for the Visual Representation of Language." *Leonardo* 17, no. 1. 1984: 8–16.

Duggan, Geoffrey B., and Stephen J. Payne. "Skim reading by satisficing: Evidence from eye tracking." In *Proceedings of the SIGCHI Conference on Human Factors in Computing Systems*. 2011, pp. 1141–1150.

Duncan, Pamela and Carlo Zapponi. "Quiz reveals deep misconceptions over numbers of Europeans in UK" in *The Guardian*. 11 June 2016. www.theguardian.com/politics/datablog/2016/jun/11/quiz-reveals-misconceptions-numbers-europeans-in-uk-eu-referendum.

Dupin, Charles. *Carte figurative de l'instruction populaire de la France*. Science, Industry and Business Library: General Collection, The New York Public Library. 1827. digitalcollections.n ypl.org/items/22a17950-5224-0136-99b4-11596a80992a.

Eccles, Ryan, Tom Kapler, Rob Harper and William Wright. *Stories in GeoTime*. In *2007 IEEE Symposium on Visual Analytics Science and Technology (VAST)*. 2007, pp. 19–26. doi: 10.1109/ VAST.2007.4388992.

Errea, Javier. *Visual Journalism: Infographics from the World's Best Newsrooms and Designers*, Gestalten, Berlin. 2017.

FDA and ISMP Lists of Look-Alike Drug Names with Recommended Tall Man Letters. ISMP Institute for Safe Medication Practices. 2010. www.ismp.org/Tools/tallmanletters.pdf.

Felton, Nicholas. *2013 Annual Report*. 2014. http://feltron.com/FAR13.html.

Few, Stephen. *Show Me the Numbers*, Analytics Press, El Dorado Hills, CA. 2004.

Fowler, Henry Watson, Francis George Fowler, and James Augustus Henry Murray. *The Concise Oxford Dictionary of Current English*, The Clarendon Press, Oxford. 1912. archive.org/details/conciseoxforddic00fowlrich.

Friendly, Michael, Juergen Symanzik, and Ortac Onder. *100+ Years of Graphs of the Titanic Data*. 2018. www.datavis.ca/papers/titanic/.

Friendly, Michael, and Howard Wainer. *A Gleam in the Mind's Eye: Visual Discovery and the Rise of Data Visualization*, Harvard University Press, Cambridge, MA. 2020.

Fry, Ben. *Tendril*. 2000. http://benfry.com/tendril/.

Gauthier, Isabel, Alan C.N. Wong, William G. Hayward, and Olivia S. Cheung. "Font tuning associated with expertise in letter perception." *Perception* 35, no. 4. 2006: 541–559.

GfK. *Final Report: National Geographic-Roper Public Affairs 2006 Geographic Literacy Study*, GfK NOP, May 2006. www.nationalgeographic.com/roper2006/pdf/FINALReport2006GeogLitsurvey.pdf.

Goffin, Pascal, Jeremy Boy, Wesley Willett, and Petra Isenberg. "An exploratory study of word-scale graphics in data-rich text documents." *IEEE Transactions on Visualization and Computer Graphics* 23, no. 10. 2017: 2275–2287.

Good, Charles E. (Verso of) *Correct Map of Boston Harbor Giving Route and Official Summer Time-Table of the Nantasket Beach Steamboat Co*, Bouve, Crawford & Co., Boston, MA. 1890.

Grainger, Jonathan, Arnaud Rey, and Stephane Dufau. "Letter perception: From pixels to pandemonium." *Trends in Cognitive Sciences* 12, no. 10. 2008: 381–387.

Gratzl, Samuel, Alexander Lex, Nils Gehlenborg, Hanspeter Pfister, and Marc Streit. "Lineup: Visual analysis of multi-attribute rankings." *IEEE Transactions on Visualization and Computer Graphics* 19, no. 12. 2013: 2277–2286.

Grimes, Seth. "Unstructured data and the 80 percent rule." *Breakthrough Analysis*, August 1, 2008.

Hailpern, Joshua, Karrie Karahalios, Laura DeThorne, and Jim Halle. "Vocsyl: Visualizing syllable production for children with ASD and speech delays." In *Proceedings of ACM SIGACCESS Conference on Computers and Accessibility*. 2010, pp. 297–298.

Haley, Allan, Richard Poulin, Jason Tselentis, Tony Seddon, Gerry Leonidas, Ina Saltz, Kathryn Henderson, and Tyler Alderman. *Typography Referenced: A Comprehensive Visual Guide to the Language, History, and Practice of Typography*, Rockport Publishers, Beverly, MA. 2012.

Hearst, Marti, and Daniela Rosner. "Tag clouds: Data analysis tool or social signaler?" In *Hawaii International Conference on System Sciences, Proceedings of the 41st Annual, IEEE*. 2008, pp. 160–160.

Hearst, Marti. *Search User Interfaces*, Cambridge University Press, Cambridge, U.K. 2009.

Hearst, Marti, Emily Pedersen, Lekha Priya Patil, Elsie Lee, Paul Laskowski, and Steven Franconeri. "An evaluation of semantically grouped word cloud designs." *IEEE Transactions on Visualization and Computer Graphics* 25, no. 1. 2019, pp. 1–14.

Heer, Jeffrey and Michael Bostock. "Crowdsourcing graphical perception: Using mechanical turk to assess visualization design." In *Proceedings of the SIGCHI Conference on Human Factors in Computing Systems*. ACM. 2010, pp. 203–212.

Heer, Jeffrey and Vadim Ogievetsky. "A tour through the visualization zoo." *Communications of the ACM* 53, no. 6. 2010: 59–67.

Heilmann, Roland, Daniel A. Keim, Christian Panse, and Mike Sips. "Recmap: Rectangular map approximations." In *IEEE Symposium on Information Visualization*. IEEE. 2004, pp. 33–40.

Helfand, Jessica. *Reinventing the Wheel*, Princeton Architectural Press, New York. 2006.

Henriques, Roberto. *Carto-SOM: Cartogram Creation Using Self-Organizing Maps*. Master dissertation. Universidade Nova de Lisboa. 2005.

Hernan, Michael. *Compact Typography: The Design of Typefaces Conceived for Small Size Applications*. MATD dissertation. University of Reading. 2009.

Hitchcock, Tim, Robert Shoemaker, Sharon Howard, Jamie McLaughlin, et al., *London Lives, 1690–1800*. Version 1.1. 24 April 2012. www.londonlives.org.

Holmes, Nigel. "Pointing the finger," *Time Magazine*, July 27, 1987. p. 27.

Holmes, Nigel. *Designer's Guide to Creating Charts and Diagrams*, Watson-Guptill, New York. 1991.

Holmes, Nigel. *Best in Diagrammatic Graphics*, RotoVision, Brighton, U.K. 1996.

Holmes, Nigel. *The Book of Everything: A Visual Guide to Travel and the World*, Lonely Planet. 2012.

Howard, Sharon. *London Lives Coroners' Inquests, 1760–1799*. August 2018. CC SA 4.0. london.sharonhoward.org/CoronersInquests.

Huyghebaert, Pierre in *L'art de Franquin*. Panel with Yves Frémion, Frédéric Jannin, Gérard Viry-Babel, Pierre Huyghebaert by Bibliotheque Centre Pompidou, 9 janvier 2017. www.youtube.com/watch?v=4O7Yyj6Jpio&t=22m12s.

Jänicke, Stefan, Greta Franzini, Muhammad Faisal Cheema, and Gerik Scheuermann. "On close and distant reading in digital humanities: A survey and future challenges." In *EuroVis (STARs)*. 2015, pp. 83–103.

Jonker, David, Scott Langevin, David Giesbrecht, Michael Crouch, and Nathan Kronenfeld. "Graph mapping: Multi-scale community visualization of massive graph data." *Information Visualization* 16, no. 3. 2017: 190–204.

Kahn, P. and K. Lenk. "Principles of typography for user interface design." *Interactions* 5, no 6. 1998: 15–29.

Kane, John. *A Type Primer*, Pearson Prentice Hall, Upper Saddle River, NJ. 2011.

Kitts, Barry. "Printed time." *Octavo: An International Journal of Typography* 6. 1988: 6–11.

Knuth, Donald. *Computer Modern Typefaces*, Addison Wesley Publishing, Boston, MA. 1986.

Kono, Eiichi, "English, Japanese and the Computer" in *Computers and Typography 2*. Rosemary Sassoon, ed. Intellect, Bristol, UK. 2002, pp. 54–68.

Krause, Thomas and Amir Zeldes. "ANNIS3: A new architecture for generic corpus query and visualization." *Digital Scholarship in the Humanities* 31, no. 1. 2016: 118–139.

Kronenfled, Barry. *Results of the 2016 U.S. Presidential Election*. commons.wikimedia.org/wiki/File:2016_presidential_election_electoral_college_cartogram.png.

Krygier, John and Denis Wood. *Making Maps: A Visual Guide to Map Design for GIS*, Guilford Press, New York. 2011.

Lane, Hobson, Hannes Hapke, and Cole Howard. *Natural Language Processing in Action: Understanding, Analyzing, and Generating Text with Python*, Manning Publications, Shelter Island, NY. 2019.

Larkin, Jill H. and Herbert A. Simon. "Why a diagram is (sometimes) worth ten thousand words." *Cognitive Science* 11, no. 1. 1987: 65–100.

Larson, Kevin. "The science of word recognition." ATypI. 2003. www.microsoft.com/typography/ctfonts/WordRecognition.aspx.

Le Corbusier. *Towards an Architecture*. 1923. Republished Getty Publications, Los Angeles. 2007.

Lee, Byungjoo, Olli Savisaari, and Antti Oulasvirta. "Spotlights: Attention-optimized highlights for skim reading." In *Proceedings of the 2016 CHI Conference on Human Factors in Computing Systems*. 2016. pp. 5203–5214.

Legros, L.A., and I.C. Grant. *Typographical Printing Surfaces, the Technology and Mechanism of Their Production*, Longmans, Green and Co., London. 1916.

Lima, Manuel. *Visual Complexity: Mapping Patters of Information*, Princeton Architectural Press, New York. 2011.

Lima, Manuel. *The Book of Circles: Visualizing Spheres of Knowledge*, Princeton Architectural Press, New York. 2017.

Lohse, Jerry. "A cognitive model for the perception and understanding of graphs." In *Proceedings of the SIGCHI Conference on Human Factors in Computing Systems*. ACM. 1991, pp. 137–144.

Lupton, Ellen. *Thinking with Type: A Critical Guide for Designers, Writers, Editors & Students*, 2nd edition, Princeton Architectural Press, New York. 2010.

MacEachren, Alan. *How Maps Work: Representation, Visualization, and Design*, Guilford Press, New York. 1995.

Mackinlay, Jock. "Automating the design of graphical presentations of relational information." *ACM Transactions on Graphics* 5, no. 2. 1986: 110–141.

Mackinlay, Jock, and Kevin Winslow. *Designing Great Visualizations*, Tableau. 2009. tableausoftware.com/files/designing-great-visualizations.pdf.

Maguire, Eamonn James. *Systematising Glyph Design for Visualization*. PhD dissertation. University of Oxford. 2014.

Maharik, Ron Israel. *Digital micrography*. PhD dissertation. University of British Columbia. 2011.

Master of the Brussels Initials. *Initial N: A Priest at an Altar*. 1389–1404. Getty Ms. 34 (88.MG.71), fol. 206v.

Mazza, Riccardo. *Introduction to Information Visualization*, Springer, London. 2009.

McCandless, David. "Brexit explained" on *Information is Beautiful*. 2019. www.informationisbea utiful.net/visualizations/the-uks-brexit-options-in-the-eurozone-landscape-visualized/.

McCurdy, Nina, Julie Lein, Katharine Coles, and Miriah Meyer. "Poemage: Visualizing the sonic topology of a poem." *IEEE Transactions on Visualization and Computer Graphics* 22, no. 1. 2015: 439–448.

McGhee, Geoff. *Journalism in the Age of Data*. 2010. Documentary film available at vimeo.com/ channels/uwdata/14777910.

McGuffie, Lewis. *Why and How to Draw a Bold Typeface to Accompany a Regular*. MATD dissertation. University of Reading. 2019.

McLean, Kate. *Smellmap Amsterdam*, Sensory Maps. 2014. sensorymaps.com/portfolio/smellmap amsterdam/.

Marchese, Francis T. "Exploring the origins of tables for information visualization." In *15th International Conference on Information Visualisation*. IEEE. 2011.

Michal, Gerhard. *Metabolic Pathways*, F. Hoffmann-La Roche Ltd. 2017. biochemical-pathways .com/#/map/1.

Michelin, Pneu. *Guide Michelin*. Michelin-Guide, Clermont-Ferrand. 1908. archive.org/details/ guidemichelinfra00pneu.

Miller, Harvey J. "Tobler's first law and spatial analysis." *Annals of the Association of American Geographers* 94, no. 2. 2004, pp. 284–289.

Misue, Kazuo. "Drawing bipartite graphs as anchored maps." In *Proceedings of the 2006 Asia-Pacific Symposium on Information Visualization*. Australian Computer Society, Inc. 2006, pp. 169–177.

Mohammad, Saif M. and Peter D. Turney. "Emotions evoked by common words and phrases: Using mechanical turk to create an emotion lexicon." In *Proceedings of the NAACL HLT 2010 Workshop on Computational Approaches to Analysis and Generation of Emotion in Text*. Association for Computational Linguistics. 2010, pp. 26–34.

Mordor Intelligence. *Data Visualization Applications Market Forecasts and Trends (2015 – 2020)*, Mordor Intelligence, Hyderabad. 2015.

Munzner, Tamara. *Visualization Analysis and Design*, CRC Press. 2014.

Nacenta, Miguel, Uta Hinrichs, and Sheelagh Carpendale. "FatFonts: Combining the symbolic and visual aspects of numbers." In *Proceedings of the International Working Conference on Advanced Visual Interfaces*. ACM. 2012.

National Geographic. *Final Report: National Geographic-Roper Public Affairs 2006 Geographic Literacy Study*. GfK NOP, New York, May 2006. www.nationalgeographic.com/roper2006/ pdf/FINALReport2006GeogLitsurvey.pdf, pp. 6–7.

Neurath, Otto. *International Picture Language: The First Rules of ISOTYPE*, K. Paul, Trench, Truber & Co, London. 1936.

Neurath, Otto. *From Hieroglyphics to Isotype: A Visual Autobiography*, Hyphen Press, London. 2010.

Nielsen, Jakob. *Tag Cloud Examples*, Nielsen Norman Group. 2009. www.nngroup.com/articles/tag -cloud-examples/.

O'Connor, Maureen. "The 5 reasons girls type like thissss," in *The Cut*, February 21, 2013. www.t hecut.com/2013/02/5-reasons-girls-type-like-thissss.html.

Osley, A.S. *Mercator: A Monograph on the Lettering of Maps, etc in the 16th Century Netherlands, etc*, Watson-Guptill Publications, New York. 1969.

Osterer, Heidrun and Philipp Stamm. *Frutiger – Typefaces: The Complete Works*, Birkhäuser, Basel. 2014.

Pang, Bo and Lillian Lee. "A sentimental education: Sentiment analysis using subjectivity." In *Proceedings of ACL.* 2004, pp. 271–278.

Paris, Matthew. *Map of Britain*, St Albans, England. 1250. The British Library, shelfmark Cotton MS Claudius D VI, 1. www.bl.uk/collection-items/matthew-paris-map-of-britain.

Parsons, Colonel. *Chronological Tables of Europe*, Printed for B. Barker at the White-Hart and C. King at the Judges Head in Westminster Hall. 1726.

Patel, Rupal and William Furr. "ReadN'Karaoke: Visualizing prosody in children's books for expressive oral reading." In *Proceedings of the SIGCHI Conference on Human Factors in Computing Systems.* 2011, pp. 3203–3206.

Payne, S.J. "Mental models in human-computer interaction." In *The Human-Computer Interaction Handbook*, Andrew Sears and Julie A. Jacko, eds. Lawrence Erlbaum Assoc., New York. 2007, pp. 80–93.

Pearlman, Nathaniel. *Death and Taxes*, Graphicacy. 2015. Available as a poster at timeplots.com.

Peter of Poitiers. *Historical Genealogy of Christ W.796*, England. 1225. The Walters Art Museum.

Pick, Eug. *Tableau De L'Histoire Universelle (Eastern Hemisphere)*, Eug. Pick, Libraire-Editeur. 1858. David Rumsey Map Collection. www.davidrumsey.com/luna/servlet/s/60w6l4.

Playfair, William. *Chronology of Public Events and Remarkable Occurrences within the Last Fifty Years*, W. Lewis, London. 1821.

Proctor, Robert and Kim-Phuong Vu. "Human information processing: An overview for human computer interaction." In *The Human Computer Interaction Handbook.* Andrew Sears and Julie A. Jacko, eds. Lawrence Erlbaum Assoc., New York. 2008, pp. 43–62.

Ramos, E. and D. Donoho. "The 1983 ASA data exposition dataset: Cars." 1983. lib.stat.cmu.edu/datasets.

Rayner, K. and A. Pollatsek. *The Psychology of Reading*, Lawrence Erlbaum Assoc., Hillsdale, NJ. 1989.

Rendgen, Sandra. *Information Graphics*, Taschen. Cologne. 2012.

Rendgen, Sandra. *Understanding the World: The Atlas of Infographics*, Taschen. Cologne. 2014.

Rendgen, Sandra. *The Minard System: The Complete Statistical Graphics of Charles-Joseph Minard*, Princeton Architectural Press, New York. 2018.

Riche, Nathalie Henry and Tim Dwyer. "Untangling Euler diagrams." *IEEE Transactions on Visualization and Computer Graphics* 16, no. 6. 2010: 1090–1099.

Roberts, S.W. and A.H. Fracker. *Rules & Regulations for Running the Trains on the North Pennsylvania Railroad.* Philadelphia. 1875. catalog.hathitrust.org/Record/100599187.

Robinson, Arthur H., Joel L. Morrison, Phillip C. Muehrcke, A. Jon Kimerling, and Stephen C. Guptill. *Elements of Cartography*, 6th edition, Wiley, Hoboken, NJ. 2016.

Ronell, Avital. *The Telephone Book: Technology, Schizophrenia, Electric Speech*, University of Nebraska Press, Lincoln, NE. 1989.

Rosenberg, Daniel and Anthony Grafton. *Cartographies of Time: A History of the Timeline*, Princeton Architectural Press, New York. 2012.

Roth, C.F.G. *Genealogical Distribution of the Arts and Sciences.* 1780. https://omeka.lehigh.edu/exhibits/show/diderot/sciences/tree.

Sanocki, Thomas and Mary C. Dyson. "Letter processing and font information during reading: Beyond distinctiveness, where vision meets design." *Attention, Perception, & Psychophysics* 74, no. 1. 2012: 132–145.

Salton, Gerard and Christopher Buckley. "Term-weighting approaches in automatic text retrieval." *Information Processing & Management* 24, no. 5. 1988: 513–523.

Sarbaugh, L.E., Richard Powers, Hugh Culbertson, and Thomas Flores. "Comprehension of Graphs." In *Bulletin*, 31 – Jan. 1961, Dept. of Agricultural Journalism, University of Wisconsin, with U.S. Dept. of Agriculture. babel.hathitrust.org/cgi/pt?id=wu.89098667975&view=2up&seq=1.

Segel, Edward, and Jeffrey Heer. "Narrative visualization: Telling stories with data." *IEEE Transactions on Visualization and Computer Graphics* 16, no. 6. 2010: 1139–1148.

Shimabukuro, Mariana. *An Adaptive Crowdsourced Investigation of Word Abbreviation Techniques for Text Visualizations*. Master's Thesis. University of Ontario Institute of Technology. 2017.

Shneiderman, Ben. "Tree visualization with tree-maps: A 2-dimensional space filling approach." In *ACM Transactions on Graphics* 11, no. 1. 1992, pp. 92–99.

Shneiderman, Ben. "The eyes have it: A task by data type taxonomy for information visualizations." In *Proceedings 1996 IEEE Symposium on Visual Languages*. IEEE. 1996, pp. 336–343.

Sievert, Carson and Kenneth Shirley. "LDAvis: A method for visualizing and interpreting topics." In *Proceedings of the Workshop on Interactive Language Learning, Visualization, and Interfaces*. 2014, pp. 63–70.

Squire, Victoria, Friedrich Forssman, and Hans Peter Willberg, *Getting it Right with Type: The Dos and Don'ts of Typography*, Lawrence King Publishing, London. 2006.

Stieler, Adolf, C. Vogel, and C. Scherrer, *Stielers Hand-Atlas*. Justus Perthes, Gotha. 1905. www.davidrumsey.com/luna/servlet/s/md55s6, see also www.davidrumsey.com/luna/servlet/s/6532c9.

Strobelt, Hendrik, Daniela Oelke, Bum Chul Kwow, Tobias Schreck, and Hanspeter Pfister. "Guidelines for effective usage of text highlighting techniques." *IEEE Transactions on Visualization and Computer Graphics* 22, no. 1. 2016: 489–498.

Stroop, J. R "Studies of interference in serial verbal reactions." *Journal of Experimental Psychology* 18, no. 6. 1935: 643–662.

Sultanum, Nicole, Devin Singh, Michael Brudno, and Fanny Chevalier. "Doccurate: A curation-based approach for clinical text visualization." *IEEE Transactions on Visualization and Computer Graphics* 25, no. 1. 2018: 142–151.

Symanzik, Juergen, Michael Friendly, and Ortac Onder. "The unsinkable Titanic data." In *Proceedings of the 2019 Joint Statistical Meetings (JSM)*. American Statistical Association (ASA), Alexandria, VA. 2019.

Thudt, Alice, Uta Hinrichs, and Sheelagh Carpendale. "The bohemian bookshelf: Supporting serendipitous book discoveries through information visualization." In *Proceedings of SIGCHI Conference on Human Factors in Computing Systems*. 2012, pp. 1461–1470.

Tschichold, Jan. *The New Typography* (R. McLean, trans.), University of California Press, Berkeley. 1928/1995.

Tse, Archie. "Why we are doing fewer interactives," at *Malofiej*. 2016. https://github.com/archietse/malofiej-2016/blob/master/tse-malofiej-2016-slides.pdf.

Tufte, Edward. *The Visual Display of Quantitative Information*. Graphics Press. Cheshire, CT. 1983.

Tufte, Edward. *Envisioning Information*, Graphics Press, Cheshire, CT. 1990.

Tufte, Edward. *Beautiful Evidence*, Graphics Press, Cheshire, CT. 2006.

Tukey, John W. "Some graphic and semigraphic displays." In *Statistical Papers in Honor of George W. Snedecor*. T.A. Bancroft, ed., The Iowa State University Press, Iowa City, IA. 1972, pp. 293–316.

Twyman, Michael. "The bold idea: The use of bold-looking types in the nineteenth century." *Journal of the Printing Historical Society* 22. 1993: 107–143.

Tyner, Judith A. *Principles of Map Design*, Guilford Publications, New York. 2014.

VanderLans, Rudy. *Emigre #16: Sound Design*. Lompa Printing, Albany, CA. 1990.

van Doesburg, Theo. *Affiche Kleine Dadasoirée*, at Collection Centraal Museum, Utrecht. 1923.

Unger, Gerard. *Theory of Type Design*, nai010 publishers, Rotterdam. 2018.

United States Bureau of Labor Statistics, *Unemployment rates by state, seasonally adjusted, Jan 2019*. Bureau of Labor Statistics, Local Area Unemployment Statistics. www.bls.gov/web/laus/mstrtcr2.pdf.

Valdés, Juan José. *National Geographic's Cartographic Typefaces*. www.nationalgeographic.com/maps/national-geographics-cartogaphic-typefaces.

Valerio, Cornelio. *Colloquia et dictionariolum*. apud Henricium Henricum ad Coemiterium B. Mariae sub Lilio. 1576. archive.org/details/bub_gb_VVBNWNTGtusC.

Vinot, Jean-Luc, and Sylvie Athenes. "Legible, are you sure?: An experimentation-based typographical design in safety-critical context." In *Proceedings of the SIGCHI Conference on Human
Factors in Computing Systems.* ACM. 2012, pp. 2287–2296.

Virgil Master. *Chart*, Paris, France. 1405.

Wallgren, Anders, Britt Wallgren, Rolf Persson, Ulf Jorner, and Jan-Aage Haaland. *Graphing
Statistics & Data: Creating Better Charts*, SAGE Publications, Thousand Oaks, CA. 1996.

Ward, John. *The Young Mathematician's Guide: Being a Plain and Easie Introduction to the
Mathematicks* (4th ed.), A. Bettesworth, and F. Fayrham, London. 1724. archive.org/details/
youngmathematic02wardgoog.

Warde, Beatrice. *The Crystal Goblet or Printing Should be Invisible* (Henry Jacob, ed.), Sylvan Press,
London. 1955.

Ware, Colin. *Information Visualization: Perception for Design*, Morgan Kaufmann, Waltham, MA.
2013.

Wattenberg, Martin and Fernanda B. Viégas. "The word tree, an interactive visual concordance."
IEEE Transactions on Visualization and Computer Graphics 14, no. 6. 2008: 1221–1228.

Weskamp, Marcos. *NewsMap.* 2004. http://newsmap.jp.

Wickham, Hadley. *ggplot2: Elegant Graphics for Data Analysis*, Springer, London. 2009.

Wilhide, Elizabeth. *How to Design a Typeface*, Conrad Octopus Ltd with The Design Museum,
London. 2010.

Wilkinson, Leland. *The Grammar of Graphics*, 2nd ed., Springer Science & Business Media, New
York. 2005.

Wilkinson, Leland. "Exact and approximate area-proportional circular Venn and Euler diagrams."
IEEE Transactions on Visualization and Computer Graphics 18, no. 2. 2012: 321–331.

Wong, Dona M. *The Wall Street Journal Guide to Information Graphics: The Dos and Don'ts of
Presenting Data, Facts and Figures*, W.W. Norton & Company, New York. 2010.

Wong, Pak Chung; Patrick Mackey, Ken Perrine, James Eagan, Harlan Foote, and Jim Thomas.
"Dynamic visualization of graphs with extended labels." In *Information Visualization.* 2005,
pp. 73–80 (IEEE Symposium on InfoVis).

Xu, Jie and Craig S. Kaplan. "Calligraphic packing." In *Proceedings of Graphics Interface.* 2007, pp.
43–50.

Yang, Qian, Gerard de Melo, Yong Cheng, and Sen Wang. "Hitext: Text reading with dynamic
salience marking." In *Proceedings of the 26th International Conference on World Wide Web
Companion.* 2017, pp. 311–319.

Index